Pro Couchbase Server

David Ostrovsky

Yaniv Rodenski

Apress®

Pro Couchbase Server

ISBN-13 (pbk): 978-1-4302-6613-6

ISBN-13 (electronic): 978-1-4302-6614-3

Publisher: Heinz Weinheimer
Lead Editor: Jonathan Gennick
Developmental Editor: Corbin Collins
Technical Reviewers: Kenneth Williams and Philipp Fehre
Editorial Board: Steve Anglin, Mark Beckner, Ewan Buckingham, Gary Cornell, Louise Corrigan, Jim DeWolf, Jonathan Gennick, Jonathan Hassell, Robert Hutchinson, Michelle Lowman, James Markham, Matthew Moodie, Jeff Olson, Jeffrey Pepper, Douglas Pundick, Ben Renow-Clarke, Dominic Shakeshaft, Gwenan Spearing, Matt Wade, Steve Weiss
Coordinating Editor: Jill Balzano
Copy Editor: April Rondeau
Compositor: SPi Global
Indexer: SPi Global
Artist: SPi Global
Cover Designer: Anna Ishchenko

To my wonderful wife, Dina, for not divorcing me despite my working weekends on this book, and my son, Adam, for being awesome in general.

— David Ostrovsky

For my wife, Morin, and my daughters, Romy and Ella—thanks for letting Daddy do this.

— Yaniv Rodenski

In loving memory of Ephraim Rodensky and Noam Sheffer.

Contents at a Glance

Contents

About the Authors

David Ostrovsky is a Senior Architect at Sela Group as well as a software development trainer, speaker, and author. He is the co-author of the "Essentials of Developing Windows Store Apps Using C#" and "Advanced Windows Store App Development Using C#" Microsoft official courses (20484, 20485), and numerous articles. David has been a computer geek since the age of 12 and a professional software developer since 1999. He specializes in big data systems and application performance tuning.

Yaniv Rodenski is a Senior Architect at Sela Group, a speaker, an author, and an all-around nerd. Yaniv has been developing software as a hobby since he was young, and professionally since 1997.Yaniv is the founder and co-manager of the Microsoft Azure User Group in Israel, the co-author of the "Developing Windows Azure and Web Services" Microsoft official course (20487), and a contributor to official Microsoft training materials on Windows Azure, Windows 2008 R2 HPC Server, and HDInsight (Hadoop) over the years.

About the Technical Reviewers

Ken Williams is a Senior Architect at Burstly, a mobile analytics and advertising company based in beautiful Santa Monica, California. He is an accomplished big data architect with extensive work experience on large-scale databases. He was an early adopter of key-value stores, specifically Couchbase, and has spoken publicly about his implementation and scaling experience, most recently at CouchConf San Francisco.

Traveling through the world of Scheme, C/C++, Ruby, and JavaScript, **Phil Fehre** enjoys all kinds of programming and their respective communities. He is writing both [software](https://github.com/sideshowcoder) and [words] (http://sideshowcoder.com) as sideshowcoder, and keeps talking about TDD, NoSQL, and the software development process in general. Over the last few years he has had the chance to work with and grow systems on the latest and greatest technologies. He saw them succeed and fail, and saw the tech being the "wrong tool," the "right tool," or the "most fun tool" for the job. He now works at Couchbase, where he explores the ins and outs of NoSQL as a Developer Advocate.

Acknowledgments

We would like to thank all the people who helped us throughout this project: Sela Group, in particular Dudu Bassa, Caro Sega, Ishai Ram, Roy Rachmany, and all our colleagues who provided support and enthusiasm. We also want to thank Sasha Goldshtein and Yuval Mazor for their feedback about the book content.

Next, we would like to thank the Apress team, as this book wouldn't have happened without Jonathan Gennick, Jill Balzano, and the rest of the great people at Apress. You guys do tremendous work. A special thanks to Gwenan Spearing for putting us in touch with Jonathan.

Of course, we'd like to thank the fine folks from Couchbase for their help and advice and for making Couchbase Server in the first place, thus giving us an awesome database to write about.

And last, but absolutely not least, we would like to thank our families for putting up with us, for feeding us as we huddled with our laptops in the kitchen and carefully stepping over power cables whenever we took over the living room.

Introduction

Ever since we decided to start writing this book, there has been one question which kept popping up whenever someone heard about it: why Couchbase Server? The immediate answer was obvious: because we absolutely love it. But putting aside our natural enthusiasm for every piece of new technology that comes out, Couchbase Server does have a few distinct characteristics that make it stand out from other NoSQL solutions.

The first distinguishing feature of Couchbase Server is that it's blazingly fast. Couchbase Server keeps coming at the top of every performance benchmark, some of which were commissioned by its competitors. This is mostly due to a solid caching layer it inherited from one of its ancestors: memcached.

Next is the fact that Couchbase Server scales exceedingly well. While the NoSQL movement promotes scalability and some products imply scalability in their name, only a few products have actually proven themselves in large scale. Couchbase Server scales and does so in a very easy and streamlined manner. Moreover, Couchbase Server can also scale down if needed, making it a perfect match to run in an elastic cloud environment.

High availability is another important aspect of Couchbase Server architecture. There is no single point of failure in a Couchbase Server cluster, since the clients are aware of the topology of the entire cluster, including where every document is located. In addition the documents are replicated across multiple nodes and can be accessed even if some nodes are unavailable.

For those reasons and many others, we found Couchbase Server to be a fascinating technology. One that is worth investing long months of studying into, just to create a solid knowledge base which others can use. We hope this book will be helpful to all who wish to make the most of Couchbase Server.

PART I

Getting Started

CHAPTER 1

■ ■ ■

Getting Started with Couchbase Server

Relational databases have dominated the data landscape for over three decades. Emerging in the 1970s and early 1980s, relational databases offered a searchable mechanism for persisting complex data with minimal use of storage space. Conserving storage space was an important consideration during that era, due to the high price of storage devices. For example, in 1981, Morrow Designs offered a 26 MB hard drive for $3,599—which was a good deal compared to the 18 MB North Star hard drive for $4,199, which had appeared just six months earlier. Over the years, the relational model progressed, with the various implementations providing more and more functionality.

One of the things that allowed relational databases to provide such a rich set of capabilities was the fact that they were optimized to run on a single machine. For many years, running on a single machine scaled nicely, as newer and faster hardware became available in frequent intervals. This method of scaling is known as *vertical scaling*. And while most relational databases could also scale horizontally—that is, scale across multiple machines—it introduced additional complexity to the application and database design, and often resulted in inferior performance.

From SQL to NoSQL

This balance was finally disrupted with the appearance of what is known today as *Internet scale*, or *web scale*, applications. Companies such as Google and Facebook needed new approaches to database design in order to handle the massive amounts of data they had. Another aspect of the rapidly growing industry was the need to cope with constantly changing application requirements and data structure. Out of these new necessities for storing and accessing large amounts of frequently changing data, the NoSQL movement was born. These days, the term NoSQL is used to describe a wide range of mechanisms for storing data in ways other than with relational tables. Over the past few years, dozens of open-source projects, commercial products, and companies have begun offering NoSQL solutions.

The CAP Theorem

In 2000, Eric Brewer, a computer scientist from the University of California, Berkeley, proposed the following conjecture:

It is impossible for a distributed computer system to satisfy the following three guarantees simultaneously (which together form the acronym CAP):

- *Consistency*: All components of the system see the same data.

- *Availability*: All requests to the system receive a response, whether success or failure.

- *Partition tolerance*: The system continues to function even if some components fail or some message traffic is lost.

A few years later, Brewer further clarified that consistency and availability in CAP should not be viewed as binary, but rather as a range—and distributed systems can compromise with weaker forms of one or both in return for better performance and scalability. Seth Gilbert and Nancy Lynch of MIT offered a formal proof of Brewer's conjecture. While the formal proof spoke of a narrower use of CAP, and its status as a "theorem" is heavily disputed, the essence is still useful for understanding distributed system design.

Traditional relational databases generally provide some form of the C and A parts of CAP and struggle with horizontal scaling because they are unable to provide resilience in the face of node failure. The various NoSQL products offer different combinations of CA/AP/CP. For example, some NoSQL systems provide a weaker form of consistency, known as *eventual consistency*, as a compromise for having high availability and partition tolerance. In such systems, data arriving at one node isn't immediately available to others—the application logic has to handle stale data appropriately. In fact, letting the application logic make up for weaker consistency or availability is a common approach in distributed systems that use NoSQL data stores.

As you'll see in this book, Couchbase Server provides cluster-level consistency and good partition tolerance through replication.

NoSQL and Couchbase Server

NoSQL databases have made a rapid entrance onto the main stage of the database world. In fact, it is the wide variety of available NoSQL products that makes it hard to find the right choice for your needs. When comparing NoSQL solutions, we often find ourselves forced to compare different products feature by feature in order to make a decision. In this dense and competitive marketplace each product must offer unique capabilities to differentiate itself from its brethren.

Couchbase Server is a distributed NoSQL database, which stands out due to its high performance, high availability, and scalability. Reliably providing these features in production is not a trivial thing, but Couchbase achieves this in a simple and easy manner. Let's take a look at how Couchbase deals with these challenges.

- *Scaling*: In Couchbase Server, data is distributed automatically over nodes in the cluster, allowing the database to share and scale out the load of performing lookups and disk IO horizontally. Couchbase achieves this by storing each data item in a vBucket, a logical partition (sometimes called a *shard*), which resides on a single node. The fact that Couchbase shards the data automatically simplifies the development process. Couchbase Server also provides a cross-datacenter replication (XDCR) feature, which allows Couchbase Server clusters to scale across multiple geographical locations.

- *High availability*: Couchbase can replicate each vBucket across multiple nodes to support failover. When a node in the cluster fails, the Couchbase Server cluster makes one of the replica vBuckets available automatically.

- *High performance*: Couchbase has an extensive integrated caching layer. Keys, metadata, and frequently accessed data are kept in memory in order to increase read/write throughput and reduce data access latency.

To understand how unique Couchbase Server is, we need to take a closer look at each of these features and how they're implemented. We will do so later in this chapter, because first we need to understand Couchbase as a whole. Couchbase Server, as we know it today, is the progeny of two products: Apache CouchDB and Membase. CouchOne Inc., was a company funded by Damien Katz, the creator of CouchDB. The company provided commercial support for the Apache CouchDB open-source database. In February 2011 CouchOne Inc. merged with Membase Inc., the company behind the open source Membase distributed key-value store. Membase was created by a few of the core contributors of Memcached, the popular distributed cache project, and provided persistence and querying on top of the simplicity and high-performance key-value mechanism provided by Memcached.

The new company, called Couchbase Inc., released Couchbase Server, a product that was based on Membase's scalable high-performance capabilities, to which they eventually added capabilities from CouchDB, including storage, indexing, and querying. The initial version of Couchbase Server included a caching layer, which traced its origins directly back to Membase, and a persistence layer, which owed a lot to Apache CouchDB.

Membase and CouchDB represent two of the leading approaches in the NoSQL world today: key-value stores and document-oriented databases. Both approaches still exist in today's Couchbase Server.

Couchbase as Key-Value Store vs. Document Database

Key-value stores are, in essence, managed hash tables. A key-value store uses keys to access values in a straightforward and relatively efficient way. Different key-value stores expose different functionality on top of the basic hash-table-based access and focus on different aspects of data manipulation and retrieval.

As a key-value store, Couchbase is capable of storing multiple data types. These include simple data types such as strings, numbers, datetime, and booleans, as well as arbitrary binary data. For most of the simple data types, Couchbase offers a scalable, distributed data store that provides both key-based access as well as minimal operations on the values. For example, for numbers you can use atomic operations such as increment and decrement. Operations are covered in depth in Chapter 4.

Document databases differ from key-value stores in the way they represent the stored data. Key-value stores generally treat their data as opaque blobs and do not try to parse it, whereas document databases encapsulate stored data into "documents" that they can operate on. A document is simply an object that contains data in some specific format. For example, a JSON document holds data encoded in the JSON format, while a PDF document holds data encoded in the Portable Document binary format.

■ **Note** JavaScript Object Notation (JSON) is a widely used, lightweight, open data interchange format. It uses human-readable text to encode data objects as collections of name–value pairs. JSON is a very popular choice in the NoSQL world, both for exchanging and for storing data. You can read more about it at: www.json.org.

One of the main strengths of this approach is that documents don't have to adhere to a rigid schema. Each document can have different properties and parts that can be changed on the fly without affecting the structure of other documents. Furthermore, document databases actually "understand" the content of the documents and typically offer functionality for acting on the stored data, such as changing parts of the document or indexing documents for faster retrieval. Couchbase Server can store data as JSON documents, which lets it index and query documents by specific fields.

Couchbase Server Architecture

A Couchbase Server cluster consists of between 1 and 1024 nodes, with each node running exactly one instance of the Couchbase Server software. The data is partitioned and distributed between the nodes in the cluster. This means that each node holds some of the data and is responsible for some of the storing and processing load. Distributing data this way is often referred to as *sharding*, with each partition referred to as a shard.

Each Couchbase Server node has two major components: the Cluster Manager and the Data Manager, as shown in Figure 1-1. Applications use the Client Software Development Kits (SDKs) to communicate with both of these components. The Couchbase Client SDKs are covered in depth in Chapter 3.

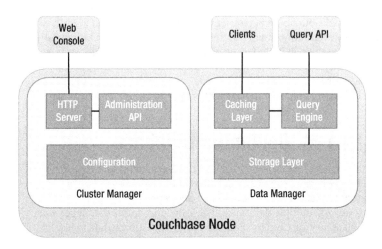

Figure 1-1. *Couchbase server architecture*

- *The Cluster Manager*: The Cluster Manager is responsible for configuring nodes in the cluster, managing the rebalancing of data between nodes, handling replicated data after a failover, monitoring nodes, gathering statistics, and logging. The Cluster Manager maintains and updates the cluster map, which tells clients where to look for data. Lastly, it also exposes the administration API and the web management console. The Cluster Manager component is built with Erlang/OTP, which is particularly suited for creating concurrent, distributed systems.

- *The Data Manager*: The Data Manager, as the name implies, manages data storage and retrieval. It contains the memory cache layer, the disk persistence mechanism, and the query engine. Couchbase clients use the cluster map provided by the Cluster Manager to discover which node holds the required data and then communicate with the Data Manager on that node to perform database operations.

Data Storage

Couchbase manages data in *buckets*—logical groupings of related resources. You can think of buckets as being similar to databases in Microsoft SQL Server, or to schemas in Oracle. Typically, you would have separate buckets for separate applications. Couchbase supports two kinds of buckets: Couchbase and memcached.

Memcached buckets store data in memory as binary blobs of up to 1 MB in size. Data in memcached buckets is not persisted to disk or replicated across nodes for redundancy. Couchbase buckets, on the other hand, can store data as JSON documents, primitive data types, or binary blobs, each up to 20 MB in size. This data is cached in memory and persisted to disk and can be dynamically rebalanced between nodes in a cluster to distribute the load. Furthermore, Couchbase buckets can be configured to maintain between one and three replica copies of the data, which provides redundancy in the event of node failure. Because each copy must reside on a different node, replication requires at least one node per replica, plus one for the active instance of data.

Documents in a bucket are further subdivided into virtual buckets (vBuckets) by their key. Each vBucket owns a subset of all the possible keys, and documents are mapped to vBuckets according to a hash of their key. Every vBucket, in turn, belongs to one of the nodes of the cluster. As shown in Figure 1-2, when a client needs to access a document, it first hashes the document key to find out which vBucket owns that key. The client then checks the cluster map to find which node hosts the relevant vBucket. Lastly, the client connects directly to the node that stores the document to perform the get operation.

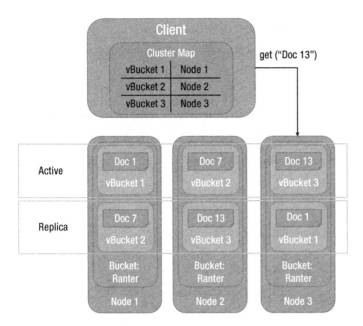

Figure 1-2. *Sharding and replicating a bucket across nodes*

In addition to maintaining replicas of data within buckets, Couchbase can replicate data between entire clusters. Cross-Datacenter Replication (XCDR) adds further redundancy and brings data geographically closer to its users. Both in-bucket replication and XCDR occur in parallel. XCDR is covered in depth in Chapter 9.

Installing Couchbase Server

Installing and configuring Couchbase Server is very straightforward. You pick the platform, the correct edition for your needs, and then download and run the installer. After the installation finishes, you use the web console, which guides you through a quick setup process.

Selecting a Couchbase Server Edition

Couchbase Server comes in two different editions: Enterprise Edition and Community Edition. There are some differences between them:

- *Enterprise Edition* (EE) is the latest stable version of Couchbase, which includes all the bugfixes and has passed a rigorous QA process. It is free for use with any number of nodes for testing and development purposes, and with up to two nodes for production. You can also purchase an annual support plan with this edition.

- *Community Edition* (CE) lags behind the EE by about one release cycle and does not include all the latest fixes or commercial support. However, it is open source and entirely free for use in testing and, if you're very brave, in production. This edition is largely meant for enthusiasts and non-critical systems.

When you are ready to give Couchbase a hands-on try, download the appropriate installation package for your system from www.couchbase.com/download.

Installing Couchbase on Different Operating Systems

The installation step is very straightforward. Let's take a look at how it works on different operating systems.

Linux

Couchbase is officially supported on several Linux distributions: Ubuntu 10.04 and higher, Red Hat Enterprise Linux (RHEL) 5 and 6, CentOS 5 and 6, and Amazon Linux. Unofficially, you can get Couchbase to work on most distributions, however, we recommend sticking to the supported operating systems in production environments.

Couchbase also requires OpenSSL to be installed separately. To install OpenSSL on RHEL run the following command:

```
> sudo yum install openssl
```

On Ubuntu, you can install OpenSSL using the following command:

```
> sudo apt-get install openssl
```

With OpenSSL installed, you can now install the Couchbase package you downloaded earlier.
RHEL:

```
> sudo rpm –install couchbase-server-<version>.rpm
```

Ubuntu:

```
> sudo dpkg -i couchbase-server-<version>.deb
```

Note that <version> is the version of the installer you have downloaded.
After the installation completes, you will see a confirmation message that Couchbase Server has been started.

Windows

On a Windows system, run the installer you've downloaded and follow the instructions in the installation wizard.

Mac OS X

Download and unzip the install package and then move the Couchbase Server.app folder to your Applications folder. Double-click Couchbase Server.app to start the server.

■ **Note** Couchbase Server is not supported on Mac OS X for production purposes. It is recommended that you only use it for testing and development.

Configuring Couchbase Server

With Couchbase installed, you can now open the administration web console and configure the server. Open the following address in your browser: http://<server>:8091, where <server> is the machine on which you've installed Couchbase. The first time you open the web console, you're greeted with the screen shown in Figure 1-3.

Figure 1-3. *Opening the web console for the first time*

Click Setup to begin the configuration process, as shown in Figure 1-4.

Figure 1-4. *Configuring Couchbase Server, step 1*

The Databases Path field is the location where Couchbase will store its persisted data. The Indices Path field is where Couchbase will keep the indices created by views. Both locations refer only to the current server node. Placing the index data on a different physical disk than the document data is likely to result in better performance, especially if you will be using many views or creating views on the fly. Indexing and views are covered in Chapter 6.

In a Couchbase cluster, every node must have the same amount of RAM allocated. The RAM quota you set when starting a new cluster will be inherited by every node that joins the cluster in the future. It is possible to change the server RAM quota later through the command-line administration tools.

The Sample Buckets screen (shown in Figure 1-5) lets you create buckets with sample data and views so that you can test some of the features of Couchbase Server with existing samples. Throughout this book you'll build your own sample application, so you won't need the built-in samples, but feel free to install them if you're curious.

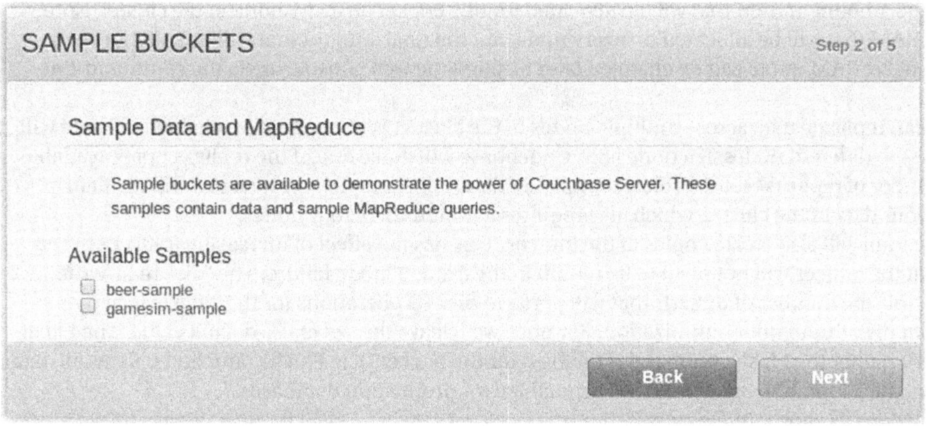

Figure 1-5. *Configuring Couchbase Server, step 2*

The next step, shown in Figure 1-6, is creating the default bucket. Picking the memcached bucket type will hide the unsupported configuration options, such as replicas and read-write concurrency.

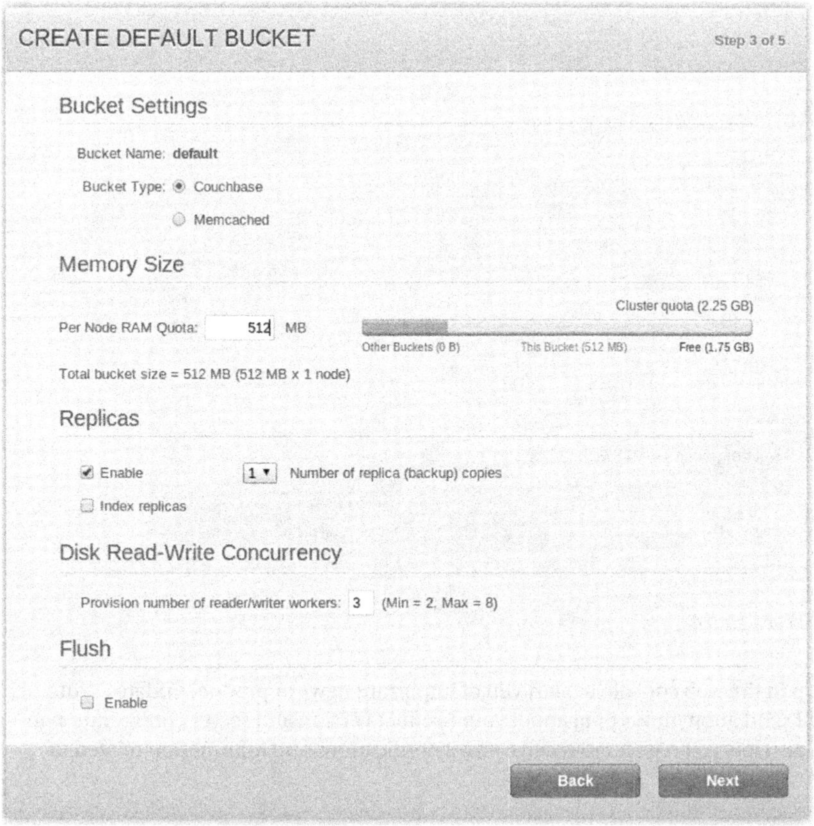

Figure 1-6. *Configuring Couchbase Server, step 3*

The memory size is the amount of RAM that will be allocated for this bucket on every node in the cluster. Note that this is the amount of RAM that will be allocated on every node, not the total amount that will be split between all nodes. The per-node bucket RAM quota can be changed later through the web console or via the command-line administration tools.

Couchbase buckets can replicate data across multiple nodes in the cluster. With replication enabled, all data will be copied up to three times to different nodes. If a node fails, Couchbase will make one of the replica copies available for use. Note that the "number of replicas" setting refers to *copies* of data. For example, setting it to 3 will result in a total of four instances of your data in the cluster, which also requires a minimum of four nodes.

Enabling index replication will also create copies of the indices. This has the effect of increasing traffic between nodes, but also means that the indices will not need to be rebuilt in the event of node failure. The "disk read-write concurrency" setting controls the number of threads that will perform disk IO operations for this bucket. Chapter 8 goes into more detail about disk-throughput optimization. For now, we'll leave this set at the default value. The Flush Enable checkbox controls whether the Flush command is enabled for the bucket. The Flush command deletes all data and is useful for testing and development, but should not be enabled for production databases.

The next step, Notifications, is shown in Figure 1-7.

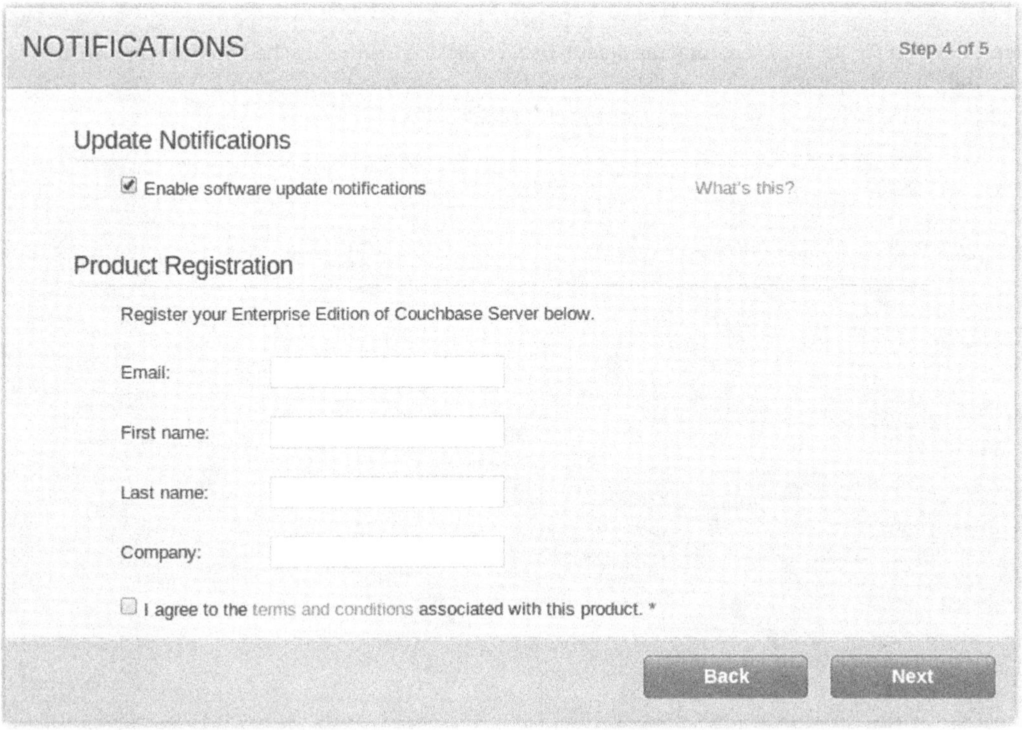

Figure 1-7. *Configuring Couchbase Server, step 4*

Update Notifications will show up in the web console to alert you of important news or product updates. Note that enabling update notifications will send anonymous data about your product version and server configuration to Couchbase (the company). This step also lets you register to receive email notifications and information related to Couchbase products.

The final step, Configure Server, as you can see in Figure 1-8, is to configure the administrator username and password. These credentials are used for administrative actions, such as logging into the web console or adding new nodes to the cluster. Data buckets you create are secured separately and do not use the administrator password.

CONFIGURE SERVER   Step 5 of 5

Secure this Server

Please create an administrator account for this Server. If you want to join other servers to this one to form a cluster, you will need to use these administrator credentials in the "join cluster" process.

Username: Administrator

Password: |

Verify Password:

[Back]   [Next]

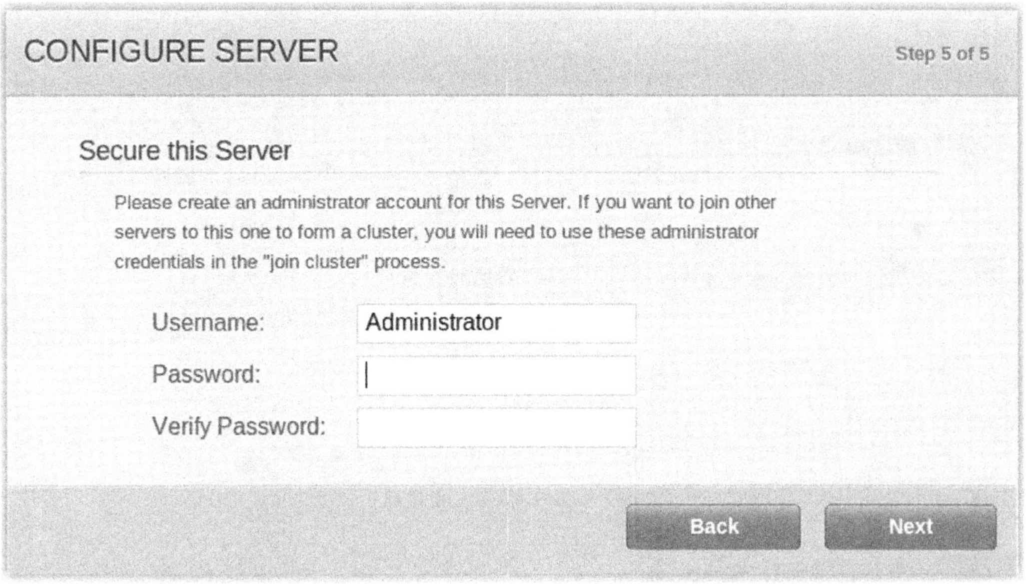

Figure 1-8. *Configuring Couchbase Server, step 5*

■ **Tip**   Avoid using the same combination as on your luggage.

Click Next to finish the setup process, and you will be taken to the Cluster Overview screen in the web console. Couchbase will need about a minute to finalize the setup process and then initialize the default bucket, after which you should see something similar to Figure 1-9.

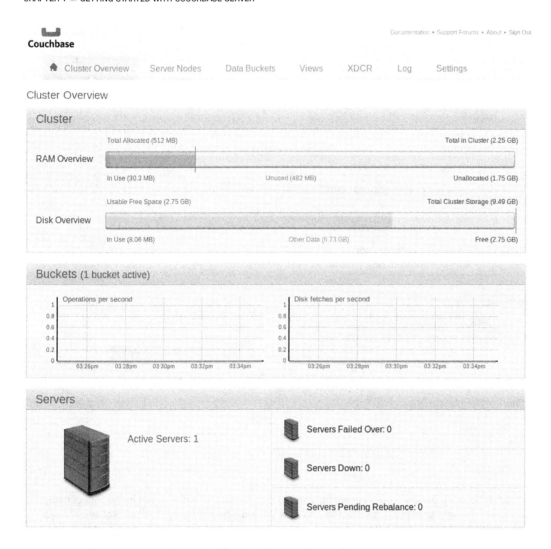

Figure 1-9. *The Cluster Overview tab of the Couchbase web console*

Congratulations—your Couchbase Server is now fully operational!

Creating a Bucket

Throughout this book, you'll be building a sample application that will demonstrate the various features of Couchbase Server. RanteR, the Anti-Social Network, is a web application that lets users post "rants," comment on rants, and follow their favorite—using the word loosely—ranters. It bears no resemblance whatsoever to any existing, well-known web applications. At all.

To start building your RanteR application, you'll need a Couchbase bucket to hold all your data. Couchbase Server administration is covered in depth in the chapters in Part III, so for now you'll only create a new bucket with mostly default values.

Click Create New Data Bucket on the Data Buckets tab of the web console to open the Create Bucket dialog, as shown in Figure 1-10.

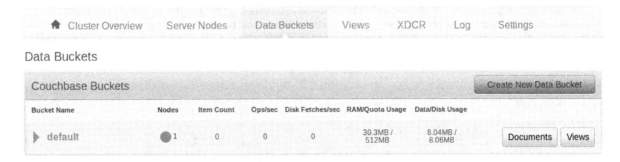

Figure 1-10. *The Data Buckets tab of the Couchbase web console*

Enter *ranter* as the bucket name, as shown in Figure 1-11, and set the RAM quota to a reasonable amount. RanteR doesn't need much RAM for now. Leave the Access Control set to the standard port. You can enter a password to secure your data bucket.

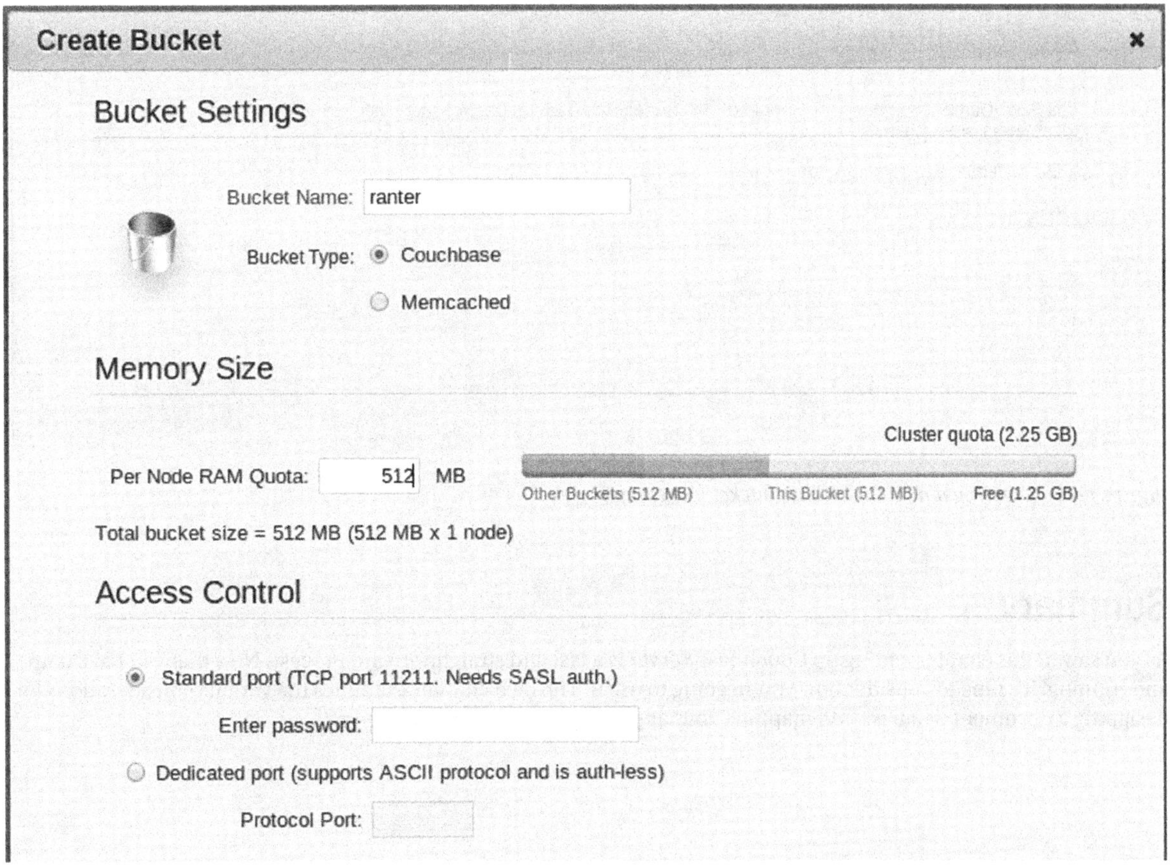

Create Bucket

Bucket Settings

Bucket Name: ranter

Bucket Type: ● Couchbase
○ Memcached

Memory Size

Cluster quota (2.25 GB)

Per Node RAM Quota: 512 MB

Other Buckets (512 MB)   This Bucket (512 MB)   Free (1.25 GB)

Total bucket size = 512 MB (512 MB x 1 node)

Access Control

● Standard port (TCP port 11211. Needs SASL auth.)

Enter password:

○ Dedicated port (supports ASCII protocol and is auth-less)

Protocol Port:

Figure 1-11. *Creating a new Couchbase bucket*

Because you only have one Couchbase node installed and configured, we cannot use replication, so make sure to uncheck the Replicas box as shown in Figure 1-12. For convenience, and because this is not a production server, enable the Flush command for this bucket. Leave the other settings at their default values for now. Click Create, and you are done.

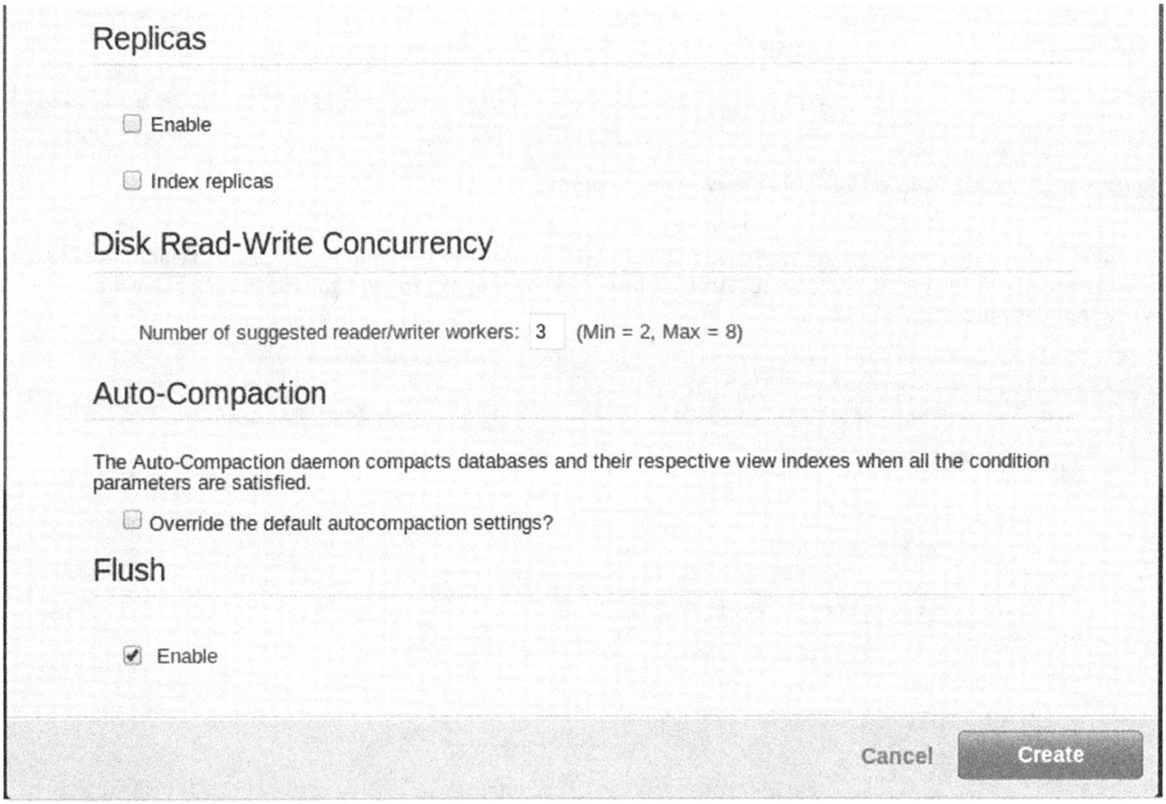

Figure 1-12. *Creating a new Couchbase bucket, continued*

Summary

As you saw in this chapter, setting up Couchbase Server is a fast and straightforward process. Now that you have it up and running, it's time to consider how you're going to use it. The next chapter examines the various considerations for designing a document database and mapping your application entities to documents.

CHAPTER 2

■ ■ ■

Designing Document-Oriented Databases with Couchbase

One of the biggest challenges when moving from relational databases to NoSQL is the shift one needs to make in the way one designs a database solution. Considering the fact that most NoSQL solutions differ from one another, this change of mindset can become frustrating. This chapter covers how to design a database using Couchbase's style of document-oriented design mixed with key-value capabilities.

We feel that in order to thoroughly cover database design, a full-blown database is needed. For purposes of demonstration, we have created an application called RanteR, an anti-social network that we will use as an example throughout this book.

RanteR: The Anti-Social Network

Much like any social application, RanteR allows users to express their thoughts publicly over the web. Unlike other applications, though, these thoughts are not intended to glorify something but rather to complain (and are therefore called *rants*). In addition, users who choose to rant through RanteR invite other RanteR users to dislike, ridicule, and even flame those thoughts.

Building the RanteR functionality step by step will allow us to explore different aspects of database design and discover how Couchbase deals with those issues. Let's start with one of the most basic tasks in designing a database: mapping application entities to the database.

One of the hardest decisions we had to make was which language to use to build RanteR. Couchbase Server relies on a set of client libraries for most operations. As of this writing, there are seven different official libraries in seven different programming languages. The different client libraries are covered in depth in Chapter 3. In the end, we decided to build RanteR as a Node.js web application, for the following reasons:

- Node.js is fun and popular among the cool kids these days. It is our attempt to appear less old and out of touch.

- We have conducted an unscientific survey among our programmer peers, looking for the most acceptable (or least offensive) programming language. Java programmers adamantly refused to read code in C#, and vice versa. PHP and Python programmers felt negatively about both Java and C#, and so on. But, surprisingly enough, most were fine with JavaScript. Except for Ruby programmers, who felt that everything was better with Rails.

- And, finally, the Node.js client library is the latest and most comprehensive Client SDK at this time, which allows us to show more features in our code samples.

Figure 2-1 shows the high-level structure of RanteR.

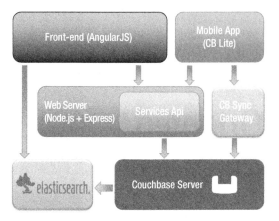

Figure 2-1. *RanteR's components*

We will use the Couchbase client libraries extensively throughout this part of the book. Most of the code samples for client libraries are taken from the services API, which is located in the API folder in RanteR.

RanteR uses Couchbase's integration with ElasticSearch through the cross-datacenter replication (XDCR) mechanism to search for rants and ranters. XDCR is covered in Chapter 13. We also cover some of the basics of ElasticSearch in Chapter 8.

Just like all major social applications, RanteR has a mobile app component, which uses Couchbase Lite for database synchronization. Couchbase Lite, which is part of Couchbase's JSON Anywhere strategy, is the world's first NoSQL mobile database. We will use Couchbase Lite in Chapters 14 and 15. Chapter 16 covers synchronizing data between Couchbase Lite databases and a Couchbase Server cluster.

As with any other type of database-centric application, one of the first challenges we need to tackle is database design. The rest of this chapter looks at how to model our data in Couchbase.

Mapping Application Entities

One of the biggest issues with relational databases is that they represent data in a way that is fundamentally different from the way the same data is represented in applications. Data that is usually represented as a graph of objects in most programming languages needs to be deconstructed into different tables in a relational model. This problem is generally referred to as *object-relational impedance mismatch*.

Let's take a look at the class representing our rant object in Java:

```
public class Rant {

        private final UUID id;
        private final String username;
        private final String ranttext;
        private final URI imageURI;
        private final Rant rantAbout;
        private final String type;
        private final List<Rantback> rantBacks;
```

```java
        public Rant(UUID id, String username, String rantText, String type, List<Rant> rantBacks,
URI imageURI, Rant rantAbout) {
                this.id = id;
                this.username = username;
                this.rantText = rantText;
                this.type = type;
                this.imageURI = imageURI;
                this.rantBacks = rantBacks;
                this.rantAbout = rantAbout;
        }

        public UUID getId() {
                return id;
        }

        public String getUsername() {
                return username;
        }

        public String getRantText() {
                return rantText;
        }

        public URI getImageURI() {
                return imageURI;
        }

        public List<Rant> getRantBacks() {
                return rantBacks;
        }

        public List<Rantback> getRantBacks() {
                return rantBacks;
        }
}

public class Rantback {

        private final UUID id;
        private final String username;
        private final String text;

        public Rant(UUID id, String username, String text) {

                this.id = id;
                this.username = username;
                this.text = text;
        }

        public UUID getId() {
                return id;
        }
```

```
        public String getUsername() {
            return username;
        }

        public String getText() {
            return text;
        }
}
```

In this example, we have two types of relations:

1. A rant can be about another rant. In this case, the rant being ranted about is shown inside the rant body.

2. A rant can have rantbacks, a list of short textual reactions to the original rant.

Let's take a look at how this model is mapped to a database, first using a relational approach and then a document-oriented approach using Couchbase.

Using a Relational Database

In a traditional relational database, the rant entity should be mapped to a row in a table representing the rant. In addition, we would add an `int` column in the same table for representing the rant the user is ranting about. Since they have a slightly different structure, rantbacks would most likely be stored in different table. Tables 2-1 and 2-2 show how we would represent a rant about another rant with two rantbacks in a relational database.

Table 2-1. *Rants Table*

Id	Username	RantText	ImageURI	RantAbout	Type
1	JerryS	Why do they call it Ovaltine...?	--	--	Rant
2	YanivR	Real Couchbase developers drink...	--	1	Rant

Table 2-2. *Rantbacks Table*

Id	RantId	Username	Text
1	2	JohnC	Well, of course, this is just the sort blinkered...
2	2	DavidO	I just watched you drink three cups of green tea...

The biggest issue with this type of representation is the fact that in order to retrieve the data needed to display a single rant in the application, you need to access up to four different records in two tables. Accessing four records might not seem like a big deal, but with larger graphs, it could affect performance.

An even bigger issue occurs when you need to scale out. Accessing multiple records distributed across a cluster can become extremely complicated and slow.

Using a Document-Oriented Approach with Couchbase

Document-oriented databases use documents in a specific format that stores data representing an object graph. For Couchbase Server, documents are stored in JSON format. The following example shows a simple rant as a JSON document:

```
{
        "id": "2d18e287-d5fa-42ce-bca5-b26eaef0d7d4",
        "type": "rant",
        "userName": "JerryS",
        "rantText": "Why do they call it Ovaltine? The mug is round. The jar is round. They should
call it Roundtine."
}
```

The first thing you should notice there is that we do not represent the fields with null values. What's important here is not that we save a little bit of space when storing our documents, but rather the fact that documents are not bound to a schema.

On its own, this rant by user JerryS has no nested data and can be stored as a single document. However, there's a more complex model we want to explore. Here we have a second rant, which has JerryS's rant nested inside it. Due to Couchbase's schemaless nature, we can store both rants as a single document, as follows:

```
{
        "id": "6e5416b7-5657-4a10-9c33-2e33d09b919c",
        "type": "rant",
        "userName": "YanivR",
        "rantText": "Real Couchbase developers drink beer.",
        "rantAbout": {
                "id": "2d18e287-d5fa-42ce-bca5-b26eaef0d7d4",
                "type": "rant",
                "userName": "JerryS",
                "rantText": "Why do they call it Ovaltine? The mug is round. The jar is round. They
should call it Roundtine."
        }
}
```

In the preceding example, YanivR's rant has JerryS's rant embedded in it. Now when we retrieve YanivR's rant, we get all the related rants in a single operation. This, of course, comes with a cost: because we are saving JerryS's rant twice, we are using much more disk space than in a normalized relational database. Also, if we wanted to update JerryS's rant, we would need to update two different documents. This is one of the tradeoffs for working with a NoSQL database, and one to keep in mind when designing our data model.

Luckily, RanteR does not allow ranters to change their rants (at least until enough people rant at the developers about being unable to edit their rants). One thing we do expect to change, and hopefully quite frequently, is the collection of rantbacks. This is a good reason to consider saving rantbacks in a separate document. Let's create a document for holding them:

```
[{
        "username": "JohnC",
        "text": "Well, of course, this is just the sort blinkered philistine pig-ignorance I've come
to expect from you non-creative garbage."
},
```

```
{
        "username": "DavidO",
        "text": "I just watched you drink three cups of green tea in a row. You are not a real
Couchbase developer."
}]
```

This document represents a JSON array, and each item in the array is a JSON document representing a rantback. This type of separation allows us to update the rantbacks without changing the original rant itself. Another potential benefit of separating data into linked documents is the fact that we can reference the same document from multiple other documents.

Although we've added an ID property for most of the documents, Couchbase Server maintains a separate key for each and every document in the database (as well as for simple type values). We discuss keys in the next section, but for simplicity we'll use the UUID formatted value of 47758bd1-8ad6-4564-97c1-a8cdf003cea3 as the key for the rantbacks document. Let's add a reference to the new rantback array document into the original rant document:

```
{
        "id": "6e5416b7-5657-4a10-9c33-2e33d09b919c",
        "type": "rant",
        "userName": "YanivR",
        "rantbacks": "47758bd1-8ad6-4564-97c1-a8cdf003cea3",
        "rantText": "Real Couchbase developers drink beer.",
        "rantAbout": {
                "id": "2d18e287-d5fa-42ce-bca5-b26eaef0d7d4",
                "type": "rant",
                "userName": "JerryS",
                "rantText": "Why do they call it Ovaltine? The mug is round. The jar is round. They
should call it Roundtine."
        }
}
```

Couchbase is optimized for key-based lookups, and you can build your document without fearing the extra roundtrips. Furthermore, embedding content inside a document allows us to access the whole JSON graph atomically.

Designing Keys

Every value in Couchbase Server, whether simple or complex, has a unique key. Unlike most other databases, Couchbase does not generate the document keys automatically. It is up to the application creating the data to supply a unique string value of up to 250 characters as the key for each document. There are several techniques we can use to create keys for our documents. Because key-based lookup is the most efficient way to access a document, selecting a strategy for creating keys will have significant impact on the way you access your data.

Natural Keys

Natural keys are unique values that are a part of the entity represented in the database. This design principle originates in relational database design and is also useful when designing keys in non-relational databases. This means that any unique value that is part of the document can be used as a key. For example, in a rant, the username is not unique. However, we can use the username as a key for the user-details document because it is unique in the context of user details.

When designing Couchbase keys, using a natural key such as the username makes sense when we have the key in advance, before performing the lookup. For example, the username and email are both unique for a document representing a user; the choice between using a username or email would be based on the data we have when accessing the document. If you use the username for login, then that would be the logical choice for the natural key. On the other hand, if the login is based on the user's email address, and the username is only used for display, having the email as a natural key makes more sense.

Creating Your First Document

It is time to start creating some documents in our database. In this section we will create documents using the Couchbase administration console. To use the administration console, open the following address in your browser: `http://<server>:8091` where `<server>` is the machine on which you've installed Couchbase. Enter the administrator username and password you configured during the Couchbase Server installation and sign in. Once signed in, click the Data Buckets link in the top navigation bar. You should see the list of buckets in your Couchbase Server cluster, as shown in Figure 2-2.

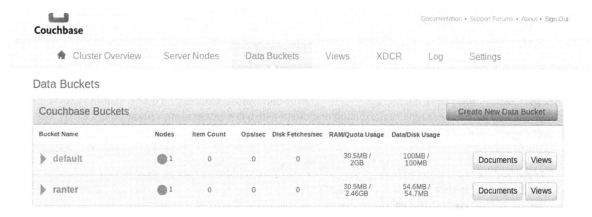

Figure 2-2. *The Data Buckets view in the Couchbase administration console*

To start creating documents, click the Documents button for the ranter bucket. Now we can create new documents in our bucket. The first document we will create is a user document. Click the Create Document button and then provide a document ID. Because RanteR uses a simplistic login system based on the combination of a username and password, enter a username for the document ID, as shown in Figure 2-3.

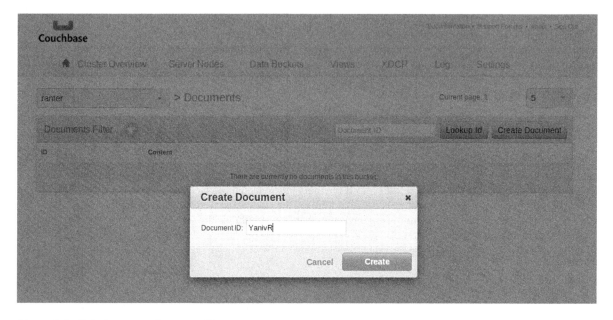

Figure 2-3. *Entering a new document ID*

Click the Create button. The Couchbase Server administration console will create a new document with some sample data in JSON format. Let's replace the default document with a document representing a RanteR user. Use the following document structure and feel free to insert your own data:

```
{
        "type": "user",
        "username": "YanivR",
        "email": "yaniv@ranter.com",
        "password": "12345",
        "shortDesc": "A software grouch",
        "imageUrl": "https://secure.gravatar.com/userimage/34395405/7856c192a706851d06f391be9050
e008.jpg?size=200"
}
```

After entering the document, click Save to save the document, as shown in Figure 2-4.

Figure 2-4. A user document in the Couchbase administration console

---

■ **Note** Saving the type of the document inside the document itself is extremely useful when working with views. We recommend always including which type of entity the document represents as one of the attributes.

Counters

Auto-incremented IDs are commonly used in relational databases. It is a simple way to ensure that each row in a table has a unique value generated by the database. As mentioned earlier, Couchbase Server does not generate values for keys, nor does it have an equivalent for tables. However, Couchbase Server does have a mechanism for storing numeric values and incrementing or decrementing them as an atomic operation. We can use this mechanism to implement counters, which are simply stored numeric values used as part of a key.

■ **Note** Currently, you cannot manage numeric values from the administration console. Chapter 4 covers numeric values and counters.

Counters are useful for iterating over a set of documents. For example, in RanteR we will want to show the last ten rants on a user's timeline. A simple way to do this would be to generate the rant keys as a string with the following pattern: rant_<username>_<countervalue>. Here, <countervalue> comes from a per-user counter. This would let us quickly retrieve specific rants made by users, as well as the total rant count.

Now we can create rants for a specific user. Because we don't have a way to create a numeric value from the administration console, we will just enter the following rant with the ID rant_yanivr_1:

```
{
        "username": "YanivR",
        "ranttext": "JavaScript is the One True Language. Why can't people see that?",
        "id": "rant_yanivr_1",
        "type": "rant"
}
```

Universally Unique Identifiers (UUID)

Universally unique identifiers (UUID) are unique values that can be generated without the need for centralized coordination. In our case, this means that an application can generate a value that is most likely to be unique without accessing the database first.

■ **Note**   Because there is a finite number of values that can be used as UUIDs, there is a small possibility that the same value will be generated twice. There are a few techniques to lower the probability of generating such values. For more information on UUIDs, see the UUID Wikipedia article: `http://en.wikipedia.org/wiki/Universally_unique_identifier`.

Generating a unique key programmatically rather than via the database can prevent excessive database roundtrips. Another useful scenario for using UUIDs is when we need a way to have the key before accessing the database. For example in RanteR we can use a UUID as the key of a rantback for a rant, which allows us to create both documents in our application before storing either, because the rantback key can be generated in advance. We can also use the rant document to get the rantback ID for retrieving the rantback document.

For example, we can add a UUID value for our rant document:

```
{
        "username": "YanivR",
        "ranttext": "JavaScript is the One True Language. Why can't people see that?",
        "id": "rant_yanivr_1",
        "type": "rant",
        "rantbacks": "3a0ac5ec-5c90-4bcd-923c-4ee9900ebba7"
}
```

■ **Note**   You can use the value 3a0ac5ec-5c90-4bcd-923c-4ee9900ebba7 as the UUID for the document. It is completely unique.

Metadata

For every value stored in the database, Couchbase Server creates metadata that is associated with that record. Couchbase metadata contains additional information that is needed for advanced data operations, as follows:

- *Expiration*: Couchbase supports temporary documents, which can only be used for a predefined period of time. Couchbase saves the expiration, or time-to-live (TTL), in UNIX epoch time (the number of seconds since Jan 1st 1970 UTC). Chapter 4 covers expiration in depth.

- *Check-and-Set (CAS)*: The CAS value is a 64-bit integer that is updated by the server whenever the associated item is modified. CAS can be used to manage concurrency when multiple clients might attempt to update the same item simultaneously. Chapter 4 covers CAS in depth.

- *Flags*: Flags are a set of SDK-specific parameters used for a variety of SDK-specific needs. For example, in some SDKs flags are used to identify the format in which the data is serialized, whereas other SDKs store the data type of the object being stored. Flags are represented as 32-bit integers.

■ **Note**   Currently, flags differ from one SDK to another. For this reason, some SDKs are not compatible with other SDKs. If you need to access the same document from different SDKs, please refer to the SDK's documentation for guidance.

In addition to the preceding list, Couchbase Server saves additional metadata for internal use:

- Id: Couchbase Server saves the document's key as part of the metadata.

- Type: Internally, Couchbase saves data in two formats:

    - JSON: Used whenever a valid JSON value is being saved in the database. JSON is also used to store counters that are created using the increment/decrement functionality in the SDKs.

    - Base64: All other data is being saved as Base64 encoded strings.

- Rev: This value is an internal revision ID used by Couchbase Server.

Just like with keys, Couchbase stores metadata in memory. Since version 2.1, Couchbase server uses 56 bytes of RAM per document for metadata. In previous versions, Couchbase Server used 64 bytes per document to store metadata.

Document Versioning

Scalability is only one aspect that influenced the NoSQL movement. Another aspect is the frequent changes to data structures. Modern applications change frequently, and so do the data sources they depend upon. For this reason, it is not surprising that most NoSQL solutions offer schemaless mechanisms to store data. Couchbase follows the same principle, which means that while certain documents represent a specific type or entity, they are not constrained to do so in the same manner as other documents. Throughout the life of the application, attributes and even whole sub-objects can be added or removed from your data. For example, in RanteR v1.0, the rant object has certain attributes, but in RanteR v1.1 we may decide to add a new creation-date field and replace the simple rantText attribute with a more complex sub-object.

As the data model of your application evolves, you can store new versions of documents without needing to change the existing documents representing older versions of the same types. However, when you retrieve older data, you might need to take precautions to ensure your code can still interpret it correctly. Changes to documents can affect your application in two scenarios: when accessing data with the Couchbase SDKs and when creating views.

Versioning Considerations when Using the Couchbase SDKs

Couchbase's SDKs are written in a variety of languages and use different mechanisms for serializing and deserializing data. Some languages have a more dynamic type system—for example, JavaScript objects do not have a strict structure, so Node.js applications can retrieve documents from different versions in different structures without a problem. However, if you try to access a property that does not exist in the version of the document you have retrieved, the property will have the value of undefined. It is up to you, the developer, to ensure that the properties you access exist before accessing them.

In statically typed languages, such as Java and C#, objects have a predefined structure, which means that when you add properties, you must have all the values in place. In this case, it's up to the serializer to decide whether the document can be deserialized. In most cases, missing attributes will be deserialized as the default value of the property. However, with more dramatic changes, such as changing a simple property to a complex embedded document, you might have to resort to custom serialization or to updating the older documents after all.

Versioning Considerations in Couchbase Views

Couchbase views are essentially a secondary index on JSON documents using MapReduce functions written in JavaScript. This allows you to create an index based on the content of your JSON document. Chapter 5 covers views in depth, but for now just remember that new views may miss older documents that don't have the indexed properties. Conversely, older views may not catch new versions of documents, whose properties differ from what the view expects.

Summary

Document-oriented databases offer simplicity when it comes to database design. We can save complex application types as monolithic documents, which simplifies the way we query our data. The shift to a non-relational mindset is often confusing, as we need to let go of some of the core concepts that dominated database design in the past three or four decades in order to achieve scalability, performance, and agility.

PART II

Development

CHAPTER 3

The Couchbase Client Libraries

Chapter 2 showed how to use the administration console to create and retrieve data from our Couchbase Server cluster. However, like any other database, Couchbase is intended to serve as a data store for applications. Unlike many traditional databases, Couchbase Server is designed to distribute data across multiple nodes, which adds complexity to storage and retrieval. To allow applications to save and retrieve data, Couchbase provides a set of language-specific client libraries, also called Couchbase Client SDKs. In this chapter you'll learn the basics of accessing data programmatically using the different Couchbase client libraries in all the supported languages.

Currently, Couchbase provides officially supported SDKs for the following seven languages and runtimes:

- Java
- .NET
- C
- PHP
- Ruby
- Node.js
- Python

Note SDKs for several additional languages, including Clojure, Go, Perl, and Erlang, are maintained by the community as open source projects. An up-to-date list can be found at the official Couchbase website: `www.couchbase.com/communities/all-client-libraries`. Couchbase is also compatible with memcached, so any memcached SDKs should be able to access Couchbase seamlessly. Of course, memcached SDKs will only be able to use the memcached features, rather than the full power of Couchbase Server.

These SDKs are used to communicate with the Couchbase Server cluster. To do so, the SDKs usually communicate directly with the nodes storing relevant data within the cluster, and then perform data operations such as insertion and retrieval. This means that the Couchbase clients are aware of all the nodes in the cluster, their current state, and what documents are stored in each node.

The best way to understand how the Couchbase SDKs work is to use them. So without further ado, we are going to start writing our first application.

For our first application using Couchbase Server, we are going to develop part of the basic functionality of RanteR: creating and retrieving user rants. For now, we will create a simple application, configure access to the Couchbase Server cluster, and then use this connection to store and retrieve data. In Chapter 4, you'll learn about the various ways to create, retrieve, and delete data in Couchbase. For now, you only need two simple operations: get and set. Get retrieves a document, and set adds or updates a document in the database.

> ■ **Note**   Because this is a book about Couchbase, rather than any particular programming language, we'll leave out the less interesting application glue code. However, the complete code samples can be found at the book's website as well as in the book's GitHub repository: `https://github.com/procouchbaseserver/example-source`.

The first SDK we will cover is the Java SDK. This section will also contain most of the background information on the client libraries. If you're only interested in one of the other languages, we recommend you read the Java SDK section before skipping ahead to your language of choice.

The Java SDK

The first step to using Couchbase in any language is to download the appropriate Client SDK. Like most modern languages, Java provides more than one way to add external dependencies. The Couchbase Java SDK is available as a manual download or through a Maven repository.

Adding the Java SDK Manually

The Java SDK is available for download from the Couchbase website (`www.couchbase.com/communities/java/getting-started`) under Step 1: Get a Client Library. Download and extract the zip file and then add the couchbase-client, netty, httpcore, jettison, spymemcached, and commons-codec libraries to your project.

Using Maven

Apache Maven is a software project management and comprehension tool. The name Maven means "knowledgeable" in Yiddish—the most powerful ranting language known to man. Maven uses a project object model (POM) file to manage, among other things, software dependencies. In order to use the Couchbase SDK in our Maven project we need to add the Couchbase SDK as a dependency in the POM file, as seen here:

```
<dependencies>
 <dependency>
   <groupId>com.couchbase.client</groupId>
   <artifactId>couchbase-client</artifactId>
   <version>1.2.2</version>
 </dependency>
</dependencies>
```

Or, if you're using a plug-in in one of the popular Java IDEs, search for Couchbase in the Maven repositories list or use the group ID *com.couchbase.client* and artifact ID *couchbase-client*.

Using the CouchbaseClient Class

Once we have all the dependencies in place, we can start using the SDK to connect to the database. The first step is to create an instance of the CouchbaseClient class, which is used to communicate with Couchbase Server clusters. We will see that this approach is common to most of the Couchbase Client SDKs: the client object is the main entry point for all data access. In order to connect to the server, we'll need to provide the client with some connection information, namely the addresses of one or more nodes in the cluster, which will be used to retrieve the cluster's configuration, the name of the bucket where the data will be stored, and a password, if one is set for the bucket.

In a multi-node cluster, it is good practice to provide the addresses of more than one node, in case one of the nodes is unavailable for any reason:

```
List<URI> nodes = Arrays.asList(new URI("http://127.0.0.1:8091/pools"));
CouchbaseClient client = new CouchbaseClient(nodes, "ranter", "");
```

In the preceding code example, we create a list of node addresses—in our case just the one node, which is installed on the local machine—and pass it to the CouchbaseClient constructor, along with the name of the bucket. We did not set a password, so the third parameter is an empty string.

Now that we have our CouchbaseClient object, it's time to store some data. Let's define a simple Rant object for our application, which will hold an ID, the user name, and the rant text itself. We'll also need a field in which to store the type of object so we can distinguish it from other document types in the database:

```java
public class Rant {
        private final UUID id;
        private final String username;
        private final String ranttext;
        private final String type;

        public Rant(UUID id, String username, String ranttext, String type) {
                this.id = id;
                this.username = username;
                this.ranttext = ranttext;
                this.type = type;
        }

        public UUID getId() {
                return id;
        }

        public String getUsername() {
                return username;
        }

        public String getRanttext() {
                return ranttext;
        }
}
```

Now that we have a Rant class, we need to make it serializable in order to save it to the database. In Java we have multiple ways to make a class serializable. For example, we can have the Rant class implement the Serializable interface, in which case the Couchbase client will use regular Java serialization to send the object to the server, where it will be stored as a binary blob. A binary value will not be indexed, and its properties can't be queried—it can only be retrieved by key and then deserialized back into an object.

While storing objects is certainly a useful feature in some cases, normally we will want to use the full range of Couchbase abilities with our data, such as querying, indexing, and more. For this, we need to serialize our object into a JSON representation before storing it in the database. Couchbase Server recognizes JSON values and treats them as documents. It is important to keep in mind that there are multiple libraries that can do this. In this example, we will use google-gson, which you can obtain through Maven by adding a dependency with the group ID com.google.code.gson and artifact ID gson. To serialize an object into JSON, we'll create an instance of the Gson class and use the toJson method:

```
Gson gson = new Gson();
Rant rant = new Rant(
                UUID.randomUUID(),
                "JerryS",
                "Why do they call it Ovaltine? The mug is round. The jar is round. They should
call it Roundtine.",
                "rant");

Boolean success = client.set(rant.getId().toString(), gson.toJson(rant)).get();
```

The set method stores or updates a document in the database. We cover operations in detail in Chapter 4.

▪ **Note**   The set method returns an OperationFuture<Boolean> object, because the Couchbase SDK is designed to be asynchronous. In a real-world application, you should use the API asynchronously, but in the code sample above we call OverationFuture.get method to retrieve the result synchronously for simplicity.

We can view or edit our stored rant in the Couchbase administration console. Figure 3-1 shows the document we've added in the previous example.

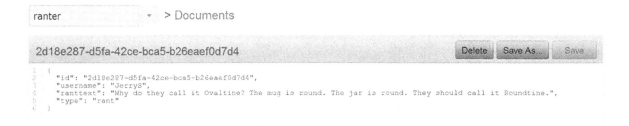

Figure 3-1. *A rant document, viewed in the Couchbase administration console*

To retrieve our newly stored rant, we call the get method of CouchbaseClient with the document ID as the parameter, which will return the document as a JSON string. We then call the fromJson method of Gson to turn it back into a Rant object:

```
Gson gson = new Gson();
String json = (String)client.get("2d18e287-d5fa-42ce-bca5-b26eaef0d7d4");
Rant rant = gson.fromJson(json, Rant.class);
```

Once we're done using Couchbase, we can call the shutdown method to shut the client down gracefully:

```
client.shutdown();
```

The Java SDK is a good example for some of the more common tasks. However, other languages have nuances specific to them. In the following sections we will introduce the different official Couchbase SDKs. At this point you can simply skip ahead to the language of your choice, or directly to the "Inside the Couchbase Client Libraries" section towards the end of this chapter.

The .NET SDK

In .NET, just like with the other languages, the first thing we need to do is download the SDK and add references to the assemblies to our .NET project. Much like in Java, this can be done either manually or by using the NuGet package manager.

Manually Referencing the Assemblies

We can download the latest SDK from the .NET Community Getting Started page on the Couchbase website: www.couchbase.com/communities/net/getting-started.

Once we have downloaded the binaries, we'll need to add references to the Couchbase.dll, Enyim.Caching.dll, and Newtonsoft.Json.dll assemblies to our project.

Using NuGet Package Manager

Like most modern development frameworks, .NET has a convenient package manager, called NuGet, which simplifies the process of adding the Couchbase SDK to the project. NuGet can be installed as an add-on in Microsoft Visual Studio 2010 and MonoDevelop and comes integrated by default into Visual Studio 2012 or later.

To install the Couchbase SDK with NuGet in Visual Studio, open the NuGet Management Console, and then run the following command:

```
PM> Install-Package CouchbaseNetClient
```

Alternatively, you can open the NuGet Package Management UI, search for the *CouchbaseNetClient* package in the online package source, and click Install.

Using the CouchbaseClient Class

Just like in Java, we will use the CouchbaseClient class to connect to the Couchbase Server cluster. Before we can use the CouchbaseClient class, we need to configure the Couchbase Server connection information in our application. A simple way to do this is by adding a new section to the application configuration file—web.config or app.config, depending on whether it's a web application or not. The relevant parts of the configuration file should look like this:

```xml
<?xml version="1.0"?>
<configuration>
 <configSections>
   <section name="couchbase" type="Couchbase.Configuration.CouchbaseClientSection, Couchbase"/>
 </configSections>
 <couchbase>
   <servers bucket="ranter" bucketPassword="">
     <add uri="http://localhost:8091/pools"/>
   </servers>
 </couchbase>
</configuration>
```

As you can see in the preceding code, the <couchbase> configuration section contains the <servers> element, which specifies the bucket that will hold our data, the password (if needed), and the address of a Couchbase node from which the client will retrieve the cluster configuration. In this example the node is installed on the local machine.

We'll need to import the following namespaces:

```
using Couchbase;
using Couchbase.Extensions;
using Enyim.Caching.Memcached;
using Newtonsoft.Json;
```

Now we can create an instance of the CouchbaseClient class to store and retrieve items from the database. The default constructor will read the configuration from the application configuration file and contact one of the specified nodes to get the cluster configuration:

```
var client = new CouchbaseClient();
```

Alternatively, we can specify the configuration programmatically at run-time:

```
var config = new CouchbaseClientConfiguration();
config.Urls.Add(new Uri("http://localhost:8091/pools/"));
config.Bucket = "ranter";

var client = new CouchbaseClient(config);
```

In the preceding code example, we create an instance of the CouchbaseClientConfiguration class, initialize the same parameters we used in the configuration snippet earlier, and then create an instance of CouchbaseClient with the configuration object as the constructor argument.

Once we have the client instance, we can use it to perform database operations. For now, let's define a simple Rant class, which will only hold the user name, the message, the type of post, and an ID. We will use this data object to store and retrieve posts.

```
public class Rant
{
        [JsonProperty("id")]
        public Guid Id { get; set; }

        [JsonProperty("userName")]
        public string UserName { get; set; }

        [JsonProperty("rantText")]
        public string RantText { get; set; }

        [JsonProperty("type")]
        public string Type { get; set; }
}
```

The astute reader might notice that we are using the JsonProperty attribute for each of our C# properties in this class. This is done to bridge between the different naming conventions in C# and JSON. In this book we use the Google JSON Style Guide as our naming convention, and therefore our JSON properties are in camel case, starting with a lowercase letter and capitalizing each subsequent word. In C#, the convention is to use Pascal case, which is starting each word with a capital letter.

■ **Note** The JsonProperty attribute is part of the Newtonsoft.Json library, which comes with the Couchbase .NET SDK.

Now that we have our Rant class, we can store it in the database. To do so, much like what you saw in the Java SDK section, we need to serialize the object. In .NET, we can decorate the class with the Serializable attribute, in which case the Couchbase client will use .NET runtime serialization, causing the object to be stored as binary data. Objects stored as binary data are not indexable, and their properties can't be queried—they can only be retrieved by key and then deserialized back into CLR objects.

To take advantage of the full range of Couchbase's abilities with our data, such as querying and indexing, we will need to convert our CLR object into a JSON representation before storing it in the database. Luckily, the Couchbase .NET SDK comes with the Newtonsoft.Json library, which does precisely that. We can use the JsonConvert class from the library to serialize objects into JSON and back:

```
var rant = new Rant
{
    Id = Guid.NewGuid(),
    Type = "rant",
    UserName = "JerryS",
    RantText = "Why do they call it Ovaltine? The mug is round. The jar is round. They should call
it Roundtine."
};

string json = JsonConvert.SerializeObject(rant);
var success = client.Store(StoreMode.Set, rant.Id.ToString(), json);
```

In this example, we create a new Rant object with some sample data, then use the static JsonConvert.SerializeObject method to serialize the object into JSON and store it in the database. We'll cover the various store modes and server operations in Chapter 4.

To simplify the work with JSON documents, the Couchbase .NET SDK has a set of built-in extension methods, which are defined in the Couchbase.Extensions namespace. These methods convert to and from JSON while performing data access. For example, we can use the convenient StoreJson method to do the JSON serialization for us:

```
bool success = client.StoreJson(StoreMode.Set, rant.Id.ToString(), rant);
```

There is one important caveat when using the *Json extension methods: when the CLR object has a property named Id, the extension methods automatically map it to the stored key and do not include this property in the resulting JSON document. This mapping works well with strongly typed views, which we talk about later in the book. However, when you use more than one type of SDK to access your data, this can be a problem, as other Client SDKs won't map the key back to the ID property.

To retrieve a rant by its key, we can use the GetJson extension method, which will get the document and deserialize it from JSON into a CLR object for us. In the next example we use a hardcoded string as the key for simplicity:

```
string key = "9538ccc8-56a6-4445-b9d2-0558287c41eb";
var rant = client.GetJson<Rant>(key);
```

The Couchbase .NET SDK provides simple database access functionality to Couchbase Server clusters for .NET applications. It is designed according to up-to-date industry practices, includes the ubiquitous Newtonsoft.Json library for JSON serialization, and is available as a NuGet package.

The C SDK

The C Couchbase SDK (libcouchbase) has additional importance beyond providing access to the database in the C language. This library is a prerequisite for the PHP, Python, Ruby, and Node.js clients, so the installation steps described in this section will be useful for all of those SDKs.

To start using libcouchbase, either in a C/C++ application or when using another SDK, we first need to install it. Since we are dealing with native C code, the installation process is platform specific. In the next few sections, we will describe how to install libcouchbase on each of the supported platforms.

Linux

The Linux version of Couchbase Server is currently supported on Ubuntu, Red Hat Enterprise Linux, CentOS, and Amazon Linux.

Ubuntu

The first thing we need to do in order to install libcouchbase on Ubuntu is to add Couchbase to the package resource list:

```
> sudo wget -O/etc/apt/sources.list.d/couchbase.list
http://packages.couchbase.com/ubuntu/couchbase-ubuntu1204.list
```

Next, we need to install the GPG key:

```
> wget -O- http://packages.couchbase.com/ubuntu/couchbase.key | sudo apt-key add -
```

And, finally, we need to install the libcouchbase package:

```
> sudo apt-get update
> sudo apt-get install libcouchbase2-libevent libcouchbase-dev
```

Red Hat

On Red Hat Enterprise Linux, CentOS, or Amazon Linux we also need to add Couchbase to the package resource list. For the 64-bit repository, run the following shell command:

```
> sudo wget -O/etc/yum.repos.d/couchbase.repo http://packages.couchbase.com/rpm/couchbase-
centos62-x86_64.repo
```

For the 32-bit repository, run the following shell command:

```
> sudo wget -O/etc/yum.repos.d/couchbase.repo http://packages.couchbase.com/rpm/couchbase-
centos62-i686.repo
```

And then install the libcouchbase package:

```
> sudo yum check-update
> sudo yum install -y  libcouchbase2-libevent libcouchbase-devel
```

You can also use the package manager GUI to search for the libcouchbase package and install it that way. Alternatively, you can download the stand-alone version of the SDK. To download the stand-alone archives, and for installation instructions for other OS versions, visit www.couchbase.com/communities/c/getting-started.

Windows

Acquiring libcouchbase in Windows is fairly straightforward. You simply download the libcouchbase archive for your planned architecture and Visual Studio toolset version from www.couchbase.com/communities/c/getting-started.

After unzipping the archive, you need to set up your Visual Studio project. To do so add <folder>\include\ libcouchbase to your project's include directories, add <folder>\lib to your project's library directories, and make sure that libcouchbase.dll, which is also located in <folder>\lib, is discoverable by the application. In this case, <folder> refers to the location where you have extracted the libcouchbase archive.

Mac OS X

For Mac OS X, libcouchbase is available for installation via homebrew (http://brew.sh) using the following shell command:

```
> brew update && brew install libcouchbase
```

Using libcouchbase

Now that we have libcouchbase installed, we can start building our first application. The general pattern for using the Couchbase SDK in a C/C++ application is similar to all Couchbase SDKs. We initialize a connection and then use this connection to store and retrieve objects from the database. However, unlike the .NET and Java SDKs, which we've already covered, the C SDK uses asynchronous callbacks for database operations. Let's create and open a connection to our Couchbase server:

```c
#include <stdio.h>
#include <stdlib.h>
#include <libcouchbase/couchbase.h>

static void error_callback(lcb_t instance,
                           lcb_error_t err,
                    const char *errinfo)
{
        printf("Error %s: %s", lcb_strerror(instance, err),
errinfo ? errinfo : "");
exit(EXIT_FAILURE);
}

int main(void)
{
        struct lcb_create_st create_options;
        lcb_t connection;
        lcb_error_t err;

        // Set the connection parameters.
        memset(&create_options, 0, sizeof(create_options));
        create_options.v.v0.host = "localhost:8091";
```

```
        create_options.v.v0.user = "";
        create_options.v.v0.passwd = "";
        create_options.v.v0.bucket = "ranter";

        // Create the connection object with the specified parameters.
        err = lcb_create(&connection, &create_options);
        if (err != LCB_SUCCESS)
        {
                printf("Error creating instance: %s\n", lcb_strerror(NULL, err));
                exit(EXIT_FAILURE);
        }

        // Set the error handler.
        lcb_set_error_callback(connection, error_callback);

        // Connect to Couchbase (asynchronously).
        err = lcb_connect(connection);
        if (err != LCB_SUCCESS)
        {
                printf("Error initializing connection: %s\n",
                  lcb_strerror(NULL, err));
                exit(EXIT_FAILURE);
        }

        // Wait for the connection process to finish.
        lcb_wait(connection);

        // Do stuff.

        // Release the connection.
        lcb_destroy(connection);

        getchar();
}
```

In the preceding example, we initialize the lcb_create_st struct with the connection parameters: the address of our Couchbase node, from which we will retrieve the cluster configuration, the bucket name, and, optionally, a username and password. Then we call lcb_create to initialize an instance of lcb_t with the specified connection parameters. We set the callback function that will be called for errors. And then we call lcb_connect with the initialized instance to begin the connection process. Because, like all database operations, the lcb_connect call is asynchronous, we use lcb_wait to wait for the connection to finish. Finally, when we're done using Couchbase, we call lcb_destroy to release the connection.

With our connection open, we can use the connection struct to perform database operations. We'll need a callback function for libcouchbase to call when the store operation completes:

```
static void store_callback(lcb_t connection,
                           const void *cookie,
                           lcb_storage_t operation,
                           lcb_error_t error,
                           const lcb_store_resp_t *item)
{
```

```
        if (error == LCB_SUCCESS)
        {
                printf("Rant stored: ");
                fwrite(item->v.v0.key, sizeof(char), item->v.v0.nkey, stdout);
                printf("\n");
        }
        else
        {
                printf("Error storing rant: %s (0x%x)\n",
                         lcb_strerror(connection, error), error);
                exit(EXIT_FAILURE);
        }
}
```

For brevity, we will use hardcoded strings as our key and sample rant:

```
// Set the store operation callback.
lcb_set_store_callback(connection, store_callback);

// Code block - for variable scoping.
{
        lcb_store_cmd_t cmd;
        const lcb_store_cmd_t *commands[1];

        commands[0] = &cmd;
        memset(&cmd, 0, sizeof(cmd));
        cmd.v.v0.operation = LCB_SET;
        cmd.v.v0.key = "2g3e45db-054b-4b7c-ba61-955ebcdae94a";
        cmd.v.v0.nkey = strlen(cmd.v.v0.key);
        cmd.v.v0.bytes = "{\"id\": \"1d3e45db-054b-4b7c-ba61-955ebcdae94a\",\"username\":
\"JerryS\",\"ranttext\": \"Why do they call it Ovaltine? The mug is round. The jar is round. They
should call it Roundtine.\",\"type\": \"rant\"}";
        cmd.v.v0.nbytes = strlen(cmd.v.v0.bytes);

        err = lcb_store(connection, NULL, 1, commands);

        if (err != LCB_SUCCESS)
        {
                printf("Failed to store: %s\n", lcb_strerror(NULL, err));
                exit(EXIT_FAILURE);
        }
}

// Wait for the set operation to finish.
lcb_wait(connection);
```

In the preceding code sample we set the store callback, which we defined earlier, initialize a new
lcb_store_cmd_t struct, and set the operation type, key, value, and the parameter lengths. Then we call lcb_store
to perform the command and use lcb_wait to wait until the operation finishes. The second parameter to lcb_store,
which is NULL in our example, is a cookie—a token that will be passed by libcouchbase to the callback function. It is
used to pass state information for different store calls and does not get sent to the server.

Next we will retrieve a document. Once again, we will need a callback function for the get operation:

```
static void get_callback(lcb_t connection,
                         const void *cookie,
                         lcb_error_t error,
                         const lcb_get_resp_t *resp)
{
        if (error != LCB_SUCCESS)
        {
                printf("Error retrieving rant: ");
                fwrite(resp->v.v0.key, 1, resp->v.v0.nkey, stdout);
                printf(" ==> %s\n", lcb_strerror(connection, error));
        }
        else
        {
                printf("Rant retrieved: ");
                fwrite(resp->v.v0.key, 1, resp->v.v0.nkey, stdout);
                printf(" ==> \n");
                fwrite(resp->v.v0.bytes, 1, resp->v.v0.nbytes, stdout);
        }
}
```

We set the callback of the get operation in the same way as we did with the store callback:

```
// Set the get operation callback.
lcb_set_get_callback(connection, get_callback);

{
        lcb_get_cmd_t cmd;
        const lcb_get_cmd_t *commands[1];

        commands[0] = &cmd;
        memset(&cmd, 0, sizeof(cmd));
        cmd.v.v0.key = "1d3e45db-054b-4b7c-ba61-955ebcdae94a";
        cmd.v.v0.nkey = strlen(cmd.v.v0.key);

        err = lcb_get(connection, NULL, 1, commands);

        if (err != LCB_SUCCESS)
        {
                printf("Failed to get: %s\n", lcb_strerror(NULL, err));
                exit(EXIT_FAILURE);
        }
}
```

```
// Wait for the get operation to finish.
lcb_wait(connection);
```

The get operation example is very similar to the store example, except we only specify the key we wish to retrieve as well as the key length. When the document is returned by the server, libcouchbase will call the get_callback function and then pass the retrieved document as the lcb_get_resp_t parameter.

Libcouchbase provides C/C++ applications with a native asynchronous API for accessing Couchbase Server. However, even if you are not using C/C++ to write your applications, there is still a good chance you will be using libcouchbase under the covers. The last four SDKs in this chapter all use libcouchbase internally. The next SDK we will cover is Node.js, which is asynchronous by nature and integrates seamlessly with the callback-based API of libcouchbase.

The Node.js SDK

For most programming languages, JSON is just a lightweight, textual data-interchange format, but for JavaScript, it plays a special role. JSON is a subset of JavaScript, which is used as the native format for object literals. This means that any JSON value can be treated as an object. For this reason, JSON-based document databases are extremely popular in the Node.js community. The Couchbase Node.js SDK provides an easy interface for accessing Couchbase Server clusters from Node.js applications.

Note   The Node.js Couchbase SDK is dependent on the libcouchbase C library. For Linux and Mac OS X users, it is necessary to install libcouchbase first. Installing libcouchbase is covered in the section "The C SDK" in this chapter.

Once the libcouchbase C library is installed on your machine, you can use the Node Package Manager (NPM) to set up the Couchbase Node.js SDK:

```
> npm install couchbase
```

Now we can start using the Node.js module in our application. In order to load the Couchbase module, we will use the require function:

```
var couchbase = require('couchbase');
```

With the module loaded, we can now use the connection method to create a new client object. Just like with the other SDKs, we need to provide a configuration object that specifies the name of the bucket, connection details, and a list of nodes that can be used to retrieve the cluster configuration, as follows:

```
var client = new couchbase.Connection({
        'bucket':'ranter',
        'host':'127.0.0.1:8091'
});
```

Once we have the client object, we can use it to perform database operations. Let's use our rant sample, which will only hold the user name, the message, the type of rant, and an ID. Unlike most languages, in JavaScript we can just use JSON as an object literal:

```
var rant = {
                "username": "YanivR",
                "rantText": "JavaScript is the One True Language. Why can't people see that?",
                "id": "8b7a5f8b-f511-4c7e-9279-9304d06e6468",
                "type": "rant"
        };
```

Now we can use the `client` object to add the post to our Couchbase Server cluster:

```
client.set(rant.id, rant, function(err, result) {});
```

In the preceding code we call the `set` method of the client. One thing that might pop out in this sample is the fact that the `set` function receives three parameters:

1. Key: The key for accessing the document.

2. Value: The object that will be stored as a JSON document in the database.

3. Callback: A function that will be called once the `set` method finishes executing.

Having a callback is typical for Node.js, which is built around the notion of asynchronous APIs. For example, this allows us to execute the get method asynchronously once the `set` method is done executing.

```
// saving the post to Couchbase
client.set(rant.id, rant, function(err, result) {

        // once the document is saved, we pull it back from the database by id
        client.get(rant.id, function(err, result){

                // writing the document to console
                console.log(result.value);

        });
});
```

Node.js is rapidly becoming the framework of choice for building IO-intensive applications for many developers and organizations. Its asynchronous model and native JSON support make Node.js ideal for interacting with JSON-based, document-oriented databases on one side and JavaScript-based front-ends on the other. The Couchbase Node.js SDK is consistent with Node.js's style of asynchronous APIs and is very natural for Node.js developers.

The PHP SDK

Just like the Node.js Couchbase SDK, the PHP SDK also relies on libcouchbase, which we will need to install, as covered in the "The C SDK" section of this chapter. Then we will install the PHP Client SDK itself.

Similar to the C SDK installation, the PHP installation process requires platform-specific development tools and external libraries. In the following sections we will describe how to install the PHP SDK for each of the supported platforms.

Linux

To install the SDK from the PECL repository, first let's make sure we have all the prerequisites. Because the installation process builds the PHP Client SDK from source, we will need to have build tools and the PHP development files installed.

On Ubuntu, we'll need the following packages: php5-dev, php5-json, php-pear, and build-essential, which can be installed with the following shell command:

```
> sudo apt-get install php5-dev php5-json php-pear build-essential
```

> ■ **Note** Depending on your Ubuntu version, you might not need to install php5-json.

On RHEL, we'll need the following packages: php-devel, php-pear, and the group "Development Tools," which can be installed as follows:

```
> sudo yum install php-devel php-pear
> sudo yum groupinstall "Development Tools"
```

Once we have the prerequisites installed, we can install the Couchbase SDK with PECL:

```
> sudo pecl channel-update pecl.php.net
> sudo pecl install couchbase
```

You can also download and build the Couchbase PHP extension from source code, which can be found here: http://pecl.php.net/package/couchbase.

Finally, we need to add the Couchbase extension to the php.ini config file. Scroll down to the extensions section of the php.ini file and add the following lines:

```
extension=json.so
extension=couchbase.so
```

If your php.ini file already loads the json.so extension, you only need to add couchbase. so after it.

> ■ **Note** On some systems, such as CentOS, we need to make sure the JSON extension loads before the Couchbase extension, so we add it to the config file as well, in the correct order.

Windows

Installing the PHP SDK on Windows is quite straightforward. You can download the appropriate Windows version of the Couchbase PHP extension from www.couchbase.com/communities/php/getting-started.

Mac OS X

As on Linux, you can install the PHP extension from the official PECL repository. First, let's make sure we have PEAR and PECL. You can download PEAR using curl, as follows:

```
> curl -O http://pear.php.net/go-pear.phar
```

Then run the install process:

```
> sudo php -d detect_unicode=0 go-pear.phar
```

After starting the installation you will be prompted to set the installation paths. First, we will set the installation base path to /usr/local/pear. To do so, type 1, press Return, and enter the desired path.

Next, we will change the binaries directory to the Mac OS X default binaries location: /usr/local/bin. To do so, type 4, press Return, and enter the desired path.

Finally, press Return to finish the configuration process. To verify that PECL was installed successfully, run the following command:

```
> pecl version
```

Now that we have PECL, let's install the Couchbase PHP SDK from the official repository:

```
> sudo pecl install couchbase
```

Alternatively, you can build the PHP extension from source. Download the source tarball from http://pecl.php.net/get/couchbase, unzip the archive, and in the created folder run the following commands:

```
> phpize
> ./configure
> make
```

Add the extension, with the full path to the file, to your php.ini file:

```
extension=/<full path>/couchbase.so
```

■ **Tip**　If you've installed the Couchbase extension with PECL, you can discover the full path to couchbase.so with the shell command: `pecl list-files couchbase`.

Finally, restart your web server.

Using the PHP SDK

Now that we have the Couchbase PHP SDK installed and configured, let's connect to the database. Create a new file named couchbase.php with the following script

```php
<?php
$couchbase = new Couchbase("127.0.0.1:8091", "", "", "ranter");
var_dump($couchbase);
?>
```

As with the other Client SDKs, we initialize a new Couchbase object with the addresses of one or more nodes, an optional username and password, and the name of the bucket to which we want to connect. To see the result, either open the web page in a browser or run the script from the command line:

```
> php couchbase.php
```

The preceding command should result in the following output, indicating that a new Couchbase client object was created:

```
object(Couchbase)#1 (1) {
  ["_handle":"Couchbase":private]=>
  resource(4) of type (Persistent Couchbase)
}
```

Next, let's create and store a new simple Rant in the database. As with most of the other SDKs, we can store a native object or an array directly, and it will be saved as a binary data. This can certainly be useful in some situations, but mostly we'll want to take advantage of Couchbase features like indexing and querying, which require that we store our data as JSON documents instead. Because we made sure to load the JSON PHP extension earlier, we can use the json_encode and json_decode functions to convert objects into JSON strings and back:

```php
<?php
$couchbase = new Couchbase("127.0.0.1:8091", "", "", "ranter");

$rant = array(
        "id" => uniqid(),
        "type" => "rant",
        "userName" => "JerryS",
        "rantText" => "Why do they call it Ovaltine? The mug is round. The jar is round. They should
call it Roundtine."
);

$cas = $couchbase->set($rant["id"], json_encode($rant));
var_dump($cas);
?>
```

That code example creates a PHP array with the ID, type, username, and rant text of our post, and calls the set method of the Couchbase object to store it in the database as a JSON document. The value returned by the set function is a CAS (Check-and-Set) ID, which is used to provide optimistic concurrency in database operations. CAS will be covered in detail in the next chapter, "CRUD Operations."

To retrieve our stored rant, we will use the get method of the Couchbase object with the ID as a parameter. In the next example we use a hardcoded ID string for simplicity:

```php
<?php
$couchbase = new Couchbase("127.0.0.1:8091", "", "", "ranter");

$json = $couchbase->get("527ce9e6ef558");
var_dump($json);

$rant = json_decode($json);
var_dump($rant);
?>
```

This code example retrieves the rant document as a JSON string and then decodes it into a PHP object.

PHP is a very popular environment and is used by a large number of products and websites. The Couchbase PHP SDK provides PHP developers with an easy-to-use API for working with Couchbase.

The Python SDK

The Couchbase Python Client SDK, like the PHP, Ruby, and Node.js SDKs, relies on the libcouchbase C library for access to the Couchbase server. So before installing the Python SDK, we need to make sure we have the C SDK installed, which is covered in the "The C SDK" section of this chapter.

Similar to the C and PHP SDK installations, the Python SDK installation process requires platform-specific development tools and external libraries. We will describe how to install the Python SDK for each of the supported platforms.

■ **Note**   The Python SDK requires Python version 2.6 or higher.

Linux

On Linux, the Python SDK requires a C compiler in addition to libcouchbase and the Python development files. The easiest way to install the Client SDK itself is through the pip package manager.

To install the pip package manager on Ubuntu or other Debian-based distributions, run the following commands:

```
> sudo apt-get install build-essential
> sudo apt-get install python-dev python-pip
```

On Red Hat, run the following shell commands:

```
> sudo yum groupinstall "Development Tools"
> sudo yum install python-devel python-pip
```

Once you have the prerequisites and pip installed, you can install the Couchbase Python SDK:

```
> sudo pip install couchbase
```

Windows

Installing the Python SDK on Windows is very straightforward. You can download the Windows package installer from the Python PyPi package index at https://pypi.python.org/pypi/couchbase#downloads.

Using the Python SDK

With the SDK installed, let's create a new script, called ranter.py, and connect to the ranter bucket in our cluster:

```
#!/usr/bin/env python
from couchbase import Couchbase
client = Couchbase.connect(host='localhost', port=8091, bucket='ranter')
print client
```

Running this script should produce the following result:

```
> python ranter.py
<couchbase.connection.Connection bucket=ranter, nodes=['127.0.0.1:8091'] at 0x7faeb928fb78>
```

We have successfully connected to our bucket, so now let's store a new rant. Python 2.6 and higher includes the JSON module, and the Couchbase SDK will attempt to convert objects into JSON by default before storing them:

```
import uuid
from couchbase import Couchbase

client = Couchbase.connect(host='localhost', port=8091, bucket='ranter')

rant = {
        'id' : str(uuid.uuid4()),
        'type' : 'rant',
        'userName' : 'JerryS',
        'rantText' : 'Why do they call it Ovaltine? The mug is round. The jar is round. They should
call it Roundtine.'
}

result = client.set(rant['id'], rant)
print result
```

As you can see in this example, we've created a dictionary with some sample post values and then called the set function, with the key and the dictionary as parameters. The Python client library automatically serialized the dictionary into JSON and stored it in the database.

Running the script in the example above should produce the following result:

```
> python ranter.py
OperationResult<RC=0x0, Key=223ac695-04c0-4c44-8cf7-93fd5c8a5f90, CAS=0x6fe6e8b3a4040000>
```

Most of the time you will want to store your data as JSON documents in order to take advantage of the indexing and querying capabilities of Couchbase Server. However, in some cases it makes sense to store your data as binary data, for example in Python's Pickle format. You can set the desired format for all operations that add or change data through the format parameter. To store our rant from the previous example in Pickle format, we would use this code:

```
from couchbase.user_constants import *
result = client.set(rant['id'], rant, format=FMT_PICKLE)
```

In this code the format parameter can be one of the following:

- FMT_JSON: Converts the value to JSON. This is the default format.

- FMT_PICKLE: Converts the value to Pickle.

- FMT_BYTES: Stores the value as a byte string. Value must already be a bytes type.

- FMT_UTF8: Stores the value as a UTF-8-encoded string.

- FMT_AUTO: Automatically decides the value conversion. For lists, tuples, dicts, bools, or None the format will be FMT_JSON, for str it will be FMT_UTF8, for byte objects it will be FMT_BYTES, for everything else it will be FMT_PICKLE.

We can change the default format for all database operations by passing one of the FMT_* values as the default_format parameter to the connect method.

To retrieve our stored rant from the database by key, we'll use the get method of the Couchbase client object. For now, we'll just pass the key as a hardcoded string for convenience:

```
from pprint import pprint
rant = client.get('223ac695-04c0-4c44-8cf7-93fd5c8a5f90');
pprint(rant.value, indent=4)
```

This should result in the following output:

```
> python ranter.py
{   u'id': u'223ac695-04c0-4c44-8cf7-93fd5c8a5f90',
    u'rantText': u'Why do they call it Ovaltine? The mug is round. The jar is round. They should
call it Roundtine.',
    u'type': u'rant',
    u'userName': u'JerryS'}
```

If we try to retrieve a nonexistent key, the default behavior of the Client SDK is to throw an exception. We can override this behavior by passing the quiet=True parameter to the connect function when initializing the database connection, or to the get function itself, in which case trying to retrieve nonexistent keys will return the value None. We can examine the result object returned by the get function to see the underlying libcouchbase error code, the error text, and the key we tried to retrieve, as follows:

```
client = Couchbase.connect(host='localhost', port=8091, bucket='ranter', quiet=True) # Quiet here
result = client.get('nosuchkey', quiet=True); # Or here
print(result.rc, result.errstr, result.key, result.value)
```

Running the preceding code example will result in the following:

```
> python ranter.py
(13, 'No such key', u'nosuchkey', None)
```

The Ruby SDK

The Couchbase Ruby SDK provides access to Couchbase Server clusters for Ruby applications. This includes simple Ruby programs and scripts as well as full-blown Ruby on Rails applications. In this section we will cover both working directly with the Couchbase Ruby client library as well as with a more elaborate Ruby on Rails sample.

The Couchbase Ruby client SDK, like the PHP, Python, and Node.js SDKs, relies on the libcouchbase C library for access to the Couchbase server. Thus, before installing the Python SDK, we need to make sure we have the C SDK installed, which is covered in the "C SDK" section of this chapter.

A Simple Ruby Script

Let's create a simple Ruby script for adding and retrieving a rant. In order to use the Couchbase Ruby SDK we need to install the Couchbase Ruby Gem:

```
> gem install couchbase
```

With the SDK installed, let's create a new script, called ranter.rb, and connect to the ranter bucket in our cluster. We will need to require the couchbase gem in our application using the `require` statement. Once we have required the gem, we can use the connection method to create a new client object. Just like with any other SDK, we need to provide configuration settings to specify the name of the bucket, connection details, and a list of nodes that can be used to retrieve the cluster configuration:

```ruby
require 'couchbase'
client = Couchbase.connect(:bucket => "ranter",
                                          :hostname => "localhost");
```

Once we have the `client` object, we can use it to perform database operations. Let's use our Ranter sample, which will only hold the user name, the message, the type of post, and an ID:

```ruby
rant = {
            :userName => "YanivR",
            :rantText => "JavaScript is the One True Language. Why can\'t people see that?",
            :id => "c287c27b-1018-4337-976a-49a73ff6f39f",
            :type => "rant"
        }
```

Now we can use the `client` object to store the post in our Couchbase Server cluster:

```ruby
client.set(rant[:id], doc);
```

And we can use the get method to retrieve our document from the database:

```ruby
dbrant = client.get(rant[:id])
puts "username: #{dbrant['userName']},
        ranttext: #{dbrant['rantText']},
        id: #{dbrant['id']},
        type: #{dbrant['type']}"
```

Run the Ruby `ranter.rb` command to execute this Ruby script. It should print the rant's information to your console window as follows:

```
> ruby ranter.rb
userName: YanivR,
        rantText: JavaScript is the One True Language. Why can't people see that?,
        id: c287c21-1018-4337-976a-49a73ff6f39f,
        type: rant
```

Building a Rails Application

We have just seen how to use Couchbase with a simple Ruby script. However, the main framework for developing Ruby applications is Ruby on Rails, which is a very prescriptive framework. In Ruby on Rails there are usually clear rules regarding the way things should be done. This is true for every aspect of software development, including database access. For this reason, there is also a separate couchbase-model gem that provides an ORM-like abstraction, consistent with the Ruby on Rails–style of data access. Let's start with creating a new Ruby on Rails project. This is done using the `rails new` command, which generates a complete Ruby on Rails project. Ruby on

Rails projects are structured to use ActiveRecord, an ORM tool. Since we will not use ActiveRecord in our project, let's create a new project without it:

```
> rails new ranter -O --old-style-hash
```

The above command will create the Ranter project directory. Locate the Gemfile file inside the Ranter folder and open it in your text editor of choice. We will add three new gems to the Gemfile:

```
# The Couchbase Ruby SDK
gem 'couchbase'

# An ORM-like library for Couchbase
gem 'couchbase-model'

# A JSON serielizer
gem 'yajl-ruby'
```

Save the Gemfile file and run the bundle install command. Next, we need to configure the Couchbase Server connection information in our application. Couchbase-model uses a YAML-style configuration file, config/couchbase.yml, which works similarly to config/database.yml. To create the config/couchbase.yml we will use the couchbase:config generator:

```
rails generate couchbase:config create config/couchbase.yml
```

The config/couchbase.yml is created already configured to access your local host, which is sufficient for development purposes. You might need to add a username and password if you have those configured for your bucket, but other than that you should be able to connect. One thing that you do need to configure is the bucket name. For now let's set the development configuration section to use the ranter bucket as follows:

```
development:
 <<: *common
 bucket: ranter
```

Unlike most SDKs, couchbase-model lets us define model classes, which will be used to access our database, instead of using the Couchbase client directly. In order to create such model classes we need to derive from Couchbase::Model. The following model class represents a rant:

```
class Rant < Couchbase::Model
 attribute :id :default => lambda{ SecureRandom.uuid }
 attribute :username, :ranttext
 attribute :type

end
```

▤ **Note**   Model classes also provide functionality for working with Couchbase Views. Views are covered in detail in Chapter 5, which also describes the implications for couchbase-model.

The couchbase-model gem is consistent with the behavior of other ORMs, such as ActiveRecord, so we can use our newly created model in our controller. The following controller exposes a simple Web API with a GET method that returns a rant and a POST method for creating a new one:

```ruby
require 'yajl'

class RantsController < ApplicationController

  def show
    id = params[:id]
    rant = Rant.find(id)

    respond_to do |format|
      format.json { render json: rant }
    end

  end

  def create
    body = Yajl::Parser.parse(request.body.read)
    rant = Rant.create!(body)

    respond_to do |format|
      format.json { render json: rant }
    end
  end
end
```

The Ruby SDK provides support for any type of application in the Ruby world, from simple scripts to full-blown Ruby on Rails applications using the couchbase-model gem. The couchbase-model gem provides additional capabilities, which are beyond the scope of this book. However, the Ruby community section of the Couchbase website, www.couchbase.com/communities/ruby, provides extensive documentation and a full Ruby on Rails tutorial. If you are going to use Couchbase from a Rails application, we encourage you to take a look at these resources.

Inside the Couchbase Client Libraries

The process of using Couchbase SDKs is very similar across the various programming languages. To start performing operations against the cluster you need to create an instance of a connection or a client object. This client is then used for communication between the application and the different nodes in the Couchbase Server cluster.

The various Couchbase clients do much more than locate nodes holding specific keys. In fact, they are constantly updated with the current cluster topology, which allows Couchbase to provide high availability and seamless scalability. Client SDKs also provide functionality for working with views, which enable querying and indexing documents based on properties other than their key. Views are covered in detail in Chapter 5.

A thorough understanding of how the Couchbase client works is important for building and maintaining real-world applications. So now we will take a closer look at some of the operations we have performed through the SDK, and understand more fully how they are implemented internally. We will also see how the clients react to topology changes in the cluster.

■ **Note**   It is important to note that the Couchbase SDKs behave differently when accessing memcached buckets. Memcached buckets do not have replicas, and therefore do not provide failover. This simplifies the way Couchbase clients interact with the cluster. For the rest of this chapter we will discuss the behavior of clients connected to Couchbase buckets only.

Thread Safety

Most programming languages provide a mechanism for concurrency, or threading, to parallelize work. Being able to reuse a single Couchbase client object from multiple threads usually improves application performance, especially since it avoids the overhead of multiple connection initializations. The .NET and Java SDKs take advantage of their respective built-in features to guarantee thread safety when reusing the client object. The C client library, on the other hand, is not implemented as thread safe. In particular, the internal IO routines and userspace buffers that libcouchbase maintains for sending and receiving responses should not be accessed concurrently. For this reason, the Python, PHP, and Ruby SDKs, which rely on libcouchbase, should not attempt to access the same client instance from multiple threads. Node.js, which also uses libcouchbase, is inherently single-threaded, so this is usually not an issue. If you use one of the multi-core Node.js modules, such as cluster, you should create a separate Couchbase connection object for each thread.

Couchbase Client Initialization

When we first create a client, the client needs to retrieve the cluster configuration. To do so, we provide the client with a list of preconfigured nodes it can connect to initially. The client then connects to one of the nodes and uses the Couchbase HTTP API to query the server for the cluster's status and configuration data.

The HTTP-based API provides very detailed information about the cluster. One of the main things for which it is used is to create the cluster map, which contains two main maps:

- ServersList: An in-memory representation of all the servers and their statuses.
- vBucketsMap: A list of all the vBuckets. Each vBucket in the list contains the index in the server map of its primary server as well as the server holding its first replica.

When performing a document operation (such as saving or retrieving), the client hashes the document key, getting a number value between 1 and 1024. This number is the number of the vBucket where the document is stored. Once the relevant vBucket is located, the client can simply locate the corresponding server and access it directly.

Once the cluster map is created, the Couchbase client begins to continuously query the node. This is done using an HTTP mechanism called HTTP chunked transfer (also known as HTTP streaming, or long polling), which means that the node returns a continuous response to the client that is waiting for changes in the cluster's configuration. This is key to the process, because whenever the cluster topology changes, the client gets notified and the cluster map gets updated to reflect those changes.

■ **Note**   The initialization process is a fairly expensive operation. This is done in order to free the client to perform only the operations needed to retrieve or manipulate the documents at runtime. For this reason, it is recommended to create the connection once and reuse it throughout the application if it is possible to do so in a thread-safe manner. When using multiple clients, it is also recommended to ensure that the streaming connections are distributed across different servers, in order to spread the load between them. One way to do this is to use a load balancer as the initialization node, which will spread the connections evenly among the existing Couchbase nodes.

Another implication of the server-map creation process is the creation of open connections between the client and each of the nodes, as you can see in Figure 3-2. Having so many open connections impacts both the clients and the servers. So, in addition to the recommendation to keep the client alive throughout the application life, it is also recommended to minimize the number of Couchbase clients in your application in order to minimize the number of open connections maintained to each node. As a best practice, try to minimize the number to one per instance of the application. The connection is opened on port 11210, used by the memcached binary protocol, and used for key-based document retrieval (views are accessed using HTTP over port 8092).

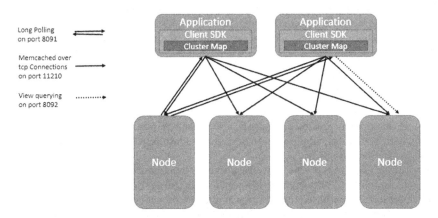

Figure 3-2. *Connections between clients and Couchbase Server cluster nodes*

Performing Operations Using the Couchbase Client

After creating a Couchbase client object, we can start performing operations against the cluster. As implied by the fact that we have a different port for view querying, Couchbase treats operations that use the document's key for access differently from view operations that can be used to retrieve ranges of documents.

For key-based access, Couchbase uses the memcached binary protocol. In fact, most of the Couchbase client libraries are built around existing memcached client libraries, such as spymemcached in Java and EnyimMemcached in .NET. When we issue a key-based operation, such as get, the Couchbase client uses the key to locate the relevant vBucket in the vBucketsMap. From the vBucket the client can retrieve the active server index in the ServersList (assuming the cluster is not going through topology changes) and use the already open connection to retrieve the document.

View operations are more complex and often retrieve ranges of items. To do so, they contain logic that must be executed on one of the servers in the cluster. For view operations, the Couchbase client uses round-robin selection between nodes in the cluster and then uses HTTP to communicate with the node that executes the operation on its behalf. The selected node will retrieve all the needed items from the other nodes, aggregate them, and return a response to the client.

■ **Note** Currently, Couchbase supports three types of view operations: non-reduced, reduced, and spatial views, each handled slightly differently. Views and their operations are covered in detail in Chapter 5.

Reconfiguration

As mentioned previously, the Couchbase client long-polls the node it used to retrieve the configuration. This is done in order to get configuration changes in near real-time. When the cluster's configuration is changed, the Couchbase client recreates the cluster map to reflect the changes. This process is not trivial, since the connections to nodes need to be managed as well. It is the responsibility of the Couchbase client to prevent multiple reconfigurations at the same time.

The Couchbase cluster configuration is managed by the Cluster Manager component, which is part of every node in the cluster. Besides storing the cluster configuration and exposing it via HTTP, the Cluster Manager also runs a watchdog process that checks the availability of all the other nodes in the cluster. With that in mind, long-polling the configuration on a single node does minimize the chances of the client to access a node that is not responsive. However, if such a call occurs, the Couchbase client library will actually ask for the configuration from the configuration node and then reload the cluster map.

Summary

Couchbase client libraries do much more than merely provide database access. In fact, many of Couchbase's defining features, such as high performance and high availability, wouldn't have been possible without the use of advanced client-side libraries.

Now that we understand the basics of the Couchbase SDKs, as well as some of Couchbase's inner workings, we can start exploring its more advanced capabilities. For the rest of this part, we will use the Couchbase SDKs in different scenarios. Chapter 4 takes a closer look at key-based operations. Chapter 5 covers views, which provide advanced querying functionality based on document content. Lastly, Chapter 6 introduces N1QL—the Couchbase document query language.

■ ■ ■

CRUD and Key-Based Operations

So far in the book, you've installed and configured Couchbase, modeled your document database, and used the Client SDKs to perform basic store and retrieve operations. Because Couchbase is both a key-value store and a document database, you can access data in two fundamentally different ways. As a key-value store, which is essentially a large hash table, Couchbase provides very fast inserts and retrievals by key. As a document database, Couchbase lets you index and query data through views, which will be covered in the next chapter. Of the two methods, key-based access is the more efficient, but is also inherently less flexible.

This chapter goes into much more detail about key-based database operations. In addition to the basic CRUD—which stands for create, retrieve, update, and delete—Couchbase has a fairly large set of commands for dealing with concurrency, document expiration, replication and persistence, and atomic operations on numeric types.

Chapter 3 looked at storing and retrieving documents by key; these operations, as well as most other Couchbase key-based operations, accept optional parameters for managing replication, concurrency, and expiration. Before we go on and dive into all the database commands in Couchbase, we need to expand upon those concepts, as they are central to working with data in a multi-user environment.

Persistence and Replication

Chapter 1 looked at the Couchbase Server architecture and saw that the Couchbase Server data manager has a memcached-based caching layer in addition to the disk-based persistence layer. When you store a document, it is actually cached in RAM first and then eventually persisted to disk. This is known as an "eventually persistent" model. Couchbase also tries to keep as many documents as possible in the RAM cache, purging less active documents to make room for more active ones. This allows Couchbase to provide very fast reads and writes, as well as high throughput up to the limit of the memory cache.

The tradeoff for the high performance of the eventually persistent model is that there may be a period during which a newly stored object exists only in the memory of a single node. If that node fails before the object is persisted or replicated, the data will be lost. Later in this chapter, you'll see what mechanisms exist to ensure data durability by explicitly specifying how it should be persisted or replicated.

Concurrency

Most databases are designed to serve multiple users, and having multiple users means that it's possible they will attempt to change the same data simultaneously. The canonical example of the importance of safe concurrency is a bank transaction, because apparently people pay closer attention when there's money involved. With that in mind, let's examine the (highly likely) scenario in which the RanteR anti-social application goes viral and its creators, David and Yaniv, become filthy rich. Having made it big, they open a shared bank account to stash their ill-gotten gains. On the morning after the IPO, both our heroes go shopping, and, in a stunning coincidence, David pays for a yacht at exactly the same moment that Yaniv is paying for his private jet.

As you can see in Figure 4-1, because the balance update operation is not atomic, both clients retrieve the balance at the same time, update it, and then set the result. Instead of the expected result of -$1,000,000, the balance ends up at $0, due to the race condition created by the poor implementation.

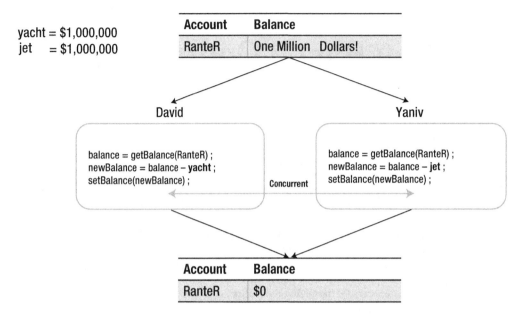

Figure 4-1. *Race condition*

To help developers implement concurrent access safely, Couchbase provides mechanisms for optimistic concurrency and pessimistic concurrency. Optimistic concurrency is an approach that assumes that collisions are unlikely and only checks whether the data has been changed by someone else as part of the update operation itself. If the data has been modified in the meantime, the update fails. This does not prevent the user from attempting a conflicting change, but it does prevent actually committing the conflicting change. Pessimistic concurrency, on the other hand, assumes that collisions are likely and actually locks the resource exclusively for the user. This way other users are prevented from accessing the resource and have to wait until it is released.

To put it another way, optimistic concurrency is a developer saying to themselves: "No worries, nobody will try to change this document while I'm editing it. But just in case, I'll remember to double-check that it hasn't changed when I try to update it later." While pessimistic concurrency is the developer thinking: "No doubt someone will try to sneak a change in just as I'm almost done editing this document. I'll lock it down so nobody but me can touch it until I'm done."

In Couchbase, optimistic concurrency is provided by the check-and-set (CAS) operation. For every item in the database, Couchbase stores a unique CAS value as part of that item's metadata. The CAS value is a 64-bit integer that is updated by the server whenever the item is modified. Most retrieve operations include a way to return the CAS value along with the item; the exact method differs from one SDK to the next. Most update operations, including the check-and-set operation itself, take a CAS value as a parameter and will fail if it differs from the server CAS value.

The pseudocode for getting a document from the database, changing it, and then saving it back safely is as follows:

```
retries = 10
while(!success && retries > 0)
{
        cas, doc = get_with_cas(key)
        new_doc = do_something(doc)

        success = update_with_cas(new_doc, cas)
        decrement retries
}
```

When optimistic concurrency is not enough, Couchbase provides pessimistic concurrency through the get-and-lock operation, which retrieves an item by key and then locks the key to prevent other clients from retrieving or updating it.

To call get-and-lock, you must provide an expiration time as a parameter. The default lock expiration time is 15 seconds, and the maximum you can specify is 30 seconds. When Couchbase locks a key, it updates the CAS value and returns the new CAS to the client. While the key is locked, the only operation you can perform with it is a check-and-set with the new CAS value, which will update the item and release the lock. Couchbase will also release the lock automatically when the timeout expires.

We cover the specifics of using CAS with various database operations later in this chapter.

Document Expiration

Part of the metadata that Couchbase stores for each item in the database is the time-to-live (TTL) value, which, as the name implies, controls when the document will expire. Unless explicitly specified, the TTL is 0 by default, meaning that the document is stored indefinitely and never expires.

The ability to have items expire automatically is a very powerful feature that can be used to purge transient data, such as temporary documents, from the database. For example, we use the ability to store temporary objects to implement an out-of-process session store for our RanteR web application. Implementing the session store on top of Couchbase gives us good performance and seamless support for scaling the web application to multiple servers.

■ **Note**   For simplicity, we use the same Couchbase bucket to store the application and session data in the code sample. In a real-life application, consider using a separate memcached bucket to implement the session store. There is no need to persist or replicate the session data, so there's no reason to waste server resources by writing the data to disk.

We examine the ins and outs of implementing an out-of-process session store on top of Couchbase Server in detail in Chapter 7. For now, you can see the relevant part of the Node.js implementation in the following code example. The CouchbaseStore.set function stores the session-state object with an expiration time that comes from the session cookie, or it defaults to one hour (3600 seconds). As you can see in the example, the expiration time is passed to the set method as part of the optional parameters object:

```
CouchbaseStore.prototype.set = function(sid, sess, fn) {
        var maxAge = sess.cookie.maxAge;
        var ttl = typeof maxAge == 'number' ? maxAge / 1000 | 0 : 3600;

        client.set(sid, sess, {expiry: ttl}, fn);
};
```

You can specify TTL values in seconds or in Unix epoch time. Values provided in seconds are limited for 30 days; any value above 30 days will be translated to Unix epoch time, which is limited to the maximum value of epoch. Most SDKs take care of the conversion from native time formats for you.

Note   Couchbase stores the TTL value as an absolute Unix timestamp, even if you specify it as a relative time in seconds.

Couchbase flags expired items as deleted but does not actually remove them from memory or disk right away. It performs expiration maintenance every 60 minutes by default, but will also remove an expired item immediately and return a "key not found" error if a client attempts to retrieve an expired key. Items that have expired, but which haven't been erased from the disk, can still show up in view results. Detecting and dealing with expired items in views are topics covered in Chapter 5.

Database Operations

At last, the time has come to talk about database operations. There are, naturally, differences in syntax and data types between the various Client SDKs when it comes to database methods. For the most part, these differences are rather trivial, such as using the native date-time object versus Unix epoch time, or method callbacks versus returned values. We will show the significant differences in APIs where relevant.

There are several broad categories of operations we can perform:

- Store: Creates new documents. Optionally returns a CAS value.

- Retrieve: Retrieves one or more documents. Optionally also returns CAS values.

- Update: Updates an item, changes TTL, or increments/decrements a counter. Optionally checks the CAS value.

- Delete: Deletes an item. Optionally checks the CAS value.

- Observe: Determines whether an item has been replicated or persisted to disk.

Note   Couchbase can't update part of a JSON document. When we talk about updating in the context of a JSON document, we actually mean replacing it with a new version.

Storing Data

In Chapter 3, we used the set operation to store a document in the database. The set method creates a new item under the specified key or overwrites it if an item with that key already exists. It is logically similar to the upsert (insert-or-update) operation in other systems. Because set overwrites the previous data, you should only use it if you're certain it's safe, or if you don't care whether old data is destroyed. For example, if you're storing a shopping cart document for an ecommerce site, you'll likely use set to create the document if it's the first item added, or update it if it already exists. We used set in the previous chapter's code examples to avoid "key already exists" errors when running the example multiple times.

The add operation creates an object in the database, similarly to set, but fails if an object with the specified key already exists. You'll want to use add, rather than set, when you need to make sure you don't accidentally destroy existing data. For example, in RanteR, we will use add to create new users to make sure we don't overwrite an existing user document with the same key. If the add operation fails, we can notify the user that another user with the same username already exists:

```
var user = {
        type: "user",
        username: req.body.username,
        email: req.body.email,
        password: req.body.password,
        shortDesc: req.body.description,
        imageUrl: req.body.image
};

// add the new user to the database
couchbaseClient.add("user-" + user.username, user, addUserCallback);
```

As you can see in the code example, we fill the user object with data from the web request, and then call the add method. Our document key consists of the string user- concatenated with the username:

```
function addUserCallback(error, result) {
        var data = {};
        var status = 200; // HTTP status: OK.

        if(error) {
                if(error.code == couchbase.errors.keyAlreadyExists) {
                        status = 409; // HTTP status: Conflict
                        data = {error: "User already exists."};
                }
                else {
                        status = 500; // HTTP status: Internal Server Error
                }
        }
        else {
                data = {
                        isLoggedIn: true,
                        name: user.username
                };

                req.session.userData = data;
        }

        res.json(data);
}
```

In the addUserCallback method, we check whether the add operation returned an error and, if not, then we store the newly added user details in the session state and return them to the client as well. If there is an error, and the error code equals to keyAlreadyExists, then a user with that username already exists, and we return the HTTP status code 409, which means *conflict*. For any other errors, we return the HTTP status code 500, which simply means *internal server error*.

Both set and add accept the same optional parameters:

- Key: The key.

- Value: The value to store, as the name suggests.

- Expiry: The expiration time, or TTL, for the inserted value. By default the TTL is 0, meaning the item is stored indefinitely.

- persist_to: Specifies the persistence requirement for the operation. By default, store methods will return the moment the data is stored in the cache layer of the active node. Passing a non-zero value in the persist_to parameter will case the operation to return only when the value has been persisted to disk on that many nodes, or if it times out before the persistence requirement has been met. The maximum possible value is 4—the master node plus up to 3 replicas.

- replicate_to: Specifies the replication requirement. The operation returns after the value has been replicated to as many nodes as specified in this parameter, or if it times out before the replication requirement has been met. The maximum value is 3, as that is the maximum possible number of replicas in a cluster.

The set operation has another optional parameter:

- cas: The CAS value to match against the server. If the cas parameter differs from the CAS value of the existing item on the server, the operation will fail.

The persistence and replication requirement parameters are very useful for ensuring that important information is stored securely. For example, you want to make sure that any sort of financial data is protected against loss by setting the replicate_to parameter to at least 1, and persist_to at least 2. That way the store operation will not return until the data has been copied to at least one other node, and persisted to disk both on the master and the replica nodes. In our RanteR application, while admittedly we don't store any particularly sensitive information, we might want to set persistence or replication requirements when storing a new user document. The flipside of using these options is that the operation takes longer to complete and return to the client. That's fine if the operation is infrequent, or important enough that the tradeoff is worthwhile, but should not be used for all data storage:

```
couchbaseClient.add("user-" + user.username, user, {persist_to: 1, replicate_to: 1}, addUserCallback);
```

The preceding code example adds a new parameter object containing the persistence and replication constraint values. In this case, the addUserCallback will be called only after Couchbase stores the document to disk once and replicates it to at least one other node.

Setting the persist_to or replicate_to constraints to a value higher than the number of nodes in the cluster will still store the document, but will also return an error. For example, attempting to replicate and persist to 3 nodes in a 1-node cluster will return the following error object in Node.js:

```
{ [Error: Durability requirements failed]

 code: 4103,

 innerError: { [Error: Durability constraints requires more nodes/replicas than the cluster
configuration allows. Durability constraints will never be satisfied] code: 33 } }
```

Some SDKs also provide multi-value versions of the set and add operations for bulk insertions. These work just like the single-value methods but accept an SDK-specific collection of values and optional parameters. A single bulk set with multiple documents is much more efficient than calling set for each document separately, because it incurs much less communication overhead.

In RanteR we store new rants as a pair of documents: one to hold the rant itself and another to hold an array of rantback response objects. The rant document holds a reference to the rantbacks document. Let's take a look at the code snippet that stores the two documents:

```
var documents = {};
documents[rantKey] = { value: rant };
documents[rantbacksKey] = { value : [] };
connection.setMulti(documents, {}, setMultiCallback);

function setMultiCallback(error, result) {
        if(error){
                res.writeHead(500); // HTTP status: Internal Server Error.
                Res.end();
        } else {
                res.json(201, rant); // HTTP status: Created.
        }
};
```

That code example creates a new document to hold the objects we want to store, which we then pass to the setMulti method. The documents object holds the values we want to store as properties named after their respective keys. Each value is wrapped in an object. In the example, it only holds the value itself under the value property, but you can also add optional parameters such as CAS and expiry time. In the setMultiCallback function, we check whether an error occurred and return HTTP status 500 if so, or HTTP status 201 and the rant object itself otherwise.

SDK-Specific Differences

In the .NET and C SDKs, the set, add, and replace operations are combined into a single method. In .NET, the Store method accepts the type of operation as the first parameter, whereas in libcouchbase, the operation type for the lcb_store method is set in the operation field of the lcb_store_cmd_t parameter struct.

Also note that the .NET SDK has two versions of most operations—one named <operation>, which returns a simple data type, and another called Execute<operation>, which returns a status object. For example, the Store method returns a bool value, which indicates whether the operation succeeded, whereas the ExecuteStore method returns an IStoreOperationResult object, with properties such as Success (same as the boolean returned from Store), Exception (the underlying exception, if any), and Cas (the CAS value of the newly stored object).

Retrieving Data

The most straightforward and efficient way to retrieve an item from Couchbase is with the get operation, which you already used in Chapter 3. It takes a key as a parameter and, depending on the particular SDK, returns either the value itself or a result object that contains the value and some additional information.

If the key isn't found in the database, the behavior of the get operation depends on the SDK. It either returns the equivalent of NULL in that language, or a special "Key not found" object, or throws an exception.

Let's take a closer look at using the get method in the RanteR login module:

```
var key = "user-" + req.body.username;
couchbaseClient.get(key, getUserCallback);

function getUserCallback(error, result) {
        var data = {};
        var status = 200; // HTTP status: OK.
```

```
        if(error) {
                if(error.code == couchbase.errors.keyNotFound) {
                        status = 404; // HTTP status: Resource not found.
                        data = {error: "User does not exist."};
                }
                else
                        status = 500; // HTTP status: Internal Server Error.
        }
        else {
                if (result.value.password !== req.body.password) {
                        status = 401; // HTTP status: Unauthorized.
                        data = {error: "Invalid username or password."};
                }
                else {
                        data = {
                                isLoggedIn: true,
                                name: result.value.username
                        };

                        req.session.userData = data;
                }
        }
        res.json(status, data);
}
```

As you can see, we get the username in the request body and use it to calculate the key of the user document. We call the get method with the key and a `callback` function, which will process the returned data. In the callback, we need to check whether the `error` parameter is NULL; if it isn't, then we check the error code to find out the type of error. If the error code is keyNotFound, then the user does not exist in the database, and we return the appropriate HTTP status and error message. If the `error` parameter is NULL, which means we retrieved the document successfully, then we can validate the password and either log the user in or return an error.

■ **Note**   In the example, we store passwords as plain text because we are lazy. Please don't do that! Use a cryptographic hash to store and validate passwords in production.

The bulk version of the get command accepts a collection of keys and returns a collection of values. If some of the keys do not exist, the behavior again depends on the SDK; most will simply return the keys that exist. It's important to note that you cannot rely on the order of returned values being the same as the order of keys you sent, because some SDKs do not provide placeholders for missing values.

Let's take a look at an example of using bulk get in RanteR. In this case, we want to retrieve all the rants about a particular user. We use a view to retrieve the IDs of the rants we want (explained in depth in Chapter 5) and then we use the getMulti method to retrieve the actual rant documents by their IDs:

```
couchbaseClient.getMulti(ids, {}, function(error, results) {
        if(error){
                res.writeHead(500);
                res.end();
```

```
    } else {
            var rants = [];
            for(var key in results) {
                    var result = results[key];
                    if(result.value)
                            rants.push(result.value);
            };
            res.json(rants); // write the rants array to the response
    }
});
```

In this code example, the ids parameter is an array of rant document IDs we retrieved earlier. The getMulti callback function accepts two parameters: an error object (or NULL if the operation succeeded) and the results object, which is a dictionary that maps the document keys to result objects. Each result object has a value property, which holds the document object if it was retrieved successfully, or an error property if the document could not be retrieved.

SDK-Specific Differences

The names and input parameters of the bulk get methods are different for some SDKs, as you can see in Table 4-1.

Table 4-1. Bulk get API

SDK	Method	Comments
Java	getBulk	
.NET	Get	Accepts an IEnumerable<string> collection of keys.
C	lcb_get	Accepts an array of commands, one per key.
PHP	getMulti	
Python	get	Accepts an array of keys.
Ruby	get	Accepts a list of keys.
Node.js	getMulti	

Get-and-Touch

You can specify an expiration parameter in the get method call, which will return the item and update its expiration at the same time. The touch operation, which we will talk about later in this chapter, can also update the expiration of a document, but get-and-touch provides better performance than using separate get and touch operations.

Get-and-touch is very useful for working with temporary values. For example, say we wanted to implement a draft post feature in RanteR, which would save unfinished posts for a certain amount of time. When the user returned to the post to continue editing, we'd use get-and-touch to retrieve the post and extend its expiration time in a single operation:

```
couchbaseClient.get(rantDraftKey, {expiry: 3600}, getCallback);
```

That example retrieves the rant document stored under rantDraftKey and sets its expiration time to 3600 seconds (1 hour) in the same operation.

SDK-Specific Differences

In Java, the get-and-touch operation is implemented as a separate method named getAndTouch.

Retrieving and Updating Data Concurrently

When talking about updating data in a multi-user environment, you must always keep concurrency in mind. There are multiple ways to update data stored in Couchbase Server, and most of them accept a CAS value as an optional parameter to provide optimistic concurrency.

Get-with-CAS

As you saw in the beginning of this chapter, Couchbase provides optimistic concurrency support through check-and-set (CAS) operations. The common use case for concurrency is to retrieve an item with its current CAS value, update the item, and then pass the updated item and the saved CAS value to an update operation that will only succeed if the server CAS value is the same as the one we passed. We use this pattern in RanteR for storing rantbacks. When a user submits a new rantback for some rant, we retrieve the rantbacks document with CAS, append the new rantback to it, and store the updated document back to Couchbase with the CAS value we got earlier. If someone else manages to update the rantbacks document in the short interval between retrieval and storage, the server CAS value will no longer match the one we have. In a scenario like this, it's common to create some sort of retry mechanism, which checks whether the operation succeeds, and, if not, it performs the get-with-CAS, update, and store flow again (and again) until it succeeds or a certain number of retries fail in a row.

In most of the SDKs, get-with-CAS is an overload of the get method, but some provide a separate method that returns the item and the CAS:

```
connection.get(rantbacksKey, function(error, result) {
        if(error)
                // Do stuff with error

        var cas = result.cas;
        var rantbacks = result.value;
        updateRantbacks(rantbacks);

        // Store rantbacks with the CAS.
});
```

The preceding code snippet shows part of the rantback document update flow. First we retrieve the document with its current CAS value, then we update it, and finally we pass the CAS value back to the server with the store operation.

SDK-Specific Differences

Different SDKs have different APIs for the get-with-CAS operation, as you can see in Table 4-2.

Table 4-2. *Get-with-CAS API*

SDK	Method	Comments
Java	gets	Returns a CASValue<Object> object, which holds the value and the CAS.
.NET	GetWithCas	Returns a CasResult<T> object, which holds the result value and the CAS.
C	lcb_get	The regular lcb_get method always returns the CAS as part of the lcb_get_resp_t struct.
PHP	get	Third parameter of the get method reads the CAS value.
Python	get	If the extended parameter is True, returns a tuple with the value, flags, and CAS.
Ruby	get	If the extended parameter is true, returns a tuple with the value, flags, and CAS.
Node.js	get	The get method always returns the CAS as part of the result object.

Check-and-Set

The check-and-set (sometimes called compare-and-swap) operation performs an update only if the provided CAS parameter matches the one on the server. If the CAS value is different—meaning the server item has been changed in the meantime—the CAS operation fails.

Some SDKs have a separate CAS method, whereas others overload the set operation with an optional CAS parameter to provide the same functionality. Let's take a look at how we use the set method to update an updated rantbacks document in RanteR:

```
connection.set(rantbacksKey, rantbacks, {cas: cas}, function (error, result) {
      if (error) {
            if( error.code == couchbase.errors.keyAlreadyExists) {
                  // Document was changed between the get and set.
            }
            else
                  // Some other type of error.
      }
      else
                  // Document saved successfully.
});
```

In the preceding code snippet, you can see a part of the rantbacks update flow. After retrieving the rantbacks document with its CAS value, we try to store the updated object back to the database with the original CAS. If the server CAS is different from the provided value, the operation returns an error with an error code equal to keyAlreadyExists.

Normally, you don't want to give up right away if a cas operation fails. Rather, you want to implement some sort of retry logic to attempt the cas operation again if it fails. Let's see the full implementation of storing rantbacks in RanteR with optimistic concurrency and retry logic:

```
var rantKey = req.params.id;
connection.get(rantKey, getCallback);

function getCallback(error, result) {
      if(error) {
            if(error.code == couchbase.errors.keyNotFound)
                  res.json(404, {error: "Rant does not exist."});
```

```
                else
                        res.json(500, {}); // Internal Server Error.
        }
        else {
                var rantbacksKey = result.value.rantbacks;
                var rantback = req.body;

                // Update the rantbacks document,
                // retry up to 10 times if the operation fails.
                updateRantbacksWithRetry(rantbacksKey,
                        rantback,
                        10,
                        updateCallback);
        }
}

function updateCallback(status, data) {
        res.json(status, data);
}
```

As you recall, we store a reference to the rantbacks in the rant document, which means that in order to add a new rantback, we first need to find the rantbacks document key. We retrieve the rant document by the ID we get in the web request and extract the rantbacks key from the rant. With the rantbacks document key and the new rantback object in hand, we call the updateRantbacksWithRetry function, which also takes a parameter for maximum number of retries to attempt, and a callback function:

```
function updateRantbacksWithRetry(rantbacksKey, rantback, retries, updateCallback) {
        connection.get(rantbacksKey, function(error, result) {
                if(error)
                        return updateCallback(500, {});

                var cas = result.cas;
                var rantbacks = result.value;
                rantbacks.push(rantback);

                connection.set(rantbacksKey, rantbacks, {cas: cas}, function (error, result) {
                        if (error) {
                                if( retries > 1 &&
                                  error.code == couchbase.errors.keyAlreadyExists) {
                                        // Document was changed between the get and set.
                                        return updateRantbacksWithRetry(rantbacksKey, rantback,
retries - 1, updateCallback);
                                }
                                else
                                        return updateCallback(500, {});
                        }
                        else
                                return updateCallback(200, {});
                });
        });
}
```

In the updateRantbacksWithRetry function, we retrieve the existing rantbacks document, which is a JSON array, push the new rantback into the array, and then attempt to store the document back to Couchbase with the CAS value that we retrieved in the get method. If there is no error, then the new rantback was stored successfully. If the error object isn't NULL and the error code equals keyAlreadyExists, then the document has been changed by someone else between the moment we retrieved it and the moment we tried to store the updated document. If that's the case, and we still have retries left, we call the updateRantbacksWithRetry function recursively, while decrementing the retry count by 1.

SDK-Specific Differences

The API for locking a document differs from SDK to SDK, as you can see in Table 4-3.

Table 4-3. *Check-and-set API*

SDK	Method	Comments
Java	cas	Multiple overloads with the same semantics as the set method, with an additional CAS value parameter.
.NET	cas	Multiple overloads with the same semantics as the Store methods, with an additional CAS value parameter.
C	lcb_store	Set the cas field of the lcb_store_cmd_t struct to a non-zero value to match it against the server.
PHP	cas, set	Has both an optional parameter for the set method and a separate cas method.
Python	set	Takes the CAS value as an optional parameter.
Ruby	set	Takes the CAS value as an optional parameter.
Node.js	set	Takes the CAS value as an optional parameter.

Pessimistic Concurrency through Locking

Sometimes optimistic concurrency is not the best solution. For example, if a document changes frequently and in quick succession, update operations may end up failing even after multiple retries. As an alternative, Couchbase provides a pessimistic locking mechanism through the get-and-lock operation. This operation retrieves an item with a new CAS value and then locks that item, preventing any operations without the correct CAS until it is unlocked. As part of the get-and-lock operation, you must provide a lock timeout parameter. The maximum length of time an item can be locked is 30 seconds, and when the lock timeout expires, Couchbase unlocks the item automatically.

To unlock the locked item before the timeout, either perform some CAS update operation on it or use the unlock operation to release the lock without changing the item.

Let's rewrite the previous code example to use locking instead of optimistic concurrency. Instead of calling the updateRantbacksWithRetry function, we'll call updateRantbacksWithLock:

```
updateRantbacksWithLock(rantbacksKey, rantback, 100, updateCallback);
```

As you can see, we're passing the same arguments, except we increased the retry count to 100. Because we're actually going to be retrying to acquire the lock, which is faster than updating the document and storing it, we can afford more attempts:

```
function updateRantbacksWithLock(rantbacksKey, rantback, retries, updateCallback) {
        connection.lock(rantbacksKey, {lockTime : 5}, function(error, result) {
```

```
            if(error)
                    // temporaryError means the document is locked
                    if( error.code == couchbase.errors.temporaryError &&
                      retries > 1)
                            return updateRantbacksWithLock(rantbacksKey, rantback, retries - 1,
updateCallback);
                    else
                            return updateCallback(500, {});

            var cas = result.cas;
            var rantbacks = result.value;
            rantbacks.push(rantback);

            connection.set(rantbacksKey, rantbacks, {cas: cas}, function (error, result) {
                    if (error)
                            return updateCallback(500, {});
                    else
                            return updateCallback(200, {});
            });
        });
}
```

As you can see, the basic flow remained the same, except now we're trying to lock the document by calling the function recursively if the lock fails with an error code of temporaryError, which means that it is already locked by someone else. If we successfully lock and retrieve the document, we update the rantbacks array and then store it back to the database by calling set with the CAS value we got from the lock method. The set operation will also unlock the document after it stores the value, so we don't need to call unlock explicitly.

If you need to unlock a locked object explicitly without modifying it, you can use the unlock method with the CAS value you got from the lock, as in the following example:

```
connection.unlock(key, {cas: cas}, function(error, result) { });
```

Which of the two approaches to concurrency to choose depends on your application logic and data-access pattern. On the one hand, if updating the object in your application is an expensive operation, using a lock may result in better performance, because while you may perform multiple lock attempts, you will only have to update the object once. On the other hand, if the object you need to update is accessed from multiple parts of your application, you may want to go with optimistic concurrency and implement retries on the update and store. This way you'll avoid having to deal with the locked object in other parts of your application.

At this point, you might be thinking that 30 seconds for a lock isn't very much time at all. For example, you cannot to lock a document, take as much time as you want to edit it in the UI, and then save and unlock it when you're done. You are absolutely correct, and this limitation is, in fact, intentional. To allow arbitrarily long locks on values goes against the distributed, scalable approach to data storage. Couchbase provides fast, scalable data access, but the tradeoff is that it is often the application developer's responsibility to ensure data integrity and resolve conflicting data changes.

SDK-Specific Differences

The API for locking and unlocking a document differs from SDK to SDK, as you can see in Table 4-4.

Table 4-4. *Lock and unlock API*

SDK	Lock	Unlock	Comments
Java	getAndLock	unlock	Returns a CASValue<Object> object, which holds the value and the CAS.
.NET	GetWithLock	Unlock	Returns a CasResult<T> object, which holds the result value and the CAS.
C	lcb_get	lcb_unlock	Set the lock field of the lcb_get_cmd_t struct to a non-zero value to get and lock the item. The exptime field of the same struct specifies the expiration timeout.
PHP	getAndLock	unlock	The second parameter of the get method reads the CAS value.
Python	lock	unlock	Returns a result object that contains the item and the CAS.
Ruby	get	unlock	Pass True as the lock parameter to lock the item.
Node.js	lock	unlock	The regular get method always returns the CAS as well.

Replace

The replace operation updates the value of an existing item and fails if an item with the provided key does not exist. In most SDKs, the replace operation works similarly to add and set and accepts the same parameters. Although the differences between add, set, and replace are small, it is sometimes useful to be able to check whether a key exists and update it as a single atomic operation. For example, if you want to update a range of keys generated with a counter, you may want to use a replace operation to make sure you don't accidentally recreate any keys that have been deleted in the meantime.

The replace operation accepts the same parameters as the add operation:

```
connection.replace(key, value, {expiry : 1, cas : cas, persist_to: 1, replicate_to: 1}, callback);
```

In the preceding code snippet, you can see a replace call with its various optional parameters.

SDK-Specific Difference

In the .NET SDK, the replace operation is implemented as a StoreMode parameter of the Store and Cas methods. In libcouchbase, replace is a flag in the lcb_store method parameter struct.

Appending and Prepending Binary Data

The append and prepend operations are used to concatenate binary data. These are atomic operations that append or prepend raw serialized data to an existing binary value. Like most update operations, append and prepend can also accept an optional CAS value parameter to check against the server CAS, as well as optional TTL, persist_to, and replicate_to parameters, similar to the store methods discussed earlier in this chapter.

■ **Note** At this point we're going to stop saying "append and prepend" and just use "append" all the time. Assume that everything said about append applies to prepend as well.

The two most common use cases for appending binary data are concatenating strings and appending raw binary data such as byte arrays. A simple example would be storing application logs from multiple sources. Because append is an atomic operation, there's no danger of losing values due to concurrency issues, even though the exact order of concurrent appends cannot be guaranteed.

Another example of using append is maintaining lists or sets of values. In RanteR, we keep a list of followers for each user by appending the user IDs of new followers to a string value. The list is actually a simple delimited string, so adding new followers is very easy. Removing followers is slightly more complicated, because there is no matching delete operation; instead we actually append the deleted value again, with a prefix that marks it as deleted. And because append is atomic, we don't need to add extra safeguards for concurrency. See the following:

```
function updateFollower(follow, follower, operation, updateFollowerCallback) {

        var key = "follow-" + follow;
        var value = (operation == "follow" ? "+" : "-") + follower;

        connection.append(key, value, appendCallback);

        function appendCallback(error, result) {

                // 'Not stored' error means it's a first time append,
                // so we need to add the key
                if( error &&
                    error.code == couchbase.errors.notStored &&
                        operation == "follow") {
                                connection.add(key, value, updateFollowerCallback);
                        }
                else
                        updateFollowerCallback(error, result);
        }
}
```

In that code sample, the updateFollower function gets the names of the followee and the follower, the operation (follow or unfollow), and a callback that processes the result and returns it to the client. The key of the document to which we want to append a new follower is follow-<username>, where username is the user being followed. The value we append is +<follower> or -<follower>, where follower is the username of the currently logged in user, and + or - denotes whether we're adding or removing it from the list. We then call the append method to append the value string to the list. If this returns a notStored error, it means the key we're trying to append to doesn't exist in the database yet, in which case we call the add method to create the key with the follower as the value.

■ **Note**   We cover the general use case of dealing with lists, including compaction and performance considerations, in Chapter 7.

It's very important to note that you cannot use append to add sections to JSON objects or arrays. Appending one JSON object to another will result in a document that contains both one after another, which most likely won't be a valid JSON object any more. Similarly, appending to the end of a serialized application object—for example, a Python array stored in Pickle format—will add the data to the end of the binary stream, resulting in an object that cannot be deserialized.

When you append a lot of data, you must be careful not to exceed the 20 MB maximum document size. There is no automatic way to do this—you must handle it in your application logic. A typical solution is to split the appended value in some way or to implement some sort of compaction logic in your application that will reduce the size of the document.

SDK-Specific Differences

Different Client SDKs behave differently when appending numerical values. For example, in Node.js, storing the number 1 and then appending another 1 to it will result in 11. Doing the same in Java will result in 257, i.e. 00000001 + 00000001 = 0000000100000001 = 257 in decimal.

Touch

In addition to updating data, you can also update some of the metadata associated with an item, specifically its expiration time. The touch operation updates the TTL of an item if it exists. This is a very straightforward method that accepts a key and the new TTL value. The rules we talked about in the "Document Expiration" section at the beginning of this chapter apply here as well: a TTL of 0 means the document never expires, and the TTL value is interpreted as being relative to the current time if it is less than 30 days, or as absolute Unix epoch time if greater than that:

```
connection.touch(key, { expiry : 3600, cas : cas, persist_to : 1, replicate_to : 1 }, callback);
```

In the preceding code snippet, the touch method is similar to the various store methods, except that it does not update the document itself, but rather the TTL metadata. All the parameters except the key are optional; if the expiry parameter is not provided, it defaults to 0, meaning no expiration.

In addition to updating the expiration time, touch can also be used as a quick way to check whether an item exists, if you don't need the item itself. In particular, if the item is large, then using touch will be much more efficient than get due to the network and serialization overhead. Exercise caution when using touch this way, as it will overwrite TTL values you set in other parts of the application, possibly breaking your application logic:

```
couchbaseClient.touch("user-" + username, userExistsCallback);

function userExistsCallback(error, result) {
      if(error) {
              if(error.code == couchbase.errors.keyNotFound) {
                      status = 404; // HTTP status: Resource not found.
                      data = {error: "User does not exist."};
              }
              else
                      status = 500; // HTTP status: Internal Server Error.

              res.json(status, data);
      }
      else {
              // Do something with the user.
      }
}
```

The preceding code uses touch as a quick way to check whether a key exists. Before performing another operation with the username, it calls the touch method without providing a TTL value. If no error is returned, then the key exists and the example function can proceed to do something. If there is an error with the error code keyNotFound, then the user does not exist. For all other types of error, the code simply returns a generic error status.

SDK-Specific Differences

In the .NET SDK, the Touch method returns void, and thus cannot be used to check whether an item exists.

Numeric Data

In addition to JSON documents and strings, Couchbase can store and manipulate simple numeric values. This is done through the increment and decrement operations, which work on positive integer values. Like append and prepend, increment and decrement actually combine three steps into a single atomic operation: get, update, and set. They ensure that no values will be lost between multiple concurrent operations, but do not guarantee the exact order in which concurrent updates will occur.

Because Couchbase stores numeric values as unsigned integers, trying to store negative values will result in an integer overflow, and the operation will actually return the overflow value. Likewise, Couchbase will not let you decrement past zero or a negative number—the result will always be zero.

▦ **Note** At this point we're going to stop saying "increment and decrement" and just talk about increment. Everything will be equally valid for decrement as well.

The increment operation accepts the following parameters:

- Key: The key of the value to increment.

- Offset: The amount by which to increment the value.

- Initial: An optional initial value, which will be set if the key does not exist yet. Trying to increment a non-existent key without supplying an initial value will fail.

- TTL: An optional expiration time for the value.

Increment updates the value and returns the new value as the result.

Chapter 2 talks about one of the most common uses for increment, which is to generate the equivalent of auto-incrementing IDs for keys. In our RanteR application, we use a counter to both track the number of rants per user and to generate incremental IDs for rant document keys. Let's take a look at how we create a new rant document:

```
var userkey = "rant-" + rant.userName;
var counterKey = userKey + "-count";
connection.incr(counterKey, {initial: 1, offset: 1}, incrementCallback);

function incrementCallback(error, result) {
        if(error) {
                res.writeHead(500);
                res.end();
        }
        else {
                var documents = {};
                var rantKey = userkey + '-' + result.value;

                // Store the rant with rantKey as the key.
        }
}
```

That sample code increments the rant-<username>-count counter by calling the incr method. If the key doesn't exist yet, it will be created with the initial value of 1—otherwise, it will be incremented by 1. In the callback function, we generate the key for the rant we want to store in the following format: rant-<username>-<count>, where count is the incremented value returned in the result object.

In general, counters have a multitude of uses. You can use counters for anything that requires an efficient Couchbase-equivalent to SELECT count(*) FROM table in T-SQL; for example, keeping track of the number of rants in total, number of rants per user, and so on. To retrieve the number of rants posted by some user, all you need to do is retrieve the counter stored under the key rant-<username>-count, where username is the user we want, as in the following code example:

```
var counterKey = "rant-" + username + "-count";
connection.get(counterKey, function(error, result) {
        console.log("Rant count: " + result.value);
});
```

SDK-Specific Differences

In most Client SDKs, increment and decrement are separate methods. In libcouchbase, however, both of these operations are implemented by the lcb_arithmethic method, which simply takes a positive or negative delta value.

The Node.js implementation of the incr and decr methods also accepts optional persist_to and replicate_to parameters, similar to the store methods.

Deleting Data

The delete operation removes the value with the specified key from the database. You can provide an optional CAS parameter to check against the server CAS value. It is important to note that delete does not actually remove the item from the server immediately but only flags it for deletion. Normally the deleted item will be cleaned up as part of the recurring hourly maintenance process. However, if a client tries to retrieve the deleted item, then it will be removed from memory immediately and the server will return a "key not found" error:

```
couchbaseClient.remove(rantKey, removeCallback);

function removeCallback(error, result) {
        var data = {};
        var status = 200; // HTTP status: OK.

        if(error) {
                if(error.code == couchbase.errors.keyNotFound) {
                        status = 404; // HTTP status: Resource not found.
                        data = {error: "Rant does not exist."};
                }
                else
                        status = 500; // HTTP status: Internal Server Error.
        }

        res.json(status, data);
}
```

The preceding code example deletes a rant in the RanteR sample application. To delete the rant document, we call the remove method with the key, stored in the rantKey variable, as a parameter. In the callback function, we check for errors and return an appropriate status message if one occurred. Otherwise, we simply return the HTTP status 200, indicating that the rant was successfully deleted.

Just like expired documents, deleted documents that haven't been erased from the disk yet can still show up in view results. Chapters 5 talks about dealing with them.

SDK-Specific Differences

In the Node.js client SDK, the remove method also accepts optional persist_to and replicate_to parameters, which work similarly to the way they do in the store method.

Flush

The flush operation deletes all the documents from a bucket. This operation is provided mostly for testing and debugging purposes and is disabled by default. To use the flush command, you must explicitly enable it in the bucket settings.

■ **Note**   Do not use flush in production. Ever. We mean it.

Observing Data

Documents in Couchbase can exist in various states. A document can be stored in memory only, it can be persisted to disk, it can be replicated to one or more nodes (and be in memory or on disk there as well), and it can even be marked as deleted but still be persisted and in memory. The observe operation retrieves information about the state of a document across the cluster. By observing an object you can, for example, verify that it meets a certain threshold of durability, such as being replicated at least twice, to protect against node failures.

As mentioned earlier in this chapter, most of the store and update operations accept an optional persistence and replication parameter. Let's take a look at the state of a stored object with and without a persistence requirement by observing it immediately after the store operation returns:

```
client.set('_test', 123, function(error, result){
        client.observe('_test', function(err, result) {
                console.log(result);
        });
});
```

That code snippet produces the following result on a single-node cluster:

```
{ _test:    [ { status: 0, cas: [Object], from_master: true, ttp: 53328337, ttr: 0 } ] }
```

Add a persistence requirement to the set operation, like so:

```
client.set('_test', 123, { persist_to : 1 }, function(error, result){
        client.observe('_test', function(err, result) {
                console.log(result);
        });
});
```

The result of the observation will be as follows:

```
{ _test: [ { status: 1, cas: [Object], from_master: true, ttp: 0, ttr: 0 } ] }
```

The status property indicates the state of the object (in hexadecimal):

- 0x00: Found, not persisted to disk.

- 0x01: Found, persisted to disk.

- 0x80: Not found.

- 0x81: Found, marked for deletion. (Equivalent to 0x01 | 0x80, meaning not found but still persisted to disk.)

The from_master property indicates whether the reply came from the master node for this object or from a replica. The ttp and ttr properties indicate the average time to persist and replicate the object, respectively, according to server statistics.

Most Client SDKs also have a bulk version of the observe method.

SDK-Specific Differences

In addition to the observe method, the Java SDK has an observePoll method, which will wait and poll the server until a certain persistence and replication condition is met, or until it times out. You can use the Observe method with optional parameters in the .NET SDK, and the lcb_durability_poll method in the C SDK to provide the same functionality as the Java observePoll method.

General SDK-Related Notes

Many of the Client SDKs provide multi-value variants for various operations, which combine multiple calls into a single operation. It is nearly always more efficient to perform one multi-operation instead of several separate operations, because it will have much less communication overhead.

The differences between the various SDKs are quite substantial. Some, like Node.js, provide multi-value variants for nearly all database operations, while others, like .NET and Java, only provide bulk get methods. Please consult the documentation of your chosen SDK for information about which multi operations it implements.

Summary

In this chapter, you've seen how to work with data through key-based operations. Key-based access in Couchbase is very fast and efficient, which means that unlike in traditional databases, you can go ahead and retrieve documents multiple times, or whenever you need them. This way, with clever data modeling, you can achieve quite sophisticated data-lookup functionality. However, despite all the cleverness you can apply, there are still various forms of queries that you simply can't perform purely through key-based operations. Chapter 5 covers how to use the advanced querying functionality of Couchbase views.

■ ■ ■

Working with Views

Key-based operations provide an efficient mechanism for accessing data, and key-value stores often provide better performance than other data-access approaches. However, relying solely on keys to access complex data can be very limiting. Document databases provide a more flexible approach for querying data based on the content of the documents they store. Every document database provides different querying techniques. In Couchbase there are two different ways to query document content: views and the N1QL query language, which is covered in Chapter 6.

Couchbase views create indexes based on the content of JSON documents stored in the database. For example, let's say you would like to show a ranter all the rants that were made about his or her rants. You can create a view with an index on the userName property of the rantAbout embedded document and then use that index for efficient queries by username.

Couchbase views are written using MapReduce, a programming model made popular in 2004 when Google's Jeffrey Dean and Sanjay Ghemawat released a paper titled "MapReduce: Simplified Data Processing on Large Clusters." MapReduce is designed for processing data in a distributed manner. Couchbase uses MapReduce to process documents across the cluster and to create indexes based on their content. There are several other techniques for distributing processing across a cluster, however, MapReduce is extremely useful for dealing with two of the more challenging aspects of distributed data processing: sorting and aggregation. By using MapReduce in Couchbase Server views you can add those two capabilities to your querying arsenal.

MapReduce 101

As the name implies, the MapReduce model (see Figure 5-1) is built around two operations: map and reduce. The map operation, which is executed on every item in the dataset, does some initial processing and filtering and then outputs the transformed result as a key-value set. The reduce operation receives the results of the map, grouped by the key, then processes and aggregates the mapped values.

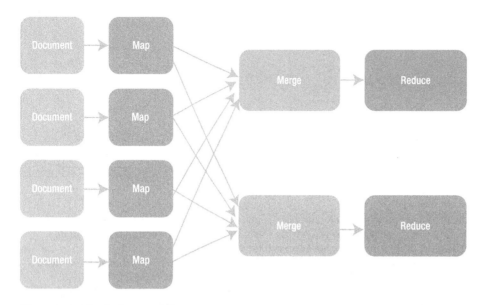

Figure 5-1. *MapReduce workflow*

The MapReduce pattern has a multitude of applications, so let's take a closer look at how MapReduce is used in Couchbase Server views.

Creating a View in Couchbase

Couchbase views are MapReduce functions written in JavaScript. Couchbase stores the views in JSON documents called *design documents*, each of which can contain one or more views. Before you can start creating views, you need to create a design document. To do so, log into the Couchbase management console and navigate to the Views tab, as shown in Figure 5-2.

Figure 5-2. *The Views tab in the Couchbase admin console*

If you have more than one bucket in your cluster, make sure you're in the ranter bucket and then click the Create Development View button.

■ **Note** Creating a view over a large dataset can impact the cluster's performance; development views reside in development design documents and allow developers to test their views using a subset of the real dataset without negatively affecting the overall cluster performance. When you're satisfied with the development view, you need to publish it as a production view, which will then work on all the relevant data.

Next, you need to enter the design document and view names. Since you're creating a development view, the design document name will be prefixed with _design/dev_. Name your design document _design/dev_rants and your view rantabouts_by_original_ranter, as shown in Figure 5-3.

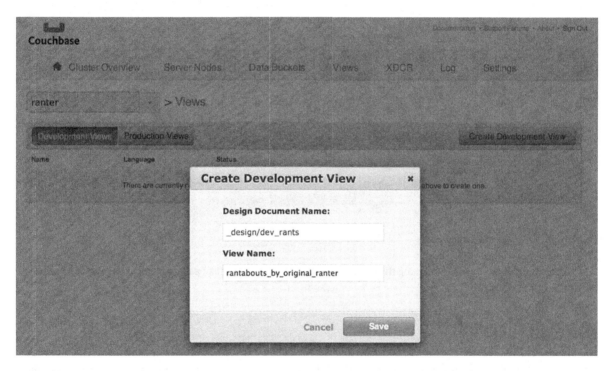

Figure 5-3. *Creating a new development view*

Now that you've created your view, you can click the Edit button to start editing it. As you can see in Figure 5-4, the view page has three sections:

- *Document preview*: This section shows a randomly selected sample document and its metadata. You can click the Preview a Random Document button to randomly select another document from the bucket.

- *View code*: This section contains the map and reduce functions.

- *Results*: This section lets you to see the output of the view, either based on the design-time subset or on the whole bucket.

Figure 5-4. The Couchbase view page

You'll now add the logic for indexing the documents in the bucket. Let's take a closer look at the map and reduce functions and how they work.

The Map Function

The MapReduce flow begins by reading the entire dataset, in parallel, across the cluster. For Couchbase views, this means processing all the documents in the bucket that the view belongs to. Each document, along with its metadata, is passed to the map function for initial processing. The following code sample shows the default map functions definition in a Couchbase view:

```
function (doc, meta) {
  emit(meta.id, null);
}
```

We'll talk about the emit function in just a moment, but first let's take a closer look at the map function and how it can be used for creating views.

Filtering in MapReduce

Since the map function is executed for each and every document, you can use it to filter the input dataset and only output the documents you need in the view. For example, in the current view you only need documents that represent rants. This is why you added the type property for each and every document in RanteR back in Chapter 2. Additionally, you're looking for rants that are about other rants, which means that they have the rantAbout property. To find these rants, add a condition in your map function to emit a result only for documents that meet the requirements:

```
function (doc, meta) {
 if(meta.type == "json" &&
    doc.type == "rant" &&
    doc.rantAbout){
        emit(meta.id, null);
 }
}
```

■ **Note**   Because not all the documents in your bucket are in JSON format, you must first filter the non-JSON documents out.

After changing the map function, click the Save button.

The emit Function

The emit function outputs the result of the map function. The output is then passed to the reduce function, if one is defined. If you do not provide a reduce function, the emit function simply outputs the key-value pairs that make up the view. In the preceding example function, you used the document id property as the key and passed null as the value. Let's take a look at the result of your view, which you can do by clicking the link next to the Filter Result caption below the View Code section. When you click the link, you should see the view output in a new web page. If you have rants in your database, you should see a result that resembles the following sample:

```
{"total_rows":1,"rows":[
{"id":"yanivr-rant-1","key":"yanivr-rant-1","value":null}
]
}
```

Every document in your view will have the following properties:

- id: This is the ID (key) of the original document. Couchbase Server provides this value in order for the SDKs to be able to retrieve the document through the view.

- key: This is the first value you passed to the emit function. This will be the key of the view. Note that this key can, and often will, be different from the original document key.

- value: This is the second parameter you passed to the emit function. The value allows you to provide a transformed version of the data. You can create the transformation logic in your view and pass the result as the value.

Currently, you have a view that allows you to retrieve a document by ID. This is hardly useful, because you can achieve the same result faster with the get operation. What you really want is to retrieve rants by the username of the person in the rantAbout document. Let's change the map function so that the key is based on the property you want to use in your index:

```
function (doc, meta) {
 if(meta.type == "json" &&
    doc.type == "rant" &&
    doc.rantAbout){
        emit(doc.rantAbout.userName, null);
 }
}
```

If your database, for example, contains three rants that have values in the rantAbout property, you'll get a result similar to the following:

```
{"total_rows":3,"rows":[
{"id":"davido-rant-1","key":"JerryS","value":null},
{"id":"yanivr-rant-1","key":"JerryS","value":null},
{"id":"davido-rant-2","key":"YanivR","value":null}
]
}
```

The preceding results have three records—two rants are about JerryS's rants and one is about YanivR's rant. You can now use the key field to retrieve rants about a specific user.

One thing you might notice is that you do not emit the rant itself. This could have easily been done by using the code emit(doc.rantAbout.userName, doc);, which emits the doc object itself instead of null as the value. It might seem tempting to emit documents, or parts of documents, to prevent round trips to the cluster. However, emitting data increases the size of the view on disk and incurs more I/O overhead when reading or calculating views, which affects overall cluster performance. On the other hand, because views always emit the id field, which is the key of the original document, you can use the ID to retrieve the documents directly. Key-based lookups in Couchbase Server are very fast. As a best practice, emit only data that cannot be accessed or calculated easily by your client application, such as aggregations.

Creating Views from Code

Although the admin console is a great tool for development, views are actually a part of your application code base. And as with any code, you need to manage it under source control. In addition, you need a way to deploy your views as you roll out new versions of your applications. Couchbase stores design document definitions, including their views, as JSON documents. You can use the Couchbase SDKs to retrieve, set, or update those definitions programmatically.

Getting a Design Document

The connection object exposes the getDesignDoc method, which retrieves the definition of a design document:

```
connection.getDesignDoc('rants', function( error, ddoc, meta ) {
        if(error) console.log(error);
        console.log(ddoc);
})
```

If you run the preceding code, you'll get a design document definition similar to the following (minus the comment):

```
{ views:
  {
        rantabouts_by_original_ranter: {
            map: 'function (doc, meta) {\n  if(doc.type == "rant" && doc.rantAbout)
            {\n  \temit(doc.rantAbout.userName, 1);\n  }\n}'
            // we can have a reduce property here
            }
  }
}
```

Setting a Design Document

The connection object also exposes the setDesignDoc method, which can be used to create or change a design document. In RanteR, you store each design document in a *.json file, and you create the views using the setDesignDoc function at start time, as follows:

```
var rants = fs.readFileSync("./utils/designDocs/rants.json");

connection.setDesignDoc('rants', rants, function(err) {
        if(err) {
                console.log( 'ERROR' + err );
        } else {
                console.log( 'Updated ' );
        }
});
```

SDK-Specific Differences

Managing design documents works pretty much the same in all SDKs, with some small syntactic differences.

Table 5-1. Design Document API Differences

SDK	Comments
Java	The methods for working with design documents are named getDesignDoc, createDesignDoc, and deleteDesignDoc.
.NET	In .NET, the CouchbaseCluster class has the CreateDesignDocument, RetrieveDesignDocument, and DeleteDesignDocument methods.
C	There are no dedicated methods for working with design documents in the C library. You can use the lcb_make_http_request function to make HTTP requests to the Couchbase API.
PHP	The Couchbase class has the getDesignDoc, setDesignDoc, and deleteDesignDoc methods, which do the same thing as in Java and .NET. The listDesignDocs method lists the design documents in a bucket.
Python	In Python, the methods are design_get, design_create, design_publish, and design_delete. The design_publish method publishes a development design doc to production.
Ruby	In ruby, the Couchbase::Bucket class has a hash of existing design documents under the design_docs property, and the save_design_doc and delete_design_docs methods for saving and deleting them, respectively.

Querying Views

Now that you have a secondary index, you can use it to query the data. To query the view use the ViewQuery object, which you get by calling the view method of the Connection object. You pass the names of the design document and view you want to query as parameters

```
var view = connection.view('rants', 'rantabouts_by_original_ranter');
```

Querying by Keys

The ViewQuery object exposes the query method for querying the view. The most straightforward way to query the view is by key. For example, let's retrieve the first 10 documents that represent rants about a specific user:

```
view.query({limit: 10, key: username}, function (error, results) {
        if(error)
            throw error;
        getRants(results,res);
});
```

In the preceding code example, you query the view for the first ten documents whose key equals the value of the username variable. The callback function provides both an error object, in case the query fails, and a results object representing the query result as outputted by the view. Since you only emitted the key and ID from your view, you need to go back to the server and retrieve the rants themselves. This is done inside the getRants method:

```
function getRants (results, res){

        // retrieve the id property from each object in
        // the results collection
        var ids = _.pluck(results, 'id');

        connection.getMulti(ids, {}, function(err, ids) {
                if(err){
                        res.writeHead(500);
                        res.end();
                } else {
                        var rants = _.pluck(rants, 'value');
                        res.json(rants); // write the rants array to the server response
                }
        });
}
```

In the getRants method, you use the underscore module to project the ID property of every object in the results array into an array of IDs, and then you use the getMulti method to retrieve all the rants in a single call to the server.

Range Querying

The ViewQuery object also allows you to query ranges of keys by specifying a start key and an end key. The following sample retrieves rants posted between two dates:

```
view.query({startkey: startDate, endkey: endDate}, function (error, results){
        if(error)
                throw error;
        getRants(results,res);
});
```

Sorting

Documents returned by Couchbase views are automatically sorted by key in the following order:

- Null
- False
- True
- Numbers
- Text, case sensitive, lowercase first, UTF-8 order
- Arrays, sorted by the values of each element, in order of the array index
- Objects, sorted by the values of keys in alphabetic order

By default, all the values are sorted in ascending order. The results can be returned in descending order by passing the descending parameter:

```
view.query({startkey: endDate, endkey: startDate, descending: true}, function (error, results){
        if(error)
                throw error;
        getRants(results,res);
});
```

■ **Note**   Because Couchbase performs the selection after sorting, you also need to switch between the start key and end key values.

Pagination

For larger result sets it might make sense to break the result into multiple pages. The ViewQuery object accepts an optional skip parameter that can be used in conjunction with the limit parameter to split the result into pages. For example, let's go back to querying rants about specific ranters. In the first example, you've limited the result to the first ten documents returned by the view. In order to retrieve the next ten results, you can use the following query:

```
view.query({limit: 10, skip: 10, key: username}, function (error, results) {
        if(error)
                throw error;
        getRants(results,res);
});
```

In addition to the skip and limit methods of pagination, which are available in most Client SDKs, some libraries, such as Node.js and Java, implement a Paginator object that can be used to page through the results. To get the Paginator object, call the firstPage method:

```
view.firstPage({limit: 10, key: username}, function (error, results, paginator) {
        if(error)
                throw error;
        getRants(results,res);
});
```

The `callback` function will return the results as well as the `Paginator` object, so you can now call the next method to retrieve the next page:

```
view.firstPage({limit: 3}, function (error, results, paginator) {
        if(error)
                throw error;

        console.log(results);
        if(paginator.hasNext()) {
                paginator.next(function (error, results) {
                        if(error){
                                console.log(error);
                        } else {
                                console.log(results);
                        }
                });
        }
});
```

In the preceding code example, you call the `hasNext` method to check if there are further pages left, and, if so, you use the `next` method to get the next page of results.

SDK-Specific Differences

There are quite a few differences in the way the various SDKs query views.

Table 5-2. *View Query API Differences*

SDK	Comments
Java	To query a view in Java, retrieve an instance of the `View` class with the `getView` method, then create a new instance of the `Query` class and set the query parameters, such as key, limits, staleness, etc. Finally, use the `query` method of the `CouchbaseClient` object to run the query on the specified view and retrieve a `ViewResponse` object, which you can use to iterate over the query results.
.NET	In .NET, get an instance of the `View` class with the `GetView` method. You can iterate over the `View` instance to retrieve the results. To sort, filter, group, etc. the view, you can chain the `Key`, `StartKey`, `EndKey`, `Group`, etc fluent methods of the `View` class together before iterating over the results.
C	In the C SDK, you use the `lcb_make_http_request` function to make HTTP requests to the view API endpoint.
PHP	The `view` method accepts an array of options, including keys, staleness, grouping, etc. and returns an array of query results.
Python	In Python, you can create an instance of the `Query` class, which contains options such as keys, grouping, etc, and use it as a parameter for creating a `View` object, which will contain the results. Alternatively, you can create the `View` object directly with the optional parameters, which will create the `Query` object implicitly. Either way, you can iterate over the `view` object to get the query results.
Ruby	In Ruby, you fetch a `view` object from the `design_docs` hash property of the `Bucket` class. You can then iterate over the view to get the results.

The Reduce Function

One of the strengths of the MapReduce model, in comparison to other distributed computational models, is the ability to perform aggregations. Aggregations are performed in the reduce function. Couchbase views have two types of reduce functions: built-in and custom.

Built-in Reduce Functions

Couchbase has three built-in reduce functions. These functions cover common use cases and can be used to perform aggregations, either for the entire result set or per group. The built-in reduce functions are implemented in Erlang, rather than in JavaScript, for better performance.

- _count: Returns the number of items

- _sum: Calculates the sum for numeric values returned in the value field of the results

- _stats: Calculates both the count and sum values, as well as minimum value, maximum value, and the sum of squares of the values ($value^2 + value^2 + \ldots + value^2$)

Let's create a new view based on the rantabouts_by_original_ranter view. To do so, open the rantabouts_by_original_ranter view (see Figure 5-5) and take a look at the Reduce pane. Click the _count link to add the _count built-in reduce function to the view. Change the emit function to output the value 1 instead of null, and then click the Save As button. Name the new view "rantabouts_count."

Figure 5-5. *Using the built-in _count reduce function in a view*

If you run the view, you will get a single row with the total number of rants that are about other rants. You need to tell Couchbase that you would like to group the view by key. To do so, you need to pass the group parameter when querying the view, as in the following example:

```
view.query({group: true}, function (error, results) {
});
```

You can also pass the group parameter to the result view in the View page of the admin console. To do so, click on the Filter Results dropdown button and check the Group box, as shown in Figures 5-6 and 5-7.

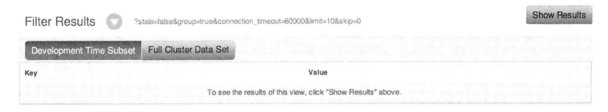

Figure 5-6. *Clicking the circled upside-down triangle button...*

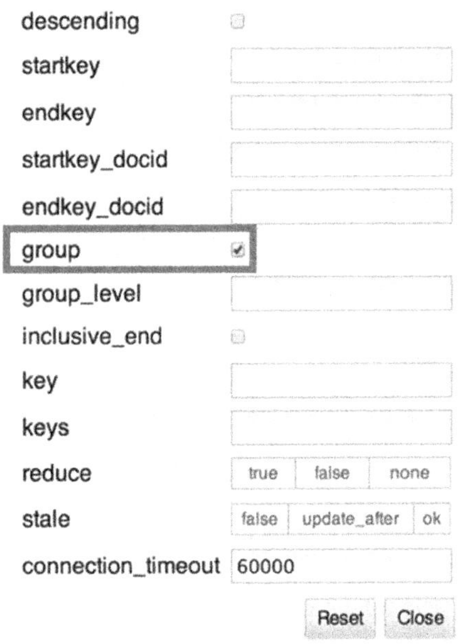

descending	☐
startkey	
endkey	
startkey_docid	
endkey_docid	
group	☑
group_level	
inclusive_end	☐
key	
keys	
reduce	true false none
stale	false update_after ok
connection_timeout	60000

Reset   Close

Figure 5-7. *opens this dropdown menu*

Couchbase will group the view results based on your key. You can click on the "Show Results" button (see Figure 5-8) or the link next to the Filter Results button to view the results. One thing you might notice is that you don't have an ID field in your results. That's because each record in the grouped view represents an aggregation of all the documents in that group.

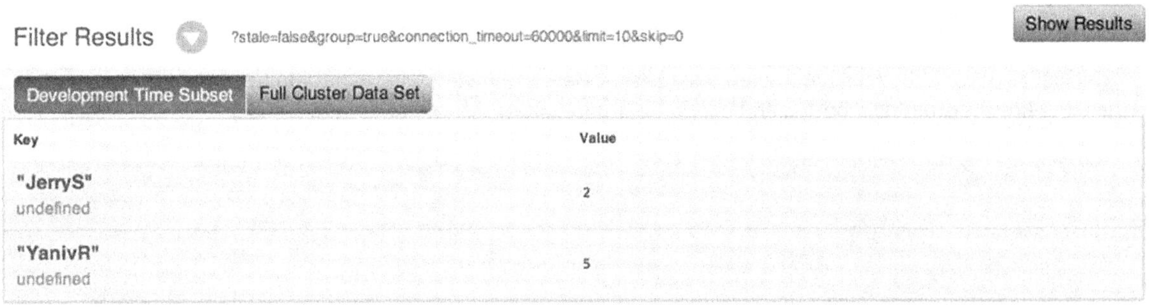

Filter Results ▽ ?stale=false&group=true&connection_timeout=60000&limit=10&skip=0   Show Results

Development Time Subset	Full Cluster Data Set	
Key		**Value**
"JerryS" undefined		2
"YanivR" undefined		5

Figure 5-8. *The result pane in the view page showing the result of a grouped view*

Compound Keys

So far in this chapter you've used simple types such as numbers or alphanumeric values as the keys in your views. Couchbase views also support compound keys, which are basically JavaScript arrays containing multiple values. Compound keys are sorted based in the order of values in the array, i.e., first sorted by all the values at index 0, then sub-sorted by the values at index 1, and so on.

When querying a grouped view with a compound key, you can specify a group level, which indicates the number of indexes in the key to be used for grouping. For example, consider a view that counts the number of rants per time unit with different levels of granularity (per day, per month, or per year). Instead of simply emitting the date as the key, you can create the view using the `dateToArray` built-in utility function, as follows:

```
function (doc, meta) {
 if(meta.type == "json" &&
    doc.type == "rant" &&
    doc.date){
        emit(dateToArray(doc.date), null);
 }
}
```

The result of this map function will contain a compound key that is an array of the year, month, day, hour, minute, and second of the rant. Obviously, you will also need to use the `_count` reduce function. Now that you have your view ready, you need to query it while providing the appropriate group level:

```
view.query({ group_level:1 }, function (error, results){
        if(error)
                throw error
        res.json(results);
});
```

The preceding sample results will show the number of rants per year. To show the same aggregation per day, all you need to do is set the group_level parameter to 3.

Custom Reduce Functions

When the built-in functions are not enough, you can write your own `reduce` function. But before we look at how to write your own `reduce`, it's important that you understand how Couchbase executes the `reduce` functions.

In order to perform aggregations on the values emitted by the `map` function, `reduce` usually accepts two parameters: the key and a collection containing all the values emitted for that key:

```
function (key, values) {
        // perform an aggregation...
}
```

For Couchbase `reduce` functions, in most cases, the key is an array containing the key itself, followed by the documents IDs.

Often, the `reduce` function will actually be executed more than once per key. This happens in one of two cases:

- In a multi-node cluster, Couchbase executes the `reduce` function once for every node.

- When the values array is large, Couchbase might split the execution into separate calls, with each call receiving part of the values.

When Couchbase executes the reduce function more than once per key, it needs to run an additional cycle of reduction to aggregate the results of all the intermediate reductions. This final execution of the reduce function is called a *re-reduce*. In order to differentiate between standard reduce executions and a rereduce, the reduce function accepts a third parameter named rereduce. Because of this behavior, custom reduce functions should usually conform to the following pattern:

```
function (key, values, rereduce) {
        if(rereduce){
                // perform the final aggregation...
        } else {
                // perform the intermediate reduce
        }
}
```

Let's implement a reduce function that will calculate the average number of rantbacks per user. In order to do so, you need to slightly change the structure of the rantbacks to contain the name of the original ranter and a document type in addition to the rantbacks array:

```
{
 "type": "rantbacks",
 "userName": "morinr",
 "values": [
   {
     "userName": "yanivr",
     "text": "I just did last April"
   }
 ]
}
```

Now you can create a view that calculates the average based on the rantbacks documents. The first step, as always, is to create a map function:

```
function (doc, meta) {
 if(meta.type == "json" &&
    doc.type == "rantbacks" &&
    doc.userName){
   emit(doc.userName, doc.values.length);
 }
}
```

The preceding map function emits the name of the original ranter and the number of rantbacks, per rantbacks document. Next you need to create a reduce function that will take the output of the map function, sum up the number of rantbacks per user, and divide that sum by the total count of rantbacks per user, to give us the average. Because reduce is likely to run in two stages, you essentially have to write two reduce functions: one to create the intermediate reduce results and another to further reduce them into the desired output. If the reduce runs as a single stage, the intermediate result is actually the desired result:

```
function (key, values, rereduce) {
 if(!rereduce){
   var sum = 0;
```

```
  for(var i=0; i<values.length; i++){
    sum += values[i];
  }

  return {
    count: values.length,
    avg: sum / values.length
  };
} else {
  var aggsum = 0;
  var aggcount = 0;

  for(var i=0; i<values.length; i++){
    aggsum += values[i].count * values[i].avg;
    aggcount += values[i].count;
  }

  return {
    count: aggcount,
    avg: aggsum / aggcount
  };

}
}
```

Let's break down what reduce actually does. Figure 5-9 uses made-up values to illustrate the point.

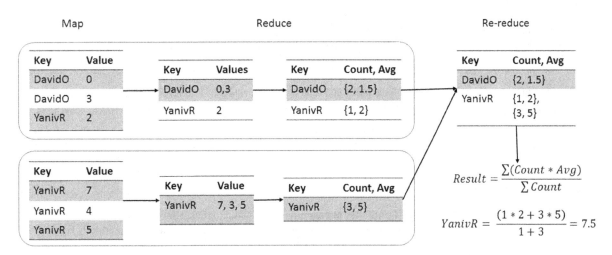

Figure 5-9. *The execution of the average reduce function, including a re-reduce*

The two parallel processes—the horizontal blocks in Figure 5-9—could be separate nodes, or Couchbase deciding to split up a large data set. The output of the map function are key value pairs, where the key is a username and the value is a collection of rantback counts per rant. Couchbase combines the results per key and passes this as the input to the reduce function, which calculates the rantback count and average for each key and outputs them as the intermediate reduce results. In this example, for user DavidO the intermediate result is also the final result: 2 rants with an average of 1.5 rantbacks each. That is what the rereduce function will output. For the user YanivR, rereduce will calculate the sum of the products of each count and average pair and divide it by the total count. This will give you the actual average number of rantbacks for each of YanivR's rants.

If you group the results by key, the output will be: DavidO : {2, 1.5} ; YanivR : {4, 7.5}

Views and Persistence

Unlike documents, which can sometimes exist purely in RAM, views are always persisted to disk. Understanding how data is persisted is key to understanding how views behave. As we've seen before, views are stored as files, where each file contains a design document, which are organized as b-trees. Each bucket stores the design documents' definitions in a metadata file. In addition to maintaining index files for the active vBuckets, Couchbase can also index replica vBuckets for faster recovery during failover. Index replication can be set up in the bucket configuration screen or during the creation of a bucket.

The metadata files are stored in the data directory under <bucketname>/master.couch.1. The index files are stored in the @indexes/<bucket name> directory. One file per design document and, if index replication is enabled, an additional file for the replica index will be created. The files are named according to the following convention:

```
main_<index signature>.view.1
replica_<index signature>.view.1
```

The index signature is a hex value calculated by hashing the design document definition with MD5. This means that design documents with the exact same definition will have the same index file.

Couchbase indexes are incremental—all changes are appended to the end of the index file. When a document is added, it is added at the end of the index file, and when a document is removed, a record is added marking the document as deleted. When a document is changed, a new value is added to the file, leaving the old value in place.

■ **Note** The incremental nature of Couchbase index and data files can eventually impact your cluster's performance and consume excessive disk space. To avoid bloated data files, consider setting up auto compaction. This is covered in depth in Chapter 11.

Updating Indexes

Documents in Couchbase can live in RAM until they are eventually persisted to disk. However, views are created and updated based only on the data stored on disk. This means that views are eventually consistent, potentially lagging behind data while it is kept only in RAM. In other words, whenever you query a view, there is a chance that you are missing documents that haven't been persisted yet.

Furthermore, indexes are not updated immediately when documents *do* get persisted. Updating an index is a costly process that affects all the views in the design document. On one hand, this means that views are potentially missing new documents. On the other hand, stale views may contain data that is outdated, and even documents that are expired or deleted, because they haven't been purged from storage yet.

> ▪ **Note**   In addition to stale indexes, expiration has another delay, which we will cover in a bit.

Indexes are updated in one of two ways: as the result of a query with the stale parameter, or automatically at preset intervals or as a result of a document update. The stale parameter has three different values that control if and when a view should be updated:

- `false`: The index is updated before the query is executed. This ensures up-to-date view data, based on all persisted documents, at the cost of delaying the execution of the query.

- `ok`: The index is not updated, providing the best performance as well as avoiding potential impact on the overall cluster performance, at the cost of accessing potentially stale data.

- `update_after`: The default value for the stale parameter; the query returns existing index data, and the index is then marked for update.

> ▪ **Note**   Using the `false` value for the stale parameter can be costly, especially when multiple users are querying the index concurrently, as this will cause the index to be updated multiple times. Using the `update_after` value whenever possible will decrease the stress on the server while still providing a reasonable chance to get up-to-date data.

Automatic index update can be set using the HTTP management API. You can get the current setting for your cluster by issuing a GET request to the following URL: `http://Administrator:Password@localhost:8091/settings/viewUpdateDaemon`, which should return the following values by default:

```
{
 "updateInterval":5000,
 "updateMinChanges":5000,
 "replicaUpdateMinChanges":5000
}
```

The preceding parameters control when automatic updates will occur. The first two control active production views. Note that development views cannot be automatically updated:

- `updateInterval`: An interval, in milliseconds, between automatic index updates.

- `updateMinChanges`: The number of document changes that will trigger an index update. If set to 0 no automatic updates will occur.

The `replicaUpdateMinChanges` parameter controls the update of replica indexes, if any exist.

To change the default settings, issue an HTTP POST request to the same URL with the new values. If the change was successful you will get a JSON document with the updated values in the response.

Views and Expiration

Couchbase Server uses a lazy erasing mechanism. It doesn't erase documents immediately when they expire; instead it only marks them as such. The actual deletion happens either when an attempt is made to access a document that is marked for deletion, or periodically by a maintenance process called the *expiry pager*.

Because views are calculated for all the document stored on disk, they might include documents that are marked for deletion. When querying a view, you can set the include_docs query parameter to true, which will cause Couchbase to return the document itself in the results of the query. The document is stored in the doc property of each result object, and will be null for expired or deleted documents. This mechanism can be a benefit if you were going to retrieve the documents in any case, or a downside if you had no intention of doing so. The alternative to using this method is to retrieve the potentially outdated query results normally and then check for keyNotFound errors while retrieving the documents you need.

In addition, in some cases Couchbase Server stores the result of built-in reduce functions as part of the view. This means that the aggregated result might be based on the content of expired documents.

Geospatial Views

In recent years, the proliferation of GPS devices in commodity hardware has made geospatial data ubiquitous. Storing location data is easy, but extracting useful information from it is actually quite challenging. Couchbase helps you work with location data by providing indexing through a specialized type of view, called a geospatial view.

Geospatial indexes are stored as R-trees, which are data structures similar to B-trees, in that they are balanced trees optimized for quick searches. Except, rather than working with scalar values, R-trees work with rectangles (hence the "R" in the name). Each node in the tree contains—or bounds—the nodes below it, and the leaf nodes represent a single location point. In this way, each level of the tree contains progressively more fine-grained location data.

Creating Geospatial Views

Being the cutting-edge, innovative, anti-social application that it is, RanteR collects geospatial data whenever possible. This includes HTML5 geolocation in browser environments, or native APIs in various mobile apps. RanteR mobile apps for various platforms are described in Part IV, "Mobile Development with Couchbase." Geolocation data is stored in the location property of the rant document.

```
{
    "type": "rant",
    "userName": "ElaineB",
    "rantText": "You ever notice how happy people are when they finally get a table? They feel so
      special because they've been chosen. It's enough to make you sick.",
    "location": {
        "type": "Point",
        "coordinates": [
            -73.97041887044907,
            40.764033329795204
        ]
    },
    "date": "2014-01-23T10:54:18.666Z",
    "rantbacks": "6207d79d-39ed-472a-8337-fe8d8c533608"
}
```

The preceding rant document stores the location as a GeoJSON point. GeoJSON is a standard format for encoding geographic data structures, which is used by Couchbase geospatial views to store location data. For additional information about GeoJSON, visit http://geojson.org/.

To index your geolocation-enabled rants, you need to add a geospatial view. You can do this by clicking the Add Spatial View button next to the development design document, as shown in Figure 5-10.

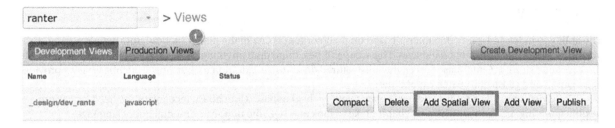

Figure 5-10. *Adding a spatial view*

The geospatial view page looks almost identical to the standard MapReduce view page, with one difference: instead of the two panes for the `map` and `reduce` functions, you have a single pane for a `spatial` function. Here is the default geospatial function implementation:

```
function (doc) {
 if (doc.geometry) {
   emit(doc.geometry, null);
 }
}
```

The main use of the `spatial` function is to perform filtering and emit GeoJSON data in addition to any data needed from the document or metadata. Since you already save the location as a GeoJSON point, all you need to do is to filter out irrelevant documents and emit the content of the location property. Because you are only interested in rants that have the location property, you will use the following function:

```
function (doc, meta) {
 if (doc.type == "rant" &&
     doc.location) {
   emit(doc.location, meta.id);
 }
}
```

■ **Note**   Unlike MapReduce views, spatial views do not emit the documents ID by default. However, the spatial function receives the document metadata as the second parameter, and you can emit the document ID as the value field.

Now that you have a spatial view, you can query it. Querying is done by supplying a bounding box, a set of values representing a rectangle, which marks the boundaries of the area you want to query. All the GeoJSON shapes contained within the bounding box will be returned. The bounding box is represented by four coordinates: the first two numbers represent the lower-left corner, and the last two numbers represent the upper-right corner.

As of this writing, geospatial views are supported natively only in the .NET and Java SDKs. However, you can still query geospatial views from the other SDKs using the HTTP API—simply issue an HTTP `GET` request to the following URL:

```
http://<server>:8092/<bucket>/_design/<design_document>/_spatial/<view_name>?bbox=-180,-90,180,90
```

and be sure to replace the `bbox` parameter value with your actual bounding box coordinates.

We have implemented a utility Node.js module in RanteR to query geospatial views. The module, spatialView.js, is located in the `utils` folder in the RanteR source code.

Summary

The ability to index and query documents based on their content is one of the main differentiators between key-value stores and document databases. These capabilities, more than anything else, mark the shift from Membase, the key-value store, to Couchbase Server, the full-featured database. In addition to indexing, Couchbase views provide aggregation and geospatial search capabilities.

While views provide a robust and useful way to query the database, Couchbase recognizes the need for a more flexible querying mechanism. The next chapter takes a look at N1QL, the new experimental query language.

◼ ◼ ◼

CHAPTER 6

The N1QL Query Language

As you've seen in the previous two chapters, you can store and retrieve documents very quickly with key-based operations and perform some pretty complex queries and aggregations with views. However, even with these two mechanisms, you are limited to finding known keys and searching in pre-defined indices within a single bucket. You can't perform ad-hoc queries programmatically, nor can you search across multiple buckets. This is where N1QL comes to the rescue! N1QL (pronounced "nickel") is a new query language with a familiar, SQL-like syntax. As of this writing, it is still not available in production and is only offered as a developer preview. We will use the most recent version, which is Developer Preview 3, to learn how to use N1QL.

Because it is still in development, the internal implementation details are certainly subject to change before the release. However, the language specifications and syntax are finalized enough so that you can begin writing code, which should work with the production release without any modifications. Currently, the query engine that powers N1QL works as a stand-alone executable that runs alongside Couchbase Server. In the final version, we expect it to be incorporated into the server itself.

Let's begin by downloading the latest version of the N1QL developer preview here: http://www.couchbase.com/communities/n1ql.

◼ **Note** If the production version of N1QL has been released by the time you read this, then use that and ignore these download and installation instructions for the development preview version.

There is no installation process for the query engine—all you need to do is run the cbq-engine executable and pass the location of our Couchbase cluster as a parameter:

```
> cbq-engine -couchbase http://<host>:8091/
```

In this case, <host> can be the address of any node in the Couchbase cluster.

The N1QL query engine process listens for query requests on port 8093. To execute queries, you can use the cbq command-line shell that comes with the developer preview or issue HTTP requests to the <cbq-host>:8093/query endpoint, where <cbq-host> is, of course, the machine where you ran the query engine. Additionally, if you use Node.js, as we do in this book, then you're in luck, because the latest SDK already has N1QL support built in. The upcoming 2.0 releases of the .NET and Java SDKs will have N1QL support as well; if you happen to read this book before they become available, you can give the developer preview versions a try. By the time the production release comes out, all supported SDKs should have built-in N1QL querying implemented.

Executing N1QL Queries

Before diving into the query language itself, let's make sure that you can actually execute queries. The simplest way to test that everything works is to use the command-line shell. Simply run cbq and provide the address of the query-engine machine as a parameter, like this:

```
> cbq -engine http://<cbq-host>:8093/
```

After opening the shell, type in "SELECT * FROM ranter" (minus the quotes) and press Enter. You'll examine the actual results later, but for now you should see some output similar to this:

```
{
    "resultset": [
        {
            "id": "davido-rant-1",
            "rantAbout": {
                "id": "yanivr-rant-2",
                "rantText": "JavaScript is the One True Language. Why can't people see that?",
                "type": "rant",
                "userName": "YanivR"
            },
            "rantText": "Static languages are always better",
            "type": "rant",
            "userName": "DavidO"
        },
        {
            ... more stuff ...
        },
... more stuff ...
    ],
    "info": [
        {
            "caller": "http_response:160",
            "code": 100,
            "key": "total_rows",
            "message": "45"
        },
        {
            "caller": "http_response:162",
            "code": 101,
            "key": "total_elapsed_time",
            "message": "261.0109ms"
        }
    ]
}
```

Wait, was that SQL just now? Well, no, but it's pretty close! As you can already guess, N1QL is designed to be very easy to pick up for anyone who already knows SQL, so most of the syntax is going to look very similar. Of course, Couchbase isn't a relational database, so it doesn't have tables, columns, and so on. Instead, it has buckets, documents with any number of other documents and arrays nested inside them, and non-document values. Querying the much more complicated data structures in Couchbase requires going beyond the SQL syntax to make things like searching inside nested arrays of documents possible. Still, if you feel comfortable with SQL, you will get into N1QL easily—you just need to learn the syntactic differences and "gotchas." If you don't know SQL at all, that's fine too—just read on!

To better understand the similarity between querying with SQL and N1QL, consider the type of objects each operates on. An SQL query operates on a two-dimensional object—a table (or multiple joined tables, which are really just one bigger table for the purposes of this comparison.) The first dimension is rows, the second is columns. For the purposes of this comparison, a bucket full of documents is equivalent to a table; each document can be thought of as a row, and the properties of the document as columns. Figure 6-1 illustrates the idea. Nested properties aren't a problem, as you can simply think of them as a column with a long name, i.e., "myDocument.outerProperty. innerProperty." In both cases, a query iterates over one dimension and retrieves values from the other. Just like "SELECT * FROM Table1" will retrieve the values of all columns in all rows of Table1, "SELECT * FROM Bucket1" will retrieve the values of all properties of all documents in Bucket1.

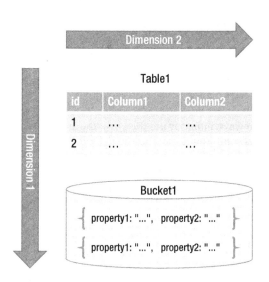

Figure 6-1. *Querying tables verus documents*

This analogy hits a snag when it reaches nested arrays of objects. The array represents a third dimension to be queried, which doesn't normally exist in SQL (as you can see in Figure 6-2).

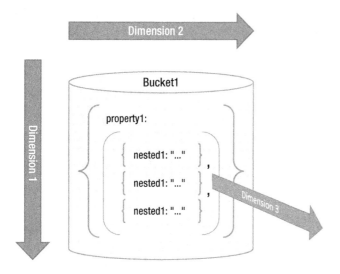

Figure 6-2. *Nested arrays as a third dimension*

N1QL introduces new syntax for dealing with arrays in one of two ways, either by iterating over the array as part of the query, or by flattening the array to turn a 3D object into a 2D one. You'll learn how to do both further along in this chapter.

Now, running queries in the shell is nice, and you'll be doing that a lot in this chapter, but to use N1QL in code you will need a way to run queries programmatically. Let's try the built-in Node.js query function first. Using it is as simple as can be—just pass the query string and the callback as parameters. Note that you now also need to pass the address of the cbq-engine to the connection object.

```
var couchbase = require('couchbase');

var client = new couchbase.Connection({
 'bucket':'default',
 'host':'127.0.0.1:8091',
 'queryhosts':'localhost:8093'
});

client.query("SELECT * FROM ranter", function(error, result) {
    console.log(result);
});
```

The preceding code should print out the same result as the query you ran in the command-line shell, but without the info array. Finally, you can use both GET and POST HTTP requests to run the query and get results as JSON. For example, you can just navigate to the following URL in a browser to get the results of the same SELECT query: http://localhost:8093/query?q=SELECT%20*%20FROM%20ranter. The query is URL-encoded and is passed in the q parameter of the query string. Of course, you should replace localhost with the actual host where the query engine is running. If you don't want to use a GET request, perhaps because the query is too long, you can also use POST and put the SELECT query in the body of the request. The response will be a JSON document in the same format you saw earlier, so you'll have to parse or deserialize it according to your language of choice. As it's not actually interesting to show this in Node.js, we'll sneak in a C# sample:

```
public static async Task<JObject> ExecuteNickelQuery(string query)
{
    var client = new HttpClient();
    var response = await client.PostAsync("http://localhost:8093/query", new StringContent(query));
    var json = await response.Content.ReadAsStringAsync();
    var result = JObject.Parse(json);

    return result;
}
```

The ExecuteNickelQuery method uses the .NET HttpClient class to post the request with the query string as the body, then parses the JSON response into a JObject. The JObject class comes from the Newtonsoft.Json library, which we talked about in Chapter 3:

```
private static async Task RunAsync()
{
    dynamic result = await ExecuteNickelQuery("SELECT * FROM ranter");

    foreach (var info in result.info)
        Console.WriteLine("{0} : {1}", info.key, info.message);

    foreach (var item in result.resultset)
        Console.WriteLine(item.userName);
}
```

One of the simplest, but not safest, ways to access the data in the JObject is to cast it into the dynamic type and then just use whatever properties you think it has. The RunAsync method prints out the key and message properties from the info array, as well as the usernames from the resultset array. The output should look something like this:

```
total_rows : 4
total_elapsed_time : 236.0187ms
ElaineB
DavidO
DavidO
YanivR
```

The N1QL Language

Now that you know how to run queries, it's time to learn the query language itself. You'll see that although the basic syntax is similar to SQL, there are quite a few additions due to the nested and unstructured nature of documents. As you saw earlier in this chapter, you use the SELECT statement to query documents in a bucket. The basic syntax is as follows:

```
SELECT [DISTINCT] <expression>
FROM            <data source>
WHERE           <expression>
```

```
GROUP BY          <expression>
ORDER BY          <expression>
LIMIT             <number>
OFFSET            <number>
```

The expression that follows the SELECT statement can be a literal value, or can specify documents and properties. For example, the query

```
SELECT "Hello world!"
```

produces the following result set:

```
"resultset": [
    {
        "$1": "Hello World!"
    }
]
```

Just like in SQL, you can also use mathematical operators and predefined functions such as ROUND, SUBSTR, and more in the expression. For example:

```
SELECT ROUND(4 / (6 + 1), 2), SUBSTR("Hello world!", 6, 5), LENGTH("N1QL")
```

That returns:

```
"resultset": [
    {
        "$1": 0.57,
        "$2": "world",
        "$3": 4
    }
]
```

You can find the full list of supported functions in the N1QL documentation at http://docs.couchbase.com/prebuilt/n1ql/n1ql-dp3/#scalar-function.html. Note that this link refers to Developer Preview 3, not the final release.

In addition to literal objects, SELECT expressions can address specific properties by name. This will return the values of only the specified properties in the result set. If you use the * wildcard in the query, the structure of the result set is much less predictable, because it will contain the entire content of all documents that match the query. Using specific property names makes the result more predictable. For example, to retrieve the rant text of all the rants in the ranter bucket, you'd use the following query:

```
SELECT rantText FROM ranter
```

That query produces a result set similar to this:

```
"resultset": [
    {},
    {},
    {
        "rantText": "Static languages are always better"
    },
    {
        "rantText": "Real Couchbase developers drink beer."
    },
    ... more stuff ...
],
```

In the result set, you can see the rantText values as well as some empty objects. The empty objects appear because some documents in the query input—the entire ranter bucket—do not have a rantText property, so its value is missing. The SELECT expression can also contain a path to nested document properties, and can address array properties by index. Finally, you can also give the selected properties an alias with the AS clause, just like in SQL:

```
SELECT rantText AS rant, rantAbout.rantText AS about, values[0] FROM ranter
```

The preceding query selects the rantText property from all the documents in the ranter bucket and gives it the alias "rant", as well as selects the rantText property of all the objects nested under the rantAbout property, which it gives the alias "about". Last, it also selects the first item in the JSON array stored under the values property, which happens to belong to the rantbacks documents in the ranter bucket. The query results should be similar to the following:

```
"resultset": [
    {
        "$1": "2d18e287-d5fa-42ce-bca5-b26eaef0d7d4"
    },
    {
        "about": "JavaScript is the One True Language. Why can't people see that?",
        "rant": "Static languages are always better"
    },
    {
        "about": "Why do they call it Ovaltine? The mug is round. The jar is round. They should call
it Roundtine.",
        "rant": "Real Couchbase developers drink beer."
    }
    ... more results ...
],
```

Because the values[0] expression doesn't have an alias, the result is stored under the $1 property in the result set. You can also use square bracket notation [] for array slicing by specifying the offsets within the array. For example, to retrieve a sub-array containing all items from the second to the fifth, you would use the following notation: property[1:4]. You can leave out one of the offsets, which means all items from the beginning or end of the array. Finally, you can use the || operation for string concatenation within the SELECT expression.

Just like in SQL, you can also use the DISTINCT keyword, or its synonym UNIQUE, to filter out duplicate results:

```
SELECT DISTINCT userName FROM ranter
```

In our example dataset, that produces the following result:

```
"resultset": [
    {
        "userName": "ElaineB"
    },
    {
        "userName": "DavidO"
    },
    {
        "userName": "YanivR"
    }
],
```

Note that the property names are case-sensitive, so in this case, "username" with a lower-case *n* would have returned a single (distinct) empty object as the result.

So far you've been retrieving the values of documents and properties in your queries, and astute readers have no doubt noticed that they didn't get the document ID as part of the results. Getting the document ID is very useful because, just like with views, you'll often want to use a query to find out the document IDs and then retrieve the documents directly with a bulk get operation. To retrieve the document ID, you can use the special META() function, which retrieves the metadata of the matched results:

```
SELECT META() AS metadata, rantText AS rant FROM ranter
```

That results in:

```
"resultset": [
    {
        "metadata": {
            "cas": 3.945622364407e+12,
            "flags": 0,
            "id": "davido-rant-1",
            "type": "json"
        },
        "rant": "You have way too much time on your hands"
    },
    ... more results ...
]
```

As you can see, the result object contains a nested metadata object that includes the document ID. Alternatively, you could have used the expression META().id AS id to retrieve just the document ID property.

Last, you can also use the CASE ... WHEN ... END expression, just like in SQL, to select different values conditionally, as follows:

```
SELECT id, CASE WHEN rantbacks IS NOT NULL THEN rantbacks ELSE "Nobody cares about your rant." END
AS replies
FROM ranter
```

This query will return the rantbacks property if it exists, or the hard-coded string if it does not:

```
"resultset": [
    {
        "id": "davido-rant-1",
        "replies": "Nobody cares about your rant."
    }
]
```

The FROM Clause

The FROM clause specifies the data source, or input, for the query. Omitting it will use an empty object as the input, which is useful for selecting object literals in the SELECT expression. The data source can be the name of a bucket, in which case the query input will consist of all the documents in that bucket. Alternatively, the data source can be a path specifying the bucket and nested document properties, in which case the input to the query will be the values of the specified properties, as in the following example:

```
SELECT VALUE() FROM ranter.rantAbout.rantText
```

The VALUE() function returns the full value of the object in the query input. In this case, the query input consists of all the values stored under the rantText property of sub-objects stored under the rantAbout property. Let's look at documents in the following format:

```
{
    "id": "davido-rant-1",
    "rantAbout": {
        "id": "yanivr-rant-2",
        "rantText": "JavaScript is the One True Language. Why can't people see that?",
        "type": ...
    },
    "rantText": ...
}
```

In this case, you'll get results such as these:

```
"resultset": [
    {
        "$1": "JavaScript is the One True Language. Why can't people see that?"
    },
    {
        "$1": "Why do they call it Ovaltine? The mug is round. The jar is round. They should call it
Roundtine."
    }
]
```

The FROM clause can be followed by a JOIN clause, which combines multiple data sources into a single input for the query. Logically, joins work very similarly to how they do in SQL—objects from the data source left of the JOIN statement are combined with objects from the data source to the right of the statement according to a specified condition, and the rest of the query operates on the resulting joined object. The main difference from SQL is that in SQL you specify which columns to join on for both sides of the statement, whereas in N1QL you specify a property or expression from the left side of the JOIN, which is then used as the primary key to look up objects on the right side.

Let's demonstrate with an example. In SQL, you would most likely store rants and users in two normalized tables, with the rants table storing the rant and the ID of the user, and the users table storing the user ID, name, address, and so on. To retrieve all rants with their corresponding user names and addresses, you would use an SQL query along these lines:

```
SELECT r.text, u.name, u.address
FROM    rants AS r
JOIN    users AS u
ON      r.userId = u.id
```

This query would match the userId value of rows from the left side of the join (i.e., the rants table) with the id value of rows from the right side (the users table) and return the combined results, as illustrated in Figure 6-3.

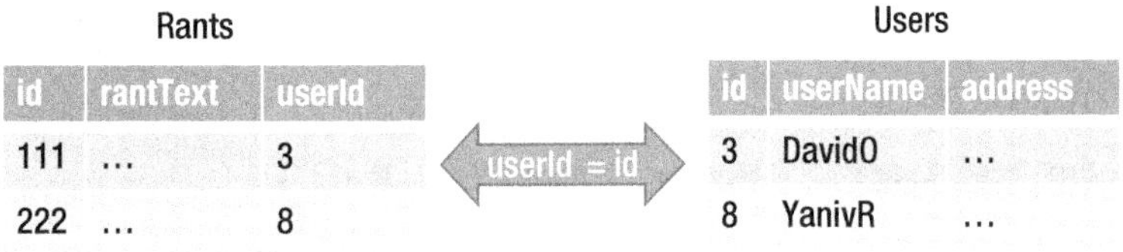

Figure 6-3. *SQL join*

In Couchbase, you can either store all rants and users in the same bucket or separate user documents into a bucket of their own. One of the best features of N1QL is that it supports cross-bucket joins, so let's assume that you actually have a separate bucket for users, and that you use the username as the document key. To perform the preceding SQL query in N1QL, you need to use the following syntax:

```
SELECT rant.rantText, user
FROM    ranter AS rant
JOIN    users AS user
KEY     rant.userName
```

The N1QL query is quite similar to the SQL one, with the main difference being that in this case the KEY clause takes the userName property from the left side of the join (the ranter bucket) and matches it with the key of the documents from the right side (the users bucket), as you can see in Figure 6-4.

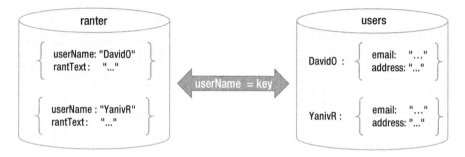

Figure 6-4. *N1QL join*

By default, N1QL performs an inner join, meaning that only objects from the left side of the join that have a matching key from the right side are selected as the input for the query. You can use the LEFT JOIN statement to perform a left join, meaning that every object from the left data source will produce at least one result object, and if a matching right-side document does not exist or has the value NULL, then the result will have the full left object plus the value MISSING or NULL, respectively, for the right object.

As you saw, you use the KEY clause to specify which document key to take from the right side of the join. You can also use the KEYS clause to specify an array of keys to match for every source object on the left. For example, if the user documents from the previous example also contained an array of followers, like this:

```
{
    "address": "Right behind you!",
    "followers": [ "YanivR", "JerryS" ],
    "userName": "DavidO"
},
{
    "address": "Who knows?",
    "followers": [ "YanivR" ],
    "userName": "JerryS"
},
{
    "address": "Why do you want to know?",
    "userName": "YanivR"
}
```

You could retrieve a list of all users with the addresses of all their followers by joining the bucket with itself and specifying the keys of the followers to join on:

```
SELECT users.userName, followers.userName AS followerName, followers.address
FROM users
JOIN users AS followers
KEYS ARRAY follower FOR follower in users.followers END
```

The KEYS clause in the query expects an array of document keys that N1QL will use to retrieve the objects for the right-side data source. The ARRAY ... FOR ... END construct unrolls the followers array, meaning that if it contained objects, you could pluck a specific property from each of those objects as the key. This is similar to the pluck method in underscore.js, or the select method in LINQ in C#. Unlike the KEY clause, KEYS can generate several result objects for each input object on the left side of the join. In this example, the user "DavidO" has two followers: "YanivR" and "JerryS," which means the right side of the join will retrieve both of those documents and join each to a copy of the document that contains "DavidO." Running this query on the three documents in the example will produce the following result:

```
"resultset": [
    {
        "address": "Why do you want to know?",
        "followerName": "YanivR",
        "userName": "DavidO"
    },
    {
        "address": "Who knows?",
        "followerName": "JerryS",
        "userName": "DavidO"
    },
    {
        "address": "Why do you want to know?",
        "followerName": "YanivR",
        "userName": "JerryS"
    }
]
```

As you can see, the user "DavidO" appears twice, in two separate result documents. N1QL extends the join operation with a cool feature called *nesting*. Using the NEST clause, you can perform a join that produces a single output for each object on the left of the join and nests all the matched objects from the right side as an array inside the result object. Let's repeat the query from the previous example using a NEST operation instead of JOIN:

```
SELECT users.userName, followers
FROM users
NEST users AS followers
KEYS ARRAY follower FOR follower in users.followers END
```

Running the query will produce the following result:

```
"resultset": [
    {
        "followers": [
            {
                "address": "Why do you want to know?",
                "userName": "YanivR"
            },
            {
                "address": "Who knows?",
                "followers": [
                    "YanivR"
```

```
            ],
            "userName": "JerryS"
        }
    ],
    "userName": "DavidO"
},
{
    "followers": [
        {
            "address": "Why do you want to know?",
            "userName": "YanivR"
        }
    ],
    "userName": "JerryS"
}
]
```

As you can see, the user DavidO no longer appears in two separate results. Instead, the result for the user DavidO, which originated in the left-side data source, contains the followers array with matching results from the right-side data source. Each follower is now a separate object within the followers array. You further can use the ARRAY ... FOR ... END clause in the SELECT expression to pluck specific properties from the objects within the nested array and return just those properties as a new array:

```
SELECT users.userName, ARRAY f.userName || ' from ' || f.address FOR f in followers END as
followedBy
FROM users
 NEST users AS followers
 KEYS ARRAY follower FOR follower in users.followers END
```

As you can see, instead of selecting the entire array of follower objects, the preceding query plucks the userName and address properties from each of the follower objects within the array, concatenates them, and returns them as a new array:

```
"resultset": [
    {
        "followedBy": [
            "YanivR from Why do you want to know?",
            "JerryS from Who knows?"
        ],
        "userName": "DavidO"
    },
    {
        "followedBy": [
            "YanivR from Why do you want to know?"
        ],
        "userName": "JerryS"
    }
]
```

The UNNEST operation, as the name suggests, does the opposite of NEST. It takes each item from a nested array and creates a new top-level object from it. Essentially, it joins the document with its own array sub-property. The resulting data source would have multiple copies of the document, one for each item in the nested array. For example, let's say you stored rantbacks as an array property of the rant document, like this:

```
{
 "id": "yanivr-rant-1",
 "type": "rant",
 "userName": "YanivR",
 "rantText": "Real Couchbase developers drink beer.",
 "rantbacks": [
    {
      "userName": "JohnC",
      "text": "Well, of course, this is just the sort blinkered philistine pig-ignorance I've come to
expect from you non-creative garbage."
    },
    {
      "userName": "DavidO",
      "text": "I just watched you drink three cups of green tea in a row. You are not a real
Couchbase developer."
    }
 ]
}
```

You could retrieve separate objects containing the username, rant text, and rantback for each of the rantbacks in each rant document in the database:

```
SELECT rant.userName, rant.rantText, rantback
FROM ranter AS rant
    UNNEST rant.rantbacks AS rantback
WHERE rant.type = 'rant'
```

As you can see, the FROM clause takes each document in the ranter bucket and UNNEST combines it with each of the documents in the nested rantbacks array. Documents that do not have a rantbacks array property are not included in the input. Running the preceding query with the single rant mentioned earlier will give the following result:

```
"resultset": [
    {
        "rantText": "Real Couchbase developers drink beer.",
        "rantback": {
            "text": "...",
            "userName": "JohnC"
        },
        "userName": "YanivR"
    },
    {
        "rantText": "Real Couchbase developers drink beer.",
        "rantback": {
            "text": "...",
```

```
        "userName": "DavidO"
    },
        "userName": "YanivR"
    }
]
```

Each of the nested rantback objects within the rantbacks array was joined with its parent document. From this input, the SELECT statement plucked the userName, rantText, and the joined rantback object. The result only contains data from objects of type "rant" that have a non-empty rantbacks array property.

Query Conditions and Expressions

You've already seen the WHERE clause used in examples in this chapter. It works exactly as you would expect from your experience with SQL, and it filters the query output according to the specified logical expression. For example, the query SELECT * FROM ranter WHERE type = 'rant' will return all documents that have a type property whose value is rant. All the common logical operators are supported, as shown in Table 6-1.

Table 6-1. *N1QL Logical Operators*

Operator	Description
=	Equal, you can also use ==.
!=	Not equal—you can also use <>.
>	Greater than.
>=	Greater than or equal.
<	Less than.
<=	Less than or equal.
BETWEEN	Value is between two other values. End value is inclusive.
NOT, AND, OR	Logical operators.
LIKE	String match operator, % matches zero or more characters, _ matches a single character.
IS NULL	Value is explicitly set to null. Inverse of IS NOT NULL.
IS MISSING	Value (property) does not exist.
IS VALUED	Value exists and is not null. Equivalent to IS NOT NULL AND IS NOT MISSING.

In addition to the regular, SQL-like operators, the WHERE clause in N1QL also supports checking conditions over an array of values. The syntax for checking a condition within an array value is similar to the ARRAY clause you've learned about earlier in this chapter:

```
SELECT id, rantbacks
FROM ranter
WHERE ANY rantback IN rantbacks SATISFIES rantback.userName LIKE 'David%' END
```

This query will retrieve the ID and rantbacks array of any document that has *at least one* rantback object with the property userName that starts with the string "David" inside its rantbacks array:

```
"resultset": [
    {
        "id": "yanivr-rant-1",
        "rantbacks": [
            {
                "text": "...",
                "userName": "JohnC"
            },
            {
                "text": "...",
                "userName": "DavidO"
            }
        ]
    }
]
```

Changing the operator ANY to EVERY in the previous query example will retrieve only those results where *every object* within the array satisfies the condition. In the preceding example, that would be an empty result set.

N1QL also lets you retrieve values by key, because Couchbase is a key-value store, after all. The KEY and KEYS clauses can be used instead of WHERE to retrieve documents directly by key. KEY accepts a single document key, while KEYS accepts an array of keys to retrieve:

```
SELECT * FROM ranter KEYS ['yanivr-rant-1', 'davido-rant-1']
```

This query will return the documents with specified keys, if they exist:

```
"resultset": [
    {
        "id": "yanivr-rant-1",
        ...
    },
    {
        "id": "davido-rant-1",
        ...
    }
]
```

You can control the number of results returned by a query with the LIMIT and OFFSET clauses. By using these clauses, pagination support is very straightforward.

```
SELECT * FROM ranter LIMIT 10 OFFSET 20
```

The preceding query will retrieve up to ten results, starting with the twenty-first result (i.e., the third page.)

Sorting and Grouping

The GROUP BY clause aggregates multiple results by the specified condition. The selected fields must either be part of the GROUP BY condition or be aggregated with one of the built-in functions, such as SUM, COUNT, AVG, etc. For example, to count how many documents of each type (rants, users, and so on) are in a bucket, you could use the following query:

```
SELECT COUNT(*) as count, type
FROM ranter
GROUP BY type
```

This query will aggregate all the documents in the ranter bucket by the type property. Documents that do not have a type property are also counted as having a value of MISSING:

```
"resultset": [
    {
        "count": 1
    },
    {
        "count": 8,
        "type": "rant"
    },
    {
        "count": 2,
        "type": "user"
    }
]
```

In the sample output, you can see that there is one document without a type property, eight documents that have the type "rant," and two that have the type "user." The optional HAVING clause, which follows the GROUP BY clause, can be used to filter items from the aggregation:

```
SELECT COUNT(*) as count, type
FROM ranter
GROUP BY type
HAVING type IS VALUED AND count(*) > 5
```

This query will only display results from documents that actually have a value in the type property, and only if there are more than five documents of that type:

```
"resultset": [
    {
        "count": 8,
        "type": "rant"
    }
]
```

Exactly as in SQL, you can sort the query results using the ORDER BY clause. By default, ORDER BY sorts items in an ascending order; you can specify the sort direction explicitly by appending the ASC or DESC clause after the sorting expression:

```
SELECT userName FROM ranter ORDER BY userName DESC
```

Unsurprisingly, this query retrieves the usernames and orders them in descending alphabetical order:

```
"resultset": [
    {
        "userName": "YanivR"
    },
    {
        "userName": "DavidO"
    }
]
```

When comparing different data types, N1QL uses the same logic as views, which you learned about in Chapter 5. The types, in ascending order, are as follows:

- MISSING

- NULL

- FALSE

- TRUE

- *Numbers*

- *Strings*

- *Arrays*: Just like in views, each array element is compared with a corresponding element in other arrays. That is, items at position 0 first, then index 1, and so on. This way longer arrays evaluate as "greater" than shorter arrays.

- *Objects*: Also like in views, objects are compared by their keys.

Indexing Properties

The vast majority of databases that allow ad-hoc querying provide some sort of mechanism for indexing parts of the data to improve query performance. Without such a mechanism, conditional queries have to search the entire data set. In SQL, specifying a condition on an unindexed column causes a full table scan. In N1QL, as you might expect, querying an unindexed property causes the server to scan the entire bucket and check this property on every document.

At the time of writing this book, the Developer Preview 3 version of N1QL actually uses regular Couchbase views behind the scenes to improve query performance. The exact details for the final implementation are still in flux, so discussing the way DP3 uses indexes isn't very useful at this point. However, the syntax for creating and using indexes is already set, and you will be able to use that when the release version of N1QL comes along.

You can create an index on a property or sub-property, or you can create a specific array index within a property. For example, to create an index named ix_userName on the userName property of documents in the ranter bucket you would use the following statement:

```
CREATE INDEX ix_userName ON ranter(userName)
```

In the developer preview, this actually creates a production view in the ranter bucket, as you can see in Figure 6-5. The map function inside the view emits a pre-processed key into the index, which depends on the datatype of the property being indexed.

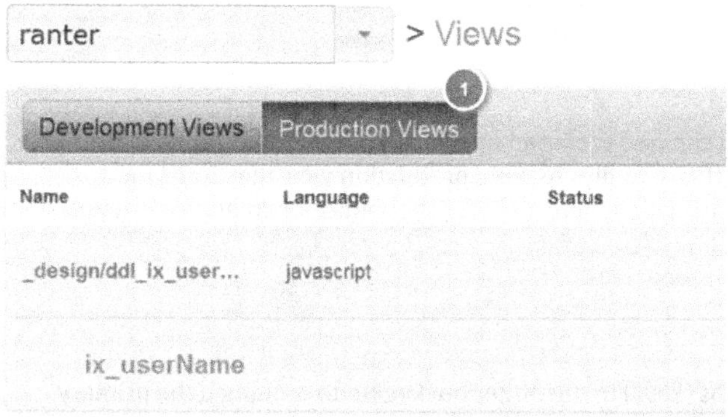

Figure 6-5. *N1QL index*

Using the index doesn't require any additional syntax—simply use the indexed property in the query condition:

```
SELECT * FROM ranter WHERE userName = 'DavidO'
```

As you can see in the query result, using the cbq shell, it now runs in under 5.5 milliseconds, instead of the 500 or so it took without the index:

```
{
    "resultset": [
        ...
    ],
    "info": [
        {
            "caller": "http_response:160",
            "code": 100,
            "key": "total_rows",
            "message": "1"
        },
        {
            "caller": "http_response:162",
            "code": 101,
            "key": "total_elapsed_time",
            "message": "5.4279ms"
        }
    ]
}
```

To delete an index, use the DROP INDEX statement with the bucket and name of the index, like so:

```
DROP INDEX ranter.ix_userName
```

This will delete the auto-generated view and will tell the N1QL query engine that it no longer exists.

■ **Note**   Don't delete the auto-generated view manually in the Couchbase console; use the DROP INDEX command in N1QL instead. The N1QL execution engine in Developer Preview 3 does not get updated if you manually delete the view and continue to try to use the index. This, of course, causes runtime errors.

In addition to secondary indexes on properties, you can also create an optimized primary index for a bucket, which accelerates queries on the document key. In DP3 this actually creates a production view that emits the document ID as an array of characters instead of as the string that it normally is. The syntax for creating a primary index is very straightforward:

```
CREATE PRIMARY INDEX ON ranter
```

This will create a primary index on the document IDs (keys) in the ranter bucket, or do nothing if the primary index already exists.

Exploring the Query Execution Details

The EXPLAIN keyword provides an insight into the inner workings of the N1QL query optimizer. Similar to the same keyword in MySQL and Oracle, prefixing a query with EXPLAIN will return the execution plan the query optimized intends to use for running the query. The execution plan includes the query parameters and information on which indexes and buckets N1QL intends to use. For example, let's compare the query from the previous topic with and without an index on the userName property:

```
EXPLAIN SELECT * FROM ranter WHERE userName = 'DavidO'
```

Running this query produces the following output:

```
"resultset": [
    {
        "input": {
            "expr": {
                "left": {
                    "left": {
                        "path": "ranter",
                        "type": "property"
                    },
                    "right": {
                        "path": "userName",
                        "type": "property"
                    },
                    "type": "dot_member"
                },
                "right": {
                    "type": "literal_string",
                    "value": "DavidO"
                },
                "type": "equals"
            },
            "input": {
                "as": "ranter",
                "bucket": "ranter",
                "ids": null,
                "input": {
                    "as": "",
                    "bucket": "ranter",
                    "cover": false,
                    "index": "#alldocs",
                    "pool": "default",
                    "ranges": null,
                    "type": "scan"
                },
                "pool": "default",
                "projection": null,
                "type": "fetch"
            },
            "type": "filter"
        },
        "result": [
            {
                "as": "",
                "expr": {
                    "path": "ranter",
                    "type": "property"
                },
                "star": true
            }
        ],
        "type": "projector"
    }
]
```

In addition to the breakdown of the SELECT expression itself, you can see that the query optimizer is going to use the #alldocs index to perform a full scan. This is a built-in index that contains all the document IDs, and N1QL will use it to retrieve each document in the bucket and check its userName property.

After creating an index on the userName property, the execution plan changes to contain the following:

```
"input": {
    "as": "",
    "bucket": "ranter",
    "cover": false,
    "index": "ix_userName",
    "pool": "default",
    "ranges": [
        {
            "high": [
                "DavidO"
            ],
            "inclusion": "both",
            "limit": 0,
            "low": [
                "DavidO"
            ]
        }
    ],
    "type": "scan"
}
```

You can see that this time N1QL will use the ix_userName index we created to retrieve only the documents with the key "DavidO" and use those as the input for the rest of the query.

Summary

The N1QL query language is a great step towards developer-friendly ad-hoc querying capabilities for Couchbase. The third developer preview version of N1QL, while not production ready, is a good tool for learning about this upcoming feature. If you are working on a long-term project that uses Couchbase Server, you can already start planning your data-access strategy around N1QL. Code that you write today will be ready to run, possibly with minor adjustments, when the production release of N1QL comes out.

CHAPTER 7

■ ■ ■

Advanced Couchbase Techniques

In the previous four chapters you've learned about the various SDKs, key-based operations, views, and the N1QL language. But just knowing how to store and retrieve data does not immediately translate into being a deadly Couchbase coding ninja. To be fair, being able to use the CRUD operations and indexed queries is enough for quite a few different applications. However, real production systems, enterprise software, and various web-scale applications have requirements beyond just using a database.

This chapter covers some important techniques that are commonly used in real-world applications, such as handling failure conditions in software, implementing two-phase commit to make up for the lack of transaction support in the database, using Couchbase as an out-of-process session container, and more.

Software Error Handling

As you'll recall from our discussion of the CAP theorem in the beginning of the book, having the application logic make up for the gaps in data-store availability is a common pattern in the world of NoSQL. Our software needs to work cooperatively with the database so that the system as a whole remains 100% available. Couchbase Server was built for high reliability and availability from the start, and, indeed, it performs admirably nearly all of the time. However, under some special circumstances part of the data can be unavailable to clients for a brief period of time. You need to know how to handle the different temporary errors until Couchbase resumes its regular service.

Out of the (hopefully) uncommon error scenarios, one you are more likely to see is node failure. When a node fails for any reason, all data in the active vBuckets on that node becomes unavailable until a failover mechanism activates a replica copy of that data on other nodes. You'll learn all about the different failover scenarios in Chapter 10, so for now let's just assume that some process takes care of activating replica copies after a delay of anywhere from only a few seconds to a few minutes, depending on configuration. If there is no failover mechanism in place, then it's possible that the node will remain unavailable indefinitely, but after reading this book you will undoubtedly know better than to go to production without failover set up.

Until failover kicks in, operations with keys that belong to active vBuckets on healthy nodes will work normally, but ones on the down node will fail with error code 0x18, "Connection failure." Your options in this case depend on your application. If the operation is not time-critical, you can simply let the failover mechanism take its time and retry the operation periodically to see if the problem gets resolved. It's a good practice in general to set a limit on the number of retries your application will attempt before reporting a failure.

Here's a very basic example in Node.js:

```
function getWithRetry(id, retries, callback) {
    client.get(id, function(error, result) {
        if(error &&
            error.code == couchbase.errors.connectError &&
            retries > 0) {
            console.log("Connection error, but don't panic, we'll try again in a second.");
```

```
            setTimeout(getWithRetry, retryDelay, id, retries - 1, callback);
        }
        else {
            callback(error, result);
        }
    });
}
```

In the code example, the getWithRetry function tries to get a document. If it encounters a connectError, which is error code 0x18 in other SDKs, and there are still retries left, it sets a timer to call itself again in retryDelay milliseconds with 1 less retry remaining. Using the function is quite simple:

```
var retryDelay = 1000; // milliseconds

getWithRetry('ranter-David0', 30, function(error, result) {
    if(error)
        console.log("Couldn't get after 30 retries. NOW you can panic!");
    // Do stuff with the result...
});
```

The getWithRetry function is initially called with 30 retries, and the retry delay is set to 1000 milliseconds, which we chose because 30 seconds happens to be the minimum automatic failover interval we can configure in Couchbase. We use a get operation in the example, but it will work with any key-based operation.

If you don't have the luxury of waiting for Couchbase to recover, and the bucket you're trying to read has replicas configured, then you can use the replica read API to get the document you want from one of the replica vBuckets.

Reading Replica Documents

As you can guess from the topic name, this mechanism only works for get operations. And, naturally, reading from a copy rather than from the active vBucket means you may get an outdated value. This can happen if the document was changed in the active vBucket, but the node failed before it had the chance to replicate the new value. The replica read operation doesn't have all the options of the regular get operation—it lets you specify the key to retrieve as well as an optional parameter that determines how the client should retrieve the document. By default, the client will request the document from all the available replica vBuckets and return the result from whichever node responds first. You can optionally tell it to read the document from a specific replica by specifying its index as the parameter. In some SDKs you can also tell the client to return results only after it gets a response from all the replicas.

You can combine replica reads with timed retries to create a "defense in depth" against node failures in your application. Unless you're using the .NET SDK, that is, because at the time of this writing it still doesn't have a replica read API. In Java, Node.js, and PHP the method name is getReplica, in C it's lcb_get_replica, and in Python and Ruby the replica read is an optional parameter of the regular get method.

Let's see an example:

```
function getWithReplicaFallback(id, callback) {
    client.get(id, function (error, result) {
        if(error &&
            error.code == couchbase.errors.connectError) {

            client.getReplica(id, function (error, result) {
                if(error)
                        getWithRetry('ranter-David0', 30, ...);
```

```
                else
                    callback(error, result)
            });
        }
        else {
            callback(error, result);
        }
    });
}

getWithReplicaFallback('ranter-David0', function(error, result) {
    console.log(error, result);
});
```

In this code example, we first try to read the document normally, then try to read any of its replicas if the regular get fails, and finally we fall back to the timed retry function we used earlier.

Handling Temporary Out-of-Memory Errors

Couchbase begins returning temporary out-of-memory (OOM) errors in response to key-based operations when its total RAM usage rises above a certain threshold, called the high-water mark, which by default is 95%. Couchbase does its best to make sure it always has room in memory to accept writes or load new documents from disk by removing less frequently used documents from its caching layer once memory use passes a certain threshold. However, in some circumstances, the server may be unable to free up memory fast enough to handle the volume of incoming writes or the number of new documents it has to load from disk—and thus move into cache—in response to get requests. The specific root causes vary by use-case, but they all pretty much boil down to "your cluster isn't big enough right now," where "big enough" can be a combination of memory, disk I/O capacity, network, etc. You'll learn about the details of cluster sizing, setting various memory thresholds, and monitoring resources in the chapters in Part III; for now just treat Couchbase as a black box that sometimes tells our application "hold on a second, I'm dealing with the stuff you sent earlier."

When your application starts receiving temporary out-of-memory errors, there are two possible outcomes that might occur, and you need to deal with both in your code. If the cluster is definitely sized correctly and is currently healthy, then usually these errors really are temporary. They most likely indicate that the database is experiencing an unusually high load spike but will return to normal soon. Your application will need to buffer outgoing write operations and retry them periodically until they succeed, and also delay any reads it needs to do—and display some sort of progress UI, if it has one—until it's able to read again. If your data has stringent durability requirements, or if the data access process is short lived, such as with a web service, you will need to have an external application mechanism that can persist and retry all the buffered operations until they go through. If, on the other hand, the cluster isn't about to recover, then this is a very bad fault condition because it will require external intervention in Couchbase. This can be an automated monitoring service of some sort that can resolve some of the simpler low-resource problems. If not, then an actual human will have to use the available administration tools to fix whatever is broken. Until that happens, the application will only be able to read and write from Couchbase at a severely reduced rate, if at all. At this point we're getting beyond the scope of this book; depending on how mission-critical this piece of the application is, you should engineer some external safeguards to deal with being unable to write to the database.

Either way, any number of temporary out-of-memory errors above zero is bad—the difference is only in how bad—so your application should log the problem and, if possible, raise an alert through whatever software mechanism you have. A well-set-up Couchbase deployment will also have some external monitoring for OOM errors, among other things, but having an additional line of defense in your application is a good idea.

If all you need is a simple error-handling mechanism, you can adapt the code example we used in the previous topic by adding code that will check if the error code equals temporaryError, which is error code 0x0B in other SDKs, and deal with logging and alerting, and then proceed to retry the operation multiple times.

Implementing Transactions with Two-Phase Commit

Unlike relational databases, most NoSQL data stores do not have built-in support for atomic transactions, because these are extremely difficult to implement in a distributed system and usually come with a heavy price regarding performance. However, sometimes the application logic requires that a sequence of operations be executed atomically—either they all succeed or they all get rolled back. For those cases it is possible to use a series of CAS-based operations in Couchbase to execute a set of changes in a way that is logically atomic and reversible. Because most of the flow is implemented in the application, it doesn't provide the isolation level of relational database transactions—other clients can read and change the intermediate values before the transaction is committed. However, the atomicity and possibility of rollback, combined with Couchbase's built-in data durability API, are enough to satisfy most use-cases.

The technique you use with Couchbase is actually an instance of a more general case, called the two-phase commit protocol (2PC), which attempts to solve the problem of atomic commits in a distributed system. We recommend reading the Wikipedia article on 2PC, at http://en.wikipedia.org/wiki/Two-phase_commit_protocol, for an overview of the protocol. Although it isn't strictly about Couchbase, it provides important background information for anyone who works with distributed systems. Besides, it's fascinating stuff! While reading that Wikipedia article in the context of Couchbase Server, think of your application as the *coordinator*, the documents participating in the transaction as the *cohorts*, and database operations as *messages* between participants.

So, how does it work? In short, you use a temporary document to hold the state of the transaction and perform changes in such a way that they can be reverted in exactly the same order. To illustrate this, we'll use everybody's favorite transaction example: transferring money between two accounts. Let's continue the example we used when we talked about concurrency in Chapter 4. After becoming ludicrously rich thanks to RanteR, the Anti-Social Network, Yaniv goes through an existential crisis. Having gotten fed up with crass materialism, he decides to give up his worldly possessions and spend the rest of his days in quiet contemplation of the cosmic oneness of being. He calls up his bank in the Tax Shelter Islands and tells them to transfer the entire bank balance to David, who happily accepts the gift because he lives his life strictly according to the Rules of Acquisition.[1] Unfortunately, the Tax Shelter Islands National Bank uses a computer system built by the lowest bidder in the 1960s, which does not support atomic transactions and tends to crash. A lot. Figure 7-1 shows how the system works.

		David	Yaniv
1)	yBalance = getBalance("Yaniv");	$1,000,000	$1,000,000
2)	setBalance("Yaniv", "$0");	$1,000,000	$0
3)	dBalance = getBalance("David");	$1,000,000	$0
4)	newBalance = dBalance + yBalance;	$1,000,000	$0
5)	setBalance("David", newBalance);	$2,000,000	$0

Figure 7-1. *A non-atomic bank transfer flow*

Consider what happens if the application crashes anywhere between steps 2 and 4. Yes, you could also move step 2 to the end, in which case a crash before that step would cause an error in the client's favor. But really, what bank would ever do that?

Now, the steps themselves are perfectly correct. All that's missing is a durable way to track which steps were already performed, so that in the event of a crash the application could either continue from the same place or roll back all the steps up to that point. Let's assume we have the two documents shown in Figure 7-2 in our Couchbase cluster, representing the accounts of our two heroes.

---

[1]This situation falls under Rules 1, 10, 21, and 285.

```
account: "David"          account: "Yaniv"
balance: 1000000          balance: 1000000
```

Figure 7-2. Initial account documents

We'll begin in step 1 by creating a third document, which will hold the transaction details. Add the new document with a state of "init," as shown in bold in Figure 7-3. As you can already guess, you're actually building a finite state machine to keep track of all the steps in the transaction.

1
```
account: "David"      account: "Yaniv"      transaction: 1
balance: 1000000      balance: 1000000      from:   "Yaniv"
transactions: []      transactions: []      to:     "David"
                                            amount: 1000000
                                            state:  "init"
```

Figure 7-3. Initialized transaction state

The transactions property, which magically appeared in the two account documents, will hold the pending transactions for each. Let's just assume it was there from the beginning and move on. Start the actual transaction process by setting its state to "pending," as shown in bold in Figure 7-4 (step 2). In a system with millions of transactions, this will help us find which transactions are in progress and which haven't started yet more efficiently.

2
```
account: "David"      account: "Yaniv"      transaction: 1
balance: 1000000      balance: 1000000      from:   "Yaniv"
transactions: []      transactions: []      to:     "David"
                                            amount: 1000000
                                            state:  "pending"
```

Figure 7-4. Starting the transaction

Next, as shown in bold in Figure 7-5 (step 3), you apply the operation specified in the transaction to one of the documents and then add a reference from the account document to the transaction state document. This is an atomic operation, because you're updating the entire document all at once.

3
```
account: "David"      account: "Yaniv"      transaction: 1
balance: 1000000      balance: 0            from:   "Yaniv"
transactions: []      transactions: [1]     to:     "David"
                                            amount: 1000000
                                            state:  "pending"
```

Figure 7-5. Updating the source account document

Do the same thing with the other account document, as shown in Figure 7-6 (step 4), except, of course, you add the amount to the balance instead of subtracting it. The order in which you update the two documents doesn't matter. What's important here is that each step both updates the balance and marks the document for rollback purposes in a single atomic operation.

4
account: "David"
balance: 2000000
transactions: [1]

account: "Yaniv"
balance: 0
transactions: [1]

transaction: 1
from: "Yaniv"
to: "David"
amount: 1000000
state: "pending"

Figure 7-6. *Updating the target account document*

With both account documents updated, in step 5 you now set the transaction state to "committed" (Figure 7-7).

5
account: "David"
balance: 2000000
transactions: [1]

account: "Yaniv"
balance: 0
transactions: [1]

transaction: 1
from: "Yaniv"
to: "David"
amount: 1000000
state: "committed"

Figure 7-7. *Committing the transaction*

Remove the transaction state reference from both of the account documents, as shown in Figure 7-8 (step 6). These are two separate operations, but we'll just show them as a single step here, because their order isn't important and doesn't affect rollback.

6
account: "David"
balance: 2000000
transactions: []

account: "Yaniv"
balance: 0
transactions: []

transaction: 1
from: "Yaniv"
to: "David"
amount: 1000000
state: "committed"

Figure 7-8. *Cleaning up the account documents*

And, finally, after cleaning up the account documents from transaction references, set the transaction state to "done" in step 7 (Figure 7-9).

7
account: "David"
balance: 2000000
transactions: []

account: "Yaniv"
balance: 0
transactions: []

transaction: 1
from: "Yaniv"
to: "David"
amount: 1000000
state: "done"

Figure 7-9. *Finished transaction*

Before covering all the failure and rollback scenarios, it's important to emphasize that each of the preceding steps is atomic and durable, because each one operates on a single document at a time. To make sure that document changes really are safe and durable, in Couchbase you use CAS values to ensure concurrent safety, as well as rely on the persistence and replication requirements API to ensure each change is stored safely before moving on to the next one. Also, note that no two states are the same, so we can always uniquely identify what state the transaction is in if we need to continue or roll back from that point.

Now, let's look at this flow in the context of failure and recovery. The failure can be an application crash or a database problem—anything that would interrupt the transaction process and leave some of the steps hanging. After a failure, your application can either try to reconstruct the state of the transaction from the data in all three documents and continue on from that point, or it can undo everything and just re-run the operation from scratch. The choice of whether to continue or to roll back depends on your exact application logic and requirements.

- If a failure occurs after step 1, it's very simple to detect the transaction state and either just delete the state document and retry or continue on to step 2.

- If a failure occurs after steps 2 or 3, that is, when the transaction state is "pending," then your choices are the following:

  - To continue, you detect the exact step by checking which of the documents contains the transaction ID in its transactions array, and then go on from that step.

  - To roll back, you set the transaction state to "canceling" and then apply the account operation in reverse to any document that has the transaction ID in its transactions array. You also simultaneously remove the transaction reference from the document. After that, set the transaction state to "canceled" to make sure no more operations will be performed with it. Then you can rerun the whole operation from the start, if you want.

At this point, it might occur to you that you could just store the original value somewhere before starting the transaction and then simply restore it if you have to roll back. The problem with this idea is that the two-phase transaction doesn't provide isolation, which means that other clients can change the document while the transaction is going on. Rolling back by restoring the original value of the document risks overwriting any other changes that happened during the transaction.

- If a failure occurs after steps 4, 5, or 6, that is, when the transaction state is "committed" and the account balances are both already updated, then your choices are the following:

  - You can just finish the transaction by cleaning up references from the account documents and setting its state to done.

  - Or you can roll back by actually running a new transaction with the same amount but with the source and destination accounts reversed. This will safely revert the account balances to what they were before the botched transaction.

As you no doubt realize, this algorithm can be used to change any number of documents via a logically atomic operation, not just two as in the example. As long as you only change each document once and do so in a predictably reversible way, you can keep adding more steps between 4 and 5 for as many documents as you want. If you have to roll the transaction back, then undo the change to each document and remove the transaction state reference, as described earlier.

The sample code demonstrating this in action is a little long, so we'll take it one step at a time. Keep in mind that this code is only meant to demonstrate how two-phase commit works, rather than teach you Node.js, and it's far from production quality. A proper application should have much better exception handling, instead of the trivial rethrow-everything cop-out we use here. Your exception-handling mechanism will be responsible for rolling back the transaction if things go wrong. We also didn't use any of the available Node.js modules that implement a state-machine for us, because that's not the point of this code example. A final note before you dive in to the example is that each step in the two-phase-commit flow depends on the result of the previous step, so implementing it in an inherently asynchronous framework results in more verbose code. In most of the other supported languages, you can write it somewhat more concisely.

The transfer function is the entry point into the transaction mechanism. It takes the transaction parameters—source, destination, and amount—and then creates a new transaction state document and moves to the next step in the flow:

```
function transfer(from, to, amount) {
    var transaction = {
        from: from,
        to: to,
        amount: amount,
        state: "init"
    };

    client.incr("transaction-counter", {initial: 0, offset: 1}, function(error, result) {
        if(error) throw error;

        var id = result.value;
        transaction.id = id;

        client.add('transaction-' + id, transaction, {persist_to: 2, replicate_to: 2},
            function(error, result)
        {
            if(error) throw error;

            updateTransactionState(transaction, "pending", updateSource);
        })
    });
}
```

In the transfer function, you build a new transaction object with the state set to "init," get a new transaction ID from Couchbase with the incr function, and save the new document in the database. At this point, you don't need to do any concurrency checking, because incr is atomic and we're saving a new document. If everything worked as expected, call the updateTransactionState function to perform the next step, which is to update the transaction state to pending. In our trivial state-machine implementation, we also pass a callback for the next step after that to the updateTransactionState function, which it will call on success:

```
function updateTransactionState(transaction, state, nextStepCallback) {
    client.get('transaction-' + transaction.id, function(error, result) {
        if(error) throw error;

        var transaction = result.value;
        transaction.state = state;

        client.replace('transaction-' + transaction.id, transaction,
            {cas: result.cas, persist_to: 2, replicate_to: 2},
            function(error, result)
        {
            if(error && error.code == couchbase.errors.keyAlreadyExists)
                return updateTransactionState(transaction, state); // Retry
            if(error) throw error;

            nextStepCallback(transaction); // Move on to the next step
        });
    });
}
```

In the updateTransactionState function, which does exactly what its name says, we retrieve the transaction-state object, update its state property, and save it back to the database. Because the cost of the update operation is trivial, and we don't actually expect anyone to compete with us for access to this document, we use the optimistic concurrency pattern we learned back in Chapter 4 for storing the document. We use the CAS value we got from retrieving the document and check for a keyAlreadyExists error—if it occurs, re-run the same function recursively using the same parameters, which will retrieve the document with the new CAS value, and then try saving it again. We don't limit the number of retries here because we're lazy, but you should.

Also, because our (sadly) fictional example deals with moving money around, we use high persistence and replication requirements in the replace operation—its callback will only be called after the data has been replicated to two additional nodes and safely stored to disk on the main and one additional node. This has two implications: first, it makes the operation significantly slower than a typical Couchbase replace, and, second, the client will return an error if Couchbase can't meet these requirements because there aren't enough nodes in the cluster. The former is the price we pay for extremely high data durability, and the latter we should deal with through better exception handling than what we show here. To pick the durability requirements in a real-world application, you will have to balance the importance of the data against the increased operation latency due to waiting for additional replication and persistence.

After saving the transaction state on the specified number of nodes, the updateTransactionState function calls the nextStepCallback function we passed to it earlier. In this case, this function is updateSource, which takes the transaction object as the parameter:

```
function updateSource(transaction) {
    client.get('account-' + transaction.from, function(error, result) {
        if(error) throw error;

        var account = result.value;
        account.balance -= transaction.amount;
        account.transactions.push(transaction.id);

        client.replace('account-' + transaction.from, account,
            {cas: result.cas, persist_to: 2, replicate_to: 2},
            function(error, result)
        {
            if(error && error.code == couchbase.errors.keyAlreadyExists)
                return updateSource(transaction);

            if(error) throw error;

            updateDestination(transaction);
        });
    });
}
```

In the updateSource function, we retrieve the "from" account document, subtract the transfer amount from the balance, and add the transaction ID to its transactions array, saving a reference to the transaction-state document for later. Finally, we save the updated account document with optimistic concurrency and the same high-durability requirements and call the updateDestination function, which is the next step in the two-phase commit:

```
function updateDestination(transaction) {
    client.get('account-' + transaction.to, function(error, result) {
        if(error) throw error;
```

```
        var account = result.value;
        account.balance += transaction.amount;
        account.transactions.push(transaction.id);

        client.replace('account-' + transaction.to, account,
            {cas: result.cas, persist_to: 2, replicate_to: 2},
            function(error, result)
        {
            if(error && error.code == couchbase.errors.keyAlreadyExists)
                return updateDestination(transaction);

            if(error) throw error;

            updateTransactionState(transaction, "committed", cleanSource);
        });
    });
}
```

The order of calling updateSource and updateDestination doesn't actually matter; we could have called them in reverse, as long as we updated the transaction state to "committed" only after updating both accounts. The updateDestination function works exactly like updateSource, except it adds the amount to the balance, instead of subtracting it, and then calls the updateTransactionState function as the next step. This time we update the state to "committed" and pass the cleanSource function to be called after successfully saving the state.

Once the transaction is committed, all that's left is to clean up the transaction-state references and then update the state one last time, to "done." Both cleanSource and cleanDestination work basically the same as updateSource, except they only remove the transaction ID from the account document's transactions array:

```
function cleanSource(transaction) {
    client.get('account-' + transaction.from, function(error, result) {
        if(error) throw error;

        var account = result.value;
        // Remove transaction reference from account
        account.transactions.splice( account.transactions.indexOf( transaction.id ), 1 );

        client.replace('account-' + transaction.from, account,
            {cas: result.cas, persist_to: 2, replicate_to: 2},
            function(error, result)
        {
            if(error && error.code == couchbase.errors.keyAlreadyExists)
                return cleanSource(transaction);

            if(error) throw error;

            cleanDestination(transaction);
        });
    });
}
```

It is much the same with `cleanDestination`:

```
function cleanDestination(transaction) {
    client.get('account-' + transaction.to, function(error, result) {
        if(error) throw error;

        var account = result.value;
        // Remove transaction reference from account
        account.transactions.splice( account.transactions.indexOf( transaction.id ), 1 );

        client.replace('account-' + transaction.to, account,
            {cas: result.cas, persist_to: 2, replicate_to: 2},
            function(error, result)
        {
            if(error && error.code == couchbase.errors.keyAlreadyExists)
                return cleanDestination(transaction);

            if(error) throw error;

            updateTransactionState(transaction, "done", function() {
                console.log("Transaction finished.");
            });
        });
    });
}
```

With both account documents cleaned up, `cleanDestination` calls `updateTransactionState` one last time to set the transaction to its final "done" state.

To transfer $1,000,000 from Yaniv to David, you'll use a very simple client that just calls the `transfer` function, like this:

```
transfer('Yaniv', 'David', 1000000);
```

To roll back the transaction after a failure, you'll use the `rollbackTransaction` function, which only needs the transaction ID as a parameter. We don't actually show the parts of the application that do the error handling, store the transaction ID for later, and so on. We'll leave that as an exercise for the reader.[2]

```
function rollbackTransaction(id) {
    console.log('Rolling back transaction id: ' + id);

    client.get('transaction-' + id, function(error,result) {
        if(error) throw error;

        var transaction = result.value;
        console.log('Transaction details: ', transaction);

        switch(transaction.state) {
            case "init":
                updateTransactionState(transaction, "cancelled", function() {});
                break;
            case "pending":
                updateTransactionState(transaction, "cancelling", rollbackSource);
```

---

[2]David has been waiting to use that line since he read his first computer textbook at the age of 9.

```
                break;
            case "committed":
                transfer(transaction.to, transaction.from, transaction.amount);
                updateTransactionState(transaction, "cancelled", function() {});
                break;
            case "done":
            case "cancelling":
            case "cancelled":
                console.log("Nothing to see here, move along.");
                break;
        }
    });
}
```

The rollback is very straightforward. We decided that our application logic wouldn't try to complete broken transactions. So after we retrieve the transaction document, we check the state just as we discussed earlier in this topic. If it's "init," we just set the transaction to "cancelled" and that's it. If the transaction state is "pending," we run the rollback flow shown below, which we'll get to in just a moment. If the transaction was already committed, the simplest way to roll it back is to mark the original transaction as canceled and just transfer the amount back to the source account in a new transaction. We left the code open to a race condition here, but in a production application the call to updateTransactionState should be conditioned on the success of the new transfer. Finally, if the transaction is in any of the end states, we do nothing.

To deal with the rollback of pending transactions, perform the flow from "initial" to "committed" in reverse:

```
function rollbackSource(transaction) {
    client.get('account-' + transaction.from, function(error, result) {
        if(error) throw error;

        var account = result.value;
        // If there's no pending transaction reference, there's nothing to do. Next step.
        if(account.transactions.indexOf(transaction.id) == -1) {
            console.log('source doing nothing');
            return rollbackDestination(transaction);
        }

        // Revert the balance
        account.balance += transaction.amount;
        // Remove the pending transaction reference
        account.transactions.splice( account.transactions.indexOf( transaction.id ), 1 );

        client.replace('account-' + transaction.from, account,
            {cas: result.cas, persist_to: 2, replicate_to: 2},
            function(error, result)
        {
            if(error && error.code == couchbase.errors.keyAlreadyExists)
                return rollbackSource(transaction);

            if(error) throw error;

            rollbackDestination(transaction);
        });
    });
}
```

The rollbackSource function retrieves the account and checks if it has a reference to the pending transaction that we are rolling back. If it doesn't, then we just call the next step, which is rollbackDestination. If it does have a pending transaction reference, we add the transfer amount back to the account balance and remove the ID from the transactions array, as follows:

```
function rollbackDestination(transaction) {
    client.get('account-' + transaction.to, function(error, result) {
        if(error) throw error;

        var account = result.value;
        console.log(account);

        function nextStep() {
            updateTransactionState(transaction, "cancelled", function() {
                console.log("Transaction rolled back.");
            });
        };

        // If there's no pending transaction reference, there's nothing to do. Next step.
        if(account.transactions.indexOf(transaction.id) == -1) {
            console.log('destination doing nothing');
            return nextStep();
        }

        // Revert the balance
        account.balance -= transaction.amount;
        // Remove the pending transaction reference
        account.transactions.splice( account.transactions.indexOf( transaction.id ), 1 );

        client.replace('account-' + transaction.to, account,
            {cas: result.cas, persist_to: 2, replicate_to: 2},
            function(error, result)
        {
            if(error && error.code == couchbase.errors.keyAlreadyExists)
                return rollbackDestination(transaction);

            if(error) throw error;

            nextStep();
        });
    });
}
```

The rollbackDestination function does the same thing, except it deducts the amount from the destination account. The last step is to update the transaction state to "cancelled."

As you can see, this results in quite a bit of code—even more if you implement it properly. While the example code is a good starting point for implementing 2PC in your own application, we don't recommend using any of the code as is. In fact, we beg you not to! In a production-quality application, you would normally implement two-phase commit as a state machine, in a module decoupled from the transaction details. That way you can use it as a service and just provide the application-specific logic as needed.

Maintaining Sets of Items

When we discussed the append and prepend operations in Chapter 4, we briefly touched upon using these operations to implement sets and presented a short example of using append to keep track of followers in our RanteR application. You can use this feature whenever we need to keep track of a constantly changing list of items in a distributed environment; for example, showing the currently logged-in users in a web application, which requires updating the list concurrently from multiple processes or machines and being able to retrieve the latest value quickly.

As we discussed in the example, the idea is very simple. We maintain the set of items as a string of tokens separated by a delimiter, with each token prefixed by either a + or a - to denote whether it was added or removed from the set. In this way, adding and removing items is essentially the same operation—appending another token to the string. Retrieving the set means getting the string, splitting it into tokens, and then iterating over the items in the order they appear to weed out the ones marked as deleted.

There are several benefits to using append to keep track of a set of items, rather than, say, a document containing a JSON array:

- Adding and removing items with append can be done in a single operation. With a document, you need to retrieve, update, and then save the result.

- Append is an atomic operation. Doing the same with a JSON document requires using a concurrency-safe mechanism with multiple retries if there is a lot of write contention.

- Adding and removing items with append is an O(1) operation, as it doesn't require parsing the existing values.

Because you keep appending to the string for both additions and removals, you need to compact it occasionally to keep the value from growing indefinitely. Depending on the access pattern, you can check the fragmentation level and compact the value either on read or on write, whichever happens more often. You'll get the fragmentation level as part of the set retrieval and parsing, so compacting after retrieval is quite convenient.

We'll demonstrate the complete flow with a code example. In this case, it checks the fragmentation level on read and performs compaction as necessary. First, we need a way to create the set and add or remove items from it:

```
function buildSet(items, operation) {
    // Concatenate the item(s), prefixed by the operation and separated by spaces.
    if(items instanceof Array)
        return operation + items.join(' ' + operation ) + ' ';
    else
        return operation + items + ' ';
}
```

The builtSet function below simply turns the item or array of items into the string we're going to append to the one in the database, formatted as +<item1> +<item2> -<item1>:

```
function updateSet(key, items, operation, callback) {
    var value = buildSet(items, operation);

    client.append(key, value, function (error, result) {
        // If the set doesn't exist yet, add it.
        if(error && error.code == couchbase.errors.notStored)
            client.add(key, value, callback);

        callback(error, result);
    });
}
```

UpdateSet takes the string we need to append and actually appends it to the stored string in Couchbase. If it gets a notStored error, which means that this is the first time we're adding items to this set, it adds the new key instead of trying to append to it. There is a potential race condition here; if we try to add the same key multiple times simultaneously, only one will succeed. Unfortunately, there's no simple way to handle this at the Couchbase level, because we can't lock or use CAS on a key that doesn't exist yet. If we knew the key we wanted to create in advance, we could create it with an empty value and then only append from then on. As it is, we can add more error handling after the add, to try appending again if the add fails because the key already exists:

```
function addToSet(key, items, callback) {
    updateSet(key, items, '+', callback);
}

function removeFromSet(key, items, callback) {
    updateSet(key, items, '-', callback);
}
```

The addToSet and removeFromSet functions are only for convenience—they just call updateSet with the relevant operation. Next, we need a way to retrieve the stored set and turn it back into an application data structure:

```
function parseSet(value) {
    // Using an object with no properties as a surrogate set
    var set = Object.create(null);

    // Parse the value string and remove the items marked as deleted
    var tokens = value.trim().split(' ');

    for(i in tokens) {
        var token = tokens[i];
        var operation = token[0];
        var item = token.substring(1);

        if(operation == '+')
            set[item] = true;
        else if(operation == '-')
            delete set[item];
    }

    // Turn our surrogate set into an array of items
    var items = [];
    for(prop in set)
        items.push(prop);

    // Calculate the fragmentation level of the original set string
    var fragmentation = 0;
    if(tokens.length > 0)
        fragmentation = (tokens.length - items.length) / tokens.length;

    return {
        items: items,
        fragmentation: fragmentation
    };
}
```

Next, parseSet takes the value of the stored set string and splits it into tokens according to the delimiter we use. It then iterates over the tokens in the order that they appear and adds or removes them from the set result that will be returned to the application. In this case, we use a JavaScript trick to create a poor man's set data structure with an empty object by adding or deleting properties to the object. We then take all the remaining properties of the object and return their names as an array of strings, because these are the unique set values we actually want. After extracting all the non-deleted values from the set string, we can calculate how much of its length is wasted due to deleted items. This is pretty simple to do: the fragmentation ratio equals the number of deleted items divided by the total number of items. The function returns both the actual items in the set and its fragmentation level:

```
function retrieveSet(key, callback) {
    client.get(key, function (error, result) {
        if(error)
            return callback(error, null);

        var set = parseSet(result.value);

        // Attempt to compact the set optimistically
        if(set.fragmentation > FRAGMENTATION_THRESHOLD)
            client.replace(key, buildSet(set.items, '+'), {cas: result.cas}, function(e,r) {});

        callback(null, set.items);
    });
}
```

In the retrieveSet function, we actually get the set string from the database, parse it into an array of unique items, and pass it to the callback function. We also check the fragmentation level of the stored set, and if it is above a certain threshold—defined elsewhere, as you can guess—then we build a new set string from just the non-deleted items and try to replace the existing value with it using the CAS we retrieved along with the original value. In this case, the replacement is done asynchronously and as a "best effort"—if the value hasn't changed in the meantime, it will be updated with the compacted set, otherwise nothing will happen. This solution is good in a high-read scenario where we don't expect a lot of write contention for the same set. In a high-write scenario, we'd either have to lock the key for compaction and handle lock errors with a retry, or try to compact the value with locking every X number of writes, instead.

The usage is very simple. To add items to a set, do the following:

```
addToSet('set-1', ['hello', 'world', '!'], function(error, result) {});
```

That will store the string "+hello +world +!" in the database.
To remove an item, do this:

```
removeFromSet('set-1', ['world'], function(error, result) {});
```

That will update the string to be "'+hello +world +! -world'".
To retrieve the set, and potentially compact it:

```
retrieveSet('set-1', function(error, result) {
    console.log(result);
});
```

That would print just the actual items in the set:

```
[ 'hello', '!' ]
```

Using CAS as an ETag

The entity tag (ETag) is an HTTP response header field, which can be used to track changes in a web resource. It can be used for mechanisms such as web caching and optimistic concurrency. Logically, it is very similar to the CAS mechanism in Couchbase, which makes it very easy to use CAS directly as an ETag in some cases.

■ **Note**   If you're unfamiliar with entity tags in HTTP, you can read the excellent Wikipedia article at http://en.wikipedia.org/wiki/HTTP_ETag and the RFC specifications for the HTTP protocol at www.w3.org/Protocols/rfc2616/rfc2616-sec3.html#sec3.11.

We'll use our RanteR web application in the example, which is written in Node.js with Express. However, this will work more or less the same in all the common web frameworks, because the core logic only requires setting and reading HTTP headers. The first scenario is using the ETag for web caching to check whether a server resource has been changed. The first time the client retrieves a resource, the server also sends the ETag, which in our case is simply the CAS value of the document we retrieved. On subsequent requests, the client sends the ETag value it got in the If-None-Match header, which we compare with the latest CAS on the server. If the value is the same, the server returns the HTTP status code 304, which means "Not Modified," instead of sending the entire resource again. If the value is different, the server returns the new version, as well as the new ETag. All modern web browsers support caching with ETags by default and will send the If-None-Match header with all subsequent requests if the first response returned an ETag.

Let's assume that we allow users to edit their rants. We need to look at the code that retrieves a single rant from the server, modified to use ETags to save bandwidth if the rant hasn't changed since the last request.

Because the CAS object in the Node.js API is actually a bit more complex than the 64-bit integer that Couchbase uses to store it internally, we'll use a helper function to turn it into a string representation for the ETag. In other languages, you can just parse the CAS value from long to string and back to compare it to the ETag:

```
function toEtag(cas) {
    return cas['0'] + ' ' + cas['1'];
}
```

Here is the server method that responds to the GET request for a rant with a specific ID:

```
app.get('/api/rants/:id', function(req, res) {
    var rantKey = req.params.id;
    connection.get(rantKey, getCallback);

    function getCallback(error, result) {

        var data = {};
        var status = 200; // HTTP status: OK.

        if (error) {
            if (error.code == couchbase.errors.keyNotFound) {
                status = 404; // HTTP status: Resource not found.
                data = {error: "Rant does not exist."};
            }
            else
                status = 500; // HTTP status: Internal Server Error.
        }
        else {
            var etag = req.headers['if-none-match'];
```

```
        if (etag && etag == toEtag(result.cas)) {
            status = 304; // HTTP status: Not Modified
        }
        else {
            data = result.value;
            res.setHeader('ETag', toEtag(result.cas));
        }
    }

    res.json(status, data);
  }
});
```

As you can see, in the server-side code we simply get the rant by its key from Couchbase. If the request contains the If-None-Match header, then we compare it with the CAS that Couchbase returned. If the ETag matches the server CAS value, we return HTTP status code 304, otherwise we return the rant data and set the ETag header to the latest CAS value.

In the preceding example, we always retrieve the document with get, even if the ETag matches, which can be wasteful if the document in question is large. Instead, we can use a touch operation to retrieve the CAS without getting the document itself, as we'll do in the next example. Because CAS is stored in the document metadata, which Couchbase always keeps in memory, using touch to retrieve the CAS will never cause Couchbase to read from disk.

The other use-case for ETags is the same as for CAS in Couchbase server—to support optimistic concurrency. We'll continue the example of editing rants and add support for optimistic concurrency to our web client. To update a rant, the client uses a PUT request to the web API with the rant ID in the URL and the new rant version in the request body. For example: PUT /api/rants/rant-David0-13 <rant_body>. To provide optimistic concurrency, the client should pass the ETag it got when retrieving the rant in the If-Match request header. We already know that the client gets the ETag from the server, because that's part of the functionality we added in the previous example. On the server side, the code that handles the PUT request checks whether the ETag value in the If-Match header matches the document's CAS value. If it doesn't, the server returns HTTP status code 412, Precondition Failed:

```
app.put('/api/rants/:id', function(req, res) {
    var rantKey = req.params.id;
    var rant = req.body;
    var etag = req.headers['if-match'];
    var data = {};
    var status = 200; // HTTP status: OK.

    if(!etag)
        return connection.replace(rantKey, rant, replaceCallback);

    connection.touch(rantKey, function (error, result) {
        if(etag != toEtag(result.cas))
            res.json(412, {error: "ETag mismatch."}); // HTTP status: Precondition failed.
        else
            connection.replace(rantKey, rant, {cas: result.cas}, replaceCallback);
    });

    function replaceCallback(error, result) {
        console.log(error, result);
        if (error) {
```

```
            if (error.code == couchbase.errors.keyAlreadyExists) {
                status = 412; // HTTP status: Precondition failed.
                data = {error: "ETag mismatch."};
            }
            else if (error.code == couchbase.errors.keyNotFound) {
                status = 404; // HTTP status: Resource not found.
                data = {error: "Rant does not exist."};
            }
            else
                status = 500; // HTTP status: Internal Server Error.
        }
        else {
            data = result.value;
            res.setHeader('ETag', toEtag(result.cas));
        }

        res.json(status, data);
    }
});
```

This example first uses touch to retrieve the current document's CAS value, which we then compare with the ETag with got from the client. We have to do this because in the Node.js API, CAS is an opaque object, so we cannot manually create a new CAS instance and pass it to the database—we have to retrieve one and use it for comparison. In most of the other languages, you can actually parse the ETag string into a 64-bit integer and use it as the CAS directly. If the ETag and the CAS match, we call replace with the new rant from the request body, otherwise we return status 412 and an error message. We pass the CAS we retrieved with touch to replace, because the document may have been changed in the interval between the two commands.

Using Couchbase as an Out-of-Process Session Store

One of the more interesting uses for memcached, and consequently Couchbase Server, is for storing the session state of web applications. This is particularly useful in a load-balanced environment, where consecutive web requests from the same client may reach different servers. If the session state is stored by the server process in memory, which is how most web frameworks work by default, then requests routed to different servers will see different versions of the session state. This is why using an external session-state provider is a popular choice for distributed web application. Storing the session externally means that every web server instance sees the same session data, which usually eliminates the need for IT workarounds like configuring the load balancer to send all requests from the same client to the same server (a.k.a. sticky session).

Unless you have a good reason to do otherwise, you should use a memcached bucket to hold the sessions. Memcached buckets do not persist items to disk and consequently have much less impact on the performance of other buckets in the cluster. In some cases, it might make sense to use a Couchbase bucket instead; for example, if you need particularly long sessions that you want to persist in case the client returns, or if you want to be able to rebalance the cluster as needed to scale it up or down as load changes throughout the day. Unlike memcached buckets, Couchbase buckets can be rebalanced.

The folks at Couchbase have thoughtfully created a custom SessionState provider for ASP.NET, which stores all sessions in a Couchbase or Memcached bucket. You can find the library at https://github.com/couchbaselabs/couchbase-aspnet. It transparently replaces the default session-state provider and is quite simple to configure and use in your ASP.NET application.

We've used Node.js with the Express framework for code examples throughout the book. Express extends a middleware framework called Connect, which supports multiple custom session stores, but sadly, not Couchbase. Fortunately, it's quite simple to create one by extending the Connect Store class. We can find the session implementation details here: www.senchalabs.org/connect/session.html

As the documentation tells us, a minimal custom session implementation requires providing the get, set, and destroy methods, as follows:

```
var couchbase = require('couchbase');
var oneDay = 86400; // in seconds
function ensureCallback(fn) {
    return function() {
        fn && fn.apply(null, arguments);
    };
}

module.exports = function(connect) {
    var Store = connect.session.Store;

    function CouchbaseStore(options) {
        options = options || {};
        Store.call(this, options);

        this.prefix = options.prefix || '';
        if (!options.client) {
            if (!options.connection) {
                options.connection = {
                    host: 'localhost:8091',
                    bucket: 'default'
                };
            }

            options.client = new couchbase.Connection(options.connection);
        }

        this.client = options.client;
    }

    CouchbaseStore.prototype.__proto__ = Store.prototype;

    CouchbaseStore.prototype.get = function(sid, fn) {
        this.client.get(this.prefix + sid, function(err, data) {
            if (err && err.code != couchbase.errors.keyNotFound)
                return fn(err, {});

            try {
                if (!data)
                    return fn();

                fn(null, data.value);
            } catch (e) {
                fn(e);
            }
        });
    };
```

```
CouchbaseStore.prototype.set = function(sid, sess, fn) {
    var maxAge = sess.cookie.maxAge;
    var ttl = typeof maxAge == 'number' ? maxAge / 1000 | 0 : 3600;

    this.client.set(this.prefix + sid, sess, {expiry: ttl}, fn);
};

CouchbaseStore.prototype.destroy = function(sid, fn) {
    this.client.remove(this.prefix + sid, ensureCallback(fn));
};

return CouchbaseStore;
};
```

As you can see, the get method retrieves the session object for a given session ID, the set method stores the session object in Couchbase with the defined TTL expiration, and the destroy method removes the specified session from the store.

To use the custom Couchbase session store module in a Node.js Express app, all we need to do is initialize the app with the cookieParser middleware and an instance of the store object:

```
app.use(express.cookieParser());
app.use(express.session({
  store: new CouchbaseStore({
    prefix : 'session-',
    connection : {
        host: 'localhost:8091',
        bucket: 'ranter'
    }
  }),
  secret: '1234567890QWERTY'
}));
```

We can now use the session as normal, and it will be stored in Couchbase and shared between the different server instances.

Summary

Quite a few advanced scenarios can be handled with Couchbase Server and a little ingenuity. We couldn't really cover all of them in this chapter, but we did show the more common and useful ones. Dealing with the various possible failure scenarios with minimal disruption to system functionality is crucial in a production environment. In addition to the inherent resilience and durability of Couchbase, we can implement additional protections in code for a multi-layered defense against unexpected failures. Lack of transaction support is one of the most common complaints raised against NoSQL databases, but in this chapter we learned how to overcome that shortcoming by implementing two-phase commits. It takes more code and is a bit more complicated than simply opening and committing a transaction in a relational database, but it's what we have to work with. And on the plus side, the 2PC protocol we implemented isn't limited to databases; we can easily adapt it to work with any distributed system. The last two techniques we covered in this chapter, maintaining sets and using CAS values as an ETag, are very useful for a surprisingly large number of scenarios. Quite a few application data needs can be solved with sets, so being able to store sets efficiently and concurrently is a great help. And because Couchbase often serves as the data store for web APIs, being able to implement ETag support with minimal effort is great.

In Chapter 8, you're going to learn the best advanced technique of them all: integrating Couchbase with ElasticSearch. The combination of using Couchbase for storage and ElasticSearch for indexing and searching the data opens up a whole new field of possibilities.

CHAPTER 8

■ ■ ■

ElasticSearch Integration

So far, you have seen how to use views and N1QL to query your data in Couchbase Server. Both of these techniques have strengths and weaknesses, but the one thing they have in common is that they focus on finding exact matches for values. For example, in Chapter 5 you used a view to retrieve rants based on ranters ranting about them. To do so, you indexed the value of the `rantAbout.userName` property and used the username of ranters to search the index. This kind of querying is typical for most databases system, which allow you to search based on exact values. But sometimes exact values are not enough. Just like most social applications, RanteR needs to allow its users to search for rants and ranters based on more flexible parameters, such as some of the rant content.

Full-text search is the ability to index text and search content based on user-defined criteria. You can find full-text search capabilities in many of the mainstream database systems, including Oracle, Microsoft SQL Server, MySQL, and many more. Most of them have built-in, proprietary, text search capabilities.

Apache Lucene is an open-source library for full-text indexing, created by Doug Cutting, who is also known for starting the Apache Hadoop project along with Mike Cafarella. Lucene was originally written in 1999 and since then has become the de facto standard library for full-text search engines outside the proprietary, closed-source databases. Lucene has the built-in capabilities to index and search documents using data structures called inverted indices. It is also very extendable, and over the years multitudes of additional capabilities were added to Lucene by the community, including support for most, if not all, spoken languages in use today.

Powerful as it might be, Lucene is still just a library. In order to use it, you need to manage a lot by yourself. For example, you need to write the code that takes a document and indexes it. If you are dealing with a large amount of data and would like to scale this across a number of clusters, you will need to do that yourself as well. ElasticSearch is an open-source, scalable search engine based on Lucene that is rapidly becoming the search product of choice for many organizations. It does much more than just full-text search and has a strong ecosystem growing around it. In addition, ElasticSearch also supports many different types of queries and is becoming ever more popular for reporting and analytics. In fact, ElasticSearch also comes with a web-UI tool called Kibana, which simplifies creating analytical reports.

For those reasons and more, Couchbase has chosen to integrate with ElasticSearch to provide advanced search capabilities that are unavailable within Couchbase itself. Setting up integration with ElasticSearch is simple and fast, and you can have your data automatically indexed by ElasticSearch to expand the capabilities of your database, as you are going to see in the rest of this chapter.

Setting Up ElasticSearch Clusters

Before we start, you need to download ElasticSearch. This can be easily done from the ElasticSearch website at `www.elasticsearch.org/download/`. On this download page you will find the latest ElasticSearch version.

In this chapter, you will run ElasticSearch from the command line. If you are running in a production environment, you should install ElasticSearch as a daemon on Linux or as a service on Windows. You can also install ElasticSearch on Linux using apt-get/yum as described here: `www.elasticsearch.org/blog/apt-and-yum-repositories/`. If you are running ElasticSearch as a service, please consult the ElasticSearch documentation for the installation paths on your OS of choice. The deb and rpm packages provided by ElasticSearch install it into the `/usr/share/elasticsearch` directory by default.

▪ **Note**   At the time of this writing, the Couchbase plugin for ElasticSearch officially supports ElasticSearch version 1.0.1. We strongly recommend checking for the latest supported version before downloading ElasticSearch and getting that specific version from the past releases and notes page on the ElasticSearch website.

After downloading ElasticSearch, you need to extract the binaries and then install the Couchbase transport plugin. To do so, go into the ElasticSearch home directory and run the following command:

```
> bin/plugin -install transport-couchbase -url http://packages.couchbase.com.s3.amazonaws.com/
releases/elastic-search-adapter/1.3.0/elasticsearch-transport-couchbase-1.3.0.zip
```

▪ **Note**   The preceding command is for a specific version of the plugin that is compatible with ElasticSearch version 1.0.1. In order to use other versions, make sure you consult the Couchbase Plugin documentation here: `www.couchbase.com/couchbase-server/connectors/elasticsearch`. If Couchbase reports the error "Failed to grab remote bucket '<bucket>' from any of known nodes," the most common cause is a version mismatch between Couchbase, ElasticSearch, and the transport-couchbase plugin.

In addition, you will use the sense-web UI, which comes with Marvel, a monitoring and administration package for ElasticSearch. To install Marvel, run the following command:

```
> bin/plugin -i elasticsearch/marvel/latest
```

▪ **Note**   Running Marvel like this in development is fine. However, unlike ElasticSearch, Marvel needs a license to run in production. If you need Marvel for your production clusters make sure you have an appropriate license. Alternatively, use a different plugin for querying, such as Head.

An ElasticSearch cluster is built out of one or more nodes, similar to a Couchbase cluster. If you installed ElasticSearch through the deb or rpm package, then the `elasticsearch` service should already be running. If you downloaded and installed ElasticSearch manually, then you will need to start your first node with the following command:

```
> [elasticsearch home directory]/bin/elasticsearch -f
```

This will start your ElasticSearch node in the foreground, emitting log information. After a few messages, if all goes well, you should see log messages announcing that the node was started and has published an address. By default, this address will use port 9200.

■ **Note**   This command changed slightly in ElasticSearch version 1.0; running in the foreground is now the default option, and you can use the -d option to run as a daemon. In addition, you can run ElasticSearch as a service on both Windows and Linux. We recommend consulting the setup guide on the ElasticSearch website before running ElasticSearch in production.

Forming a Cluster

Now that the node is running, you actually have an ElasticSearch cluster you can use. However, just like Couchbase, ElasticSearch is intended to run as a multi-node cluster. Adding nodes to a cluster begins with configuring the cluster.name setting in the elasticsearch.yml file. When running from the command line, the elasticsearch.yml file is located in the config directory, under the ElasticSearch home directory. When installed from a deb or rpm, it can be found in the /etc/elasticsearch directory. The default value is elasticsearch, which might be confusing since by default ElasticSearch nodes try to join a cluster automatically when starting, and this can possibly cause unrelated nodes to form a cluster. We recommend that you give your cluster a proper name. For example, for the ranter production cluster we will set the following:

```
cluster.name : elasticsearch-ranter-prod
```

Automatically discovering a cluster is the default behavior of ElasticSearch nodes and is based on a network multicast mechanism. This means that when a node starts, it uses multicast to send a message to all the nodes in the network, publishing its configuration and trying to join the cluster it is configured with. While this behavior makes it extremely easy to get started with ElasticSearch, it does have some drawbacks. Besides the fact that it is possible for a node to accidently join a cluster, multicast also adds a lot of complexity on the network level. First of all, you need multicast support, which is not always available. And even if it is supported, multicast doesn't work well on complex networks. For all those reasons, the default discovery module in ElasticSearch, called zen, also supports a unicast mode for discovery.

You can change zen discovery to use unicast mode by setting the value of the discovery.zen.ping.multicast.enabled property in the elasticsearch.yml configuration file to false and then configuring a list of other nodes in the cluster using the discovery.zen.ping.unicast.hosts setting as shown here:

```
discovery.zen.ping.unicast.hosts: ["host1:port", "host2:port"]
```

On cloud deployments, discovery can become even more complicated. For this reason, ElasticSearch has separate modules that provide advanced discovery for AWS, Microsoft Azure, and Google Compute Engine. If you plan on running ElasticSearch on a cloud platform, make sure you use the right discovery module for it.

Setting Up Replication between Couchbase and ElasticSearch

Now that you have both clusters up and running, you can configure replication between the Couchbase Server cluster and the ElasticSearch cluster. The Couchbase plugin for ElasticSearch allows Couchbase clusters to use cross-datacenter replication (XDCR) to replicate all the data in a specific bucket to an ElasticSearch cluster. (XDCR is covered in depth in Chapter 13.) In order to do so, the plugin allows ElasticSearch clusters to act as Couchbase Server clusters as far as XDCR is concerned. The plugin adds the two configuration settings that specify the administrator credentials Couchbase will need in order to authenticate with the ElasticSearch cluster. We also need to set the couchbase.username and couchbase.password properties in the elasticsearch.yml configuration file. For example, in RanteR you will use the following settings:

```
couchbase.username: Administrator
couchbase.password: 123456
```

In addition to the above settings, you can also configure the following:

- `couchbase.port:` This is the port on which the plugin will listen for incoming XDCR connections; the default value for this setting is 9091.

- `couchbase.defaultDocumentType:` This is the default document type ElasticSearch will use to store documents received from Couchbase. It defaults to `couchbaseDocument`. For more elaborate mappings, you can use an index template, covered later in this chapter.

- `couchbase.checkpointDocumentType:` The document type to store replication checkpoint documents, which defaults to `couchbaseCheckpoint`. Checkpoints and all things related to XDCR in general are covered in Chapter 13.

- `couchbase.num_vbuckets:` Because XDCR performs replication directly between vBuckets, ElasticSearch must pretend it too has vBuckets. The `couchbase.num_vbuckets` setting holds the number of vBuckets that ElasticSearch should pretend to have; the default is 64 on OS X, 1024 on all other platforms. This value *must* match the number of vBuckets on the source Couchbase cluster.

- `couchbase.maxConcurrentRequests:` This is the number of concurrent requests that the plugin will allow. The default value for this setting is 1024.

Next, you need to set up a template, which is a JSON document with basic configurations and default mappings that ElasticSearch will use when creating new indices. You can use a template to configure settings such as the number of shards in an index. In addition, you can use the template to automatically create type mappings when creating a new index. This allows you to map JSON documents into well-known types and control the way each type is indexed. As part of the installation of the Couchbase transport plugin, you will get a template file that tells ElasticSearch to map all documents except ones that are sent as part of the checkpoint process in XDCR. You can use this template as is, or extend it to add your desired mappings. To use the default template that comes with the Couchbase transport plugin, run the following command:

```
> curl -XPUT http://localhost:9200/_template/couchbase -d @plugins/transport-couchbase/couchbase_
template.json
```

The next thing you need to do is create an index, which is a container for documents in ElasticSearch, analogous to buckets in Couchbase. This index will be used to store the data from your Couchbase bucket. To do so, just issue an HTTP POST or PUT request to your cluster with the name of the index at the end of your ElasticSearch cluster URL, as follows:

```
> curl -XPUT http://localhost:9200/ranter
```

Now your ElasticSearch cluster is ready, and you can configure XDCR from Couchbase to start replicating data. To do so, open the Couchbase management console and go to the XDCR tab. On the XDCR page, click on the Create Cluster Reference button to open the Create Cluster Reference dialog box. In this dialog box, add the following details:

- *Cluster Name:* This is the display name of your remote cluster.

- *IP/hostname:* This is the address of your ElasticSearch cluster, including the port number for the Couchbase transport plugin.

- *Username:* The username you configured in the `couchbase.username` property.

- *Password:* The password you configured in the `couchbase.password` property.

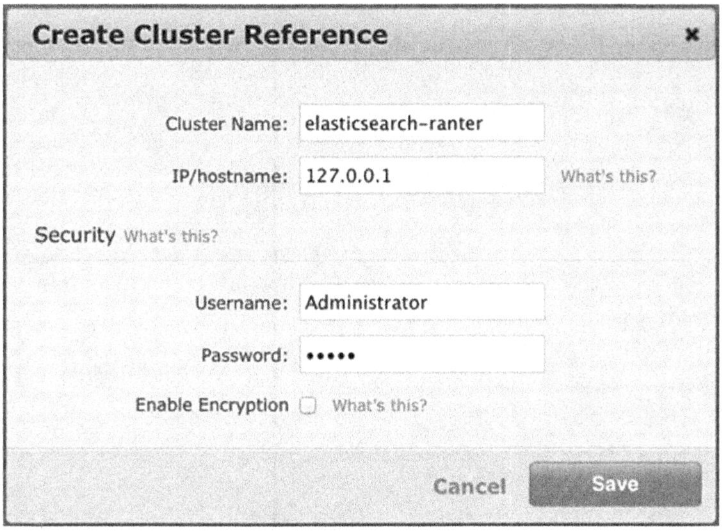

Figure 8-1. *The Create Cluster Reference dialog*

You can use the cluster reference to create one or more replications, which are the actual processes that send data to the remote cluster. To create a new replication, simply click on the Create Replication button in the XDCR tab to open the Create Replication dialog. Once there, select the Couchbase bucket to take data from and the remote cluster and bucket to replicate to. The remote bucket is actually the name of the ElasticSearch index we created previously. In addition, you need to click on the Advanced Settings link and change the XDCR protocol to version 1. Click the Replicate button to start the replication.

■ **Note** XDCR is covered in depth in Chapter 13, which includes detailed explanations for everything we are doing here. This chapter focuses on the integration between ElasticSearch and Couchbase, so we recommend you revisit these steps after reading Chapter 13.

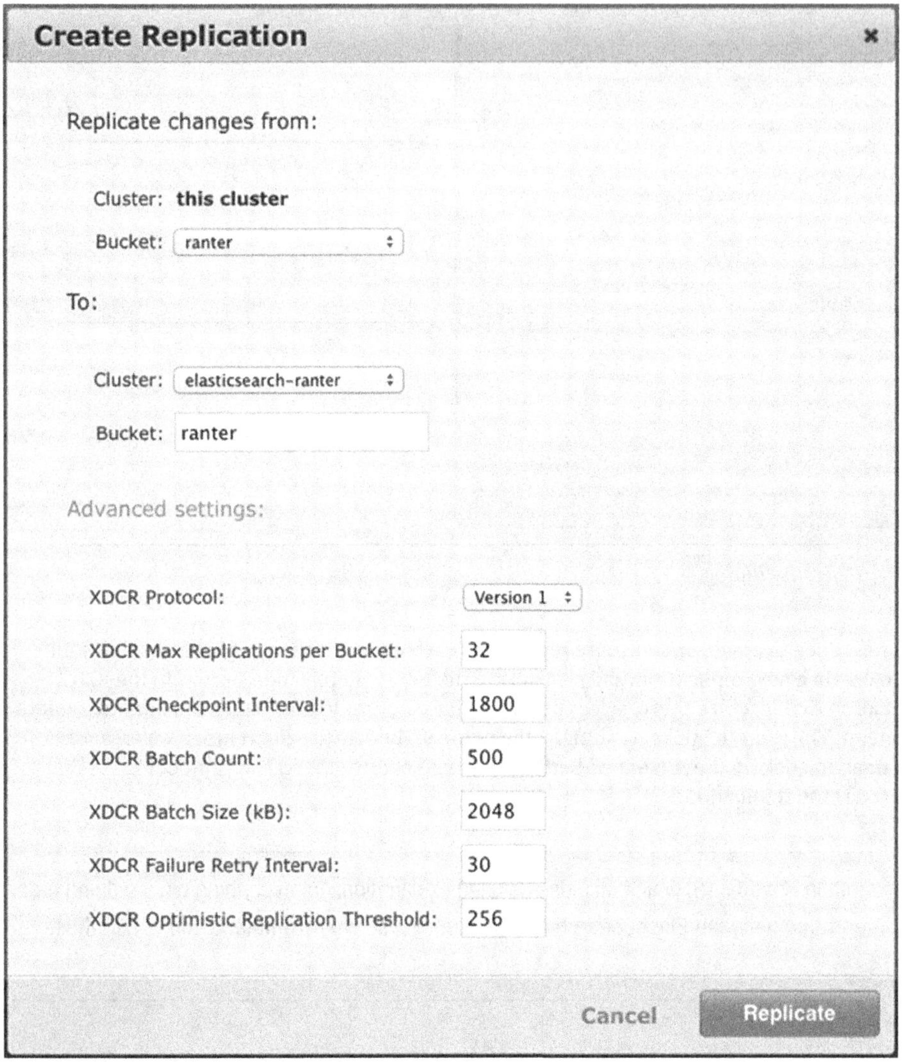

Figure 8-2. *The Create Replication dialog box*

Now that you have XDCR replicating your documents to ElasticSearch, you can use ElasticSearch to search and query them.

Querying with ElasticSearch

As discussed at the beginning of this chapter, ElasticSearch is a search engine designed for full-text indexing and searching. In addition to SDKs in multiple languages, ElasticSearch exposes an HTTP API for searching, which can be accessed from any programming language or even a browser. Assuming you've followed the book and have run all the code samples, you can execute the following query from a browser and come up with some results. Simply paste the following URL into the browser: `http://127.0.0.1:9200/ranter/couchbaseDocument/_search?q=Ovaltine`.

■ **Tip**   You can add the &pretty=true parameter to format the JSON document. This is true for any ElasticSearch HTTP request you make.

The preceding query searches for the word "Ovaltine" in all your documents. In response, ElasticSearch should return a JSON document similar to this:

```
{
  "took": 2,
  "timed_out": false,
  "_shards": {
    "total": 5,
    "successful": 5,
    "failed": 0
  },
  "hits": {
    "total": 2,
    "max_score": 0.55235815,
    "hits": [
      {
        "_index": "ranter",
        "_type": "couchbaseDocument",
        "_id": "jerrys-rant-92112221002",
        "_score": 0.55235815,
        "_source": {
          "meta": {
            "id": "jerrys-rant-92112221002",
            "rev": "2-000015b163b666c50000000000000000",
            "flags": 0,
            "expiration": 0
          }
        }
      },
      {
        "_index": "ranter",
        "_type": "couchbaseDocument",
        "_id": "yanivr-rant-1",
        "_score": 0.3912621,
        "_source": {
          "meta": {
            "id": "yanivr-rant-1",
            "rev": "2-000017b2f2719cf70000000000000000",
            "flags": 0,
            "expiration": 0
          }
        }
      }
    ]
  }
}
```

■ **Note** The examples in all chapters are based on sample data inserted when first running RanteR against an empty Couchbase bucket. The raw data can be found in the `setup/data.js` file in RanteR.

Looking at the above result, you can learn a lot about how ElasticSearch works. The first thing you can see is that you get two different results, or "hits," for your search phrase. You can also see some data for each hit, including the name of the index and the type of document, which implies ElasticSearch's ability to search across indices and document types. You also get the original document's metadata, including the document ID. This allows you to access the original document directly in your Couchbase Server cluster.

One of the most interesting properties of the result is the `_score` field. Among the biggest challenges in search engines is the ability to not simply find the occurrence of a word in text, but also to estimate the relevance of the text to the query. This capability is what made Google the search empire that it is. ElasticSearch is built around Lucene, which uses a scoring mechanism known as "term frequency/inverse document frequency" (TF/IDF) for scoring search relevance. Scoring is affected by many factors; the term *frequency factor*, for example, is based on the number of times the searched term was found in a document. The inverse document frequency factor is based on how many times the term is found in all the documents. The more rare the document is, the higher the score.

Lucene's scoring system is more complex than just these two factors and includes the following as well:

- *The type of the document ("document boost"):* The type of document can influence the score of the term. For example, when searching RanteR, you want to give a higher score to terms that appear in rants than to those that appear in rantbacks.

- *The field where the term was found ("field boost"):* The field itself can affect the relevance of the document. For example, in the search above you get two results—one is a rant by JerryS that rants about the product Ovaltine, and another is a rant that rants about JerryS's rant. It is reasonable to have a lower score for, or even ignore entirely, terms found in the `rantabout.rantText` field, since they do not make the rant relevant to a search on their own.

- *The length of the field ("length norm"):* The length of the field also matters. For example, terms found in shorter fields are considered more relevant than those found in longer fields.

- *The number of search terms found in a document ("coord"):* This factor boosts the score of documents containing a lot of search terms.

ElasticSearch has various mechanisms you can use to control the way documents are indexed and scored. These include using the ElasticSearch query domain-specific language (DSL) and document mapping.

The ElasticSearch Query DSL

ElasticSearch has a very powerful DSL for controlling every aspect of search. Using this elaborate language you can control scoring as well as the way terms are matched. The ElasticSearch DSL is based on HTTP and JSON and is quite easy to get started with.

Endpoints

The first term you need to understand is an *endpoint*. ElasticSearch arranges data in a hierarchical manner, the first level of which are indices. Indices can contain multiple document types and are analogous to databases. Inside an index are documents, which have different types that represent different document structures and are analogous to tables. Searches in ElasticSearch can be performed on every level of this hierarchy. This behavior is controlled by the endpoint. For example, the following query will execute on all the indices and documents in the cluster:

```
http://127.0.0.1:9200/_search?q=Ovaltine
```

To search the ranter index only, you can use an endpoint representing the index with the following query:

```
http://localhost:9200/ranter/_search?q=Ovaltine
```

An endpoint can represent multiple indices. For example, the following query searches both the ranter and wiki indices:

```
http://localhost:9200/ranter,wiki/_search?q=Ovaltine
```

And, finally, an endpoint can represent a specific type or types within an index. The following query searches only documents of type couchbaseDocument in the ranter index:

```
http://localhost:9200/ranter/couchbaseDocument/_search?q=Ovaltine
```

URI and Request Body Search

ElasticSearch has two HTTP-based methods for executing searches. The simpler of the two is a URI-based search. You used some very simple URI searches in the previous section; however, URI searches offer more control over the execution of the query. It's time to take a closer look at some of the capabilities of this method.

Let's examine the basic syntax for both techniques, for example, the following query searches for the term *JerryS*:

```
http://localhost:9200/ranter/couchbaseDocument/_search?q=JerryS&pretty=true
```

This returns five documents as a result. If you take a look at the result below, you can find one user document, two rants by JerryS, and two rants by other users, which are in fact rants about JerryS's rants.

```
{
  "took" : 5,
  "timed_out" : false,
  "_shards" : {
    "total" : 5,
    "successful" : 5,
    "failed" : 0
  },
  "hits" : {
    "total" : 5,
    "max_score" : 1.0469097,
    "hits" : [ {
      "_index" : "ranter",
      "_type" : "couchbaseDocument",
      "_id" : "user-JerryS",
      "_score" : 1.0469097, "_source" : {"meta":{"id":"user-JerryS","rev":
"1-0000145d716f8eab0000000000000000","flags":0,"expiration":0}}
    }, {
      "_index" : "ranter",
      "_type" : "couchbaseDocument",
      "_id" : "jerrys-rant-92112221002",
      "_score" : 0.74027693, "_source" : {"meta":{"id":"jerrys-rant-92112221002","rev":"2-000015b163b
666c50000000000000000","flags":0,"expiration":0}}
```

```
    }, {
      "_index" : "ranter",
      "_type" : "couchbaseDocument",
      "_id" : "jerrys-rant-92112221001",
      "_score" : 0.55332816, "_source" : {"meta":{"id":"jerrys-rant-92112221001","rev":
"2-000023f06a82f18b0000000000000000","flags":0,"expiration":0}}
    }, {
      "_index" : "ranter",
      "_type" : "couchbaseDocument",
      "_id" : "yanivr-rant-1",
      "_score" : 0.55332816, "_source" : {"meta":{"id":"yanivr-rant-1","rev":
"2-000017b2f2719cf70000000000000000","flags":0,"expiration":0}}
    }, {
      "_index" : "ranter",
      "_type" : "couchbaseDocument",
      "_id" : "davido-rant-1",
      "_score" : 0.49351797, "_source" : {"meta":{"id":"davido-rant-1","rev":
"2-00000533c63df6500000000000000000","flags":0,"expiration":0}}
    } ]
  }
}
```

You can also execute a similar query using the request-body search API. To do so, you can use the sense-web UI, which is installed together with the Marvel plugin. To do that, open `http://127.0.0.1:9200/_plugin/marvel/sense/index.html`, which will open a web page similar to the one shown in Figure 8-3.

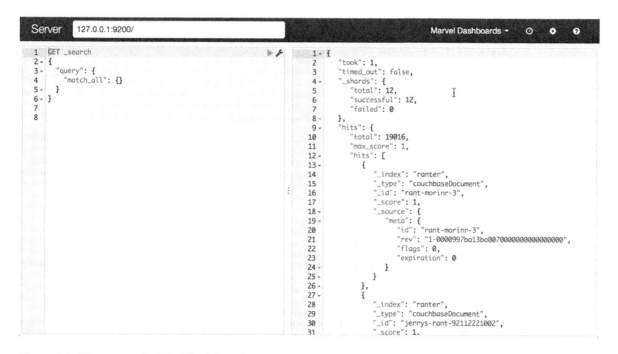

Figure 8-3. *The sense-web UI for ElasticSearch*

Using the sense UI, you can issue the following HTTP POST request, which is the request-body query API equivalent of the URI query you previously executed:

```
POST /ranter/couchbaseDocument/_search
{
 "query" : {
      "query_string": {
           "query": "JerryS"
        }
     }
}
```

Both of the preceding querying techniques are simple and straightforward. However, the ElasticSearch query DSL has over 30 different query types, each of which controls the interaction with Lucene. The query DSL allows you to control how a term is matched and how documents are scored. The following sections take a closer look at some of the basic query types.

Term Queries

In the examples so far in this chapter, you looked for a term in all the fields of the documents accessible via the endpoint you were searching on. However, under the covers a more elaborate mechanism is at work. Let's try to run the same query, only this time for the term *jerrys*. Running this query returns the exact same results as searching for the term *JerryS*. The reason for this is that ElasticSearch, or rather Lucene, indexes all the terms in lowercase. However, in order for ElasticSearch to match the term *JerryS* to the index entry of *jerrys*, it analyzes the term it searches before looking for it in the underlying Lucene indices. This type of querying, in which ElasticSearch analyzes the term before it searches, is called match querying. Before we take a look at the some of the analysis offered by match queries, let's talk about its simpler sibling: term queries.

Term queries search for documents or fields containing the exact, unanalyzed term you have entered. Let's try to run the following query:

```
POST _search
{
 "query" : {
    "term": {
      "doc.userName": "jerrys"
      }
   }
}
```

There are two things to notice about this query. The first is that it searches a specific field: doc.userName. This syntax is common to most query types in the ElasticSearch query DSL, and you can replace the field name with the reserved keyword _all to search all the fields. The second thing to notice is that you are looking for the term in lowercase. Combining the two together, we get two documents in the result, both containing the term *jerrys* in a userName field, which is located at the root level of the document:

```
{
  "took": 0,
  "timed_out": false,
  "_shards": {
     "total": 12,
     "successful": 12,
     "failed": 0
  },
```

```
"hits": {
   "total": 2,
   "max_score": 2.7047482,
   "hits": [
      {
         "_index": "ranter",
         "_type": "couchbaseDocument",
         "_id": "jerrys-rant-92112221002",
         "_score": 2.7047482,
         "_source": {
            "meta": {
               "id": "jerrys-rant-92112221002",
               "rev": "2-000015b163b666c50000000000000000",
               "flags": 0,
               "expiration": 0
            }
         }
      },
      {
         "_index": "ranter",
         "_type": "couchbaseDocument",
         "_id": "jerrys-rant-92112221001",
         "_score": 2.5040774,
         "_source": {
            "meta": {
               "id": "jerrys-rant-92112221001",
               "rev": "2-000023f06a82f18b0000000000000000",
               "flags": 0,
               "expiration": 0
            }
         }
      }
   ]
}
}
```

■ **Note** The result doesn't contain the actual property that contains the matched term, only information about the document where it was found.

However, if you attempt to run the same query using the term *JerryS* instead, you will get no results at all. This is because term queries do not analyze the term at all before searching the underlying index; they perform very simple matching.

Match Queries

Match queries might seem similar to term queries at first sight. However, they have one major difference from term queries: they analyze the term before searching the underlying Lucene indices. In Lucene, this preprocessing is known as an "analysis." It is important to understand that during the indexing process, ElasticSearch also analyzes the documents. This means that you can control the analysis process both on the indexing side and on the retrieval side. The default analysis process in ElasticSearch contains the following analyses:

- *Lowercase:* As we seen before, when analyzing a term, ElasticSearch converts it to lowercase.

- *Tokenizing:* As part of the analysis, ElasticSearch breaks the search term into separate words.

- *Boolean:* Queries execute as a boolean expression using an operator between the different words. By default, when searching for a term containing more than one word, ElasticSearch uses a boolean query with the operator "or" between the different words in the term. This behavior can be controlled by adding the operator field to the body of the request. For example, the following query will return results only for documents containing both the words "do" and "nothing" in their rantText field:

```
{
    "match" : {
        "doc.rantText" : {
            "query" : "do nothing",
            "operator" : "and"
        }
    }
}
```

Although the preceding are the default analyses in ElasticSearch, additional analyses can be applied, including the following:

- *Stop words:* After tokenizing the search terms, ElasticSearch also takes out the stop words, which are mostly short function words such as, "the," "and," "or," etc., which can either be omitted or might have a different meaning when included in a search.

- *Stemming:* Stemming is the process of reducing derived words to their root or base form. For example, the word "stemming" is derived from the root "stem."

- *Fuzziness:* Fuzziness allows for searching for an approximate match to a term, rather than an exact match. Fuzziness in ElasticSearch is type sensitive. For example, when searching a date value in a fuzzy manner, it will search for dates in a range from the date stated in the term and actually act as a date-range query. But when searching a string value, fuzziness will use the Levenshtein distance between words to find words that have a certain number of changes from the search term.

Multi-Match Queries

As we have seen before, match queries let you search either all the fields of the indexed documents or a specific field. It is sometimes useful to search several, but not all, fields of the documents. This can be easily done using multi-match queries. Let's take a look at the following query, which searches both the rantText and the rantAbout.rantText fields:

```
GET _search
{
  "query" : {
    "multi_match": {
      "query": "doing nothing",
      "fields": ["doc.rantText", "doc.rantAbout.rantText"]
    }
  }
}
```

Running the preceding sample returns two documents in the result, the first of which is DavidO's rant about JerryS's rant, which is the second document. This ranking is done based on the score of the document. However, it is possible that you would want certain fields to have a bigger impact on the score. You can do this by boosting the score for a specific field using the caret (^) sign. In the following query we have boosted the doc.rantText field to be twice as important as the doc.rantAbout.rantText field.

```
POST _search
{
  "query" : {
    "multi_match": {
      "query": "doing nothing",
      "fields": ["doc.rantText^2", "doc.rantAbout.rantText"]
    }
  }
}
```

Filters versus Queries

Up to this point, we have looked at some basic queries, which are in fact full-text searches. It is important to know that in addition to full-text queries or searches, ElasticSearch also supports a mechanism called filters. Filters allow you to search for exact values and return results that are independent of other searches. Let's take a look at the following filter:

```
POST ranter/couchbaseDocument/_search
{
    "filter" : {
      "term" : { "doc.userName": "jerrys"}
  }
}
```

This filter is a term filter, and it resembles the term query you executed earlier. However, in looking at the results of the filter you can see an important difference. The score for all the results is 1. Take a look at the results:

```
{
  "took": 1,
  "timed_out": false,
  "_shards": {
    "total": 5,
    "successful": 5,
    "failed": 0
  },
```

```
"hits": {
   "total": 2,
   "max_score": 1,
   "hits": [
      {
         "_index": "ranter",
         "_type": "couchbaseDocument",
         "_id": "jerrys-rant-92112221002",
         "_score": 1,
         "_source": {
            "meta": {
               "id": "jerrys-rant-92112221002",
               "rev": "2-000015b163b666c50000000000000000",
               "flags": 0,
               "expiration": 0
            }
         }
      },
      {
         "_index": "ranter",
         "_type": "couchbaseDocument",
         "_id": "jerrys-rant-92112221001",
         "_score": 1,
         "_source": {
            "meta": {
               "id": "jerrys-rant-92112221001",
               "rev": "2-000023f06a82f18b0000000000000000",
               "flags": 0,
               "expiration": 0
            }
         }
      }
   ]
}
}
```

ElasticSearch is not scoring the results of the filter. This means that running the same filter multiple times will return the same results, as long as the underlying data does not change. This allows ElasticSearch to cache the filter results, thus improving its performance in the following runs. In fact, because they deal with exact matches and do not calculate a score, filters are always much faster than searches, even without caching. By using filters you can add complex querying capabilities to your Couchbase application. On one hand, you can use filters for more elaborate querying while enjoying the benefits of caching. On the other hand, you can also use filters without caching. You can change the default behavior of filters by setting the _cache property to false, as shown in the following code:

```
POST ranter/couchbaseDocument/_search
{
    "filter" : {
      "term" : { "doc.userName": "jerrys"},
      "_cache" : false
   }
}
```

The ElasticSearch query DSL is vast and powerful. In fact, we didn't even scratch the surface of what it can do. It supports over 30 types of queries, including regular expressions, range queries, fuzzy queries, wildcard queries, and many more. One query type that extends the capabilities of Couchbase Server really well is the geospatial query. Geospatial queries in ElasticSearch are much more powerful and elaborate than geospatial views in Couchbase. We will take a closer look at geospatial filtering in a bit; however, before we do, it is important to note that ElasticSearch does not interpret GeoJSON properties as geospatial locations automatically. This is a good opportunity to take a closer look at mapping documents and how you can control mapping between Couchbase and ElasticSearch.

Mapping

ElasticSearch stores documents under types, which are stored in indices. This serves as both a conceptual, hierarchical method of organizing documents as well as a more structural purpose. ElasticSearch supports multiple data types, not only text. To allow this, document types in ElasticSearch have schemas that map the different data types of the fields in a document. Most of the time, ElasticSearch does a good job of creating these mappings automatically based on the structure of the documents that are being stored for a type. Let's take a look at the mapping ElasticSearch has created automatically for our couchbaseDocument type. To do so, you can simply execute the following get request from the sense-web UI:

```
GET ranter/couchbaseDocument/_mapping
```

In response to this request, you should get a JSON document similar to the following:

```
{
  "ranter": {
    "mappings": {
      "couchbaseDocument": {
        "_source": {
          "includes": [
            "meta.*"
          ]
        },
        "properties": {
          "doc": {
            "properties": {
              "date": {
                "type": "date",
                "format": "dateOptionalTime"
              },
              "email": {
                "type": "string"
              },
              "id": {
                "type": "string"
              },
              "location": {
                "properties": {
                  "coordinates": {
                    "type": "double"
                  },
```

```
                    "type": {
                        "type": "string"
                    }
                }
            },
            "rantText": {
                "type": "string"
            },
            ... more properties ...
        }
    }
 }
}
```

We have taken out a lot of the property mappings from the above document for brevity, but you can still find properties from rants, such as `location` and `rantText`, as well as from user documents, such as email. This is because ElasticSearch automatically creates a schema, which maps all the types of properties or fields from all the documents that are being stored in the `couchbaseDocument` type, i.e., all the documents in our ranter Couchbase bucket.

While ElasticSearch manages to create the mappings automatically for most types, one type of property ElasticSearch has problems mapping is GeoJSON objects. This property needs to be mapped to the `geo_point` type in ElasticSearch in order to be used in geospatial querying or filtering.

There are several techniques for controlling mappings. The first, which we've already seen, is using a template. If you provide a mapping in your template, this mapping will be added to all indices that match the template and are created after the template was set. The next option you have is to create the mapping explicitly when creating an index. To do so, simply create the index using an HTTP POST request and pass the mapping JSON as the entity body for the request, as shown in the following example:

```
> curl -XPOST http://127.0.0.1:9200/ranter -d '{
    "settings" : {
        # .. index settings
    },
    "mappings" : {
        "couchbaseDocument" : {
            # mapping for couchbaseDocument
        }
    }
}'
```

■ **Note**   You don't have to provide the JSON body in the command line. You can use the `-d @/path/to/file.json` parameter to read the request body from a file instead.

In order to create the index correctly, you can get the mapping created automatically by ElasticSearch and change the definition of the `location` property to the following one. Note that you must delete the existing index before recreating it. See as follows:

```
"location": {
        "properties": {
            "coordinates": {
                "type": "geo_point"
            },
```

```
        "type": {
           "type": "string"
        }
     }
  }
```

Lastly, you can use the mapping PUT request API to change existing types, with some restrictions. For example, you can easily use a PUT request to add new property mappings. The following command will add the property foo to the mapping of the couchbaseDocument type, and it will tell ElasticSearch to store the property data, as opposed to executing the default behavior defined in the indices template:

```
PUT ranter/couchbaseDocument/_mapping
{
  "couchbaseDocument" : {
      "properties" : {
          "foo" : {"type" : "string", "store" : true }
      }
   }
}
```

You can also change an existing mapping, within certain limitations. First, trying to update an existing mapping will fail by default, due to a conflict. This can be handled by adding the ignore_conflicts=true query string to your request URI. This will allow you to change the type of an existing mapping, but it still has one major limitation: you cannot change mappings that are already indexed. So, for your purposes, the only solution is to re-create your index with the correct mapping.

Geospatial Filters

In Chapter 5, you saw how geospatial views can be used to query locations inside a bounding box. This capability is sufficient for some use cases, but applications often have more complex geospatial search needs. ElasticSearch offers a set of powerful geospatial query tools, far beyond Couchbase's geospatial views.

Geo-Binding Box Filters

Just like Couchbase, ElasticSearch lets you filter by locations within a specified bounding box. In our sample data, we have the following rant, made by ElaineB:

```
{
 "type": "rant",
 "userName": "ElaineB",
 "rantText": "You ever notice how happy people are when they finally get a table? They feel so
special because they've been chosen. It's enough to make you sick.",
 "location": {
   "type": "Point",
   "coordinates": [
     -73.97041887044907,
     40.764033329795204
   ]
 },
 "date": "2014-01-23T10:54:18.666Z",
 "rantbacks": "6207d79d-39ed-472a-8337-fe8d8c533608"
}
```

The preceding rant was created using the RanteR mobile application and includes a location in the `coordinates` property. Since you have mapped the `coordinates` property as a geo_point in ElasticSearch, you can now use it for querying using a binding box. The following geo_binding_box filter works exactly like it would using a geospatial view in Couchbase.

```
POST ranter/_search
{

    "query" : {
        "match_all" : {}
    },
    "filter" : {
        "geo_bounding_box" : {
            "doc.location.coordinates": {
                "top_left" : {
                    "lat" :   40.776191,
                    "lon" : -73.977668
                },
                "bottom_right" : {
                    "lat" : 40.7640333,
                    "lon" : -73.9704189
                }
            }
        }
    }
}
```

Geo-Distance Filter

Another useful type of query is to search for points within a certain distance from a specific location. For example, if you would like to allow ranters to view rants posted from within 5 kilometers of their current location—so they could, for example, go and reply in person—you could use the geo_distance filter, as shown here:

```
POST ranter/_search
{
    "query" : {
        "match_all" : {}
    },
    "filter" : {
        "geo_distance" : {
            "distance" : "5km",
            "doc.location.coordinates":
            {
              "lon" : -73.97041887044907,
              "lat" : 40.764033329795204
            }

        }
    }
}
```

ElasticSearch also supports distance-range filters, so potentially you can search for rants that were made no closer than X kilometers and no farther than Y kilometers.

ElasticSearch has even more robust geospatial features. For example, we can search for locations inside an arbitrarily defined polygon, not just a box. In addition, we can save predefined shapes, such as a set of polygons describing a city or a country, and use them in query conditions.

Summary

ElasticSearch is a scalable, enterprising, and web-ready search engine. With great performance and features, it is no wonder ElasticSearch is rapidly taking over the search-engine market, challenging veteran competitors such as apache SolR. ElasticSearch has great tools and some of the best integration with the leading cloud platforms available today.

For these reasons Couchbase has elected to use it as the full-text solution of choice for their clients. Integrating Couchbase and ElasticSearch is easy and helps applications to add both text search and complex, high-performance querying on their data.

We didn't even scratch the surface of ElasticSearch and its vast ecosystem. If you are going to integrate ElasticSearch in your application, make sure to check out the great tools included with it, including Kibana, Marvel, and logstash.

In the next few chapters we are going to put the development world aside. One of the great strengths of Couchbase Server is its ability to run in large-scale production deployments. In the next part of this book we are going to learn in depth how to deploy, administer, and optimize your Couchbase Server cluster in production.

PART III

Couchbase at Scale

CHAPTER 9

■ ■ ■

Sizing and Deployment Considerations

In Part I, you installed Couchbase Server and used the admin console to create a new bucket (among other things). In this chapter, you'll learn about the technical aspects of deploying a Couchbase Server cluster. In Chapter 10, you'll read about the available admin tools and learn how to perform important administrative tasks. Then in Chapter 11 you'll learn about monitoring the health of a Couchbase cluster, making sense of the massive amounts of runtime data available to you, and configuring advanced features.

Throughout this chapter, you'll be using the Couchbase command-line tools and HTTP API. You will find these tools in the following locations:

- *Windows:* `\<install dir>\Couchbase\Server\bin`

- *Linux:* `/opt/couchbase/bin`

- *OS X:* `/Applications/Couchbase Server.app/Contents/Resources/couchbase-core/bin`

The Couchbase tools include the open-source cURL utility, which we'll use to post custom requests to the HTTP API in our examples. Of course, you can use any other HTTP client tool, if you prefer, such as the Postman extension for the Chrome browser, or Fiddler.

What you have at this point is a single-node cluster, which is really an oxymoron. Couchbase isn't designed to work with just one node outside of a testing and development environment; some of the best features—replication, horizontal scaling, and data rebalancing—all require multiple nodes. It's time to take this single node and turn it into a real cluster.

Now, before you rush to buy brand new, shiny servers, the first thing you need to do is actually design your Couchbase cluster. You need to decide how much RAM and CPU it needs, how many nodes should be created initially, what sort of storage should be used, and how the network infrastructure should be configured for the deployment. Once you have a good idea of how the cluster is going to work, you will get to the fun part, which is spending your yearly budget on hardware and installing and adding more nodes.

Planning the Couchbase Cluster

Your application and data-access patterns greatly affect the hardware resource requirements of the cluster. Let's consider some of the key hardware factors and how they relate to database performance.

RAM

Couchbase relies on an extensive memory-cache layer for its high throughput and low read/write latency. Couchbase keeps all the document keys and metadata in memory, and as much as possible of the working set—the frequently accessed data—as well. If, after subtracting the RAM taken up by the keys and metadata, there is not enough left for the whole working set, Couchbase will evict some of the documents from memory. Active documents that exist only on disk take much longer to access, which creates a bottleneck both for reading and writing data. This usually makes RAM the most crucial factor in the performance of each node individually and of the cluster as a whole.

The type, or, more specifically, the speed of the storage device also affects memory use. Because I/O operations are queued by the server, faster storage helps drain the queue faster, thus requiring less RAM in total.

During the normal course of operation, documents are added or read into the RAM cache. When the amount of RAM used by the node passes a point called the high-water mark, which is 85% of total RAM by default, Couchbase will begin evicting items from memory until the total RAM use falls below the low-water mark, which is 75% of total RAM by default. When calculating the amount of RAM required for the cluster, the goal is to have all the document IDs, all the metadata, and the entire working set, if possible, in RAM at the same time. This means that the size of document IDs + metadata + working set should be just below the high-water mark, or 85% of the cluster RAM. Of course, this isn't always possible—for example, all documents could be accessed with equal frequency, making it impractical to keep the entire working set in memory.

You can use the following guidelines to approximate how much RAM you'll need for each bucket. Note that the total RAM needed for the cluster is the total sum of memory needed for all the buckets.

First, let's define the following parameters:

- *Documents:* The number of items in your total data set. As this number changes, you'll need to readjust your total RAM either by changing how much is allocated to the bucket or by adding more nodes to the cluster.

- *ID:* The average size (in bytes) of your document IDs (keys). Remember that Couchbase keeps all the keys in memory.

- *Item:* The average size (in bytes) of your data items.

- *Copies:* The number of replicas you want to keep for each data item + 1 (for the actual item).

- *Working Set %:* The percentage of the total data set that is frequently accessed (the working set). This parameter is often subject to change; for example, in a globally available application, the working set percentage changes throughout the day, as people in different time zones wake up and begin using the application.

- *Metadata:* This is the amount of memory taken by the metadata of each item. In Couchbase 2.1+ it is a constant 56 bytes.

- *Headroom:* Additional memory overhead required to store metadata and the I/O queues. The Couchbase team recommends setting this to 25% for SSD storage and 30% for HDD storage, due to the difference in expected disk queue length.

- *High-Water Mark:* The percentage of RAM at which Couchbase begins evicting items from cache.

Using these parameters, we can calculate an approximate lower bound for our bucket RAM requirements:

- *Total Metadata* = Documents × (ID + Metadata) × Copies

- *Total Data* = Documents × Item × Copies

- *Working Set* = Total Data × Working Set %

- *Bucket RAM Required* = (Total Metadata + Working Set) × (1 + Headroom) / High Water Mark

- *Cluster RAM Required* = ∑(Bucket RAM)

As you can see, you can calculate the minimum required RAM per bucket by combining the memory required by keys and metadata with a rough estimate of the memory required by the part of the data that comprises your working set. You can adjust this estimate to account for both the extra headroom required by the server and the high-water mark setting. The sum of memory required for all the buckets is the minimum required cluster RAM.

Of course, this number is only an initial estimate, and it will have to be adjusted as data grows and changes. But now you can use the total RAM requirement to help you estimate how many Couchbase nodes you'll need to provision in your cluster.

■ **Note** You cannot allocate all the RAM available on a machine to Couchbase. You must leave enough room for the operating system and other running processes. As a general guideline, you should leave at least 20% of the system RAM for non-Couchbase use.

As Chapter 5 mentions, unlike documents, which are cached in memory, views are stored and accessed only on disk.[1] However, although Couchbase itself doesn't cache views, it takes advantage of the operating system's file system I/O caching mechanism. Therefore, if your application uses views, you should leave enough free RAM on each node for the OS to cache the index data in memory. There is no exact guideline for how much free RAM you should leave—you will have to experiment and discover the right balance between memory allocated to Couchbase and memory reserved for the file system cache.

Let's look at a concrete example:

- An application with a data set of 100 million items.

- At any point in time, about 10% of the data is actively used.

- An average document size of 2 KB.

- Keys based on a UUID with a short prefix, for an average length of 44 bytes.

- Using Couchbase 2.1+, so the metadata for each item is 56 bytes.

- A replication factor of 1, which is one replica copy for each active item.

- Servers with 16 GB of RAM each.

- Spinning drives (HDD), so we'll need a headroom of 30% for the I/O queues.

- Using the default high-water mark of 85%.

- All data is in a single bucket, and there are no other buckets.

Let's calculate how much RAM we'll need in our cluster:

- *Total metadata* = $100{,}000{,}000 \times (56 + 44) \times 2 = 20{,}000{,}000{,}000 \sim= 19$ GB

- *Total data* = $100{,}000{,}000 \times 2048 \times 2 = 409{,}600{,}000{,}000 \sim= 381$ GB

- *Working set* = $381 \text{ GB} \times 0.1 \sim= 38$ GB

- *RAM required* = $(38 \text{ GB} + 19 \text{ GB}) \times 1.3 / 0.85 =$ **87.2 GB**

---

[1]This is true for Couchbase version 2.5.1 and earlier, but may change in the future. One of the upcoming features is accessing views in memory.

Given all of the initial conditions above, our bucket must have at least 87.2 GB of RAM available for normal operations. Our servers have 16 GB of RAM, and we're leaving about 20% of that for the OS, other processes, and the file system cache. Rounding up a bit, that leaves us 13 GB of RAM for Couchbase per machine. So, 87.2 GB / 13 GB = 6.7, which means we need at least 7 nodes in the cluster.

One very important consideration to keep in mind is that the desired replication factor has an enormous effect on the RAM required of your cluster. Using a replication factor of 2 in the example above would increase the memory requirement to 130 GB, which is a minimum of 10 nodes. Forgetting to take replication into account and only considering the active data is a common mistake, especially in the initial testing stages of a Couchbase deployment. Then, when you start loading data into the database, a sudden drop in cluster performance usually results and a lot of head scratching ensues.

■ **Note**   We strongly recommend erring on the side of caution and provisioning a larger cluster than required. You can gradually scale it down later, when you're certain that it can handle the amount of data and the processing load.

Storage

Although Couchbase does a great job of caching data in memory, eventually most data needs to be written to disk. Items that need to be persisted first go into the node's disk-write queue. The type of storage affects throughput and, as noted in the previous topic, memory usage for the I/O queue.

The job of reading data from storage and writing data from the I/O queue is performed by the reader and writer threads. You may recall that in Chapter 1, when you created the default and ranter buckets, you were asked to set the number of read/write workers but left it at the default value of 3. By default, two of these threads are used for reading and one for writing data to disk. You can change these settings per bucket to better match your I/O pattern. If your server disk utilization is very high, and you're seeing a lot of read or write contention, you can decrease the number of worker threads. This will relieve the I/O pressure at the expense of the increased RAM required for the write queue. On the other hand, if your disk utilization is low, you can increase the number of worker threads to get better disk utilization.

As you've seen earlier, you can set the number of worker threads when creating a new bucket. If your nodes meet the minimum hardware requirements—which are 2 GHz dual-core CPUs with 4 GB RAM and HDDs—then the default 3 threads are usually a good choice for most deployments. For more powerful hardware, and especially for SSD-based storage, increase the number of worker threads to the maximum of 8. After deploying your cluster, monitor the disk utilization, in particular the write-queue size and drain rate, and then adjust the number of worker threads accordingly. We'll talk about monitoring disk and memory utilization in Chapter 11.

You can change the number of worker threads for an existing bucket through the web admin console or through the HTTP API. In the web admin console, go to the Data Buckets tab, expand the bucket you want to edit, and click the Edit button on the right (as shown in Figure 9-1).

Couchbase Buckets								Create New Data Bucket	
Bucket Name	Nodes	Item Count	Ops/sec	Disk Fetches/sec	RAM/Quota Usage	Data/Disk Usage			
▼ ranter	● 1	100026	0	0	41.3MB / 256MB	99.1MB / 99.3MB		Documents	Views
Access Control: Authentication		Replicas: disabled		Compaction: Not active				Compact	Edit

Figure 9-1.   Editing a bucket

Enter the desired number of worker threads (as shown in Figure 9-2) and click Save.

Disk Read-Write Concurrency

Number of suggested reader/writer workers: 3 (Min = 2, Max = 8)

Figure 9-2. *Changing the number of worker threads*

■ **Note** Changing the number of workers will cause the bucket to be restarted and go through the warm-up process again, which will disconnect all clients and take some time to complete.

You can also change the number of workers through the HTTP API. To do so, issue a POST command to the URL http://<server>:8091/pools/default/buckets/<bucket> with the following data: threadsNumber=<X>&ramQuotaMB =<R>, where X is the number of threads and R is the RAM quota for the bucket in megabytes:

```
> curl -X POST -u Administrator:123456 http://localhost:8091/pools/default/buckets/ranter -d
threadsNumber=8 -d ramQuotaMB=200 -v
```

Couchbase assigns each reader thread to a static range of vBuckets at startup to avoid synchronization issues when reading data into the RAM cache. You can check the worker settings through the HTTP API by sending a GET request to the URL http://<server>:8091/pools/default/buckets/<bucket> or through the cbstats command-line tool:

```
> cbstats localhost:11210 -b ranter raw workload
```

```
ep_workload:num_readers: 5
ep_workload:num_shards:  5
ep_workload:num_writers: 3
ep_workload:policy:       Optimized for read data access
```

As you can see from the output, the ranter bucket now uses three writer and five reader threads. The vBuckets are split into five sub-ranges, referred to as "shards" in the example above, each assigned to one of the reader threads.

Storage Performance

One of the most straightforward ways to improve storage performance is to create striped logical volumes from multiple physical disks, or cloud storage drives. You can use RAID or software tools to build striped volumes. Depending on the volume configuration, the performance gains from striping may come at the cost of an increased chance of data corruption due to disk failure.

> ▪ **Tip** To learn how to create a striped volume in Windows, read the following TechNet article:

```
http://technet.microsoft.com/en-us/magazine/ff382722.aspx
```

For Linux, read the Ubuntu wiki article on LVM:

```
https://wiki.ubuntu.com/Lvm
```

Or the CentOS LVM Administrator's Guide:

```
www.centos.org/docs/5/html/Cluster_Logical_Volume_Manager/
```

As we've mentioned before, views are stored and read from disk. One option for boosting runtime view query performance is to store the indexed data on a RAM drive. Of course, unless you create some sort of write-through mechanism to dump the RAM drive to permanent storage, the index data will be lost on reboot. This means that you will be trading improved query performance for the added load of rebuilding all indexes after each node restart. Couchbase rebuilds indexes at runtime, so after the node becomes available and begins to service requests, there will be a period of time during which your views will return an empty result.

The simplest way to create a RAM drive on Linux is by using the tmpfs temporary file system mechanism, which was introduced in kernel 2.4. To create a RAM drive-based folder, mount the tmpfs file system into some directory, as follows:

```
> mkdir /tmp/ramdisk;
> chmod 777 /tmp/ramdisk
> mount -t tmpfs -o size=1024M -o noatime tmpfs /tmp/ramdisk/
```

To remount the RAM drive after a reboot, add the following line to the /etc/fstab file:

```
tmpfs    /tmp/ramdisk    tmpfs    defaults,noatime    0 0
```

Note that, although you can create a tmpfs disk larger than the available RAM, the data that doesn't fit into memory will be swapped to disk, greatly reducing performance.

For Windows, there are any number of RAM disk utilities you can use to achieve the same result.

CPU

Most operations in Couchbase are memory and disk, rather than CPU-bound. That being said, Couchbase generally requires at least two cores. If you have multiple MapReduce views that perform heavy computation, you may need to provision more CPU resources. There are no exact guidelines for CPU utilization, but as a general rule of thumb for optimal performance, you should have four cores, plus one for every design document in production and for every XDCR stream. Use the CPU statistics, which are available both in the web console and through command-line tools, to help you decide when to add more CPU resources.

Nodes

Now that you have a good estimate of how much RAM, storage, and CPU you need, the next question you need to answer is whether you should have just a few large nodes or many small nodes. With many small nodes you distribute the I/O load to more machines and reduce the impact of any individual node failing, because less data will need to be rebalanced to the rest of the cluster. On the other hand, having more nodes increases the network bandwidth required for inter-node communication and creates more potential points of failure. Additionally, Couchbase clients keep an open connection to each node, so having more nodes increases the load on the client.

The lowest bound on the number of nodes is set by your data durability requirements, meaning how many replicas of the data you need. The minimum number of nodes in a cluster is `<number of replicas> + 1` (for the active data). However, having the absolute minimum number of nodes is usually a bad practice, because if one or more nodes fail, there will not be enough nodes left to hold all the replica copies. If your cluster size isn't driven by RAM or storage requirements, then having at least two nodes over the minimum is a good idea so that in the event of node failure, you still have a safety buffer.

If your cluster has enough RAM to hold the working set, the consideration shifts to a tradeoff between network bandwidth, I/O throughput, and reliability. If your data set generates a heavy disk-write load, you will want to spread your data set to many small nodes to increase to total I/O bandwidth; for example, if your application primarily aggregates data from multiple sources and performs offline analysis. If your application has a smaller data set, but generates a lot of queries and updates, leading to a lot of inter-node communication and thus network bandwidth use, then you may want to deploy on fewer nodes, possibly with fewer replica copies and more RAM for buffering the write and replication queues. If you have a very large data set, but your application uses only a small portion of it at any given time, you may want to deploy to fewer nodes with a lot of storage and RAM for each. For example, a social network application stores a lot of historical data, but mostly needs the recently created data. The frequently used data—the working set—will be cached in RAM, while the historical data will exist in storage and will take longer to access if requested.

Network Topology

Couchbase uses bandwidth to exchange data with clients and between nodes. You can calculate a rough estimate of the required bandwidth with the following formula:

- *Operations* = Reads + Writes × Copies

- *Bandwidth per Second* = Operations × Item + Rebalancing Overhead

As a general rule, a 1 GB network is sufficient for most small-to-medium-sized production deployments. Clusters with over 20 nodes may require higher network bandwidth.

Beyond the bandwidth requirement, there are important topology-related decisions we need to make before deploying our Couchbase cluster.

In some data centers, a top-of-rack switch represents a single point of failure that can make all the machines hosted in the rack unavailable. (Or the rack could spontaneously combust. It happens.) To avoid data loss in the event of a large-scale failure, Couchbase Server v2.5 (Enterprise Edition) introduced a rack-awareness feature. This feature lets you organize nodes into multiple groups, and Couchbase then ensures that no single group contains all existing copies of the same data. Assigning nodes that reside on the same physical rack into a group means that in the event of a whole rack failing, there will still be a replica of the data in another group, on another rack. Note that this is not a cross-datacenter feature; it's meant to be used within the same location, because Couchbase expects very low latency between nodes in the cluster.

To configure rack awareness, go to the Server Nodes tab of the web console and click on the Server Groups button, which was added in v2.5 (as shown in Figure 9-3), to switch to the Server Groups view.

Server Node Name		Group	RAM Usage	Swap Usage	CPU Usage	Data/Disk Usage	Items (Active / Replica)		
▶ 10.0.1.4	Up	Group 1	14.7%	N/A	2.26%	155MB / 183MB	1 M/ 0	Fail Over	Remove

Figure 9-3. Rack-awareness server groups

Click the Create Group button to create new server groups (as shown in Figure 9-4).

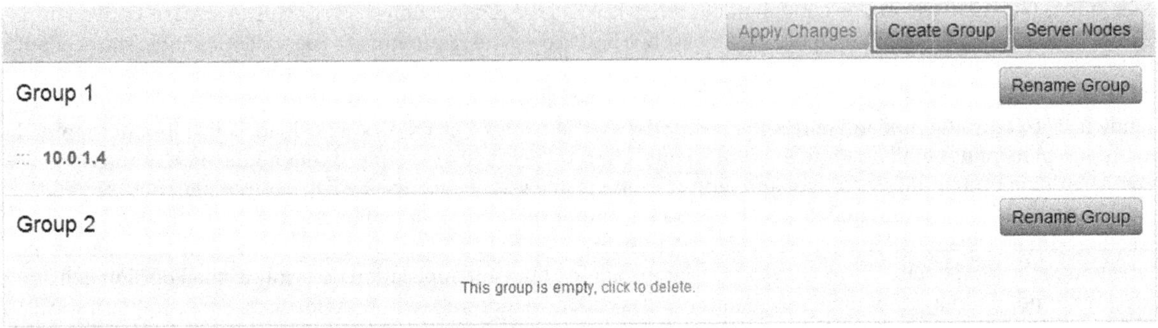

Figure 9-4. *Editing rack-awareness server groups*

You can drag and drop nodes between groups to assign them to groups. Click Apply Changes to save the new group configuration and then rebalance the cluster. When adding new nodes to the cluster, you can select which group the node will belong to (as shown in Figure 9-5).

Figure 9-5. *Assigning a new node to a server group*

▪ **Note** You must rebalance the cluster after making changes to the rack-awareness configuration.

For rack awareness to work, you must have at least two nodes, in two different server groups. Furthermore, it is highly recommended to have an equal number of nodes in each group to keep the load balanced. If the number of servers in different groups is not the same, Couchbase will make its best effort to balance the vBuckets between the available nodes within each group. This means that the smaller group will have a proportionally higher average load across its nodes.

Firewall Configuration

Couchbase Server requires several ports for communicating with the clients and between nodes, for administration, and for cross-datacenter replication (XDCR).

You must configure your firewall to open the following ports:

Port	Used for	Nodes	Clients	Cluster	XDCR
8091	Web Administration	X	X	X	X
8092	Couchbase API	X	X		X
11209	Internal Buckets	X			
11210	Buckets	X	X		
11211	Client SDK		X		
4369	Erlang Port Mapper	X			
21100–21199	Inter-node Data	X			
11214	XDCR Incoming SSL				X
11215	XDCR Outgoing SSL				X
18091	Internal HTTPS				X
18092	Internal CAPI HTTPS				X

Windows MaxUserPort

By default, Windows limits the number of outgoing ports to 5000, which may not be enough for a Couchbase node. On Windows Server, the Couchbase installer will prompt you as to whether you want to increase the number of ephemeral ports to 60,000 (as shown in Figure 9-6). Click Yes and then reboot the system after the installation completes for the setting to take effect.

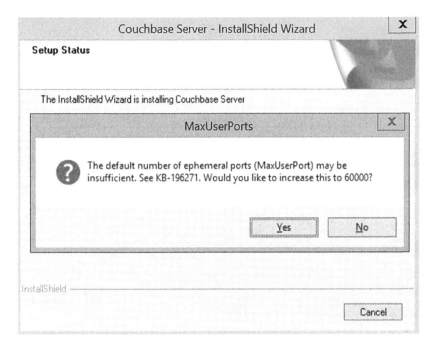

Figure 9-6. *Increasing the maximum number of ephemeral ports*

Replication

Deciding how many replicas to use in your bucket depends on two factors: how much durability your data requires and how large your planned cluster is. The tradeoff here is between data resilience on the one hand, and storage space, disk I/O load, RAM usage, and network bandwidth on the other. Multiple replicas will drastically lower the chance of data loss in the event of node failure and will also make recovery faster, because there are multiple copies of the data in the cluster. However, for each replica copy, the data item will be placed in the replication queue, transmitted over the network, placed in the disk-write queue on the replica node, and then finally persisted on disk.

For critical data, such as financial records and customer details, you'll want a high level of resilience, meaning at least two replica copies, and three for larger clusters. For important, but not critical, data—user posts, product catalogs, etc.—a single replica copy provides enough safety margin for most applications. Transient data, such as system messages, logs, or shopping carts on e-commerce sites, most likely doesn't require replication at all.

Conversely, the size of your cluster affects how many replicas you can support. As we discussed earlier in the "Nodes" topic, you will want to have more nodes than the number of copies in your cluster so that you'll be able to rebalance the cluster if nodes fail. Barring any additional resilience and size constraints, you can use the following general guidelines for picking the number of replicas in a cluster:

- A cluster with five nodes will support one replica copy with enough spare capacity to rebalance the cluster after node failover.

- A cluster with up to ten nodes will safely support up to two replica copies.

- A cluster with more than ten nodes will safely support up to three replica copies.

Often, you can utilize a hybrid approach to data resilience. Create a separate bucket with high replication settings for the critical data and a separate bucket with fewer replica copies for the rest of your data. The downside of this approach is that it's impossible to create views that query data cross-bucket. If you need to query both buckets together, you will have to get clever with your data modeling to support retrieving data from both buckets together. You will still need enough nodes in the cluster to provide room for failing nodes over.

■ **Note** You cannot change the number of replicas in a bucket after it has been created. Make sure you know how many replicas you need before you create the bucket.

Swap Space

All the operating systems supported by Couchbase have a memory paging mechanism, which moves inactive pages from memory to disk. You should always have some swap space—pagefile on Windows—allocated on each Couchbase node to ensure that even if the physical memory on the machine is exhausted, Couchbase can continue to operate without out-of-memory errors, albeit with reduced performance.

On Linux machines the swap behavior is controlled by the swappiness parameter, which accepts values from 0 to 100. A swappiness of 0 means no swapping until all physical memory is exhausted. By default, most Linux systems have a swappiness setting of 60, which can negatively affect Couchbase performance. You can use the following command to check the swappiness on a machine:

```
> cat /proc/sys/vm/swappiness
```

For optimal Couchbase performance, set the swappiness level on all nodes to 0. You can use the following command to change the setting for the current session:

```
> sudo sysctl vm.swappiness=0
```

To make the change permanent, edit the /etc/sysctl.conf file with root privileges, and add the following line to the end of the file:

```
vm.swappiness = 0
```

Unfortunately, at the time of this writing, there doesn't seem to be a way to control the swappiness of the Windows pagefile.

Summary

In this chapter, you've learned the various considerations for sizing your Couchbase cluster before deployment, as well as some tips and tricks for improving performance. Because Couchbase is very memory bound, in most cases increasing the amount of RAM available to your cluster will have the largest performance impact. For some disk-bound scenarios, such as applications that make heavy use of views, adding more nodes to the cluster to spread the I/O load is the most straightforward way to improve performance. And beyond the purely resource-based considerations, your data-durability requirements will also dictate the minimum number of nodes in your cluster.

CHAPTER 10

Basic Administration

Before we dive into the intricacies of Couchbase Server administration, we must learn the number one, irreplaceable, absolutely crucial Couchbase troubleshooting technique: turning it off and on again.

On Linux, Couchbase is configured to run as a daemon during installation. The startup script is located in:

```
/etc/init.d/couchbase-server
```

To start or stop the server manually, run the script with the appropriate argument:

```
> sudo /etc/init.d/couchbase-server [start|stop]
```

On Windows, Couchbase is installed as a service. You can control it from the Services panel or through the command line. To open the services panel, go to the Start ➤ Run dialog and enter "services.msc," then press Enter. Find the CouchbaseServer service and use the actions available in the toolbar to start, stop, or restart it.

Alternatively, open a command window as an administrator and use the following command to start or stop Couchbase Server:

```
> net [start|stop] CouchbaseServer
```

On OS X, Couchbase is installed as a regular application that runs in the background. You can control Couchbase Server from the menu bar item that is added at startup.

Building the Cluster

Now that we've got the theory out of the way, it's finally time to create our cluster. The first step is installing and configuring a single node, as we did in Chapter 1. To make things more interesting, let's insert some sample data into our first node so that we can see how Couchbase deals with existing data when later adding and removing nodes. We'll use the cbworkloadgen command-line tool that comes with Couchbase to generate 1000 sample data items, as follows:

```
> cbworkloadgen -n localhost -b default -j -u <username> -p <password> -i 1000
```

The -n parameter is our node address, -b is the bucket that will hold the data, -j tells cbworkloadgen to generate JSON documents rather than binary data, -u and -p are the login credentials of the administrator account, and -i specifies the number of items to generate. We'll come back to cbworkloadgen in the next chapter and use it to generate some load on the cluster so that we can explore the various Couchbase monitoring tools.

We are finally ready to add a second node to our cluster.

Adding a Node to the Couchbase Cluster

We can add a node to an existing cluster either as part of the initial node setup or after it's been configured as a stand-alone node. To join a cluster during the setup process, select "Join a cluster now" in the first step of the configuration wizard and enter the login details and the IP address of one of the nodes in the cluster, as you can see in Figure 10-1.

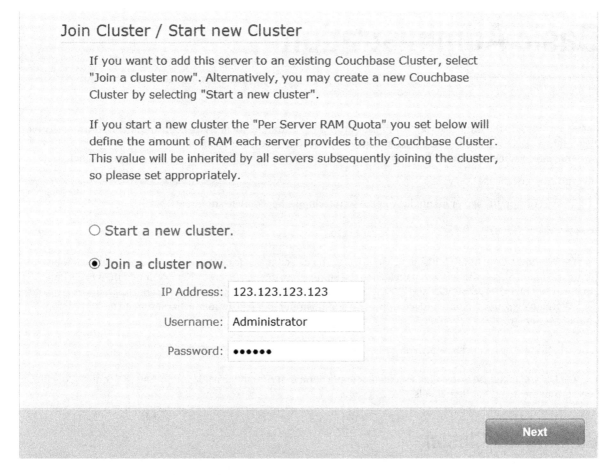

Figure 10-1. *Joining a cluster during node setup*

To add an existing stand-alone node to the cluster from the web administration console, go to the Server Nodes tab and click Add Server, as shown in Figure 10-2. Note that you must use the web console of one of the existing nodes in the cluster, not the web console of the node to be added.

Figure 10-2. *Server Nodes tab*

Enter the IP address and login details of the node you want to add to the cluster and click Add Server, as shown in Figure 10-3.

Figure 10-3. *Adding a server to the cluster*

■ **Note** All data on the node being added to the cluster will be destroyed. Normally, this isn't a problem with a newly installed node, though.

Couchbase will negotiate with the new node and add it to the cluster. However, the node will not become active until you rebalance the cluster to redistribute the data between all the nodes. You can see the new node in the Server Nodes tab of the web console by clicking the Pending Rebalance button, as shown in Figure 10-4. We cover rebalancing a little later in this chapter.

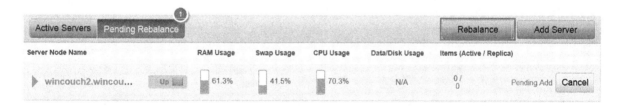

Figure 10-4. *Pending node rebalance*

You can also use the couchbase-cli command-line tool to add a node to the cluster:

```
> couchbase-cli server-add -c <cluster_host> -u <cluster_user> -p <cluster_password> --server-add=<node_host> --server-add-username <node_user> --server-add-password <node_password>
```

The parameters, in order, are: the host address of any existing node in the cluster, the administrator username and password of the cluster, the host address of the new node, and the administrator username and password of the new node.

If everything goes well, you will see the following message from the client:

```
SUCCESS: server-add <node_host>:8091
```

To add a node through the HTTP API, issue an HTTP POST request to the following URL:
http://<cluster_host>:8091/controller/addNode

Use basic authentication to provide the cluster login information and supply the following x-www-form-urlencoded data: hostname=<node_host>, user=<node_user>, and password=<node_password>. For example, using cURL, you can add a node with the following command:

```
> curl -u Administrator:123456 localhost:8091/controller/addNode -d
"hostname=node2&user=Administrator2&password=654321"
```

Alternatively, you can use the HTTP API on the new node to have it join a cluster. Use the following HTTP POST request:

```
> curl -u Administrator:123456 -d clusterMemberHostIp=<cluster_node_IP> -d clusterMemberPort=8091 -d
user=Administrator2 -d password=654321 http://<node_host>:8091/node/controller/doJoinCluster
```

The clusterMemberHostIP is the IP address of any existing node in the cluster, and the <node_host> parameter is the host address of the new node.

Removing a Node from the Cluster

Before we get to rebalancing data in the cluster, let's take a look at how to remove nodes. Both adding and removing nodes from the cluster require a data rebalance for the changes to take effect. You can mark a node for removal through the web admin console. Go to the Server Nodes tab and click the Remove button next to the target node, as shown in Figure 10-5.

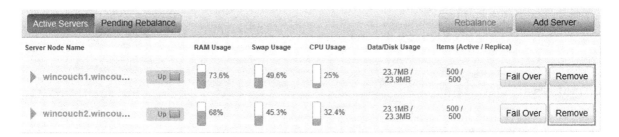

Figure 10-5. *Removing a node from the cluster*

You can see the nodes marked for removal in the Pending Rebalance view, as shown in Figure 10-6.

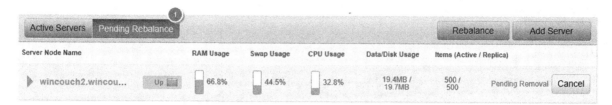

Figure 10-6. *Pending rebalance due to node removal*

There is no command-line or HTTP API option for marking a node for removal. Instead, the rebalance command can also accept a list of nodes to remove as part of the rebalance operation, as we'll see in the next topic.

■ **Note** Before removing a node, make sure your cluster has enough nodes remaining to hold all the replica copies defined in all buckets. If you need to remove multiple nodes, remove them one at a time and monitor the cluster behavior after each removal to ensure that the performance of the cluster remains acceptable.

Rebalancing

After making changes to the cluster topology, you must rebalance the data between nodes. When a rebalance is required, you will see a notification in the Server Nodes tab of the web console, as shown in Figure 10-6. Because the rebalance operation potentially moves a lot of data around, which can severely impact the cluster's performance, you must manually initiate the rebalance.

The rebalance operation is managed by a special process, called the "Orchestrator," which calculates a new vBucket map according to the new cluster topology. The Orchestrator then directs nodes to move data around until the cluster matches the new vBucket map. The rebalance process updates the current vBucket map incrementally as vBuckets get moved around in the cluster. You will recall from Chapter 3 that Couchbase clients continuously poll the server for updates in the cluster topology. This means that during the rebalance clients quickly become aware of changes in vBucket locations and can access data in the new location, which helps spread out the load on the cluster. In addition to redistributing data throughout the active nodes, the rebalance process also synchronizes replica copies to account for the new data locations. During the rebalance, data is moved out of the nodes being removed from the cluster so that they can be safely disconnected.

■ **Note** Even though Couchbase is designed to continue serving clients during a rebalance, it's best to perform the rebalance during the period of lowest activity in the cluster, if at all possible.

You can start the rebalance from the web admin console by clicking the Rebalance button on the Server Nodes tab, as shown in Figure 10-7.

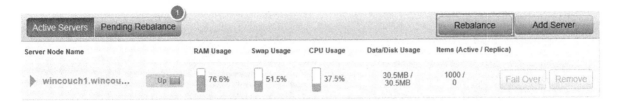

Figure 10-7. *Starting the rebalance*

Alternatively, you can use the couchbase-cli command-line tool to start the rebalance:

```
> couchbase-cli rebalance -c <host> -u <user> -p <password>
```

The <host> parameter can be any existing node in the cluster, and <user> and <password> are the administrator credentials. You can also specify nodes to add or remove from the cluster as part of the rebalance:

```
> couchbase-cli rebalance -c <host>:8091 -u <user> -p <password> --server-add=<new_host> --server-
add-username=<new_host_user> --server-add-password=<new_host_password> --server-remove=<host2>
--server-remove=<host3>
```

The command above will add <new_host> using the provided administrator credentials, remove <host2> and <host3>, and then rebalance the cluster.

To rebalance the cluster through the HTTP API, issue a POST request to the following URL: http://<host>:8091/controller/rebalance. Then supply the administrator credentials with basic authentication.

You can track the progress of the rebalance operation from the Server Nodes tab of the web console, as Figure 10-8 shows.

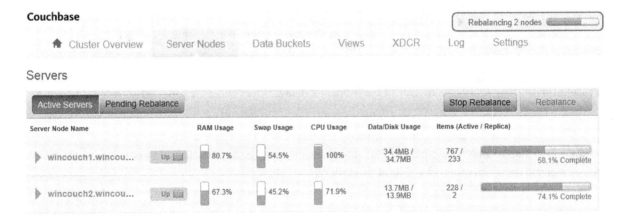

Figure 10-8. *Rebalance progress*

You can use the couchbase-cli tool to check the rebalance progress:

```
> couchbase-cli rebalance-status -c localhost -u Administrator -p 123456
```

Alternatively, with the HTTP API, issue the following request:

```
> curl -u Administrator:123456 "localhost:8091/pools/default/rebalanceProgress
```

This will return a response similar to the following:

```
{
        "status":"running",
        "ns_1@wincouch2.wincouch.f5.internal.cloudapp.net":{"progress":0.091796875},
        "ns_1@wincouch1.wincouch.f5.internal.cloudapp.net":{"progress":0.03125}
}
```

We'll talk about monitoring the rebalance process in more detail in Chapter 11.

It's safe to stop the rebalance at any point; any data that has already been moved will be part of the current vBucket map. Rebalancing the cluster again will continue from the point where the last rebalance stopped. To stop the rebalance, click the Stop Rebalance button or use the following command:

```
>couchbase-cli rebalance-stop -c localhost -u Administrator -p 123456
```

When the rebalance completes, you should see something similar to Figure 10-9 in the Server Nodes tab of the administration console.

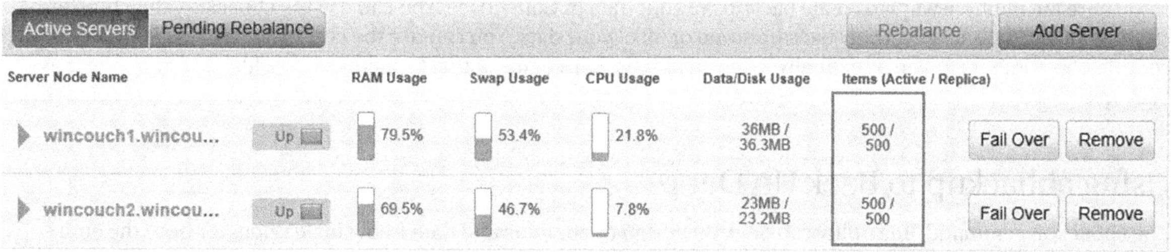

Figure 10-9. *Rebalance complete*

Swap Rebalancing

When the number of nodes being added and removed during a rebalance is the same, Couchbase will swap data directly between these nodes. This is called a swap rebalance, and it is an automatic feature that cannot be controlled externally. Because a swap rebalance only affects the added and removed nodes, it is faster and has less impact on the cluster performance.

A swap rebalance is very useful for performing live upgrades. It is, in fact, the preferred mechanism for upgrades, because it minimizes disruption and maintains the cluster capacity throughout the upgrade process. To perform a swap rebalance upgrade, install the new version of Couchbase Server on a new machine that is not yet part of the cluster. Add the new node to the cluster and remove one of the old nodes, then perform a rebalance. Because the number of nodes being added and removed is the same, Couchbase will perform a swap rebalance directly between the two. Repeat this process until all nodes have been upgraded to the new Couchbase version. You can use more than one machine at a time, as long as you add and remove the same number of nodes.

Changing the Data and Index Path

You can only set the data and index paths during the initial node setup; there is no way to change the configured paths while a node is running. With that in mind, the steps for changing the data or index location on a specific node are:

- Remove the node from the cluster. As we learned in this chapter, removing a node involves rebalancing the cluster. The removed node will end up in the initial setup state.

- Configure the node as you would a brand-new Couchbase Server installation. Set the desired data and index paths on the node, either in the web console, through the couchbase-cli command-line tool, or through the HTTP API.

- Add the node back to the cluster and rebalance again.

You can simplify the process by performing a swap rebalance with a replacement node: prepare a new node with the desired data and index paths and swap it with the node you wish to reconfigure. This way you avoid increasing the load on the cluster due to having one less node while you perform the setup, and only perform one swap rebalance, instead of two regular rebalance operations. Of course, you also need to have an extra machine for swapping nodes.

Backing Up and Restoring

Even though Couchbase is designed with durability and reliability in mind, data loss can still occur due to large-scale failures or user error. Backing up your data regularly is an important mechanism for ensuring that you do not lose any information due to unpredictable circumstances.

There are multiple ways to create backups of your data in Couchbase. You can use the cbbackup and cbrestore command-line tools to selectively back up some or all of your data. You can use the cbtransfer tool to create a copy of your data in another cluster. And, finally, you can make copies of the actual Couchbase data files and store them as backups.

Using cbbackup to Back Up Data

The cbbackup command-line utility can back up design documents and data from single nodes, or from the entire cluster, as well as from specific buckets. The design documents are stored as a JSON file, while the data is stored as a SQLite database file. The backup folder contains one subfolder per bucket, and each bucket subfolder holds the design document file as well as a folder per cluster node. Each node backup folder contains one or more cbb files, which hold the actual document data.

As you can see in Figure 10-10, the data is easily readable by any application that can access SQLite files. The cbbackup tool has the following usage:

```
> cbbackup <source> <target> [options]
```

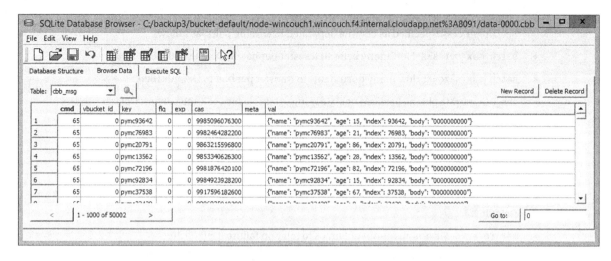

Figure 10-10. *Couchbase backup data file open in SQLite Browser*

The <source> is either a URL of a node in the cluster or the path of the Couchbase data directory. To specify a path, you must pass it as a URL using the couchstore-files protocol. For example, on Windows:

```
"couchstore-files://C:\Program Files\Couchbase\Server\var\lib\couchbase\data"
```

Or on Linux:

```
couchstore-files:///opt/couchbase/var/lib/couchbase/data
```

The <target> is a directory path where the backup will be stored. This must be either an empty directory or a non-existent one, in which case cbbackup will create it.

The [options] are optional parameters.

Specifying a source and a target will back up the data from all the buckets in the entire cluster. You can make more granular backups, as well as control various aspects of the stored data, by specifying optional parameters.

The optional parameters are as follows:

- -b <bucket>: Specifies which bucket to back up.

- --single-node: Only back up the data from the source node specified in the URL.

- -i <vBucket id>: Only back up items from the vBucket with the specified ID.

- -k <key regexp>: Only back up items whose key matches the specified regular expression.

- -n: Perform a dry run, which will validate the source, target, and optional parameters, but won't transfer any data.

- -u <username>: The cluster administrator username.

- -p <password>: The cluster administrator password.

- -t <threads>: The number of worker threads to use for the backup operation.

- -v: Print more verbose messages; very useful in combination with -n.

- -x: Extra optional config parameters, which give you very fine-grained control of the backup process. Specified as comma-separated key=value pairs, as follows:

- batch_max_bytes=X: How many bytes to transfer per batch. Default 400000.

- batch_max_size=X: How many documents to transfer per batch. Default 1000.

- cbb_max_mb=X: Split the backup (*.cbb) file into multiple files of X megabytes. Default 100000Mb.

- conflict_resolve=[0|1]: Enables or disables conflict resolution. This setting is inherited from cbtransfer and doesn't actually do anything in cbbackup. Default 1.

- data_only=[0|1]: A value of 1 will back up only the data (not design docs). Default 0.

- design_doc_only=[0|1]: A value of 1 will back up only the design docs (not data). Default 0.

- max_retry=X: Maximum number of times to retry on failure. Default 10.

- nmv_retry=[0|1]: Specifies whether to retry backup after a NOT_MY_VBUCKET error. A value of 0 means do not retry. Default 1.

- recv_min_bytes=X: Number of bytes per TCP transfer call. Default 4096.

- rehash=[0|1]: A value of 1 means cbbackup will rehash data, which is needed when transferring from Mac OS X to Linux/Windows. Default 0.

- report=X: Specifies how often to update the backup progress in the console, in number of batches transferred. Default 5.

- report_full=X: Specifies how often to write a full progress report in the console, in number of batches transferred. Default 2000.

- try_xwm=[0|1]: Tells cbbackup to transfer documents with their metadata. A value of 0 is only needed when transferring from Couchbase version 1.8.x to 1.8.x. Default 1.

Let's examine some common backup scenarios. Note that because of the eventually persistent nature of Couchbase Server, you can never get a perfectly up-to-date backup from a live cluster. To back up the entire cluster, use the following command line:

```
> cbbackup http://<host>:8091 /<backupfolder> -u <username> -p <password>
```

In our ranter application example, this would produce the following output:

```
[###################] 100.0% (10118/10114 msgs)
bucket: default, msgs transferred...
        :                total |     last |     per sec
batch :                 2082 |     2082 |       466.9
byte  :               688069 |   688069 |   154310.2
msg   :                10118 |    10118 |     2269.1
.
bucket: ranter, msgs transferred...
        :                total |     last |     per sec
batch :                 2083 |     2083 |      1030.7
byte  :               688069 |   688069 |   340459.7
msg   :                10118 |    10118 |      5006.4
done
```

The byte row shows the size of the backed-up data, and the msg row shows the number of backed-up items. To back up a single bucket:

```
> cbbackup http://<host>:8091 /<backupfolder> -u <username> -p <password> -b <bucket>
```

To back up all data on a single node:

```
> cbbackup http://<host>:8091 /<backupfolder> -u <username> -p <password> --single-node
```

Note that this will only back up the data on the specified node. To back up all data in the cluster in this way, you will have to repeat the process on every node.

When backing up data on a single node, it's faster to use a file-store reference rather than a node URL, because cbbackup will copy the data from the data files directly:

```
> cbbackup couchstore-files://<data path> /<backupfolder>
```

Later in this chapter, we'll see how using cbbackup to create a backup directly from Couchbase data files is very handy for retrieving and restoring data from nodes that have been failed over.

To back up all documents with keys that match the pattern user*:

```
> cbbackup http://<host>:8091 /<backupfolder> -u <username> -p <password> -k '^user.*'
```

To split the backup data into *.cbb files of 10 MB each:

```
> cbbackup http://<host>:8091 /<backupfolder> -u <username> -p <password> -x cbb_max_mb=10
```

To back up only the design documents from all buckets:

```
> cbbackup http://<host>:8091 /<backupfolder> -u <username> -p <password> -x design_doc_only=1
```

Using cbrestore to Restore Backed-Up Data

The cbrestore command-line utility restores data and design documents for a single bucket, which must already exist because cbrestore does not create or configure buckets—it only inserts data. To restore multiple buckets, you must call cbrestore multiple times. By default, cbrestore will overwrite any existing items when restoring from backup. Also, unlike cbbackup, cbrestore cannot restore data to just a single node, because there is no way to guarantee that the cluster topology is the same as when the backup was created, or that it's even the same cluster.

The cbrestore tool has the following usage:

```
> cbrestore <backup> <target> [options]
```

The <backup> is the root backup folder and the <target> is a URL of a node in the cluster. cbrestore accepts all of the optional parameters that cbbackup does, plus a few more, as follows:

- -a: Use add instead of set to store documents in order to avoid overwriting existing items.

- -B: Specifies a different destination bucket. By default, the destination bucket is the same as the source bucket specified by the -b parameter.

- -x conflict_resolve=[0|1]: Specifying a value of 0 is the same as using the -a parameter, which will prevent overwriting existing documents.

To restore the backup data into the specified bucket:

```
> cbrestore <backupfolder> http://<host>:8091 -u <username> -p <password> -b <bucket>
```

In our ranter example, we'd see the following output:

```
[####################] 100.0% (10116/10116 msgs)
bucket: default, msgs transferred...
         :            total |       last |     per sec
batch :                 11 |         11 |        13.2
byte  :             688069 |     688069 |    824034.7
msg   :              10116 |      10116 |     12115.0
done
```

To restore into a different bucket than the original source:

```
> cbrestore <backupfolder> http://<host>:8091 -u <username> -p <password> -b <old_bucket> -B
<new_bucket>
```

To restore only keys that do not exist in the destination bucket:

```
> cbrestore <backupfolder> http://<host>:8091 -u <username> -p <password> -b <bucket> -a
```

To restore only keys that match a specific regular expression:

```
> cbrestore <backupfolder> http://<host>:8091 -u <username> -p <password> -b <bucket> -k "<regexp>"
```

For example, to restore only items with keys that start with the string "pymc," which is the prefix for items generated by the cbworkloadgen tool, we'll use the following command:

```
> cbrestore /backup-20140221 http://localhost:8091 -u Administrator -p 123456 -b default -k
"^user.*"
```

Assuming we want to restore the data into the default bucket, we're running the command on one of the machines in the cluster, and the backup is located in the /backup-20140221 folder.

That produces the following output:

```
2014-02-21 08:04:26,086: w0 skipping msg with key: abc4
2014-02-21 08:04:29,618: w0 skipping msg with key: abc3
2014-02-21 08:04:32,763: w0 skipping msg with key: abc2
2014-02-21 08:04:36,269: w0 skipping msg with key: abc1
 [####################] 100.0% (100000/100004 msgs)
bucket: default, msgs transferred...
         :            total |       last |     per sec
batch :                101 |        101 |         7.5
byte  :            6968860 |    6968860 |    520919.4
msg   :             100000 |     100000 |      7475.0
done
```

Using cbtransfer to Transfer Data

The cbbackup and cbrestore utilities are built on top of cbtransfer, which is a lightweight extract-transform-load (ETL) tool that handles transferring data between Couchbase nodes, clusters, and backup files.

You can use cbtransfer to perform backup and restore operations, as well as to transfer data directly between two live Couchbase clusters. In addition to the command-line options we've already seen for cbbackup and cbrestore, you can use the following three optional parameters:

- `--source-vbucket-state=X`: Tells cbtransfer to only transfer data from vBuckets with the specified state, which can be `active` or `replica`. This option only works with a cluster as a data source, and not with a backup file. Default `active`.

- `--destination-vbucket-state=X`: Tells cbtransfer to only transfer data into vBuckets with the specified state, which can be `active` or `replica`. This option only works with a cluster as the target. Default `active`.

- `--destination-operation=X`: Specifies which operation to use for storing the data, which can be `set` or `add`. The default is `set`.

You can use cbtransfer to transfer data between two Couchbase clusters, using the following command:

```
> cbtransfer http://<source>:8091 http://<destination>:8091
```

It's possible to use cbtransfer to create a hot standby by backing up data from the active cluster to the standby. For simple use cases, where loss of some data is tolerable—for example, storing various server and operation logs—this is an adequate solution. However, there is a much better way of creating a hot standby, or a continuous off-site backup that you can restore from, by using XDCR. It's somewhat more complicated to set up, and more resource intensive to keep up, but it allows for much greater backup concurrency, as well as more flexibility in what exactly is backed up. We'll talk about using a second cluster as a backup in Chapter 14.

Backing Up and Restoring Using Data Files

In addition to using the backup and restore utilities, you can back up your data manually by simply copying the data files to another location. To do so, copy the config and data folders to your backup location. By default, the config and data folders are located under /opt/couchbase/var/lib/couchbase on Linux, and under C:\Program Files\Couchbase\Server\var\lib\couchbase on Windows. To restore data from file copies, shut down your cluster, copy the config and data folders back into the couchbase folder, and then start the cluster up again.

While this method of backing up data is extremely simple, it has severe limitations:

- You must shut down the cluster to restore the data.

- The cluster configuration and vBucket map must be identical.

- The node names or IP addresses must remain the same.

- You must have the same version of Couchbase Server installed.

Because of the limitations of this backup method, it is only suitable for non-mission-critical or test deployments. We highly recommend using the cbbackup, cbrestore, or cbtransfer tools for production systems.

Database and View Compaction

Couchbase uses an append-only model to store data and index files. All writes are appended to the end of the file, deleted items are marked as such but remain on disk, and document updates actually mark the old data as invalid and append a new copy at the end of the file. The writer threads take all write requests from the disk-write queue, resolve duplicates, such as when a document is updated multiple times before it's written to disk, appends the document data to the end of the appropriate vBucket file, and updates the mappings between the document ID and its location in the file. Because of their append-only nature, the data and index files become fragmented over time, with unused data still residing where it was first written in the file and the size of the data on disk increasing with each update.

To deal with the fragmentation, Couchbase has a compaction mechanism, which copies all live data into a new file, then switches to using that file and removes the old one. Compaction happens while the cluster is live, so as it runs, new data is appended to the end of the current (old) data file. When Couchbase finishes compacting a file, it copies the newly accumulated data over as well.

Couchbase stores the data for each vBucket in a separate data file. Each file is compacted separately, and the compaction process can be stopped and resumed later:

```
/opt/couchbase/var/lib/couchbase/data/default> ls
0.couch.2      264.couch.2  44.couch.2   635.couch.1  820.couch.1
1000.couch.1   265.couch.1  450.couch.1  636.couch.1  821.couch.1
1001.couch.1   266.couch.1  451.couch.1  637.couch.1  822.couch.1
1002.couch.1   267.couch.2  452.couch.1  638.couch.1  823.couch.1
1003.couch.1   268.couch.1  453.couch.1  639.couch.1  ...
```

Dealing with Compaction

There are several ways to monitor data fragmentation and to trigger compaction. The simplest but most labor-intensive way is to manually monitor your buckets and views and launch compaction from the web administration console. We'll talk about monitoring all aspects of your cluster in the next chapter, so for now we'll only see how to monitor statistics related to data fragmentation.

In the administration console, click on the name of a node in the Server Nodes tab, or on the name of a bucket in the Data Buckets tab, to open the monitoring view for that node and bucket. In the monitoring view, you will discover an overwhelming number of graphs showing every possible statistic about your cluster. The ones we're specifically interested in are the document data and view size indicators under the Summary category and the per-view statistics found just below that, as shown in Figures 10-11 and 10-12.

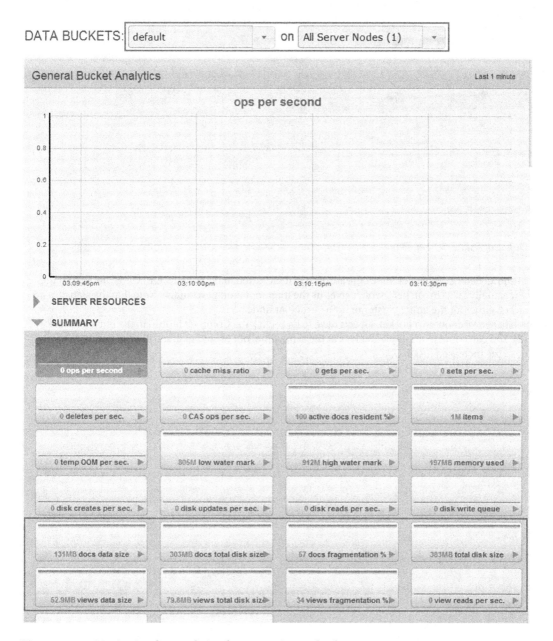

Figure 10-11. *Monitoring data and view fragmentation per bucket*

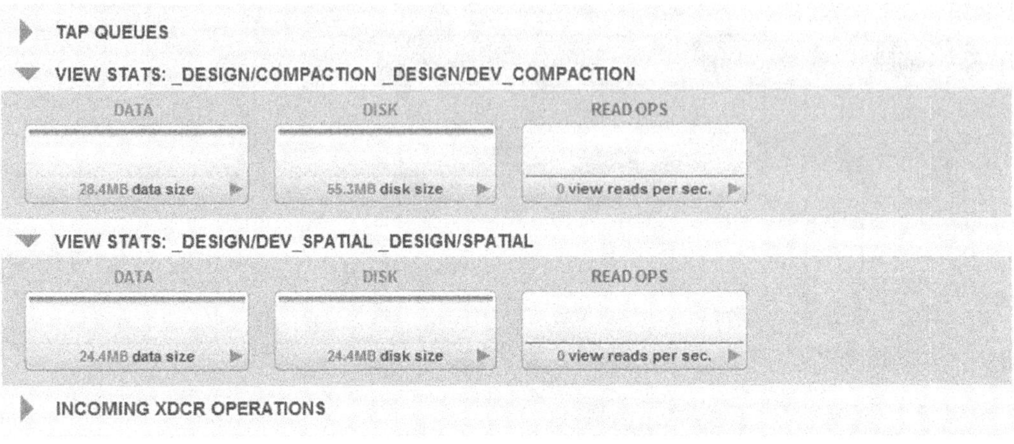

Figure 10-12. *Disk usage statistics per view*

Figure 10-11 shows detailed statistics about the amount of data stored in documents and views, and about the amount of space it actually takes up on disk, which gives us the fragmentation percentage. Note that the statistics are displayed per bucket, either for the entire cluster or for a particular node.

To perform data compaction on a bucket, all you have to do is click the Compact button in the bucket details (see Figure 10-13). You can compact multiple buckets at the same time, but of course that will impact cluster performance due to the increased disk I/O.

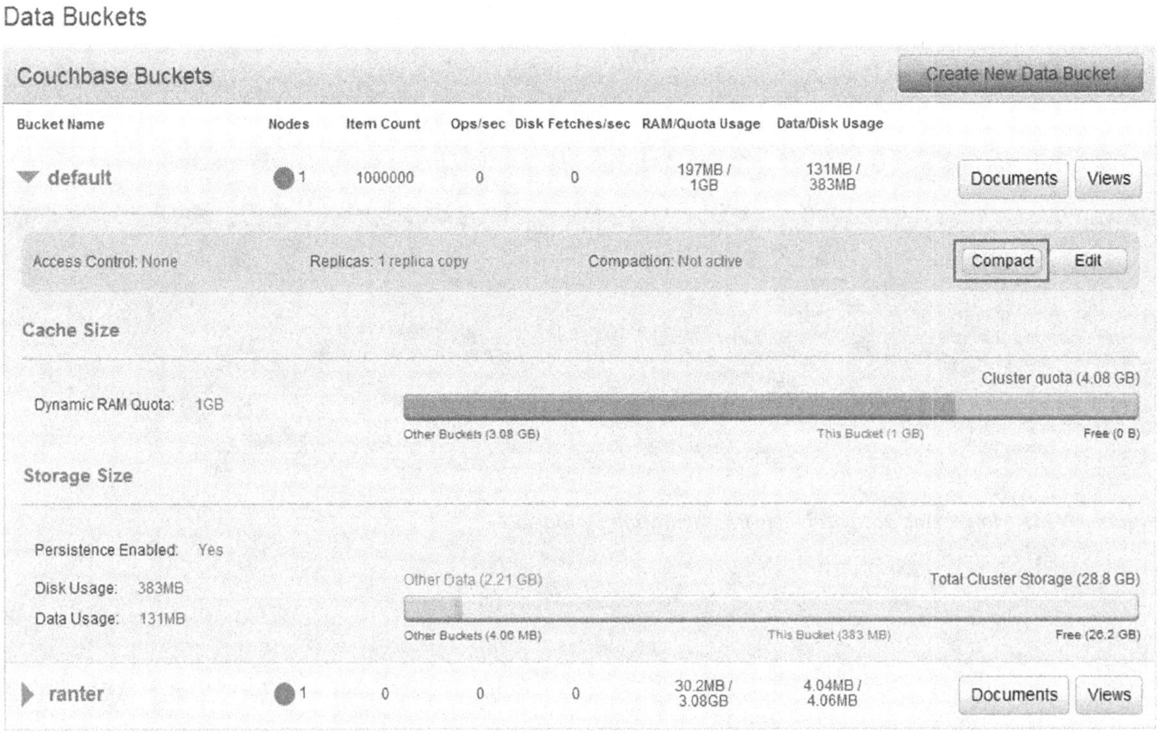

Figure 10-13. *Compacting a bucket*

Because compaction actually copies all data into a new location, it can potentially require 100% more disk space than is taken up by your data and views to store side-by-side copies of the fragmented and defragmented data.

Auto-Compaction

Manually running compaction is not a very reliable way of dealing with data and view fragmentation, especially in a large or very active cluster. Couchbase provides a way to perform compaction automatically when fragmentation reaches a certain level. By default, auto-compaction is enabled globally and is set to run whenever a bucket reaches 30% fragmentation.

As you can see in Figure 10-14, you can configure auto-compaction to run when the fragmentation percentage of a bucket or view reaches a predefined level. For example, assuming you have a bucket with 100 MB of data, with the default 30% fragmentation setting compaction would be triggered when the bucket's data occupies 130 MB or more. Additionally, you can set an auto-compaction trigger based on the size, in megabytes, of the data on disk.

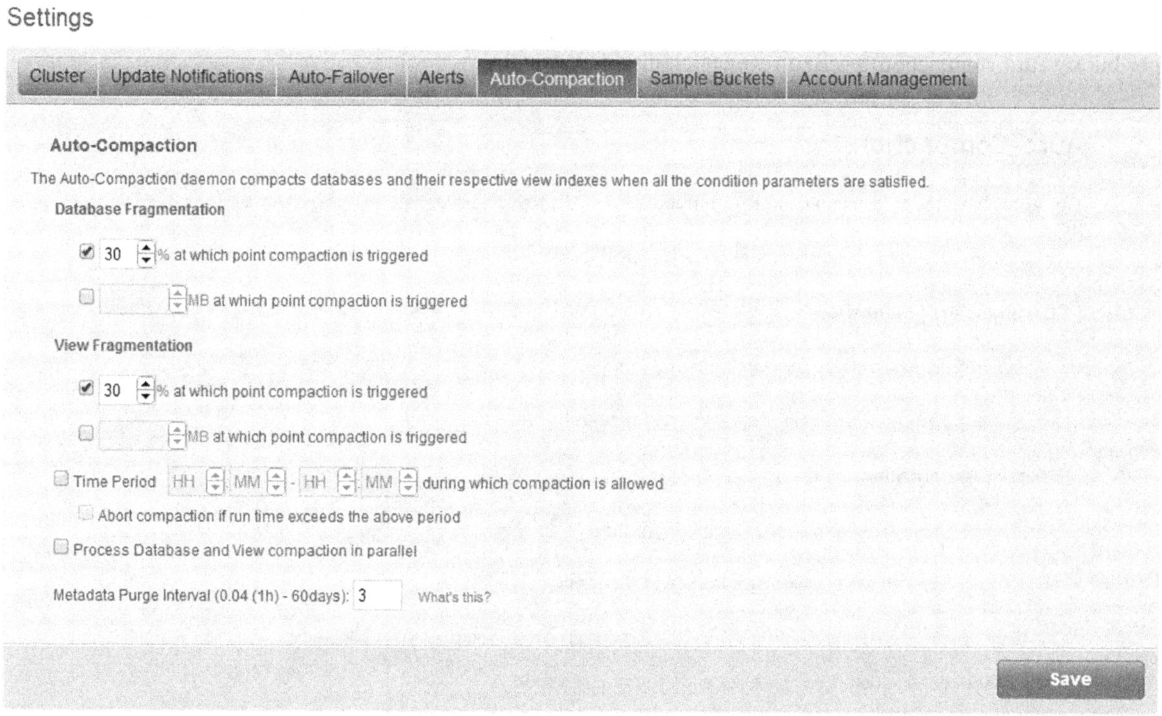

Settings

| Cluster | Update Notifications | Auto-Failover | Alerts | Auto-Compaction | Sample Buckets | Account Management |

Auto-Compaction

The Auto-Compaction daemon compacts databases and their respective view indexes when all the condition parameters are satisfied.

Database Fragmentation

☑ 30 ⬍ % at which point compaction is triggered

☐ ⬍ MB at which point compaction is triggered

View Fragmentation

☑ 30 ⬍ % at which point compaction is triggered

☐ ⬍ MB at which point compaction is triggered

☐ Time Period HH ⬍ : MM ⬍ - HH ⬍ : MM ⬍ during which compaction is allowed

    ☐ Abort compaction if run time exceeds the above period

☐ Process Database and View compaction in parallel

Metadata Purge Interval (0.04 (1h) - 60days): 3   What's this?

Save

Figure 10-14. *Default auto-compaction settings*

Because compaction is a very CPU- and I/O-intensive process, it's usually best to compact your database during off-peak hours. You can specify the time during which auto-compaction can be started. If Couchbase detects that the fragmentation threshold has been reached, it will delay automatic compaction until the specified time. If you also enable the "abort compaction" setting, then auto-compaction will be stopped once the allocated time period elapses. Otherwise, compaction will run to completion, which can extend beyond off-peak hours and degrade the cluster performance for longer than expected.

Keep in mind that if you have a consistently high write load, and you set an auto-compaction time window that is too short, it is possible that compaction will never catch up to the fragmentation because it will keep getting interrupted each day. If you see that auto-compaction lags behind the database fragmentation level, this is a sign that you may need to add more nodes to the cluster to spread out the disk I/O load. However, if your write load is inconsistent, you can deal with spikes in fragmentation by configuring auto-compaction to run incrementally. For example, let's say that your normal write activity requires one hour of compaction a day, but every Monday your application updates a large chunk of the data that requires five hours to defragment. You can set auto-compaction to run for two hours every night and then be automatically aborted. This way the Monday fragmentation spike will be gradually defragmented over most of the week, rather than in one long, performance-crushing session.

In addition to the fragmentation level and time settings, you can enable parallel data and view compaction. If your Couchbase Server is configured to store data and views on separate volumes, which is highly recommended, then compacting data and views in parallel will reduce the total time it takes for the process to complete.

The last setting in the auto-compaction tab controls the metadata purge interval. Couchbase stores "tombstones"—markers in the data files—for deleted and expired items, which it uses to maintain consistency in XDCR and view processing. Tombstones hold the key and some metadata of the removed item, which can cause the data files to grow quickly if there are many deletions from the database. After each purge interval elapses, Couchbase will remove the tombstones when it compacts the database. Setting the purge interval much lower than the default three days may result in inconsistent items showing up in views or clusters connected through XDCR. Setting it much higher will cause the data files to use much more disk space than is strictly necessary.

You can override the global settings when creating or editing a bucket, as shown in Figure 10-15. If you configure per-bucket auto-compaction, it will run even if it is disabled globally.

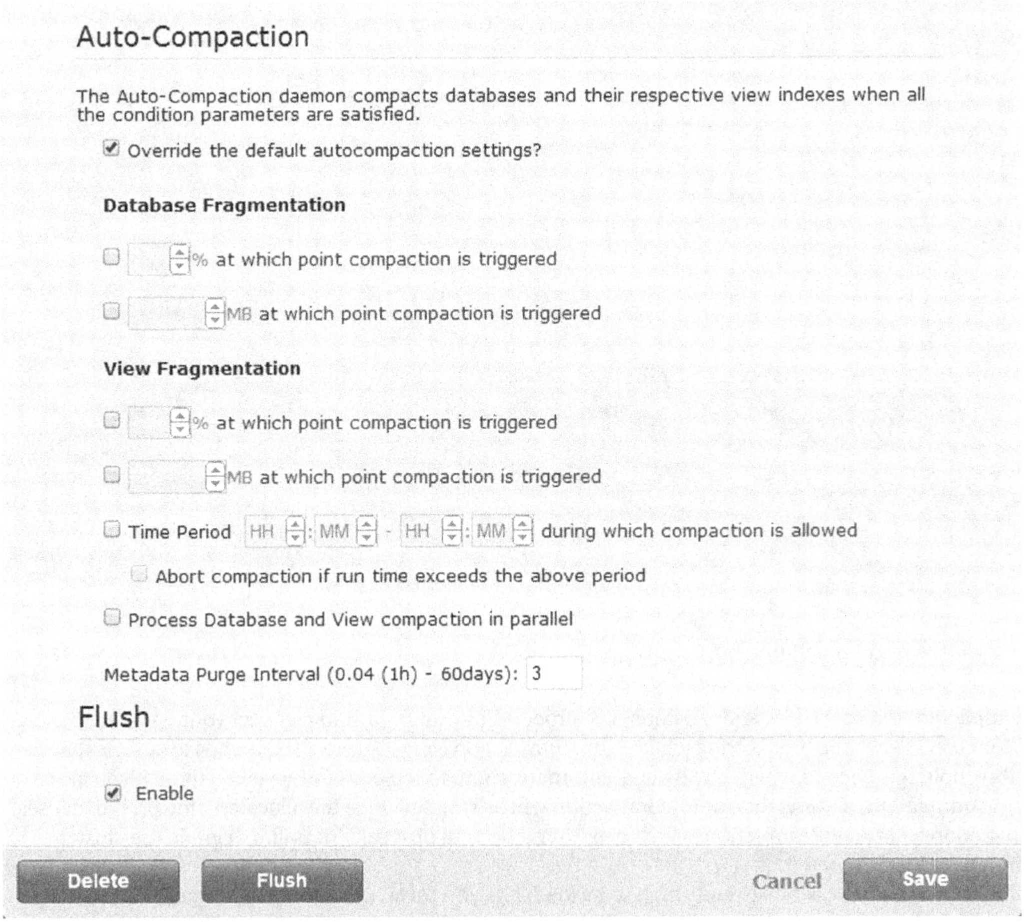

Auto-Compaction

The Auto-Compaction daemon compacts databases and their respective view indexes when all the condition parameters are satisfied.

☑ Override the default autocompaction settings?

Database Fragmentation

☐ [⇕]% at which point compaction is triggered

☐ [⇕ MB] at which point compaction is triggered

View Fragmentation

☐ [⇕]% at which point compaction is triggered

☐ [⇕ MB] at which point compaction is triggered

☐ Time Period [HH ⇕]: [MM ⇕] - [HH ⇕]: [MM ⇕] during which compaction is allowed

  ☐ Abort compaction if run time exceeds the above period

☐ Process Database and View compaction in parallel

Metadata Purge Interval (0.04 (1h) - 60days): 3

Flush

☑ Enable

[Delete]   [Flush]   Cancel   [Save]

Figure 10-15. Overriding auto-compaction per bucket

If you have multiple buckets configured for timed auto-compaction, we recommend staggering the time periods during which each bucket performs its compaction to spread the disk I/O load more evenly.

■ **Note**   Spatial views are not compacted automatically, so you must compact them manually using the HTTP API. We'll talk about the command-line tools and the HTTP API for compaction in just a moment.

To adjust auto-compaction settings from the command line, use the couchbase-cli tool with the setting-compaction option. You can provide the following parameters:

- `--compaction-db-percentage=X`: Trigger data compaction when fragmentation reaches X percent.

- `--compaction-db-size=X`: Trigger data compaction when data size on disk reaches X megabytes.

- `--compaction-view-percentage=X`: Trigger view compaction when fragmentation reaches X percent.

- `--compaction-view-size=X`: Trigger view compaction when view size on disk reaches X megabytes.

- `--compaction-period-from=HH:MM`: Delay compaction until the specified time.

- `--compaction-period-to=HH:MM`: Do not trigger compaction after the specified time.

- `--enable-compaction-abort=[0|1]`: Set to 1 to abort compaction when the specified time period ends.

- `--enable-compaction-parallel=[0|1]`: Set to 1 to compact data and views in parallel.

For example, to set auto-compaction to run only between midnight and 2AM, if the fragmentation level reaches 40%, and to defragment data and views in parallel, you would use the following command:

```
> couchbase-cli setting-compaction -c <host> -u <user> -p <password> --compaction-db-percentage=40
--compaction-view-percentage=40 --compaction-period-from=00:00 --compaction-period-to=02:00
--enable-compaction-abort=1 --enable-compaction-parallel=1
```

That should result in the following output:

```
SUCCESS: set compaction settings
```

■ **Note**   The setting-compaction option overwrites the auto-compaction settings, which means that you must specify all of the parameters you want to enable. All other parameters will be set as disabled, i.e., running the command `couchbase-cli setting-compaction` without any parameters will turn auto-compaction off.

Triggering Compaction Externally

Couchbase provides command-line tools and an HTTP API for monitoring and performing compaction. You can get data and view fragmentation statistics for a particular bucket through the HTTP API and use those statistics to decide when to run compaction.

To retrieve bucket statistics, issue a GET request to the following URL: http://<host>:8091/pools/default/buckets/<bucket_name>/stats

This will return a very large JSON document containing detailed statistics about the bucket, including data and view fragmentation. By default, Couchbase returns statistics for the last minute, at a resolution of one second. You can increase the time span with the zoom or haveTStamp parameters. The zoom parameter defines the interval for which Couchbase will return the data and can be: minute, hour, day, week, month, or year. The haveTStamp parameter specifies the time, as a UNIX epoch timestamp in milliseconds, from which Couchbase will return the data. Combining both parameters will cause Couchbase to return data for a specific time span. For example, to get statistics for the hour starting from midnight of 1/1/2014, we would use the following GET request:

```
> curl -u <user>:<password>  -d 'zoom=hour&haveTStamp=1388534400000' http://<host>:8091/pools/
default/buckets/<bucket_name>/stats
```

The relevant data in our case will look similar to the following:

```
{
  "op":{
    "samples":{
      "couch_docs_fragmentation":[53,53,53,53, ...],
      "couch_views_fragmentation":[8,8,8,8, ...],
      ... more statistics ...
    },
    "samplesCount":900,
    "isPersistent":true,
    "lastTStamp":1388534400000',
    "interval":1000
  },
}
```

We omitted all the other statistics in the JSON document for brevity, but they include things like CPU and disk usage, number of items in the disk-write queue, and so on. You can use all of these statistics to decide when compaction is necessary, and also when it will be the least disruptive to cluster performance.

You can start compaction on a particular bucket with the command-line tool or through the HTTP API. To start compaction on a particular bucket with the couchbase-cli utility:

```
> couchbase-cli bucket-compact -c <host> -b <bucket_name>
```

You can also specify the --data-only or --view-only parameters to compact only the bucket data or views, respectively.

To compact a bucket with the HTTP API, issue the following POST request:

```
> curl -u <user>:<password> -X POST
http://localhost:8091/pools/default/buckets/<bucket_name>/controller/compactBucket
```

To stop compaction:

```
> curl -u <user>:<password> -X POST
http://localhost:8091/pools/default/buckets/<bucket_name>/controller/cancelBucketCompaction
```

As mentioned earlier, spatial views can only be compact manually. To compact a spatial view, you must issue a POST request, with Content-Type header of application/json, to the following URL:
http://<host>:8092/<bucket_name>/_design/<design_doc_name>/_spatial/_compact

Note that in this case the port is 8092, which is the port used by view queries. The <design_doc_name> parameter is the name of the design document that contains the spatial view you want to compact.

Compaction in Action

Let's look at an example of database fragmentation and compaction in action. The default auto-compaction threshold in Couchbase is 30% fragmentation, so we'll leave it as is for now. We'll start by creating a brand-new bucket, named default, and check how much disk space the data files take:

```
> du -h
4.0K    ./.delete
1.4M    ./default
1.5M    .
```

As you can see, other than some basic scaffolding files, the new bucket uses practically no disk space, which is as expected.

Next, load one million JSON documents into the bucket using the cbworkloadgen tool:

```
[dr-evil@secretlair]> cbworkloadgen -j -i 1000000 -t 4
 [###################] 100.0% (4209528/estimated 4210524 msgs)
bucket: default, msgs transferred...
        :                total |      last |    per sec
byte    :           301384000 | 301384000 |  834729.4
done

> du -h
4.0K    ./.delete
157M    ./default
157M    .
```

Looking at the bucket in the web console, you can see that there is already some data fragmentation. As you can see in Figures 10-16 and 10-17, 131 MB of data actually take up 164 MB on disk, which is 20% fragmentation.

Data Buckets

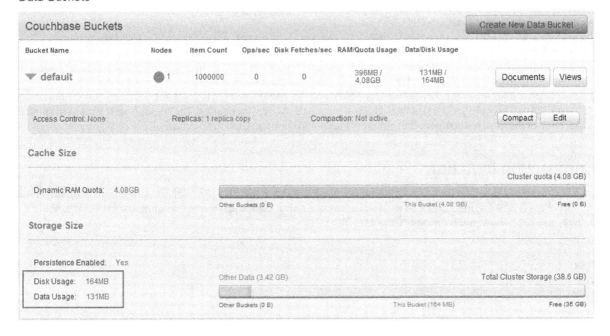

Figure 10-16. *Bucket disk usage*

Figure 10-17. *Bucket fragmentation percentage*

We run cbworkloadgen again and insert the same one million items. Because cbworkloadgen creates key names based on the item index (pymc0, pymc1, ... pymc1000000), this actually updates each item once. About a quarter of the way through the process, data fragmentation passed the 30% threshold and auto-compaction kicked in (see Figure 10-18).

Figure 10-18. *Auto-compaction*

As cbworkloadgen continues to update items, fragmentation will repeatedly pass 30%, and so auto-compaction will run multiple times. This second cbworkloadgen run also takes much longer because of the continuously running compaction in the background. If we increase the auto-compaction threshold, or turn it off entirely, the process will finish much faster, but the increase in fragmentation will mean that the data will take up much more space on disk.

After the cbworkloadgen run finishes we'll have some, but less than 30%, fragmentation. We can compact the bucket manually, which, if no other document changes happen in the meantime, will bring fragmentation close to 0%.

As you can see in Figure 10-19, the data fragmentation after compaction is only 1%. The extra disk use is now due to the access log file, which is how Couchbase tracks the most frequently accessed items so they can be loaded into memory during server warm-up. It resides in the data folder and wasn't present before we started updating existing items:

```
-rw-rw---- 1 couchbase couchbase 22999040 Feb 21 10:00 access.log
```

Figure 10-19. *After compaction*

■ **Note**   One thing to take away from this experiment is that if you intend to do a large bulk data insert, or if you want to benchmark the performance of your cluster, it may be a good idea to temporarily turn off auto-compaction to avoid prolonging the process due to repeated compactions. Couchbase will perform a full compaction after you turn it back on, which will have less total impact on performance.

Now let's take a quick look at view fragmentation. We create a design document with two simple views: one indexes our generated data by the age property and the other by the name property:

```
function (doc, meta) {
 emit(doc.age, null);
}

function (doc, meta) {
 emit(doc.name, null);
}
```

We then publish the views to production, which causes Couchbase to index our existing one million items. As you can see in Figure 10-20, this produces 36.5 MB of index data without any fragmentation.

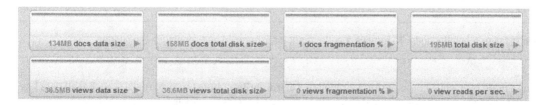

Figure 10-20. *Freshly created views*

Next, we turn off auto-compaction and update each of the million documents, which causes Couchbase to update the index as the items are inserted. As you can see in Figure 10-21, the index fragmentation level rises to just over 50%—which makes sense, since we essentially created a new copy of each item in the index, doubling its size on disk.

Figure 10-21. *View fragmentation after bulk update*

When we re-enable automatic view compaction, Couchbase will immediately compact the design document that holds our views, as you can see in Figure 10-22.

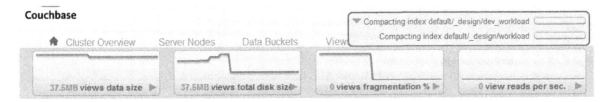

Figure 10-22. *View compaction*

Failover

When you create a data bucket with one or more replicas, Couchbase stores copies of each item on multiple nodes. Then, if a node fails, we can put it into a "failover" state, which causes Couchbase to promote the replicated data on other nodes to active status. Putting a node into failover immediately removes it from the cluster. Note that failover does not trigger a rebalance, so until you rebalance the cluster, all the active data that was on the failed node will effectively have one less replica copy in the cluster. This also means that the maximum number of nodes you can fail over safely, without rebalancing the cluster in between, is determined by the smallest number of replica copies you configured for buckets in your cluster—that is, if you have a bucket with two replicas, failing one node promotes replicas of all the vBuckets that belonged to that node to active. Failing a second node will promote copies of that node's vBuckets to active. At this point, at least some of the vBuckets will only have the active data set available, and no more copies remaining, so failing over a third node will likely result in data loss.

It is important to understand that failover is completely different from removing a node from the cluster, as we discussed earlier. When you mark a node for removal, it continues to operate and serve clients until you rebalance the cluster, which safely moves all the data to other nodes and updates the cluster map accordingly. Only then is the node actually removed from the cluster. There is no interruption of service and no chance of data loss during the removal process. On the other hand, when a node is failed over, it is removed immediately, and any data on that node that hasn't been replicated or persisted to disk will most likely be lost.

■ **Note** Never fail over a healthy node. To remove a node, mark it for removal and rebalance the cluster.

After failing a node over, you should perform a rebalance at the earliest opportunity to make sure that all data has the expected number of copies and that the load is equally distributed across the cluster.

Automatic Failover

You can configure Couchbase to fail a node over automatically under certain conditions. To enable automatic failover, in the Web Console go to the Settings tab, click on Auto-Failover, and check the Enable auto-failover box, as shown in Figure 10-23. The only other setting you can change is the time (in seconds) that the cluster will wait before failing an unresponsive node. The minimum timeout is 30 seconds; during this time, Couchbase pings the suspected node multiple times to make sure that the node is actually down, rather than just temporarily unavailable or busy.

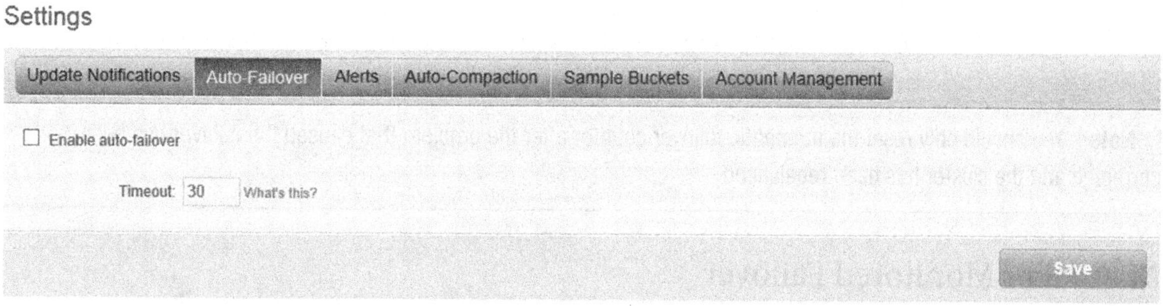

Settings

| Update Notifications | Auto-Failover | Alerts | Auto-Compaction | Sample Buckets | Account Management |

☐ Enable auto-failover

Timeout: 30   What's this?

Save

Figure 10-23. *Automatic failover*

Automatically failing nodes is not without problems. Because failing over a node increases the load on the rest of the nodes, letting auto-failover run unchecked could potentially result in a chain reaction that would take down the entire cluster, also known as the Thundering Herd problem. In a network partition scenario, each side of the partition could fail over the nodes on the other side, and thus form two separate clusters. Assuming there is enough capacity on each side, the two clusters would quickly lose consistency with each other and would be very difficult to reconcile afterwards. In both of these cases, a better solution would be a manual or monitored failover, which we'll talk about in just a moment.

To avoid failure cascades and nodes deciding to form clusters of their own, Couchbase will only ever automatically fail over one node in a row. After one node is failed over automatically, the failover counter must be reset to 0 in order to resume auto-failover functionality. Furthermore, automatic failover will only work on clusters with at least three active nodes.

In addition to using the web console to configure automatic failover, you can use the command-line tool:

```
> couchbase-cli setting-autofailover -c localhost  -u Administrator -p 123456 --enable-auto-
failover=1 --auto-failover-timeout=30
```

Pass 0 as the enable-auto-failover parameter to disable auto-failover, or 1 to enable it. Or issue the following POST request to the HTTP API:

```
> curl -i -u <username>:<password> -d 'enabled=true&timeout=30' http://<host>:8091/settings/
autoFailover
```

Change the enabled and timeout parameters appropriately. To get details about the automatic failover configuration, issue the following GET request:

```
> curl -u <username>:<password> http://<host>:8091/settings/autoFailover
```

This returns a JSON object, similar to the following:

```
{"enabled":true,"timeout":30,"count":0}
```

The count property indicates whether a node in the cluster has been automatically failed over. A count of 1 means a node has been failed over and that no further automatic failovers will occur until the counter has been reset. You can reset the counter through the HTTP API like so:

```
> curl -X POST -i -u <username>:<password> http://<host>:8091/settings/autoFailover/resetCount
```

■ **Note**   You should only reset the automatic failover counter after the problem that caused the failover has been corrected and the cluster has been rebalanced.

Manual or Monitored Failover

Because of the potential implications of node failover, such as data loss or interruption of service, some organizations mandate that human intervention is required. In such cases, a monitoring solution of some sort is needed to notify the responsible parties of the need for failover. We'll talk about configuring alerts and notifications in Couchbase later in this chapter. You can fail a node over manually at any time by using the web console, the couchbase-cli command-line tool, or the HTTP API.

Alternatively, you can use an external monitoring system to track the state of your Couchbase cluster. Unlike internal Couchbase monitoring, which is only concerned with the state of nodes in the cluster, and external system would be able to take other factors into account when deciding whether to fail a node over. For example, an external system could detect a network partition or partial failure, and determine that failing some of the nodes in the cluster will not actually do anything useful. Or check the total load on the machines in the cluster, and decide whether it will support the increased load caused by failing a misbehaving node, before failing that node. Such an external solution can use the monitoring HTTP API to retrieve statistics about the cluster, and make changes when necessary. We'll learn more about the various ways to monitor Couchbase further in this chapter.

To fail a node through the web console, click the Fail Over button next to the desired node on the Server Nodes tab, as shown in Figure 10-24.

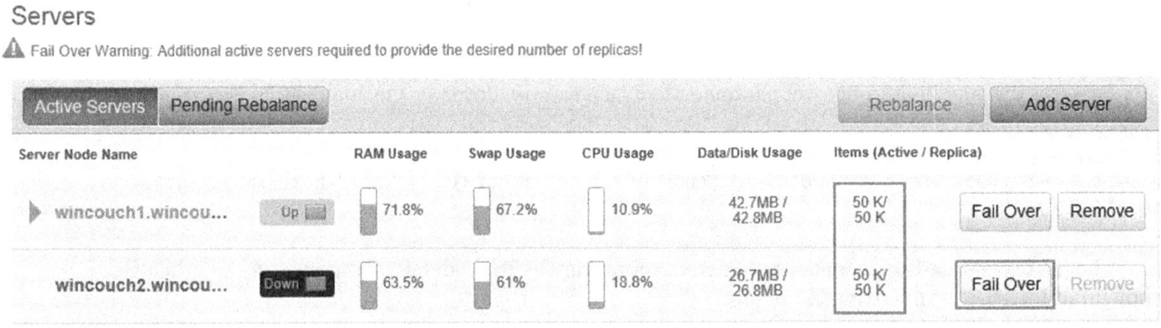

Figure 10-24. Triggering node failover

As you can see in Figure 10-25, after failing a node over, the replica items in the remaining nodes become active.

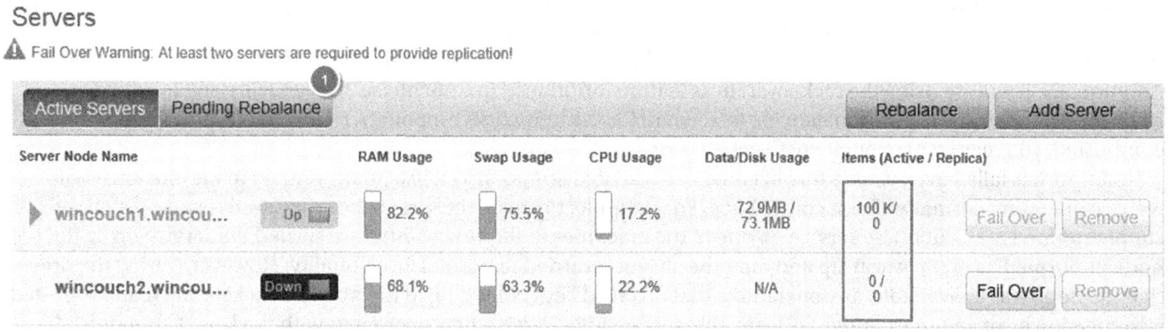

Servers

⚠ Fail Over Warning: At least two servers are required to provide replication!

Server Node Name			RAM Usage	Swap Usage	CPU Usage	Data/Disk Usage	Items (Active / Replica)		
▶ wincouch1.wincou...	Up		82.2%	75.5%	17.2%	72.9MB / 73.1MB	100 K/ 0	Fail Over	Remove
wincouch2.wincou...	Down		68.1%	63.3%	22.2%	N/A	0 / 0	Fail Over	Remove

[Active Servers] [Pending Rebalance ①] ... [Rebalance] [Add Server]

Figure 10-25. *After node failover*

Alternatively, use the following couchbase-cli command where <host> is the address of a working node in the cluster, and <failed_host> is the address of the node to fail over:

```
> couchbase-cli failover -c <host> -u <username> -p <password> --server-failover=<failed_host>
```

Or use the following POST request to the URL http://<host>:8091/controller/failOver and provide the otpNode parameter, which is the internal name of the node to fail over:

```
> curl -v -X POST -u <username>:<password> http://<host>:8091/controller/failOver -d otpNode=<otp_name>
```

In this case <otp_name> is the internal node name, which is usually in the format <ns_x@host>. To get the internal node names, use a GET request to retrieve the following URL: http://<host>:8091/pools/default. This will return a JSON object with detailed information about the cluster, including the internal node names, like the results below:

```
{
    "storageTotals": ...,
    "name": "default",
    "alerts": [],
    "alertsSilenceURL": "/controller/resetAlerts?token=0",
    "nodes": [
        {
            "otpNode": "ns_1@127.0.0.1",
            "hostname": "127.0.0.1:8091",
            ... more details ...
        }
    ],
    ... more details ...
}
```

Dealing with Failed Nodes

When a node fails, the capacity of the cluster is reduced. If you determine that after failing over a node the remaining capacity is sufficient to continue normal operation, you should perform a rebalance as soon as possible. If the remaining capacity is insufficient, you will want to add one or more nodes to the cluster first and then rebalance. Additionally, if you are using the rack-awareness feature introduced in Couchbase 2.5, you will need to adjust or re-create server groups before rebalancing to account for the new cluster topology. (If the whole rack spontaneously combusted, you may want to put it out first.)

Unless it is failed over, a node that becomes unavailable temporarily will actually remain in the cluster; it will resume operating normally after it comes back. For example, to create the screenshot you saw in Figure 10-24, we simply stopped the Couchbase service on one of the machines in the cluster. After we started the service up again, the node performed its initial warm-up and then the cluster returned to normal functionality. However, during the time that the node was unavailable, any operations that involved keys belonging to the node's vBuckets failed and returned a connection error. In our example, we were able successfully create a new document with the key "3," but not "1," because the key "1" happened to belong to a vBucket on the stopped node.

When you do fail a node over, once you have corrected the problem with the node you may want to have it rejoin the cluster. Assuming the storage device wasn't the cause of failure, the persisted data will still exist on the node. However, because the node was removed from the cluster on failover, replicas of its vBuckets were activated on other nodes, and the cluster map was updated accordingly. Thus the data on the failed node is no longer synchronized with the rest of the cluster and cannot be brought back into sync. When you add a failed-over node back to the cluster, Couchbase will treat is just like any new node and will destroy any existing data files.

You have the following options for preserving the data on the failed node before you add it back to the cluster. You can copy the data files somewhere as a backup. You can use the cbbackup or cbtransfer command-line tools, which we covered in the previous chapter, to restore documents from the data files of the failed node. With cbbackup, you can create a backup file in the condensed Couchbase backup formatfrom the data files, and later use this backup to restore the data to the cluster. With cbtransfer, you can copy data directly from the data files to a functioning cluster. Note, however, that there is no built-in conflict-resolution mechanism for restoring backed-up documents that have been changed in the active cluster—your options are to overwrite, not restore, or write your own custom mechanism for reconciling conflicting changes. In the event of data loss, such as when you had fewer replica copies than failed nodes, you can either restore all documents, skipping the ones that already exist, or filter by vBucket or key.

Another option for dealing with data loss due to failed nodes is to recover data from a remote cluster with the cbrecovery command-line tool. We talk about using XDCR as a backup in Chapter 13.

Couchbase will detect when a failed-over node has come back online and will display a notification in the web console, offering to add it back to the cluster, as you can see in Figure 10-26. This is essentially the same as adding the node back manually—it will still be treated as a brand-new node.

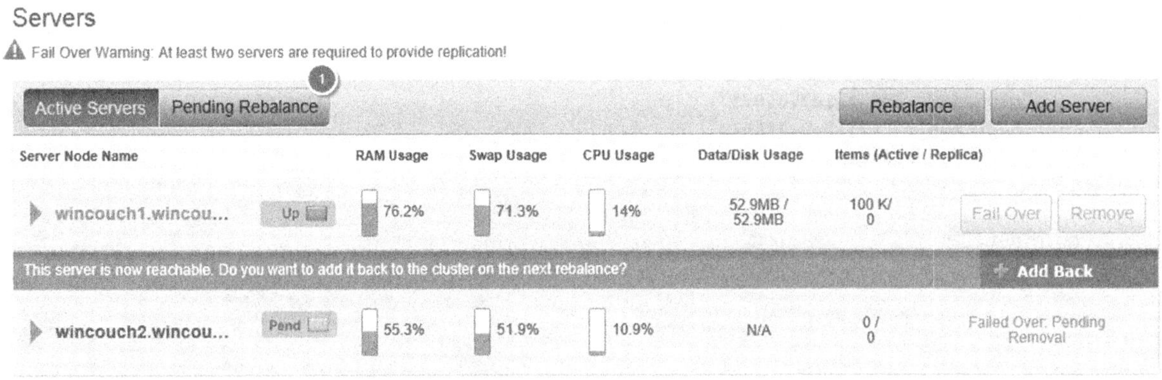

Servers

⚠ Fail Over Warning: At least two servers are required to provide replication!

Server Node Name		RAM Usage	Swap Usage	CPU Usage	Data/Disk Usage	Items (Active / Replica)	
▶ wincouch1.wincou...	Up	76.2%	71.3%	14%	52.9MB / 52.9MB	100 K/ 0	Fail Over Remove
This server is now reachable. Do you want to add it back to the cluster on the next rebalance?							✛ Add Back
▶ wincouch2.wincou...	Pend	55.3%	51.9%	10.9%	N/A	0 / 0	Failed Over: Pending Removal

[Active Servers] [Pending Rebalance] [Rebalance] [Add Server]

Figure 10-26. Adding back a failed node

Summary

We covered quite a few administration-related topics in this chapter. We learned how to perform the crucial administration operations of adding and removing nodes from a Couchbase cluster, both of which require performing a rebalance. The rebalance operation moves active and replica data around so as to spread the load evenly across all nodes. It also restores missing replica copies of data, which have been promoted to active following a node failover. This brings us to dealing with node failures and various approaches to manual and automatic failover, which we covered at the end of this chapter. Along the way we learned how to back up and restore data and how to export data for external use. In addition, we examined the implications of Couchbase's file-storage mechanism, which requires periodic data compaction to reclaim wasted disk space.

CHAPTER 11

Monitoring and Best Practices

Couchbase Server has a slick and user-friendly UI, which makes it easy to set up and use, but under the deceptively simple surface lies a whole system of complex and interconnected mechanisms. Luckily, this complex system offers multiple ways to monitor its behavior along with a huge number of switches and settings to tweak, ranging in effect from subtle to very profound.

You need to monitor Couchbase at the machine level, including system RAM and CPU use, disk I/O, and network throughput for every node, as well as for the cluster as a whole. You also need to monitor what's going on inside each node, including RAM use per bucket, client operations and number of connections, disk reads, and data fragmentation. And, going even deeper, you need to monitor a range of statistics, such as the size of the disk-write and replication queues, the queue fill and drain rates, the actual working set as a percentage of items resident in memory, XDCR traffic and processing, view reads, and more. Using all of this information, you can diagnose the behavior of your Couchbase cluster and even predict and prevent problems before they happen.

Less Obvious Couchbase Mechanisms

In addition to exhaustively detailed statistics, Couchbase also gives you a host of (metaphorical) buttons to push and knobs to tweak—everything from the obvious, like RAM quotas and number of read/write threads, to the obscure, like the exact threshold at which Couchbase begins to return out-of-memory errors to clients.

Before we get to the fun part of looking at dozens of little graphs moving up and down, we need to talk about some of the less obvious Couchbase mechanisms.

Replication and Queues

We've talked about replication in Couchbase buckets and the fact that the in-memory caching layer is decoupled from disk I/O. Changes are replicated to other nodes in the cluster through a replication queue and also persisted to disk through a write queue. However, the increased reliability that replication provides comes with a cost—the higher the replication factor, the more data Couchbase will need to transfer between nodes and persist to disk. Replication is one of the biggest factors in the performance of your cluster and needs to be monitored carefully.

Replication within a Couchbase cluster is handled in a peer-to-peer manner. There is no special master node that decides how to route the data. Each node holds both active and replica data. The active data are items that belong to one of the active vBuckets for that node and have been sent directly to the node from a client; the replica data are items that belong to one of the replica vBuckets for that node and have been sent from other nodes. When an item is sent from a client to a node, it adds or updates the item in the memory cache, inserts it into the disk-write queue, and also into the replica queue. As it processes the replication queue, the node consults the cluster map and sends the item to the node or nodes responsible for that item's replica vBucket. When the replica copy of the item arrives at another node, it will be placed or updated in the memory cache and then inserted into that node's disk-write queue.

Couchbase uses the TAP protocol for internal data transfers. Nodes in a cluster use TAP streams to send data, such as replication and rebalance traffic, to each other. When data is sent to a node, it puts both active and replica items into the same disk-write queue. If there are too many items waiting to be written to disk, a node can send a "back off" message to other nodes, which will cause them to reduce the rate at which they send replica items from their queues to the node in question. The back-off message pauses the replication and rebalance TAP streams for five seconds. Because this behavior essentially prioritizes active data incoming from clients over replica data incoming from other nodes, if the disk-write throughput is insufficient to keep up with both active and replica writes, nodes will keep sending back-off messages to each other. This will help the nodes to persist active data to disk faster, but will cause TAP queues throughout the cluster to grow continuously. By default, nodes will begin sending back-off messages when the disk-write queue reaches 1 million items, or 10% of the total items in the destination node, whichever is highest.

Changing these values can help you fine-tune the behavior of your cluster. Lowering the threshold will, on the one hand, effectively prioritize writing active items to disk faster, because when the write queue reaches the back-off threshold, replication will be slowed down. On the other hand, increasing the back-off threshold will increase data durability by ensuring that data is replicated to other nodes faster, at the cost of increasing the time it takes for active items to be persisted to disk. Of course, this is only relevant when the amount of incoming data exceeds the immediate disk-write capacity.

You can change the back-off behavior per bucket, per node, using the cbepctl tool. Here's how to change the minimum number of items in the disk queue before nodes begin sending back-off messages to each other:

```
> cbepctl <host>:11210 -b <bucket> -p <bucket_password> set tap_param tap_throttle_queue_cap
<number>
```

Note that the command uses port 11210, which is the default binary statistics port. The number parameter can be any positive integer, or the string infinite, which will remove the back-off threshold entirely. To change the threshold as a percentage of items in the destination node:

```
> cbepctl <host>:11210 -b <bucket> -p <bucket_password> set tap_param tap_throttle_cap_pcnt <number>
```

The number parameter in this case is a positive integer between 0 and 100.

In addition to the size of the disk-write queue, you can also set a memory-usage-based threshold for delaying TAP queues. To set the percentage of memory that has to be in use before a node begins sending back-off messages, use the command:

```
> cbepctl <host>:11210 -b <bucket> -p <bucket_password> set tap_param tap_throttle_threshold
<number>
```

where the number parameter is a positive integer between 0 and 100.

■ **Note** The TAP queue back-off changes are configured on a per node, per bucket basis. If you want to change the behavior of every node in the cluster, you will need to repeat the command for every node and/or bucket.

You can check the current value of the various tap-related parameters with the cbstats tool:

```
> cbstats <host>:11210 -b <bucket> -p <bucket_password> all | grep tap
```

```
ep_tap_ack_grace_period:                300
ep_tap_ack_initial_sequence_number:     1
ep_tap_ack_interval:                    1000
ep_tap_ack_window_size:                 10
ep_tap_backfill_resident:               0.9
ep_tap_backlog_limit:                   5000
ep_tap_backoff_period:                  5
ep_tap_bg_fetch_requeued:               0
ep_tap_bg_fetched:                      0
ep_tap_bg_max_pending:                  500
ep_tap_keepalive:                       300
ep_tap_noop_interval:                   20
ep_tap_requeue_sleep_time:              0.1
```
ep_tap_throttle_cap_pcnt: **10**
ep_tap_throttle_queue_cap: **1000000**
ep_tap_throttle_threshold: **90**

Working-Set Management and Ejection

As mentioned in Chapter 9, Couchbase holds the keys and metadata of all items in memory and fills most of the remaining memory with the *working set*—documents that are being actively used. Couchbase constantly tracks the frequency with which items are accessed and periodically frees up memory by removing items from RAM in a process known as *ejection*. You already learned that Couchbase uses two parameters for determining when to begin eviction and how many items to evict: when memory use exceeds the high-water-mark threshold, Couchbase runs a background process that ensures that the least frequently used items in memory have been persisted to disk and then removes them from the caching layer. This ejection continues until memory use—the total amount of RAM consumed—drops below the low-water-mark threshold. The ejection process removes both active and replica items from memory, at a ratio of 40% active to 60% replica items.

If a node receives new items faster than it can persist and eject old items, at some point it will begin returning "temporary out-of-memory" errors to clients. The temporary OOM error threshold is 95% RAM usage by default.

You can control the two water-mark parameters, the OOM error threshold, and the ratio of active-to-replica items ejected with the cbepctl utility:

```
> cbepctl <host>:11210 -b <bucket> -p <bucket_password> set flush_param <parameter> <number>
```

The number argument is the desired percent value, between 0 and 100. The parameter argument can be:

- mem_high_wat: The high-water mark, as a percentage of total RAM used

- mem_low_wat: The low-water mark, as a percentage of total RAM used

- pager_active_vb_pcnt: The percentage of active items ejected from RAM

- mutation_mem_threshold: The threshold of RAM usage at which nodes start sending temporary OOM errors to client, as a percentage

As a rule, we do not recommend increasing the OOM error threshold above the default 95%. If your data traffic includes large spikes you should consider lowering the high-water mark and OOM error thresholds somewhat to leave more room for disk and TAP queues to grow. Lowering the percentage of active items ejected will keep more of the active working set in memory, but will mean that in the event of a failover it will take longer to begin serving the promoted replica data because fewer replica items will reside in RAM at the time.

To check the current values of the various ejection-related parameters, use the cbstats utility:

```
> cbstats <host>:11210 -b <bucket> -p <bucket_password> all | egrep "wat|mut|pager"
```

```
ep_exp_pager_stime:              3600
ep_expired_pager:                0
ep_mem_high_wat:                 85
ep_mem_low_wat:                  75
ep_mutation_mem_threshold:       95
ep_num_expiry_pager_runs:        5
ep_num_pager_runs:               0
ep_pager_active_vb_pcnt:         40
ep_storage_age_highwat:          0
```

Controlling the Purge Interval

As you've learned already, Couchbase does not delete expired items immediately. Instead, a purge process periodically removes expired items from disk. By default, the purge process runs every 60 minutes, but you can change this interval with the following command:

```
> cbepctl localhost:11210 set flush_param exp_pager_stime <seconds>
```

Lowering this interval will reduce the chance of getting expired or deleted items in view-query results, but will increase server load. Experiment with the setting to get the best results depending on your data access pattern and query needs.

Monitoring

Until version 2.2, Couchbase had a very simple access-control mechanism: you configured the administrator user when creating the cluster, and that user had permission to do everything. If reading the last sentence made you cringe in terror—well done. That's why in version 2.2 the Couchbase team has added 100% more users. Specifically, you can now create another user that has read-only access to the web console and the HTTP API. This user can see the cluster, node, and bucket overviews; examine, but not edit, design documents and views; and read the system log and cluster settings. It cannot access documents, query views, or change any settings at all.

To configure the read-only user, go to the Settings tab in the web console and click on Account Management. Enter the desired user credentials and click Create. Once the read-only user has been created, you can reset its password, or delete the user entirely, from the same web console screen.

Monitoring Couchbase at the System Level

The web console provides an at-a-glance overview of the important statistics. The first tab, which you can see in Figure 11-1, provides an overview of the cluster as a whole. The second tab, shown in Figure 11-2, shows per-node information, such as RAM and disk quotas, number of stored items, and rebalance progress. The third tab, shown in Figure 11-3, shows per-buckets statistics, including additional information, during operations such as data compaction.

Cluster Overview

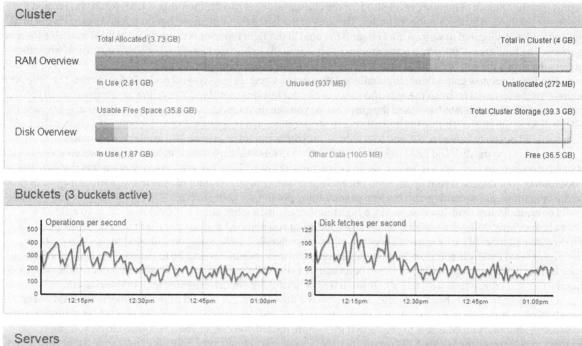

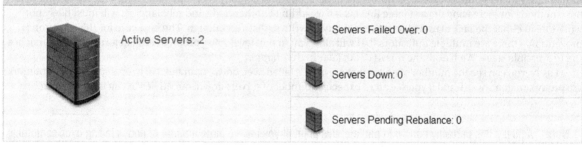

Figure 11-1. *Cluster overview*

As you can see in Figure 11-1, the Overview tab shows the total RAM and storage space available for the cluster, which is the total RAM and storage in all the nodes together, not a per-node average. The entire RAM Overview graph represents the amount of memory configured for the cluster, which is usually the value you set when you created the first node, multiplied by the number of nodes. The area to the left of the vertical red bar on the RAM graph is the total amount of RAM allocated to various buckets, and the area to the right represents the amount of RAM available for new buckets. The blue area of the graph is the memory that is actually being used for data, keys, and metadata, while the green area shows the rest of the RAM allocated for buckets, but not yet occupied by data.

The Disk Overview graph shows the combined disk usage across all buckets and nodes in the cluster. The blue area represents the space taken by all the data and views of all your buckets combined, the yellow area represents all the other non-Couchbase-related data, and the gray area, as you can no doubt guess, represents the free space available on all the disks in the cluster. During the normal course of operation, in a properly-sized and -configured cluster, the RAM usage should fluctuate between 75% and 85% of total, and there should be at least 50% available disk space.

In addition to the disk and RAM usage overviews, this tab has two important indicator graphs, which show database operations and disk fetches per second over the past hour. These two graphs give you a general idea of the condition of your cluster. If your application normally performs a steady amount of operations, a sudden spike or drop in the operations-per-seconds graph is a sign of something potentially going wrong.

For example, in a read-heavy scenario, a high number of disk fetches often indicates that either you didn't size your cluster correctly or your working set grew beyond what you planned and so your client reads are now generating an excessive number of cache misses. There are other, more detailed, indicators you will need to check in order to determine what exactly is going on. In this case, a straightforward solution would be to increase the RAM available to your bucket or cluster so as to cache a larger percentage of your data set in memory. There are actually other ways to handle this situation, which we'll talk about when we get to working-set management later in this chapter.

Conversely, in a write-heavy scenario, an unexpected drop in ops per second in combination with RAM usage over 95% often indicates that Couchbase is unable to eject unused items from memory fast enough, and thus it resorts to sending temporary OOM errors to clients that try to store data. If you don't have unallocated RAM you can use to immediately increase the bucket RAM quota, then this scenario is actually very difficult to deal with. At this point, the best methods for increasing the available RAM, such as adding another node and rebalancing, will most likely not work due to either the lack of memory or the inability to write to disk fast enough. The best cure for this situation is prevention—there are multiple indicators that will alert you to the developing problem long before it actually reaches the irreversible stage. We'll examine this in detail later in the chapter.

Lastly, you can see the number of nodes that are active, failed over, down, or in need of a rebalance. These counters are pretty straightforward, and if you see an unexpected number of servers down, our advice to you is: *don't panic!*

■ **Note**   Actually, it is perfectly normal to panic at this point. If you have a large amount of nodes failing over, something really bad is going on.

On the Server Nodes tab, as shown in Figure 11-2, you can see the status of individual nodes, including the node state—up, pending, or down; RAM, swap (pagefile), and CPU usage; the amount of data versus the amount of actual disk space being used; and the number of active and replica items stored on the node. Clicking on the triangle icon to the left of the node expands a more-detailed view, which includes the server uptime, OS version, as well as RAM and disk-usage graphs for that node. During a rebalance, you will also see how many items and vBuckets will be transferred to and from the node.

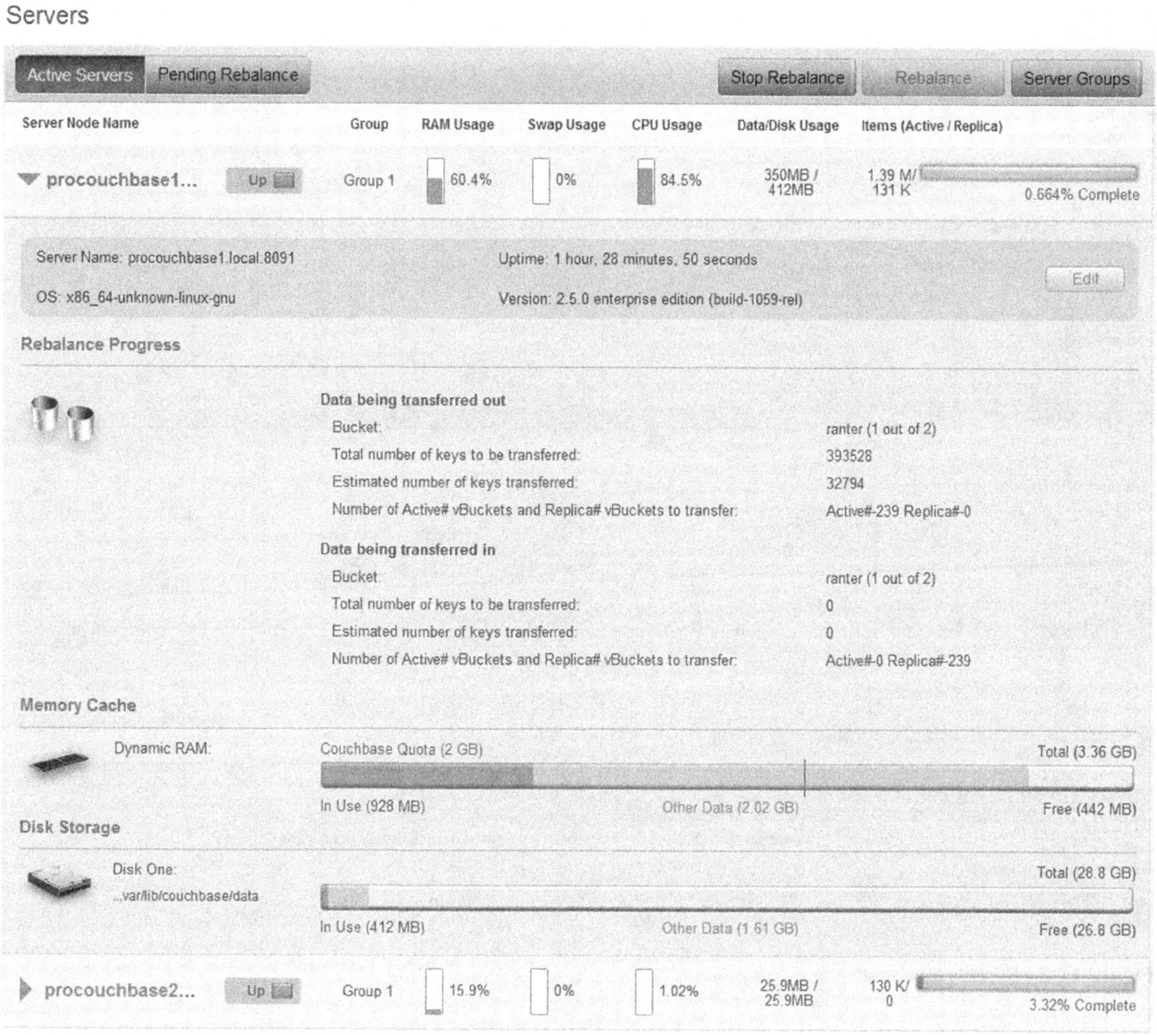

Servers

Figure 11-2. *Node overview*

Next we will take a look at the Data Buckets tab, which gives you bucket-specific information, as you can see in Figure 11-3. For Couchbase buckets this includes the number of items in the bucket, operations and disk fetches per second, and RAM and disk usage. Memcached buckets, shown in a separate category, replace the disk-fetches statistic with hit ratio—the percentage of requests that were actually found in the cache bucket. Expanding a bucket will show you the same data in graph form, as well as some additional information, such as compaction progress and the number of replicas configured for that particular bucket.

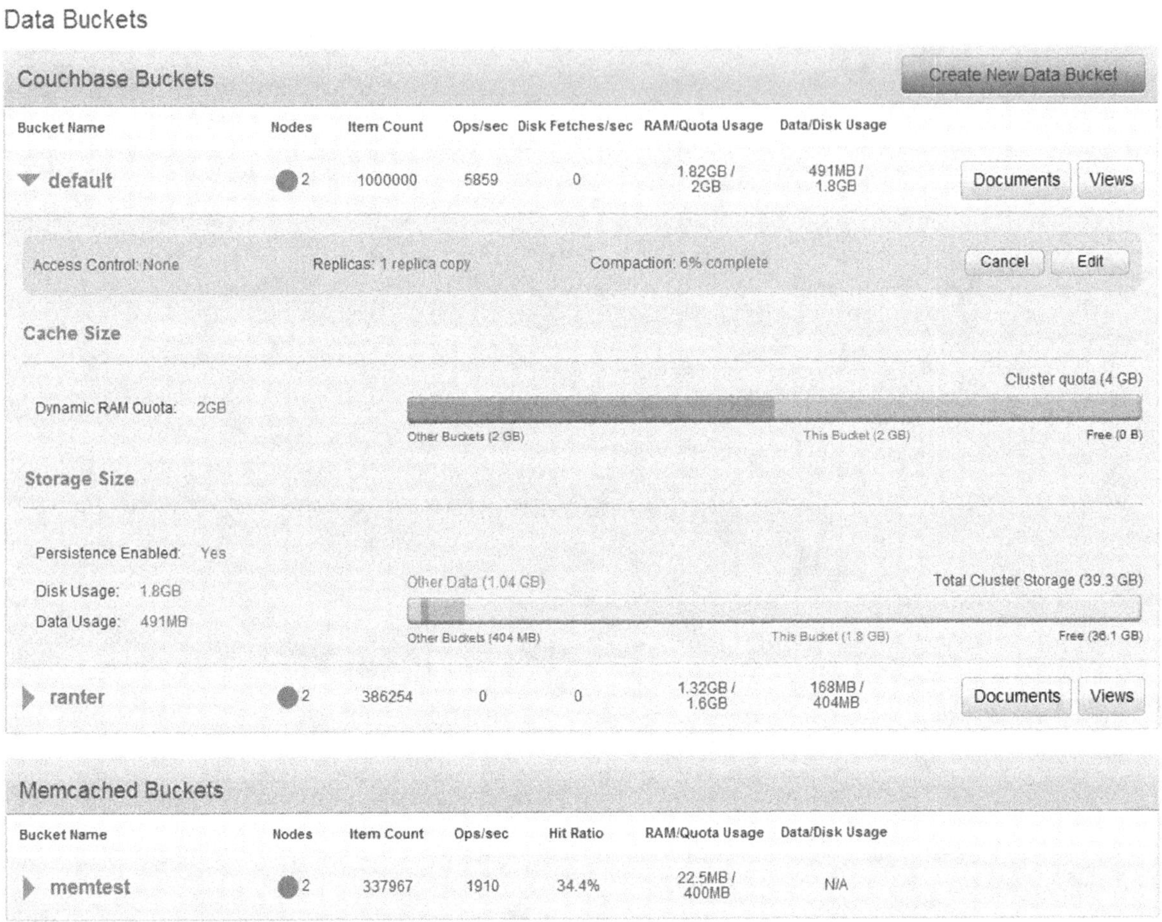

Data Buckets

Figure 11-3. *Buckets overview*

Similar to the Overview tab, this tab lets you monitor for anomalous behavior at the bucket level. For example, seeing a high number of disk reads in the cluster is an important indicator, but when you have multiple buckets defined, you'll want to know exactly which bucket is responsible for this behavior. If you see one of your buckets reading from diskoften, while the others do not, you may want to reallocate the available RAM between buckets, giving a larger share to the bucket that's experiencing a lot of cache misses. After you alleviate the immediate problem, you should consider whether you need to add another node to the cluster.

Detailed Per-Bucket Monitoring

The high-level statistics you get from the three overview tabs in the web console are very useful, but if you rely on them exclusively, all too often you will miss early signs that could warn you of potential problems long before they occur. For a much more detailed view of what's going on under the hood of a Couchbase Server cluster, clicking on the name of any node or bucket will take you to the bucket-monitoring view. Figure 11-4 shows a collapsed view of a Couchbase (as opposed to memcached) bucket.

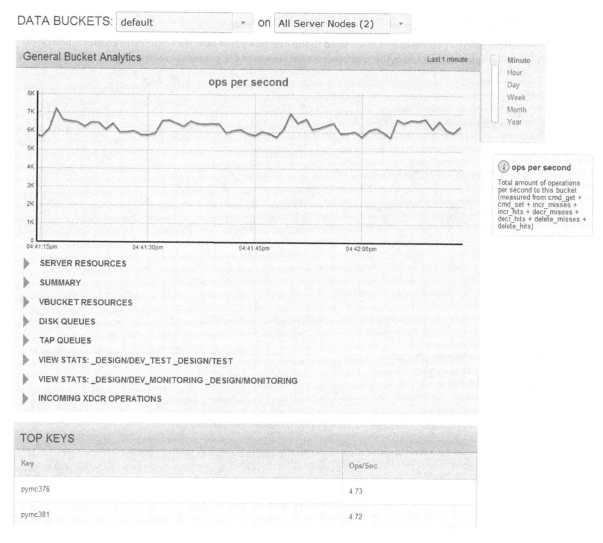

Figure 11-4. *Bucket statistics*

This view shows you statistics for a single bucket, either for the entire cluster or for a specific node. You can switch between the buckets and nodes using the two dropdown lists at the top of the page. To the right of the graph you can see the time window toggle, which lets you select how far back to display the bucket statistics, and a brief description of the currently selected metric. The description also tells you which counters are used to calculate the metric in question—these counters are available directly through the cbstats tool and from the HTTP API. In the web console you can only see statistics for a specified interval back from the present moment. To get information about a specific time period in the past, you have to use the statistics HTTP API, which we'll talk about later in this chapter.

Below the main graph view are numerous very small graphs grouped by category. Depending on your cluster configuration, you may have different categories present. Below the graph categories you can see a list of the most active keys. Knowing which keys are being accessed the most can sometimes be useful in diagnosing the behavior of your application.

Server Resources

The Server Resources category contains metrics related to the machines that host the Couchbase cluster. Clicking on the small graph will display that metric in the main graph view on top of the page, as shown in Figure 11-5.

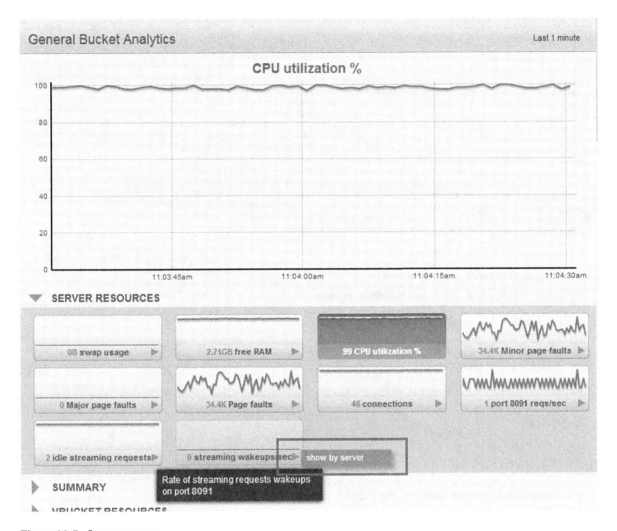

Figure 11-5. *Server resources*

Moving the mouse over the blue arrow icon under any of the small graphs will pop up a menu offering to view a breakdown of that metric by individual server, which you can see in Figure 11-6.

CPU utilization % for bucket: default

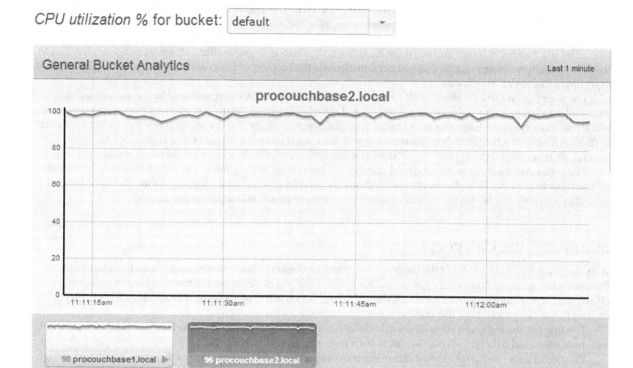

Figure 11-6. *Metric breakdown by server*

The swap-usage graph shows the amount of swap space (Linux) or page file (Windows) in use across the servers. As mentioned in Chapter 9, you can control the memory swapping behavior on Linux machines through the vm.swappiness setting. You want to make sure that you do have a swap file configured so that if, for some unexpected reason, the server requires more RAM than is physically available to it, Couchbase will not send out of memory errors. However, the swappiness should be set to 0 to make sure that no data will be swapped out of RAM as long as some free memory remains. During the normal operation of your cluster, the swap usage should be exactly 0 bytes. If you see that the swap usage is more than that, this could indicate that other processes on the server are using an abnormal amount of RAM. Alternatively, this could mean that Couchbase is running out of memory due to a high rate of incoming writes and cannot keep up by ejecting unused documents from RAM to make room for the new items. Start by checking the processes running on the server to see if you can quickly identify the reason for the abnormally high RAM usage. If nothing stands out, examine the various memory- and queue-related metrics in Couchbase, which will be covered in just a moment.

If you're using Windows machines to host Couchbase they will inevitably swap some data from RAM to disk because there is no way to control the swappiness. In this case, there is no hard and fast rule for how much swap space your servers should normally use. You should monitor your server under normal conditions to find the baseline statistics and then check the other metrics if the cluster behavior deviates significantly.

The free RAM is the total unused machine memory (i.e., not Couchbase) on all the servers in the cluster together. For example, the cluster in Figure 11-6 contains two nodes, and each one has approximately 1.35 GB of free RAM, as reported by the operating system.

The CPU utilization percentage refers to the total of all the CPU cores, averaged across all nodes in the cluster. When the CPU usage is close to 100%, it begins adversely affecting many other internal functions, including flushing disk and TAP queues, calculating indexes, and processing XDCR replication. A temporary peak in CPU usage can be caused by any number of things and will most likely not have a lasting negative effect. However, consistently high CPU usage is an important warning sign that you need to increase the capacity of your cluster, either by adding more nodes or by upgrading the existing nodes.

The page fault statistics—minor, major and total—refer to the page faults experienced by the server machine. Page faults do not (necessarily) indicate a problem and are usually part of the normal memory management process of the operating system. A large number of major page faults may indicate that the server is needing to swap memory to disk too much, which negatively impacts server performance. If you want to learn more about page faults in general, we recommend the appropriate Wikipedia page: http://en.wikipedia.org/wiki/Page_fault.

The connections graph displays the total number of connections to the Couchbase server, including incoming connections from Couchbase clients, internal TAP queues used for replication, XDCR, and more. The three metrics related to port 8091 display the number of requests, streaming requests, and wakeups per second.

Summary (the Category)

Wait, don't go! This isn't the end of the chapter—we're talking about the Summary category, which contains metrics that give you a quick overview of the current bucket status. Here you can monitor the most important indicators of cluster health and quickly discover potential warning signs, which will lead you to further investigate the in-depth metrics in the categories below this one.

The ops-per-second graph shows the total number of operations on the currently selected bucket, including get, set, increment, and delete. This number includes requests for non-existent keys.

The cache-miss ratio graph is often one of the most important indicators of cluster efficiency. A high percentage of cache misses indicates that the bucket does not have enough memory to hold the actual working set, which requires loading data from disk. Ideally, a correctly sized cluster will have a cache-miss ratio that is close to 0, because all the actively-used data will be cached in memory. Of course, it may not always be practical, or even possible, to size the cluster to fit the entire working set in memory; for example, your application may have a very large data set and use all data with equal frequency. In such cases, a consistent rate of cache misses is to be expected. If you see more cache misses than expected, the next step is to examine the metrics related to active and replica items resident in RAM, which we'll talk about in the next topic. The next four graphs show the number of get, set, delete, and CAS operations individually. Because CAS operations incur extra processing overhead, it is sometimes useful to know how many of these operations the server receives, compared to regular operations.

The percentage of active resident item is exactly what it sounds like—how many items are cached in RAM out of the total number of items in this bucket. The same graph is also shown in the next category, vBucket Resources. This metric is one of the more important indicators of cluster performance and can alert you to potential problems. If you have a good idea of what the size of your working set should be, then when the percentage of resident active items drops below the percentage of items expected to be in your working set you should increase the amount of RAM allocated to this bucket. Conversely, if you don't know what your actual working set is, then you can use the percentage of active items, the cache-miss ratio, the number of ejections from RAM, and the low-water mark metrics to get an idea of whether this bucket is sized correctly.

Because of the way Couchbase manages document ejection from RAM, the expected behavior for the resident active items percentage is to increase gradually until RAM usage reaches the high-water mark, then drop by a fairly constant amount as the server removes the least-used documents from RAM until usage drops to the low-water mark.

The items graph is quite straightforward—it shows the number of active items in the bucket.

The next graph, temp OOM per second, is one of the most important indicators of cluster health. It shows the number of temporary out of memory errors sent to Couchbase clients per second. This value should always be 0. If Couchbase starts generating temporary OOM errors, it means that it is unable to free RAM through document ejection fast enough, and that RAM usage exceeds the mutation_mem_threshold value, which by default is 95% of the bucket's allocated memory.

The most common scenario for the temporary OOM condition is when the server is unable to persist incoming items fast enough due to insufficient disk throughput. This means that in addition to the fact that the disk-write queue keeps growing, Couchbase can't eject the unpersisted items to free up RAM. If the bucket also has a non-zero number of replicas defined, then the TAP queues will continue to grow and take up even more memory, because nodes will send back-off messages to each other to delay replication. If this is caused by a temporary increase in writes, then increasing the bucket's RAM allocation may be enough to resolve the immediate problem and provide enough headroom to handle future spikes. If the increase in writes is not temporary—for example, due to software changes or node failure causing a relative increase in load on the rest—then the problem is much harder to deal with. You should still increase the RAM allocated to the bucket as soon as possible (you did leave some spare RAM when you configured the cluster RAM quota, right?) to deal with the increase in writes, and then you should add one or more nodes to the cluster and rebalance. Simply increasing the RAM size will likely not be enough, as the incoming data will eventually use all the newly allocated memory as well. If your Couchbase cluster is deployed in a cloud service, you can most likely provision additional disk resources for the existing nodes, either by adding more disk volumes or by increasing the disk-throughput allocation directly. Otherwise, you will need to change your IT infrastructure to increase the available write capacity.

If you have unallocated RAM in the cluster, you can edit the bucket in question and simply increase its RAM quota. If you don't have any unallocated RAM, you will need to check if you can shrink one of the other buckets temporarily. Editing a bucket's RAM quota does not require a restart and does not interrupt normal server operation. If you cannot reallocate RAM between buckets, you will need to increase the cluster RAM quota first. One of the reason we strongly recommend allocating no more than 80% of the machine's RAM for Couchbase is that—in addition to operating system and file cache—the rest can be used in an emergency to temporarily give more RAM to Couchbase.

Starting with Couchbase version 2.5+, you can change the cluster RAM quota from the web console. You can do so in the Settings tab, under the Cluster sub-category, change the Per Server RAM Quota value and click Save. If you have an earlier version of Couchbase, or want to maintain your geek-cred by using the command-line, you can change the RAM quota with the couchbase-cli utility as follows:

```
> couchbase-cli cluster-init -c <host> -u <user> -p <password> --cluster-ramsize=<RAM>
```

In this command, <RAM> is the desired RAM quota in megabytes. If the value you specify is too low, or too high, you will get an error message that will include the minimum and maximum RAM quota values possible on this machine.

You can also use the HTTP API to change the memory quota—issue a POST request to http://<host>:8091/pools/default and specify the memoryQuota value as the post data:

```
> curl -X POST -u <user>:<password> -d memoryQuota=<RAM> http://<host>:8091/pools/default
```

After increasing the cluster RAM quota, you can allocate this spare memory to the bucket.

As a general rule, if your Couchbase cluster needs to handle a high rate of writes, we highly recommend that you build a robust mechanism for dealing with OOM and other temporary errors on the software level. One of the most common ways to tackle this is to have a separate queue to which your application can write data that it was temporarily unable to store, and then have a periodic or event-based process that will try to empty this overflow queue into Couchbase. This may sound like overkill, and if you monitor and maintain your cluster well, it will most likely never be used. But, depending on the importance of your data, it's better than coming to work in the morning to discover that last night's TPS reports got lost in transmission.

The next two graphs show the low- and high-water mark memory thresholds for this bucket. The one after that shows the memory used by the bucket—it should normally fluctuate between the low- and high-water marks as documents get cached and ejected from RAM.

The disk-creates and updates-per-second graphs show the number of new and updated items, respectively, that are written to disk. This includes active, replicate, and pending (rebalance) items. The disk-reads graph, exactly as the name implies, shows the number of disk reads per second. This graph is related to the cache-miss ratio—they both rely on the same basic metric. As with the cache misses, ideally we want the number of disk reads to be as low as possible.

The disk-write queue graph shows the total number of items in the queue, including active, replica, and pending. Depending on your data traffic pattern, in a long-running cluster the size of the disk queue should be fairly stable. Even if your application experiences traffic spikes, the disk queue should drain after a while. As we talked about earlier in this chapter, when the disk queue reaches the TAP throttle threshold, nodes will starting sending back-off messages to each other in order to limit the rate of incoming replica items. This mechanism does a great job of dealing with spikes of incoming data, but it should not be needed during routine operation. You should keep an eye on the disk queue size to make sure it doesn't routinely exceed the TAP throttle threshold.

The next seven graphs—docs data size, docs total disk size, docs fragmentation %, total disk size, views data size, views total disk size, and views fragmentation %—show various statistics related to disk space. The docs data size graph shows the net size of all the items on disk. The docs total size graph shows the actual amount of disk space taken up by the items. As you recall, Couchbase data and index files are append-only, which means that updated or deleted items leave "holes" behind, and the files need to be periodically defragmented to reclaim this wasted space. This brings us to the next graph, docs fragmentation, which shows the wasted space as a percentage of the total. For example, Figure 11-7 shows that 436 MB of actual document data take 1.36 GB of disk space. This means that $1 - 436/1392 = 0.687$, or 69% of the disk space taken by the data files is wasted due to fragmentation. The total disk size graph shows the total disk space taken by the data and index files together. The views data, total size, and fragmentation graphs are the same, except for views.

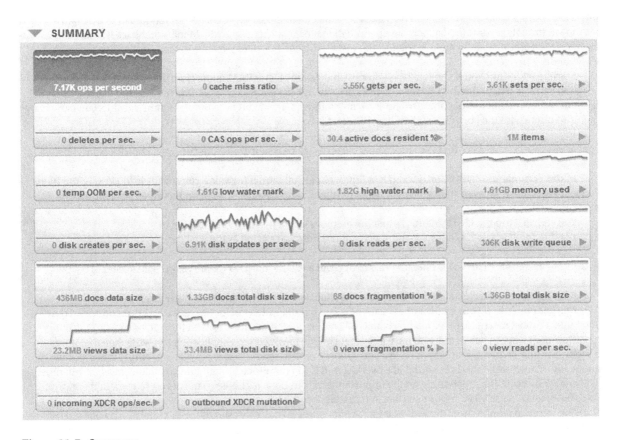

Figure 11-7. Summary

The view reads per second show the total for all views defined in this bucket. We'll look at per-view statistics in a moment. Because view queries are read from disk, this metric is important in deployments, which rely heavily on views. (You did put data and views on separate physical drives, right?)

The last two graphs in the summary category—incoming and outgoing XDCR—show the number of incoming XDCR operations per second, as well as the size of the outgoing XDCR queue. The expected behavior of these two metrics depends on what exactly you are doing with XDCR. For example, if you're using the second cluster as a hot backup for the main, then you would expect the outbound-queue graph to mirror your incoming data pattern.

Even though the bucket-statistics view defaults to showing results for the last minute, in a long-running deployment you can usually get a better sense of the overall cluster health by looking at the statistics for the last hour and checking for any abnormalities. Figure 11-8 shows what you would normally expect to see in a healthy cluster with a steady flow of incoming and outgoing data and a high auto-compaction threshold—80% in this case.

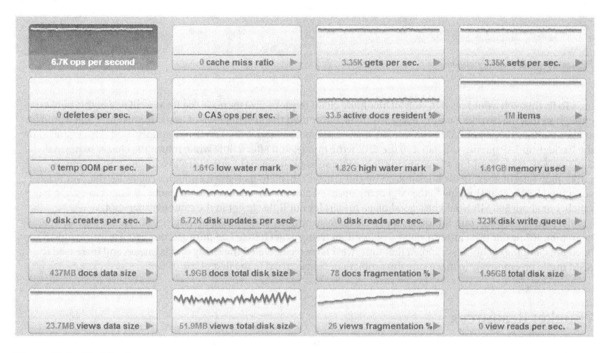

Figure 11-8. *Healthy cluster*

As you can see, the cache-miss ratio is 0, there is a steady flow of get and set operations, and the active documents and memory-used graphs fluctuate between the low- and high-water marks and no more than that. The disk-write queue is holding steady at around 300,000 items, and the total data size and fragmentation percentage fluctuate up to about 80% fragmentation.

In contrast, Figure 11-9 shows a cluster in trouble. As you can see, it has a high cache-miss ratio, which means that Couchbase keeps loading items from disk. Because clients keep requesting items that are on disk, rather than in cache, these items get added to the cache and increase the RAM usage. Until just a few moments before the screenshot was taken, updated items were also being written to the cluster, further increasing RAM and disk usage. The pager process was unable to eject items from RAM fast enough to keep up, so once the memory use climbed above the 95% threshold, Couchbase started rejecting all writes with temporary OOM errors.

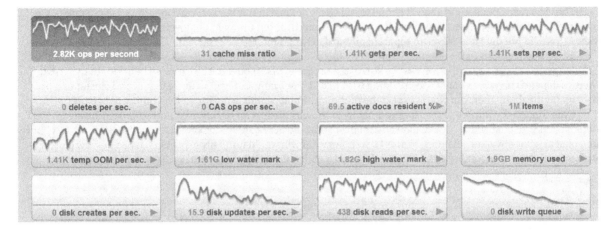

Figure 11-9. *Unhealthy cluster*

To fix this, you would need to stop all incoming client requests and increase the RAM available to this bucket enough so that the current memory usage would be lower than the new high-water mark. In this case, that would be at least another 100 MB of RAM to ensure the high-water mark is above the 1.9 GB of memory used. This would allow the backed-up TAP queues to drain into the disk-write queue, and after a little while return the cluster to normal functionality. Now, stopping all incoming client requests is probably not a good idea in a production system, so rather than only increasing the bucket RAM by 100 MB, we'd need to increase it enough to allow for the overhead of continued RAM expansion due to the data being updated and read from disk into the cache. It's hard to estimate how much, but about 500 MB would be a good place to start for our little cluster in the example snapshot.

Of course, this "fix" only addresses the immediate symptoms of the problem, not the root cause. Had we actually been monitoring our test cluster properly, rather than trying to get it to fail on purpose, our first warning would have been the climbing cache-miss ratio. At that time, we'd have recalculated the sizing of this bucket and increased its RAM quota preemptively to make sure the problem never occurred in the first place.

vBucket Resources

Data in Couchbase buckets is divided into 1024 virtual buckets, plus another 1024 for every replica copy. At any given time, some or all of the documents can be resident in memory or only on disk. Monitoring the state of data in all the vBuckets is important for understanding how Couchbase is using the available memory. The vBucket Resources category contains statistics by vBucket state: active, replica, pending, and total for all three states.

As you no doubt recall, Couchbase buckets can be configured to store up to three replicas of each item. Because items in a bucket are divided into 1024 vBuckets, Couchbase actually stores 1024, times the number of copies, vBuckets, which are spread equally throughout all the nodes in the cluster. Figure 11-10 shows a snapshot of a cluster in the middle of rebalancing after adding a second node. Until the second node was added, there weren't enough nodes to create replicas, so there were only the 1024 active vBuckets. After the second node was added, the rebalance process started moving active vBuckets to the new node, as well as creating replica vBuckets of the ones that remained active on the first node.

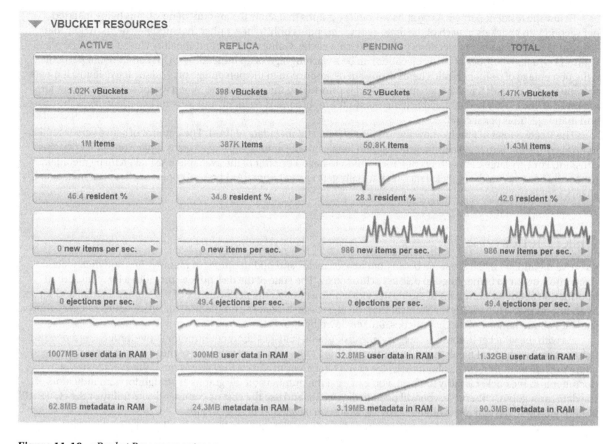

Figure 11-10. *vBucket Resources category*

Of the four columns of graphs in Figure 11-10, the first column shows statistics for all the active vBuckets of the bucket in question, the second for replica vBuckets, the third for vBuckets that are in the process of being moved as part of the rebalance, and the last column shows the totals for the first three.

The first graph shows the total number of vBuckets in each state. Because the screenshot was taken during the rebalance right after we added a second new node to a cluster of one, we can see that there are 1024 (1.02k) active vBuckets in the cluster and 398 replica vBuckets, which were already created by the rebalance; as you can no doubt guess, the rebalance is at approximately 40% progress at this point. The pending column shows that 52 vBuckets are in the process of being moved from one node to the other. In a healthy, rebalanced cluster, we would expect to see 1024 active vBuckets and <number of replicas> * 1024 replica vBuckets.

The second row of graphs shows the number of items that belong to the vBuckets in each of the three states, as well as the total. The third row shows the percentage of items that are cached in memory—as we already mentioned, ideally, we want this to be equal or greater than our application's working set to make sure that Couchbase can serve all requests from RAM, rather than from disk. As you'll recall from earlier in this chapter, the pager_active_vb_pcnt parameter specifies the ratio of active-to-replica items that are ejected from memory, and is set to 40% ejected active items to 60% replica items. This explains why 46% of the active items are cached, as opposed to 34% of the replica items—replica items get ejected more often, so fewer of them are cached.

Below the resident percentage graphs we can see graphs that show the amount of new items being inserted per second into vBuckets in each of the three states. This refers only to new rather than updated items. Below that are graphs for the number of ejections per second from cache. Going back to our unhealthy cluster example from Figure 11-9, a high number of cache ejections can be a warning sign of an impending OOM condition. In particular, if the percentage of resident replica items drops out of proportion to the percentage of resident active items, it means that the bucket doesn't have enough memory and is prioritizing the active items. When we took the screenshot for Figure 11-9, the cluster had 68% active items versus 0% replica items resident, and was still experiencing cache misses and many ejections per second.

The last two rows of graphs show the amount of data and metadata in RAM. The amount of active versus replica in RAM corresponds to the percentage of resident items, but the amount of active versus replica metadata remains constant. For very large data sets, it's not uncommon to have a quarter of the available RAM taken up by metadata. Especially because, unlike replica data which usually gets ejected from RAM first, all copies of all replica metadata are always kept in memory.

Disk Queues

As we've mentioned throughout the book, Couchbase creates and updates items in memory first and then places them into a queue to be persisted to disk asynchronously. The state of the disk queues provides a lot of important information about the condition of the cluster as a whole as well as the performance of the storage system, and serves as an important early warning mechanism that will alert us of impending problems. The Disk Queues category shows statistics about the state of the disk queues, broken down by vBucket state.

As with the vBucket Resources category, the disk-queue statistics show columns for active, replica, and pending items, as well as the total for all three. An important thing to keep in mind is that all of these graphs show the item count and tell us nothing at all about their size or the total amount of data they represent. If the average size of documents in the bucket is fairly uniform, you can treat the numbers on the graphs as straightforward indicators of the data throughput. Otherwise, you will need to dig deeper and use the cbstats command-line utility or the HTTP API to find out the actual size of the queues in bytes, which we cover later in this chapter.

The first row of graphs is rather straightforward—it shows the number of items in all the queues waiting to be persisted to disk. The expected number of items in the queue depends on a great number of factors, including your data traffic pattern, the settings for compaction, the number of views in the bucket, and many others. For this reason, there's no exact guideline for how the queue should behave. However, a number of warning signs can point to potential problems. Over a long enough time period—an hour to a day, depending on your data throughput—the queues should drain down to some low baseline amount of items. If the number of items in the queues remains consistently high, or worse yet, keeps climbing, it is a strong indication that you need to increase the available disk-write throughput. Furthermore, as we talked about at the beginning of this chapter, if the total number of items in all the queues exceeds a predefined threshold—1 million items or 10% of the total data set by default—nodes will begin delaying each other's TAP queues, to make sure they can persist the active data as soon as possible, at the expense of replication. If you expect the write queue to spike above 1M items as part of the normal operation of your application, for example if you perform bulk data inserts regularly, you can increase the threshold for TAP backoff. Otherwise, you should take this as a strong indication that your current write capacity is insufficient.

The second row of graphs shows the fill rate, as number of items per second, for the three types of data queues. The active queue fill rate is directly related to how quickly clients send data to the cluster. If it drops unexpectedly, you should first check to make sure there's no problem that is preventing the clients from communicating with Couchbase, and then you should check the temporary OOM statistics to see if there is a problem with the cluster itself. In a properly functioning cluster, the replica queue fill rate should be equal to the active queue fill rate, multiplied by the bucket replica factor. In practice, the TAP queues that handle replication are the first to be throttled whenever Couchbase experiences unusual load, such as high memory usage or a spike in the amount of writes. In Figure 11-11, you can see an active cluster with a replication factor of 1 in the middle of a server rebalance. Clients sending data to the server kept the active queue fill rate at a fairly constant six thousand items per second. However, the replica queue was repeatedly throttled due to the rebalance and—though you can't see it in the screenshot—due to the automatic compaction of the bucket, as well as ongoing index processing. Because server rebalance is a resource-intensive operation, the fact that the replication queue was throttled is not necessarily alarming. However, if this behavior continues after the rebalance ends, or at any time during normal operation, then you should check other indicators, such as memory usage, cache-miss ratio, total queue size, and the TAP statistics that we'll talk about in the next topic. The pending queue fill rate, as you can guess, represents the rate of items being added to the write queue of buckets that are in the process of being transferred from one node to another. The total fill rate is a handy indicator of the write throughput required to handle the current workload.

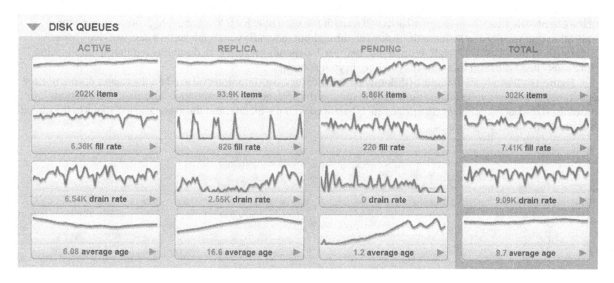

Figure 11-11. *Disk Queues category*

There is one factor that directly affects the fill rate, but unfortunately cannot be monitored from Couchbase itself, and that is the network bandwidth. Clients send and receive data from the cluster, and, depending on the replication factor, nodes within the cluster send the received data to each other up to three times. There is also the overhead for internal cluster management and monitoring, and possibly also XDCR traffic. The available network bandwidth places a hard cap on the amount of data it's possible to read and write to the database, but if you rely only on Couchbase monitoring, you won't directly discover that you've hit the network bandwidth cap. Of course, it's not particularly hard to find out how much bandwidth a node is using. On Linux, there are dozens of command-line and graphical utilities for monitoring various network-related statistics, including bwm-ng, nethogs, bmon, ifstat, iptraf, iftop, and many more. We're partial to the first two, so if you don't have a favorite utility already, you can install these utilities with apt-get or yum and give them a try. On Windows, you can use the Task Manager or Resource Monitor for a quick network overview, or use performance counters for more in-depth monitoring. And there are plenty of more-advanced external monitoring tools as well.

The next row of graphs tells you how many items are written to disk from the queues per second. Unlike the fill rate, the individual drain rate of the various queues isn't really as interesting as the total drain rate. The total drain rate is the best overall indicator of the effective disk-write throughput available to Couchbase at any given moment. Because there are multiple mechanisms that compete for the available write capacity within the cluster, including compaction, indexing, and disk reads, the total drain rate is likely to vary over time. If you want to test the write performance of different cluster and hardware configurations, you'll need to isolate the different variables that affect the drain rate. For example, if you want to test how different volume-striping settings affect the disk throughput, you can first run a test with auto-compaction turned off, without any views defined, with one bucket, and only write operations. Then you can test the effect of indexing in addition to the write traffic, then the effect of different numbers of write threads per bucket to find the optimal setting for our hardware, and so on.

If you want a simple way to monitor disk throughput, you can use the bwm-ng, iotop, and iostat utilities on Linux, or the Resource Monitor on Windows. Of course, there are more-comprehensive solutions available, and if you're using a cloud service to host your Couchbase cluster, they offer excellent monitoring tools as well.

The last row of graphs shows the average age of the items waiting to be written to disk in the various queues. As you would expect, this metric strongly correlates to the difference between the fill and drain rates. The average age of items in the queue gives you a rough indication of how long it takes for a newly added item to be persisted to disk, which ensures it's not lost if the node fails. In the event of node failure, you would lose data from a time period approximately double the average age of data. If you use the persistence and replication requirement parameters of the Client SDK, that is how long the client will wait for the store operation to return. A high average age is an indication that you need to increase the disk-write throughput to handle your application's data workload faster. Defining how high exactly is "high" is up to you, because it depends on your data durability requirements and what extra safety and validation mechanisms you have in your software.

Figure 11-12 shows an example of disk-queue statistics for a two-hour interval in a healthy cluster during normal operation. The regular spikes in the number of items and the average age correspond to automatic compaction running on the bucket data files. The drain rate is balanced with the fill rate, and the average age of items in the queue is consistently under 0.5 seconds.

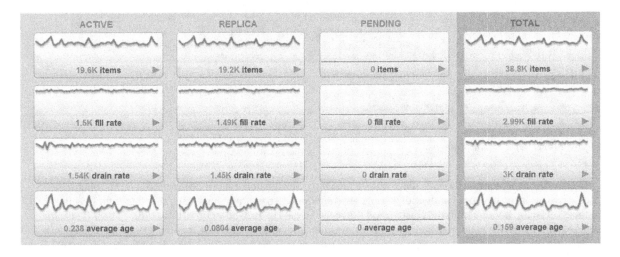

Figure 11-12. *Healthy disk queues*

TAP Queues

Monitoring the TAP queues, which is how nodes exchange data, gives you insight into the internal data flow of your Couchbase cluster. Irregularities in the data transmission can indicate problems in communications, storage, or memory usage. The TAP Queues category contains statistics about the state of the queues that hold the data waiting to be replicated, rebalanced, or sent to clients.

The first row of graphs shows the current number of TAP queues used for replication, rebalance, sending data to clients, and the total for all three. The number of replication queues depends on the number of nodes in the cluster.

The second row in the TAP Queues category shows the number of items remaining in each type of queue. Normally this number should be very low, because nodes continuously send the items to be replicated. This metric is closely linked to the next two—the drain rate and the back-off rate. The drain rate is exactly what you expect—the amount of items per second that are removed from the queue and sent over the TAP protocol to their destination. If the drain rate is insufficient, which can be caused by very high CPU load on the node, lack of available network bandwidth, or high network latency, then items will continue to accumulate in the TAP queue.

As mentioned earlier, when the total disk-write queue exceeds a certain number of items, or the memory usage of the bucket goes above the predefined threshold, nodes will begin delaying replication by sending back-off messages to each other. When a node receives a back-off message, it stops processing the TAP queues for a number of seconds in order to give the target node time to deal with its own load. The length of the back-off period is determined by the ep_tap_backoff_period parameter. You should monitor the back-off rate of the nodes in your cluster carefully and investigate the cause of the load as soon as you see a non-zero amount of back-off messages.

Figure 11-13 shows a cluster that has ended up in a very unhealthy state—we deliberately overloaded it with updates, causing its memory usage to go above the high-water mark. At that point, we actually stopped sending new data to the cluster, but it was already too late. In this state, nodes refused to accept any data from the replication TAP streams—you can see that the drain rate is equal to the back-off rate, because nodes responded to all items sent to them with a back-off message. We actually managed to recreate a rare fault condition, and unless we increase the bucket RAM quota, the cluster will actually remain in this dead-end state indefinitely. This happens when the bucket memory use increases rapidly, causing it to eject many items from RAM. By default, it prioritizes replica items for ejection. At some point, Couchbase ejects all replica data from the cache, but due to (we suspect) a fault in the ejection algorithm, it keeps trying to eject replica items instead of active ones. Since there are no more replica items left to eject, the bucket's memory use never decreases below the high-water mark, which also causes the TAP queues to remain permanently paused due to repeated back-off messages. Furthermore, as soon as RAM use passes the default 95% threshold, Couchbase also starts rejecting new writes from clients with temporary OOM errors. The solution to this condition is to increase the bucket RAM quota temporarily, which lets it load some replica items into the cache, and then it resumes ejecting both active and replica items from RAM. Of course, this requires the rate of incoming data to be slowed enough that the same fault condition doesn't occur again.

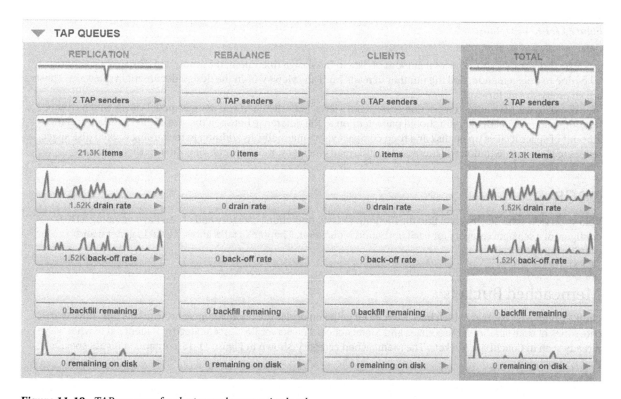

Figure 11-13. *TAP queues of a cluster under excessive load*

In addition to streaming any new incoming data to the target, the TAP protocol can also backfill existing items from the source and stream them to the target. This is used, for example, to send the contents of an existing vBucket during rebalance. The backfill remaining graph shows the number of items in the TAP backfill queue waiting to be sent. This should be 0 for replication queues, because they only stream new data, but is likely to be a larger value in TAP queues used for rebalancing.

Finally, the last row of graphs shows the number of items remaining on disk that still need to be read into the TAP queue and sent over. For example, these could be items that are persisted to disk but are not currently in the memory cache that need to be transferred to another node as part of as rebalance.

Views

If the bucket you're monitoring has views, then below the TAP Queues category you will find a separate category per design document, similar to what's shown in Figure 11-14.

Figure 11-14. *View statistics*

The three graphs show the total amount of data in the design document, the amount of disk space it actually takes due to fragmentation, and the number of reads from any views within the design document in question. These are all pretty straightforward.

If you do not have auto-compaction enabled for views, in particular if you use geospatial views, which cannot be compacted automatically, you should pay attention to the difference between the size of the view data and the amount of space it takes up on disk and then compact views manually. In addition to reclaiming wasted disk space, reducing view fragmentation will increase the disk-read efficiency, making large view queries slightly faster.

XDCR

Below the view statistics, you will find the incoming XDCR operations category and, if you have outgoing XDCR configured, a separate category for each outbound replication. Chapter 13 talks about XDCR in general and monitoring specifically.

Memcached Buckets

Unlike Couchbase buckets, which have a whole lot going on under the hood, memcached buckets only have two categories of statistics: Server Resources and Memcached. The Server Resources category is identical to what we've already seen in Couchbase buckets. The Memcached category, shown in Figure 11-15, contains statistics specific to that type of bucket.

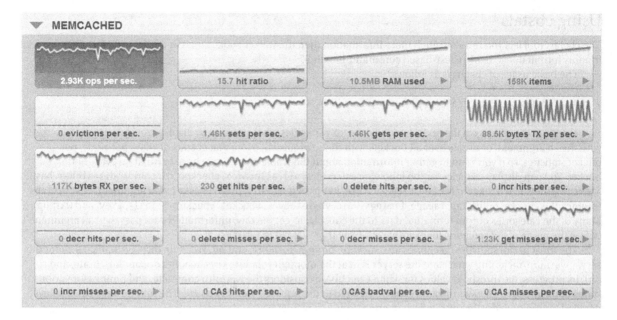

Figure 11-15. *Memcached bucket statistics*

The ops per second graph shows the total amount of operations received by the bucket, including both hits and misses. M*isses* are requests with a key that does not exist in the bucket. Because memcached buckets, as the name implies, usually serve as a data cache for applications, it is expected that not all requests will find data. Of course, a cache miss usually means that the client will have to retrieve the required data from another, presumably slower, data source. Therefore, the ratio of cache hits to cache misses is a very important metric, as it tells you how effective your caching strategy is at the moment. Ideally, you want the hit ratio to be as high as possible, and if it isn't, you should consider what you can do to improve it. The most straightforward way to raise the cache-hit ratio is usually to increase the size of the cache, which means allocating more RAM to the memcached bucket.

Next we have the RAM used and items graphs, which are rather self-explanatory. The evictions per second graph shows how many items are removed from the cache per second. Unlike Couchbase buckets, memcached buckets do not have a persistence layer, so items removed from the cache are gone permanently. When new items are added, Couchbase removes the least-frequently accessed items from the memcached bucket as needed to free up space, which is what the evictions per second graph shows. The sets per second and gets per second graphs are also rather obvious. The bytes TX and bytes RX per second graphs show the amount of data sent from and written to this bucket, respectively.

The next four graphs show the amount of successful—meaning the item was found in the cache—get, delete, increment, and decrement operations per second. The four graphs after that show the reverse—the amount of get, delete, increment, and decrement operations that were a cache miss. The last three graphs show how many CAS operations were successful cache hits, how many had a CAS value that did not match the server, and how many generated a cache miss.

Statistics and Cluster Health

Although the web console lets you monitor well over a hundred different indicators, Couchbase actually collects a lot more data, which isn't shown by the bucket monitor view.

Using cbstats

The cbstats tool lets you retrieve much more information than the web console, albeit in a somewhat less user-friendly format due to being a text-based command-line tool.

The basic usage of cbstats is as follows:

```
> cbstats <host>:11210 [category]
```

<host> is the address of the node, and the category specifies what statistics to display. You can specify a bucket with the -b argument, or iterate over all buckets with the -a argument. Note that cbstats displays per-node, per-bucket statistics, so if you want to gather information about the whole cluster, you have to run it on every node/bucket. You can display statistics for the following categories: all, allocator, checkpoint, config, dispatcher, hash, items (memcached bucket only), key, klog, kvstore, kvtimings, memory, prev-vbucket, raw argument, reset, slabs (memcached bucket only), tap, tapagg, timings, uuid, vb-takeover, vbucket, vbucket-details, vkey, and warmup. Many of the categories output formatted data to the console; to get the raw, unformatted data pass the raw argument before the name of the category, for example, raw timings instead of timings.

The most useful statistics categories are *warmup*, *timings*, *memory*, and *all*. *Warmup* displays statistics about the server warmup, including what state the server is in at the moment (reading keys, reading documents, done, and so on), its progress, the threshold values for when Couchbase considers the warmup complete, and timings for various states of the process. *Memory* displays statistics related to the bucket's memory usage. The *timings* category displays detailed timing statistics for various system operations as a histogram:

```
> cbstats <host>:11210 timings
```

The preceding command will print a large number of text-based histograms similar to the following histogram of the timing breakdown for the store command:

```
store_cmd (2191672 total)
   4us - 8us    : ( 38.59%)  845694 #######################
   8us - 16us   : ( 86.02%) 1039587 ##############################
  16us - 32us   : ( 93.33%)  160250 ####
  32us - 64us   : ( 94.67%)   29324
  64us - 128us  : ( 95.17%)   10901
 128us - 256us  : ( 98.16%)   65593 #
 256us - 512us  : ( 99.75%)   34752 #
 512us - 1ms    : ( 99.84%)    2067
   1ms - 2ms    : ( 99.88%)     788
   2ms - 4ms    : ( 99.91%)     770
   4ms - 8ms    : ( 99.95%)     893
   8ms - 16ms   : ( 99.99%)     738
  16ms - 32ms   : (100.00%)     249
  32ms - 65ms   : (100.00%)      65
  65ms - 131ms  : (100.00%)       1
  Avg           : (   24us)
```

The count is individual for each row, whereas the percentages are cumulative, so in the preceding example the store command returned within 8 to 16 microseconds 1039587 times—which is actually 47.44% of all operations. The percentage in parentheses includes all rows above it as well, so in this case 86.02% of all store commands returned within 16 microseconds. It's important to note that these are server timings, so they do not represent how long the operation actually took on the client side, because they do not include things like network latency or client-side serialization and processing.

Passing the category all to cbstats will display 278 (as of this writing) different counters. You can find the full list, with descriptions of each, at https://github.com/membase/ep-engine/blob/master/docs/stats.org.

It's a good idea to use *grep* to filter the statistics to find the ones you're actually interested in. For example, if you want to retrieve queue-related statistics, you would use a command similar to this:

```
> cbstats <host>:11210 -b <bucket> all | grep queue
```

On Linux systems, you can use the watch command-line utility to continuously monitor the output of cbstats and highlight any changes in reported values. To continue the previous example, to refresh the queue statistics every second you can use the following:

```
> watch -d -n 1 "cbstats <host>:11210 -b <bucket> all | grep queue"
```

Retrieving Statistics from the HTTP API

The HTTP API exposes total and per-node bucket statistics in JSON format. As Chapter 10 explains, you can get total bucket statistics from http://<host>:8091/pools/default/buckets/<bucket>/stats, and you can control the granularity and time frame of the report with the haveTStamp and zoom query parameters. The JSON document returned will have the following structure:

```
{
  "op": {
    "samples": { ... },
    "samplesCount": 60,
    "isPersistent": true,
    "lastTStamp": 1396001227234,
    "interval": 1000
  },
  "hot_keys": [ ... ]
}
```

The hot_keys array holds statistics about the most-frequently accessed keys, as objects in the following format:

```
{
  "name": "pymc452189",
  "ops": 4.482295E-4
},
```

The samples object has over 200 properties corresponding to various counters. The value of each property is an array of samples; you can find out the number of samples and the sampling interval from the samplesCount and interval properties of the parent object, respectively:

```
"samples": {
  "couch_total_disk_size": [ ... ],
  "couch_docs_fragmentation": [ ... ],
  "couch_views_fragmentation": [ ... ],
  "hit_ratio": [ ... ],
  "ep_cache_miss_rate": [
...
  "cpu_utilization_rate": [ ... ],
  "hibernated_requests": [ ... ],
```

```
    "hibernated_waked": [ ... ],
    ...
    "proc/beam.smp/page_faults": [ ... ],
    "proc/memcached/cpu_utilization": [ ... ],
    "proc/memcached/major_faults": [ ... ],
    ...
},
```

There is a lot of overlap between the counters returned by the cbstats all command and the HTTP API, but they're not identical. Cbstats exposes more internal counters, but it only provides data from the moment it was called. On the other hand, the HTTP API returns additional data about the Couchbase system processes—beam.smp and memcached—including memory usage and page faults.

In addition to the total bucket statistics, you can retrieve data about a bucket from a specific node. To discover the URLs for per-node statistics, first retrieve the node details from http://<host>:8091/pools/default/buckets/default/nodes, which will return a JSON document similar to the following:

```
{
  "servers":[
      {
          "hostname":"procouchbase2.local:8091",
          "uri":"/pools/default/buckets/default/nodes/procouchbase2.local%3A8091",
          "stats":{
              "uri":"/pools/default/buckets/default/nodes/procouchbase2.local%3A8091/stats"
          }
      },
      {
          "hostname":"procouchbase1.local:8091",
          "uri":"/pools/default/buckets/default/nodes/procouchbase1.local%3A8091",
          "stats":{
              "uri":"/pools/default/buckets/default/nodes/procouchbase1.local%3A8091/stats"
          }
      }
  ]
}
```

The value of the uri property is the endpoint you need to call in order to retrieve the per-node bucket statistics. As you can see in the preceding example, it will normally be in the following format: http://<host>:8091/pools/default/buckets/<bucket>/nodes/<hostname>/stats. The JSON document you get from the per-node endpoint is the same as the one returned by the bucket statistics endpoint.

Generating a Cluster Health Report with cbhealthchecker

The cbhealthchecker command-line tool generates a report about the cluster health in HTML, text, and JSON format. You can specify the time frame for the report, from a minute up to a year. The tool retrieves statistics for the specified time frame, compares them to its predefined norms, and generates alerts about abnormal values as well as warnings about potential problems.

To generate a report, use the following command:

```
> cbhealthchecker -c <host> -u <username> -p <password> [-b <bucket>] [-s <scale>]
```

<host>, <username>, and <password> are, of course, the address of a node in the cluster and the administrator credentials. If you don't specify a bucket, the tool will generate a report for all buckets in the cluster. The <scale> parameter controls the time frame for the report: minute, hour, day, week, month, and year. By default, cbhealthchecker generates reports for all six scales.

The alerts generated by cbhealthchecker are based on a set of predefined thresholds that are appropriate for the majority of Couchbase deployments. However, if your cluster is radically different, some of the examples will be irrelevant. For example, if you have a huge data set of historical data, but only a very small working set, then the alert you see in Figure 11-16 will always show up, even if your cluster is actually performing well, because cbhealthchecker expects at least 30% of all active items to be resident in memory.

Figure 11-16. *Cluster health alerts report*

In addition to alerts and the general cluster overview, the report also contains warning indicators based on internal Couchbase statistics such as timings. If your cluster is running on hardware that matches the recommended requirements and is sized according to guidelines, then you should certainly investigate the warning indicators in order to discover the root cause. For example, Figure 11-17 shows part of a report from our test cluster, which uses NAS (Network Attached Storage) disks that naturally have higher latency than local drives. The average load time refers to how long it takes Couchbase to load an item from the persistence layer. Our test cluster uses just one blob disk as the data storage, and blobs in Azure are actually accessed over the network, which adds latency. One thing we could do to increase data access performance is to create a striped volume from several blob disks. Unfortunately, there currently isn't much we can do about the access latency of any individual blob. We'll talk about deploying Couchbase on various cloud platforms in Chapter 12.

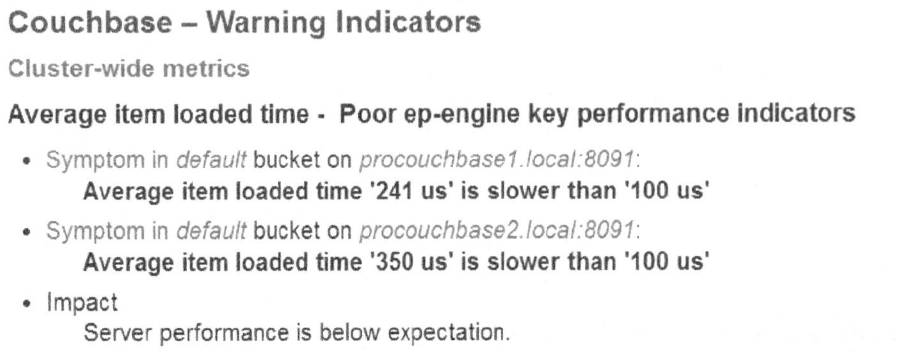

Couchbase – Warning Indicators

Cluster-wide metrics

Average item loaded time - Poor ep-engine key performance indicators

- Symptom in *default* bucket on *procouchbase1.local:8091*:
  Average item loaded time '241 us' is slower than '100 us'
- Symptom in *default* bucket on *procouchbase2.local:8091*:
  Average item loaded time '350 us' is slower than '100 us'

- Impact
  Server performance is below expectation.

Figure 11-17. *Cluster-performance warnings*

Server Warmup

When a Couchbase node or bucket is restarted it needs to go through a warmup process before it can begin serving client requests. During the warmup, Couchbase loads all the keys and metadata into RAM and then fills the rest of the memory up to the low-water mark with documents from disk. Normally Couchbase keeps track of how frequently documents are accessed and periodically saves that data in the access log. If the access log exists and isn't disabled, then the warmup process will use it to determine the order in which it will load items into memory, otherwise it will simply read items from disk sequentially. The warmup process will continue loading documents into RAM until one of the following conditions occurs:

- All items are loaded into RAM.

- All items listed in the access log are loaded into RAM.

- Total RAM use passes the low-water mark.

- The percentage of RAM use passes the value specified by the ep_warmup_min_memory_threshold parameter.

- The number of items loaded into RAM passes the value specified by the ep_warmup_min_items_threshold.

Because loading so many documents before the server can begin serving requests can take quite a long time, you can change the thresholds for when Couchbase considers the warmup complete to speed up the process. The cbepctl utility, which we've already used in this chapter to control various internal parameters, can also change the warmup thresholds. Use these commands:

```
> cbepctl <host>:11210 set flush_param warmup_min_memory_threshold <percent>
> cbepctl <host>:11210 set flush_param warmup_min_items_threshold <items>
```

To change the memory, use percentage and number of loaded items, respectively. The cbepctl utility sets parameters on a per-node per-bucket basis, so you will need to repeat these commands for every bucket and every server node.

■ **Note** The latest version of Couchbase at the time of this writing, 2.5.0, doesn't seem to save these threshold values between server restarts. So if you want to set them permanently, you'll need to configure a task to run the two cbepctl commands every time on server startup.

By default, the access log scanner process runs every 24 hours, starting from 02:00 UTC. If your data access pattern changes more frequently throughout the day, or if you want to schedule the access-log scanner to run when the load on the cluster is lowest, you can use cbepctl to change the scanner interval and start time. To change how often the scanner will run:

```
> cbepctl <host>:11210 set flush_param alog_sleep_time <minutes>
```

To change the start time, in UTC:

```
> cbepctl <host>:11210 set flush_param alog_task_time <hour_of_day>
```

Logs

Couchbase maintains separate log files for different internal components. By default, the logs are located in the following folders:

- *Windows*: `C:\Program Files\Couchbase\Server\log`

- *Linux*: `/opt/couchbase/var/lib/couchbase/logs`

- *OS X*: `~/Library/Logs`

The log files are cyclical and are limited to 10 MB in size. By default, Couchbase creates up to 20 files per log component. You can change the log directory path, as well as the size and maximum number of log files, by editing the `/opt/couchbase/etc/couchbase/static_config` file. The `error_logger_mf_dir` variable controls the log path, `error_logger_mf_maxbytes` is the maximum size of each individual log file, and `error_logger_mf_maxfiles` is the number of files Couchbase will create for each subsystem. The same file also contains the log-level variables for each of the logged subsystems; the available log levels are debug, info, warning, and error. After changing the log levels in the configuration file, you must restart Couchbase on the node in question.

Couchbase creates the following log files:

- `couchcb`: The database persistence system, including storage, views, indexes, events related to compaction, and so on

- `debug`: All debug-level log messages, except the ones in the couchdb, xdcr, and stats files

- `info`: All info-level log messages, except the ones in the couchdb, xdcr, and stats files

- `error`: All error-level log messages, except the ones in the xdcr file

- `xdcr_error`: XDCR-related error messages

- `xdcr`: XDCR-related log messages

- `mapreduce_errors`: Map/Reduce-related errors, such as JavaScript syntax errors

- `views`: View-related messages

- `stats`: Periodic reports of the various internal counters

- `memcached.log`: Memcached-related log messages, such as TAP protocol requests

The Log tab in the web console (Figure 11-18) shows a digest of the latest messages from the log files.

♠ Cluster Overview	Server Nodes	Data Buckets	Views	XDCR	Log	Settings

Log   Generate Diagnostic Report

Event	Module Code	Server Node	Time
Bucket "memtest" loaded on node 'ns_1@procouchbase2.local' in 0 seconds.	ns_memcached001	ns_1@procouchbase2.local	**11:17:14** - Fri Mar 28, 2014
Bucket "memtest" loaded on node 'ns_1@procouchbase1.local' in 0 seconds.	ns_memcached001	ns_1@procouchbase1.local	**11:17:14** - Fri Mar 28, 2014
Created bucket "memtest" of type: memcached [{ram_quota,67108864},{auth_type,sasl},{flush_enabled,false}]	menelaus_web012	ns_1@procouchbase1.local	**11:17:14** - Fri Mar 28, 2014
Port server moxi on node 'babysitter_of_ns_1@127.0.0.1' exited with status 0. Restarting. Messages: 2014-03-28 07:36:50: (cproxy_config.c.315) env: MOXI_SASL_PLAIN_USR (13) 2014-03-28 07:36:50: (cproxy_config.c.324) env: MOXI_SASL_PLAIN_PWD (6) EOL on stdin. Exiting	ns_log000	ns_1@procouchbase2.local	**11:16:58** - Fri Mar 28, 2014

Figure 11-18. *Web console log*

Alerts

You can configure Couchbase to alert you about important events and conditions. In the Web Administration console, under the Settings tab, select the Alerts view. Alerts are disabled by default, and we highly recommend enabling them for all production deployments. As you can see in Figure 11-19, setting up alerts is quite straightforward: enter the address and credentials of your mail server, set the alert email recipients, test that it works, and click Save. Unless you have a very good reason to ignore one of them, you should leave all the alert categories checked.

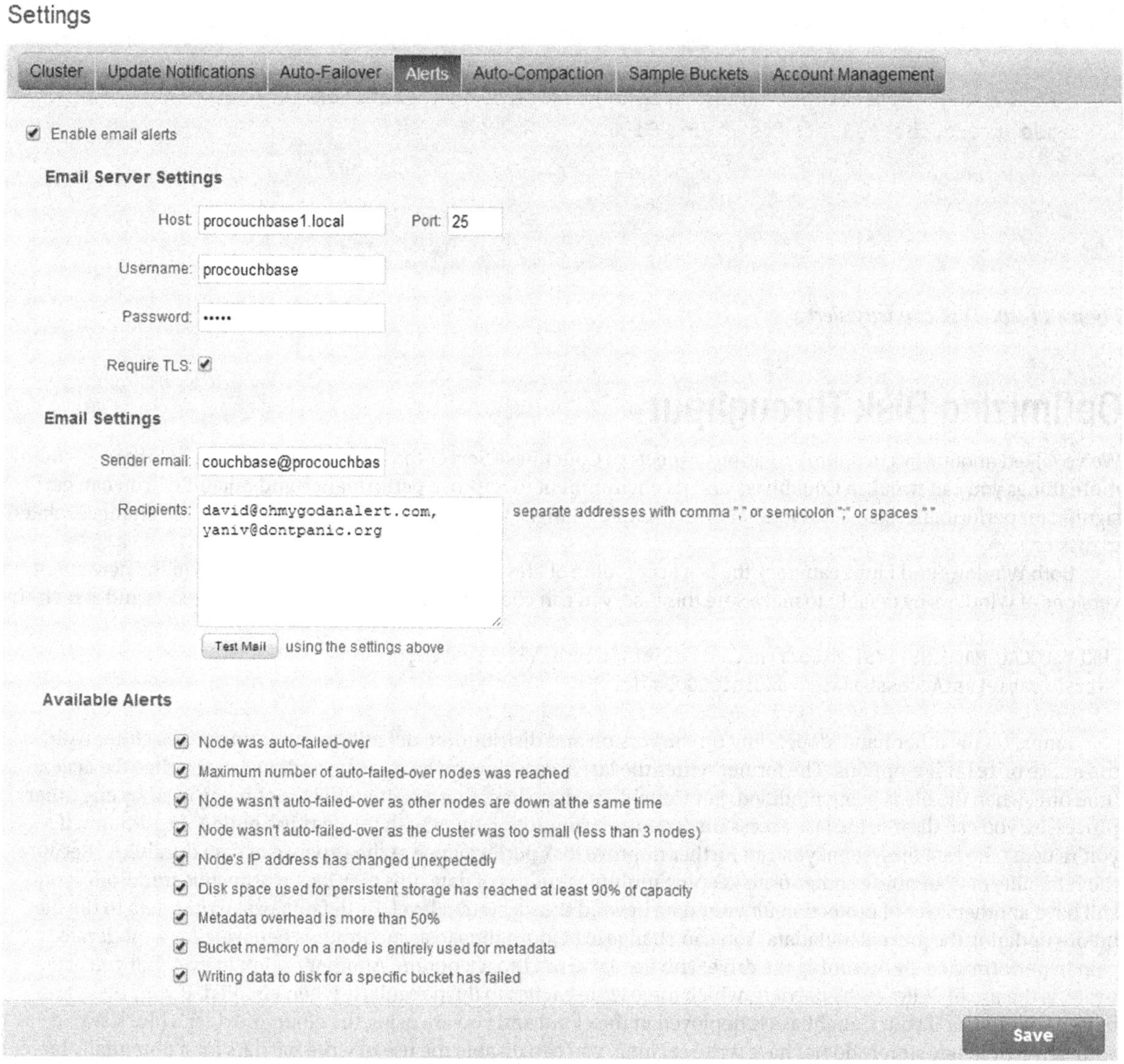

Settings

| Cluster | Update Notifications | Auto-Failover | Alerts | Auto-Compaction | Sample Buckets | Account Management |

☑ Enable email alerts

Email Server Settings

Host: `procouchbase1.local`   Port: `25`

Username: `procouchbase`

Password: `•••••`

Require TLS: ☑

Email Settings

Sender email: `couchbase@procouchbas`

Recipients:
```
david@ohmygodanalert.com,
yaniv@dontpanic.org
```
separate addresses with comma "," or semicolon ";" or spaces " "

[Test Mail] using the settings above

Available Alerts

☑ Node was auto-failed-over

☑ Maximum number of auto-failed-over nodes was reached

☑ Node wasn't auto-failed-over as other nodes are down at the same time

☑ Node wasn't auto-failed-over as the cluster was too small (less than 3 nodes)

☑ Node's IP address has changed unexpectedly

☑ Disk space used for persistent storage has reached at least 90% of capacity

☑ Metadata overhead is more than 50%

☑ Bucket memory on a node is entirely used for metadata

☑ Writing data to disk for a specific bucket has failed

[Save]

Figure 11-19. *Setting up alerts*

In addition to sending out an email, alerts also pop up in the web console, as you can see in Figure 11-20, and in the Couchbase log. If you do not want email alerts, you can still see console alert popups—just enable alerts in the settings and do not provide any mail server details.

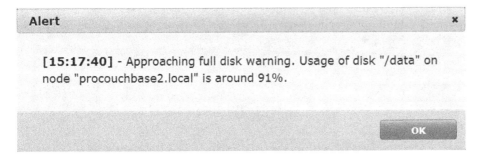

Figure 11-20. *Disk-capacity alert*

Optimizing Disk Throughput

We've talked about ways to optimize various aspects of Couchbase Server throughout this chapter, but there are many more things you can tweak in Couchbase and its environment to improve performance and reliability. You can get significant performance gains through relatively simple changes to the operating system, in particular changes related to disk I/O.

Both Windows and Linux can track the last access time of files on disk. This behavior is disabled in the newer versions of Windows by default; to make sure this is so, you can check that the following registry key exists and is set to 1:

```
[HKEY_LOCAL_MACHINE\SYSTEM\CurrentControlSet\Control\FileSystem]
"NtfsDisableLastAccessUpdate"=dword:00000001
```

Linux, on the other hand, depending on the version and distribution, defaults to mounting drives either with the atime or relatime options. The former writes the last access time on every read, and the latter writes the access time only when the file is being modified. For Couchbase data disks that are (hopefully) not being used by any other processes, you can disable the last-access timestamps by mounting them with the noatime option. In addition, if you're using the ext4 filesystem, you can further improve disk performance at the expense of data durability. Because the reliability of Couchbase comes from keeping multiple replicas of data, this may be a worthwhile trade-off—you still have another layer of protection for your data beyond the filesystem level. By default, ext4 writes data to the file before updating the journal metadata. You can change ext4 journaling to asynchronous behavior, for a moderate gain in performance, by mounting the drive with the data=writeback option. Another option in ext4 that you can tweak is the use of write-cache barriers, which force write caches to flush regularly when enabled. If your disks are battery-backed, or if your Couchbase is deployed in the cloud and you are using the cloud provider's block storage as your drive, or if they simply do not have write caching, you can disable the use of write barriers for a potentially large improvement in write performance by mounting the disks with the barrier=0 option.

With all options enabled, your /etc/fstab configuration would look something like this:

```
/dev/sdb1   /data   ext4   defaults,noatime,data=writeback,barrier=0   0 0
```

■ **Warning**   Because the data=writeback and barrier=0 mount options affect data persistence reliability, you should only use them if you have a good understanding of how the ext4 file system works. You may want to consult your resident Linux guru.

Summary

Phew! This was a long chapter, wasn't it? It started out talking about monitoring and fine-tuning replication queues, as well as about configuring various parameters related to working-set management and cache ejection. Both of those are major aspects of Couchbase's normal operation, and understanding how they work is crucial to making sure your cluster operates at peak efficiency. We then examined all the various monitoring options in exhaustive detail, including all the web console indicators, using the cbstats command-line tool to retrieve even more internal statistics and accessing summary statistics with the HTTP API. Along the way we discussed the implications of different performance metrics, how to detect potential problems early, and how to deal with various failure scenarios when they occur. We learned to generate a cluster health report with the cbhealthchecker tool, monitor Couchbase logs, and set up email alerts. And finally, we rounded out the chapter by geeking out on filesystem performance tweaks, some of which trade disk performance for data durability.

In Chapter 12, you'll learn about the various options for deploying Couchbase in the cloud.

CHAPTER 12

■ ■ ■

Couchbase Server in the Cloud

Cloud computing has been one of the main catalysts for the growth of data. In fact, cloud computing and the data explosion have been feeding each other for years. The capability to grow on demand allows companies to plan for growth without the need to invest in hardware upfront. But this rapid growth does not come without cost. To thoroughly understand the influence of the two on each other, we need to better understand what cloud computing is.

As with NoSQL, there is no formal definition for cloud computing. However, one of the characteristics influencing the data explosion is the introduction of self-service, on-demand computing. Cloud infrastructure allows applications and developers to request resources on an as-needed basis. This might seem like a trivial capability, but it provides applications with new means to scale.

With the rise of cloud computing, it has become easier for applications to scale out by simply requesting more resources, and also to scale back when those resources are no longer needed. This dynamic approach to computing resources is commonly known as *cloud elasticity*. Dealing with elasticity requires applications to be able to scale with ease. This is not simple for any application, and even less so for databases. In contrast to other databases, Couchbase Server deals very well with such scenarios, as Chapter 9 discusses. This allows Couchbase to take better advantage of cloud infrastructure and to simplify migrations to the cloud.

Today's marketplace has a wide variety of cloud providers, each with its own distinct capabilities and limitations. Because of the differences between the various cloud providers, deploying Couchbase Server is very specific to the particular cloud platform. In this chapter, you'll learn how Couchbase can be deployed on two of the leading platforms today: Amazon Web Services and Microsoft Azure.

Couchbase Server on Amazon Web Services

Amazon Web Services (AWS) is the oldest and biggest cloud provider today. AWS is available globally, located in eight different regions—three in the United States and one in each of the following: Brazil, Ireland, Singapore, Japan, and Australia. Each region has several separate data centers called Availability Zones.

AWS offers a variety of services, including the following:

- *Amazon Elastic Compute Cloud (EC2)*: EC2 provides on-demand virtual machines. EC2 virtual machines, referred to as instances, are created based on Amazon Machine Images (AMI), which are created by either Amazon, the community, or external vendors.

- *Elastic Block Store (EBS)*: EBS provides persistent storage for EC2 server volumes. EBS volumes are persisted independently of the lifecycle of the instance and can be transferred between instances in the same region.

- *AWS Marketplace*: The AWS Marketplace is a centralized online store for software and services that can be run and/or consumed by AWS applications. These services are offered in one of two formats: Software as a Service (SaaS), or pre-configured Amazon Machine Images (AMI). Using the AWS Marketplace AMIs might also include fees for the software installed on them.

- *Amazon CloudFormation*: Amazon CloudFormation provides a way to create a collection of AWS resources that can be created and managed together.

- *Amazon CloudWatch*: Amazon CloudWatch is a monitoring service that provides developers and administrators with information about AWS cloud resources. CloudWatch metrics can be viewed from a web-based management console. You can also set triggers for when a specific resource consumption reaches a specific threshold, at which point CloudWatch will send you a notification and/or perform autoscaling.

- *Amazon Simple Storage Service (S3)*: S3 is an unlimited cloud storage solution exposed when using a web services API. By using the web services API you can store, read, and delete objects up to 5 terabytes in size from anywhere.

- *DynamoDB*: DynamoDB is a fully managed NoSQL data store. DynamoDB has built-in strong consistency and fault tolerance.

The preceding list is just a small subset of the services provided by AWS. This chapter discusses the first four services. However, it is important to know that as a complete cloud solution, AWS provides much more.

Considerations for Deploying Couchbase Server on AWS

As we will soon see, it is very easy to set up a Couchbase Server cluster on AWS. However, there are some things to be considered before running a production cluster in the cloud. Factors like configuration management, sizing, and security work differently in any cloud environment. Let's take a closer look at the things we need to consider when planning an AWS-based deployment.

Location of the Nodes

AWS provides a variety of regions and availability zones for you to select from. The location of the nodes can affect the overall performance of your application. When looking at a Couchbase cluster, there are two types of communication paths you need to consider: communication between the application servers and the cluster nodes, and internal node-to-node communication within the cluster. As Chapter 3 mentions, Couchbase clients communicate directly to all the nodes in the cluster. It is recommended to co-locate application servers in the same data center as your cluster nodes. In addition, Couchbase nodes communicate with each other for many reasons, such as replicating data, monitoring, and querying views. For this reason, it is crucial that all the nodes in the same cluster be co-located in the same availability zone.

■ **Note** Data locality across geographic regions (that is, different data centers) can be achieved by replicating data with XDCR. XDCR is covered in Chapter 13.

Disk Storage

As you've seen throughout this book, all the documents in Couchbase buckets are eventually written to disk. In addition, views use disk I/O extensively to read data changes, to store index information, and to query the indexes. This makes the performance of your nodes' disk a major factor in the overall performance of the cluster, especially in heavy-write scenarios or when using multiple views. EC2 has a variety of disk storage options that can be used for Couchbase nodes.

Chapter 9 talks about the performance benefits of placing your document and index data on different drives. The same concept can be applied to EC2 instances. In addition, it is important to understand the difference between two types of drives, or volumes, that can used in EC2 nodes: instance store and Elastic Block Storage (EBS).

Instance stores are temporary drives that are usable by a single instance during its lifetime. Data in instance stores is persisted through reboot. On instance-store backed instances—that is, instances that use instance stores as their root device—data will be lost when the instance is terminated (deleted). On EBS-backed instances, data stored on instance stores will be lost if the instance is stopped. In addition, data on instance stores can be lost due to drive failure. Because of its ephemeral nature, it is not recommended to store long-term data, such as document data, on instance stores. However, at the time of this writing Amazon is offering a new generation of SSD-based instance storage, which can be used for index data and improving view performance.

Elastic Block Storage (EBS) provides highly available and reliable drives, which can be attached to EC2 instances in the same availability zone. EBS drives persist independently of the lifecycle of the instance they are attached to and are recommended when data changes frequently and requires long-term persistence. EBS drives, or volumes, have two different flavors: standard and provisioned IOPS (I/O Operations per Second). Standard volumes provide moderate I/O performance but cost less, while provisioned IOPS volumes are designed to provide better I/O performance at a higher cost. It is important to note that provisioned IOPS volumes are designed for I/O-intensive workloads, particularly database workloads, and therefore are recommended for Couchbase Server deployments.

To put the differences between the two EBS flavors in numbers, with standard EBS volumes you currently get around 100 I/O operations per second (IOPS), whereas provisioned IOPS volumes can provide up to 4,000 IOPS. In addition, you can use software volume striping to improve performance by combining multiple EBS drives into a single logical volume. Table 12-1 shows the expected performance using different EBS configurations.

Table 12-1. *EBS Performance*

EBS configuration	Expected IOPS
Standard EBS	~100
Striped standard EBS with 8 volumes	~800
Provisioned IOPS	Up to 4,000
Striped provisioned IOPS with 8 volumes	Up to 32,000

■ **Note** EC2 instances access EBS volumes over the network, which can impact the performance you get from your EBS drives. In order to receive the best performance from the EBS volumes, EC2 provides EBS-optimized instances with dedicated network capacity for EBS I/O. When working with EBS volumes, make sure you select instance types that can provide EBS-optimized support, and check the EBS-optimized checkbox in the Instance Details screen when requesting the instance.

Security Groups

Amazon EC2 security groups act as firewall configuration for all instances that are configured to use that security group. Security groups allow you to define firewall rules based on the following parameters: communication protocol to be used, ports, and sources/destinations for incoming/outgoing communication, which can be a specific IP, an IP range, or another security group. Configuring security groups depends on your application topology, but the minimum rules you need for a Couchbase cluster are shown in Table 12-2.

Table 12-2. *Security Configuration for a Couchbase Cluster*

Usage	Protocol	Ports	Sources
Node-to-node communication	TCP	8091, 8092, 11209, 11210, 4369, 21100-21199	To allow communication from other nodes, use the nodes security group as a source, thus ensuring only nodes in the cluster are allowed through the firewall.
Client communication	TCP	8091, 8092, 11210, 11211	If the client application runs inside AWS, use a security group assigned to your application servers, otherwise, use the public IP addresses.
XDCR	TCP	8091, 8092	Use a security group assigned to the replicated cluster. This might be the same security group used for your cluster or a different one.
XDCR with SSL	TCP		Use a security group assigned to the replicated cluster. This might be the same security group used for your cluster or a different one.
Administration	TCP	8091	This port needs to be accessed remotely by the cluster administrators. You can add it to the security group as needed with a specific IP and remove it when done.
Administration SSH	SSH	22	This port needs to be accessed remotely by the cluster administrators. You can add it to the security group as needed with a specific IP and remove it when done.

Setting up Couchbase Server on AWS

There are multiple ways to provision EC2 instances with Couchbase Server: you can create an instance based on an Amazon Machine Images (AMI) of one of the supported operating systems and then install Couchbase manually. Another option is to use AWS CloudFormation to provision one or more instances. AWS CloudFormation allows you to pre-configure those instances as a new Couchbase Server cluster, or to join an existing cluster. You can also use the AWS Marketplace to provision pre-configured licensed instances of Couchbase. In addition, some external services to AWS, such as RightScale and Chef, can be used to deploy Couchbase Server, both on AWS and other clouds.

Manually Creating EC2 instances

EC2 provides you with a variety of instance specifications and base images you can use for your Couchbase Server cluster nodes. Although installing Couchbase Server on EC2 is exactly the same as on any other machine, the process of creating an EC2 instance that is fitted to be a Couchbase Server node in a production server does take some special attention. In this section you will learn how to create such EC2 instances.

■ **Note** Couchbase Server installation is covered in depth in Chapter 1.

To create new EC2 instances, log on to the AWS management console and click the EC2 link, as shown in Figure 12-1.

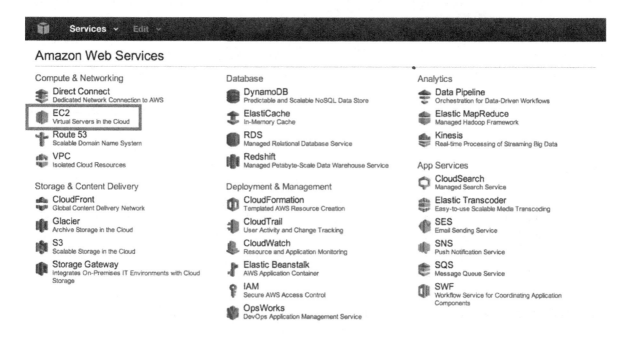

Figure 12-1. *EC2 on the AWS management console*

Before you start creating instances, you need to select your region. Do this in the dropdown menu in the right-hand side of the top bar, as shown in Figure 12-2.

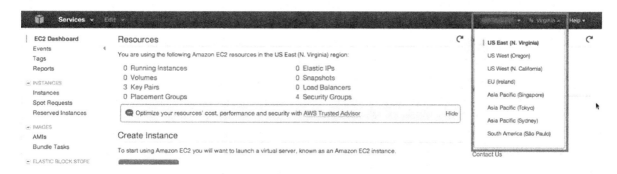

Figure 12-2. *Selecting a region in AWS*

Next, click on the Launch Instance button, as shown in Figure 12-3, to start to process of creating a new instance.

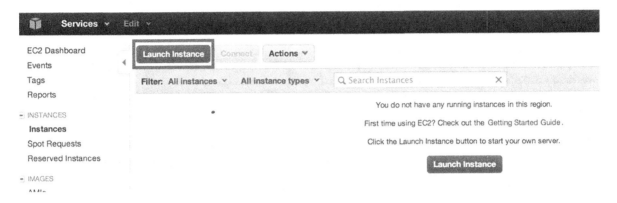

Figure 12-3. *The Lounch Instance button*

The instance-creation process begins with selecting an Amazon Machine Image (AMI). This is the base image from which your instance will be created. There are a several options to choose from. For example, in the Community AMIs tabs there are a number of images containing a preinstalled version of Couchbase. The AWS Marketplace also contains AMIs created by Couchbase, covered in the next section. For now, we will select an image from the Quick Start tab, which contains a variety of operating systems. You can select any operating system supported by Couchbase; for now we will select the Amazon Linux AMI, as shown in Figure 12-4.

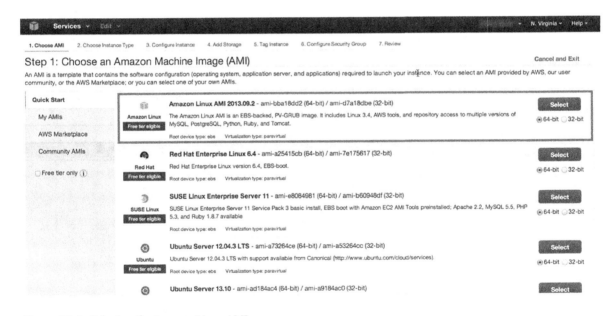

Figure 12-4. *Selecting the Amazon Linux AMI*

The next step is choosing an instance type. Just like with AMIs, AWS has a variety of instances to choose from. The instance types are divided into the following categories:

- *Micro-instances*: Micro-instances are low-cost instances with limited CPU power and memory. Micro-instances are not recommended for Couchbase.

- *General purpose*: General purpose contains a few options for instances with balanced resources in different sizes and specifications.

- *Memory optimized*: Memory-optimized instances are high-memory instances with the lowest cost per GB of RAM in comparison to other Amazon EC2 instance types. Because RAM is usually the resource in highest demand for Couchabse, memory-optimized instances will probably be the most cost-effective choice for running Couchbase in AWS.

- *Storage optimized*: Storage-optimized instances provide direct-attached storage options optimized for applications with high disk I/O needs. For Couchbase installations, storage-optimized instances might be a good fit when views are used intensively, or when the write throughput is extremely high and disk I/O can become a bottleneck.

■ **Note**   The direct attached storage is an instance store, which means there is no long-term guarantee for your data. When using an instance store for storing Couchbase data files, make sure you back up the data regularly, and be prepared for potential data loss in your cluster.

- *Compute optimized*: Compute-optimized instances have a higher ratio of CPUs to memory than other instance families, and the lowest cost per CPU in comparison to other EC2 instance types. Normally CPU is not a bottleneck for Couchbase Server clusters. However, if for some reason you do need high CPU utilization as part of your cluster activity, compute-optimized instances might be the most cost-effective choice for you.

In addition to the resource specifications of the instance types, there are two parameters you should consider:

- *EBS-optimized available*: This parameter states whether instances of this specific size can be set as EBS-optimized. As discussed earlier in this chapter, EBS-optimized instances are needed to provide dedicated network capacity when accessing EBS volumes.

- *Network Performance*: Network performance can affect not only the latency between clients and your cluster, but also the communication between nodes.

For this book, we decided to use the general purpose m1.xlarge instance, which provides 4 CPUs, 15 GB of RAM, is EBS-optimized, and has high network performance. Once you have selected the instance type (see Figure 12-5), click the Next: Configure Instance Details button.

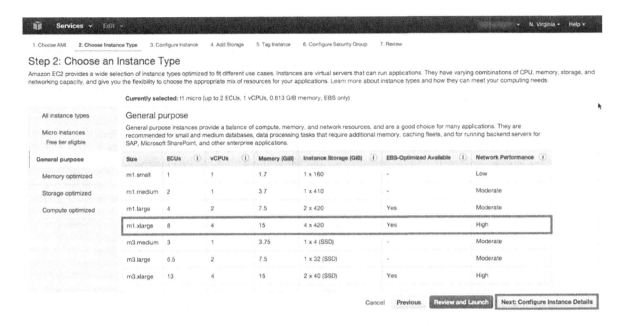

Figure 12-5. *Selecting an instance type*

Next, you'll configure the instance details (Figure 12-6). The first parameter you can set is the number of instances. If you intend to create a cluster, you can set this to the number of nodes you need to create. Then you need to select an availability zone and check the Launch as EBS-optimized instance box. Click the Next: Add Storage button.

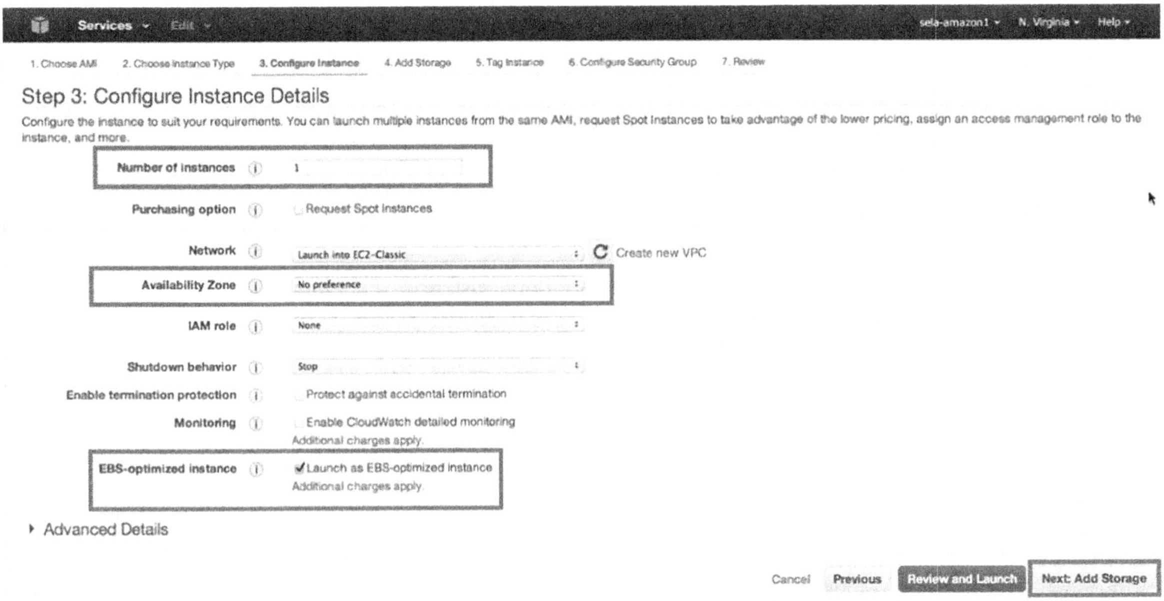

Figure 12-6. *Configuring instances*

The Add Storage screen (Figure 12-7) allows you to add additional storage devices to your instance. This can be either an instance store or an EBS volume. Let's add a new provisioned IOPS EBS volume. To add a volume, click the Add New Volume button. The AWS management console will automatically add a standard EBS volume, with 8 GB of space. To change the volume to be EBS provisioned, select Provisioned IOPS from the Volume Type list. Once you have changed the type of the volume to Provisioned IOPS you can specify the IOPS rate provided by the volume.

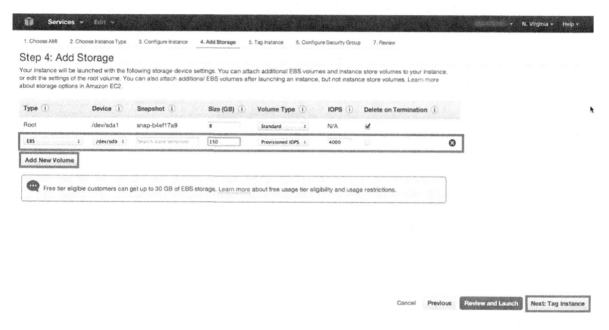

Figure 12-7. *Adding storage to EC2 instances*

▨ **Note** IOPS-provisioned EBS drives must have at least 1GB for every 30 IOPS. For example, to add a volume with 3000 IOPS, it must be at least 100 GB in size.

The Tag Instance page allows you to add a short description that can help you identify the instances in the AWS management console later. For example, tag your instance as Couchbase Server Node and click the Next: Configure Security Group button (Figure 12-8).

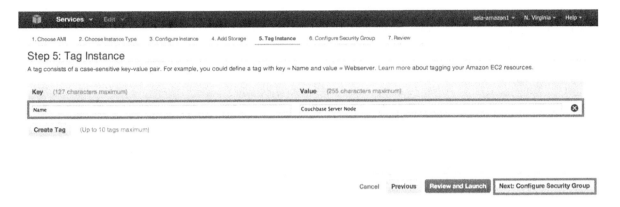

Figure 12-8. *Tagging an instance*

Next, you need to set up a security group. You'll open the communication ports between your cluster nodes, as well as for incoming traffic from clients. To do so, select the Create a New Security Group option and give it a name and a description. To enable communications to and from your cluster, you'll need to add the rules shown in Table 12-3.

Table 12-3. *Security Rules for a Couchbase Node*

Protocol	Type	Port	Source
SSH	TCP	22	0.0.0.0/0
Custom TCP Rule	TCP	8091-8092	0.0.0.0/0
Custom TCP Rule	TCP	11210-11211	0.0.0.0/0
Custom TCP Rule	TCP	4369	0.0.0.0/0
Custom TCP Rule	TCP	11209	0.0.0.0/0
Custom TCP Rule	TCP	21100 - 21199	0.0.0.0/0

■ **Note** Specifying 0.0.0.0/0 in the rules source opens the port to the public Internet and is not recommended for production use. Make sure you specify a source that is controlled by you, such as a security group. For example, once the instance is launched, the security group will be created and assigned an ID. We strongly recommend changing the source in the rules for ports 4369, 11209, and 21100-21199 to the group's ID.

Once you have created the rules for the security group, click the Review and Launch button and then click the Launch button (Figure 12-9).

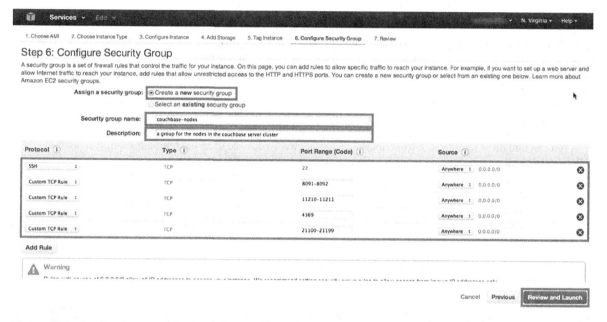

Figure 12-9. *Configuring a security group for Couchbase Server nodes*

Before you launch your instance, you will need to set a key pair, which is a set of cryptographic keys you can use to authenticate when connecting to your instance. If you do not have an existing key pair, create a new one and download the key pair before launching the instances.

Once you have launched the instance, you can use the key to connect to it through a secure shell (SSH). To do so, you first need to get the instance's public DNS name: click on the View Instances button and locate the instance. Select the instance row to see its public DNS, as shown in Figure 12-10.

	Name		Instance ID	Instance Type	Availability Zone	Instance State	Status Checks	Alarm Status	Public DNS		Public IP
			i-33256e12	m1.xlarge	us-east-1d	running	2/2 check...	None	ec2-174-129-130-66.co...		174.129.130.66
	Couchbase ...		i-79e0bf57	m1.xlarge	us-east-1c	running	2/2 check...	None	ec2-54-234-137-184.co...		54.234.137.184

Instance: i-79e0bf57 (Couchbase Server Node) | Public DNS:

Figure 12-10. *Getting a public DNS for an instance*

Once you have the instance's public DNS, you can use it to SSH to your instance and install Couchbase. To do so, use the key pair to authenticate for the user ec2-user as follows:

```
> ssh -i keypair.pem ec2-user@public-dns
```

As you can see, setting up instances manually can be tedious. AWS offers a service called CloudFormation that helps you automate this process. Let's take a closer look at how to automate Couchbase deployment with AWS CloudFormation.

Deploying Couchbase Using AWS CloudFormation

AWS CloudFormation provides a way to deploy, update, and delete a group of resources, called a *stack*, which lets you treat multiple resources as a single unit. A stack can represent more than one type of resource; you can create a stack that is composed of your application servers, as well as of database servers and any other component you need. For brevity, we will concentrate on stacks containing Couchbase Server nodes only.

The first thing needed to create an AWS CloudFormation is a template. You can create your own template, but the Couchbase team has already created a repository of such templates, which not only create the resources needed—that is, the EC2 instances installed with Couchbase—but also configure the nodes and add them to a cluster.

You can find these templates in Couchbase's git repository. To download all the templates simply issue the following git pull command:

```
> git clone git://github.com/couchbaselabs/cloud-formation.git
```

This will create a local directory called `cloud-formation` containing a script that will help you generate new templates, and a sub-folder called `packs`. Inside the packs folder you will find templates for various Couchbase versions, with various amounts of nodes.

To create a cluster using AWS CloudFormation, log on to the AWS management console and click the CloudFormation link, as shown in Figure 12-11.

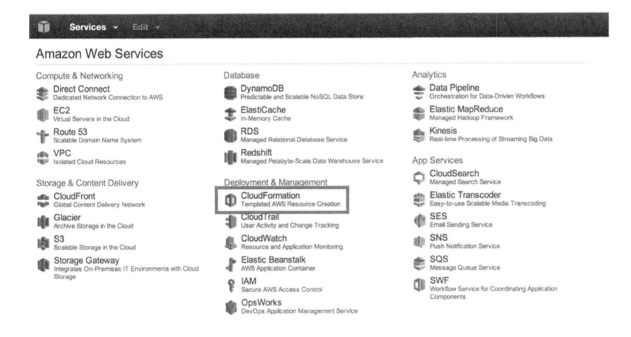

Figure 12-11. *The CloudFormation link on the AWS management console*

Next, click on the Create Stack button, as shown in Figure 12-12.

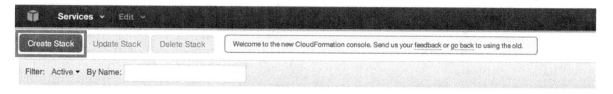

Figure 12-12. *The Create Stack button*

To create a stack, you need to give the stack a name, for example, "Couchbase," and supply a template. For now, browse to the *packs\couchbase-2.0.0-enterprise-64bit\2-pack-couchbase template*, select it, and click the Next Step button, as shown in Figure 12-13.

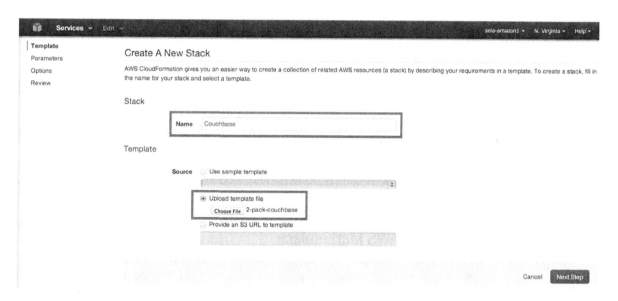

Figure 12-13. *Creating a new CloudFormation stack*

In the next screen, you can specify parameters for your CloudFormation template. In this example, we'll set the following:

- ExistingClusterHostPort: The Couchbase stack can create a new cluster or join an existing one. If you wish to join an existing cluster, you must specify the IP address and port number of that cluster in the ExistingClusterHostPort parameter. For now, let's leave it blank.

- KeyName: A cryptographic key pair that you can use to authenticate with the created instances. Let's use the Couchbase key pair we created previously in the "Manually Creating EC2 Instances" section.

- RESTPassword: A password for the Administrator user.

After setting the parameters, click the Next Step button, as shown in Figure 12-14.

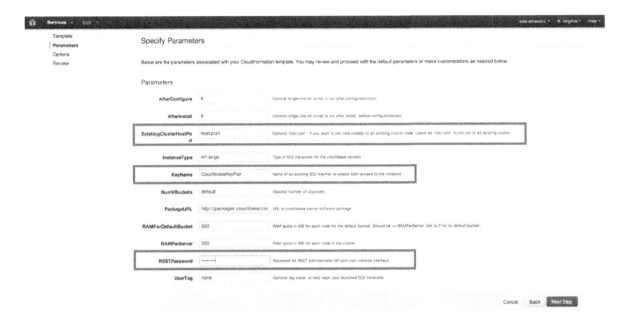

Figure 12-14. *Specifying the stack's parameters*

In the Options screen, press the Next Step button again. In the Review screen, you can review the stack you are about to create. Click the Create button to create your stack.

Deploy Couchbase Using the AWS Marketplace

The AWS marketplace offers a simple way to create EC2 instances that are preinstalled and preconfigured with Couchbase Server. In addition, the pricing for instances deployed from the AWS marketplace includes licensing, so if you choose Couchbase Server Enterprise Edition Standard or Premium, you do not need to purchase the licenses separately.

You can use the AWS marketplace search feature to find the Couchbase Server edition you want to deploy, then select it. In the product page, you can select the region and click Continue, as shown in Figure 12-15.

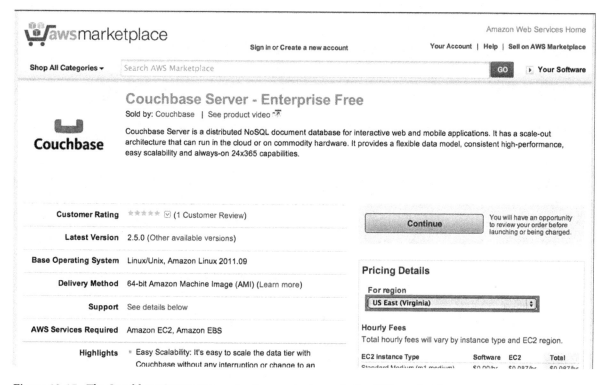

Figure 12-15. *The Couchbase Server–Enterprise Free product page in the AWS marketplace*

Next, on the 1-Click Launch page, shown in Figure 12-16, you can select the instance configuration, including a preconfigured security group. Once you have configured your instances, you can use the Launch with 1-Click button to deploy your instances.

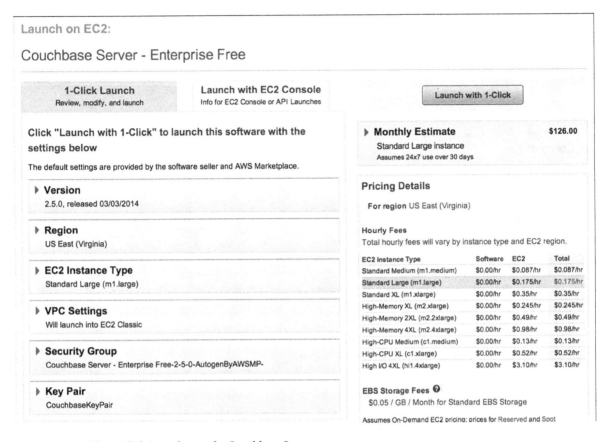

Figure 12-16. *The 1-Click Lounch page for Couchbase Server*

Couchbase Server on Microsoft Azure

Microsoft Azure is Microsoft's cloud platform. Microsoft Azure is available globally and has data centers located in eleven different regions as part of its service offering. Currently Microsoft Azure has four data centers in the United States, one each in Dublin, Amsterdam, Hong-Kong, Singapore, and Brazil, and two in Japan. In addition, Microsoft Azure has services running in China for two additional data centers.

Microsoft Azure offers a variety of services, including:

- *Microsoft Azure Virtual Machines*: The Microsoft Azure Virtual Machines service provides on-demand virtual machines, hosting a variety of operating systems including Windows and Linux.

- *Microsoft Azure Cloud Services*: Microsoft Azure Cloud Services offer a Windows-based Platform as a Service (PaaS) solution for multi-tier applications. Cloud Services offer a management and configuration layer on top of Windows-based virtual machines for applications that are written using a set of templates and APIs to run as cloud service applications.

- *Microsoft Azure Web Sites*: Microsoft Azure Web Sites offer a PaaS solution for IIS-based applications. This includes configuration and management services for such applications and integration with source-control solutions for applications that can run under IIS.

- *Microsoft Azure Virtual Network*: Microsoft Azure Virtual Network offers a Virtual Private Network (VPN) service for connecting networks and computers from different locations, including on premises, in Microsoft Azure, and on other cloud providers.

- *HDInsight*: HDInsight is a Hadoop as a Service solution based on Microsoft's Hadoop distribution.

- *Microsoft Azure Blob Storage*: Microsoft Azure Blob Storage is a cloud storage solution exposed through an HTTP-based web services API. Using the web services API you can store, read, and delete files from anywhere. Microsoft Azure Blob Storage offers two types of blobs:

    - *Block blob*: Block blobs are optimized for streaming workloads and provide better read throughput for scan operations. Block blobs are limited in size to 200 GB.

    - *Page blob*: Page blobs are optimized for random access and are useful in files that are used for seek operations. Page blobs are limited in size to 1 TB.

- *Microsoft Azure Table Storage*: A simple, storage-based key-value store.

The preceding list is just a small subset of the services provided by Microsoft Azure. This section uses Microsoft Azure virtual machines to set up Couchbase Server. However, it is also important to understand some of the other services and how they can be used in applications using Couchbase Server as a database.

Considerations for Deploying Couchbase on Microsoft Azure

As with AWS, it is very easy to set up a Couchbase Server cluster on Microsoft Azure. And just as with AWS, there are some things to be considered before running a production cluster. Let's take a closer look at the things you need to consider when planning a Microsoft Azure–based deployment.

Downtime in Microsoft Azure Virtual Machines and Availability Sets

As with any other cloud service provider, downtime in Microsoft Azure can happen at any time. Unexpected downtime can occur due to software or hardware failure. In addition, Microsoft Azure performs scheduled maintenance at regular intervals—for example, to install security updates for the host OS, which requires a reboot.

■ **Note**   Currently, security updates are applied at least once a month.

To deal with both planned and unplanned downtime, Microsoft Azure groups virtual machines in two ways:

- *Upgrade domains*: Upgrade domains are logical groups of deployments. Upgrade domains are updated one at a time; spreading virtual machines across upgrade domains ensures the availability of some virtual machines during upgrades and maintenance jobs.

- *Fault domains*: Fault domains are groups of resources dependent on the same single point-of-failure components in the data center—for example, racks that use the same top-of-rack switch, power supply, and so on. Spreading virtual machines across fault domains ensures no single failure will affect all of them.

To spread virtual machines across upgrade and fault domains, Microsoft Azure provides a feature called an *availability set*. Availability sets are used to group resources, such as virtual machines, that perform the same function. Placing multiple resources in an availability set tells the Microsoft Azure Fabric Controller management service to distribute the resources across fault and upgrade domains. This ensures that at least some of the resources within the same availability set will remain available at all times.

Virtual Machine Sizes

Microsoft Azure offers multiple VM sizes for different prices. The sizes and prices are subject to change, and Microsoft is constantly adding new hardware configurations to Microsoft Azure. To get the latest information about virtual machine sizes and specifications, see the "Virtual Machine and Cloud Service Sizes for Microsoft Azure" page in MSDN: http://msdn.microsoft.com/en-us/library/windowsazure/dn197896.aspx. Microsoft Azure VMs fall into two categories:

- *Standard Instances*: Standard instances offer a balanced distribution of resources. If you're using standard instances for Couchbase Server, we recommend using A3 (Large) instance size or bigger to get a minimum of 4 CPU cores and 7 GB of RAM.

- *Memory-Intensive Instances*: Memory-intensive instances offer a higher RAM-to-CPU core ratio. Because RAM is usually the most crucial resource for Couchbase, memory-intensive instances are usually the best choice for hosting Couchbase Server. If you're using memory-intensive instances, we recommend using A6 instance size or bigger to get a minimum of 4 CPUs and 26 GB of RAM.

■ **Note**   Microsoft Azure currently offers another class of CPU intensive instances, which can only be created as part of a Windows HPC cluster and not as standalone VMs. Therefore, they cannot be used for running Couchbase Server.

Disk Storage

We've talked about the importance of disk I/O throughout this book; it affects data durability, view performance, and XDCR. Microsoft Azure doesn't have as many storage options as EC2, which makes understanding how to get more performance out of the available storage even more important.

In general there are two types of drives in Microsoft Azure: temporary drives, which are backed by local disks on the host machine, and data disks, which are drives backed by Microsoft Azure Blob Storage.

Microsoft Azure Temporary Storage Drives

Temporary storage drives are created automatically when a Microsoft Azure virtual machine is created. On Windows-based virtual machines, the temporary drive is available as the "D:" drive, and on Linux VMs it is created as the "/dev/sdb1" device, and usually mounted to the "/mnt/resources" folder. By default, temporary drives are used to save the system pagefile, but can store any type of temporary data.

Because temporary drives are located on the same physical machine that runs the virtual machine, they can provide higher IOPS and lower latency than data disks, which are persisted to the Microsoft Azure Blob Storage.

■ **Note**   The size of temporary storage drive depends on the virtual machine size and is subject to change. To get the latest specification of virtual machine sizes and specifications, see the same "Virtual Machine and Cloud Service Sizes for Microsoft Azure" page in MSDN.

Data Disks

Data disks are virtual hard drive (VHD) files, with up to 1 TB of space, which are stored in Microsoft Azure Blob Storage and can be attached to a running virtual machine to store application data. You can upload disks that already contain data to Microsoft Azure Blob Storage and attach them to a virtual machine, or you can direct Azure to create and attach an empty disk.

Data Disk Performance

Because data disks reside in the blob storage, they have limited performance. Currently, Microsoft Azure disks provide roughly 500 IOPS per blob. You can use software striping to improve performance by combining multiple data disks into a single logical volume resulting in disk performance of roughly 500 * <number of disks> IOPS.

■ **Note** Just like temporary drive sizes, the number of disks you can attach to a virtual machine depends on the virtual machine size and is subject to change. To get the latest specifications of virtual machine sizes, see the same "Virtual Machine and Cloud Service Sizes for Microsoft Azure" page in MSDN.

Another limitation of the Microsoft Azure Blob Storage is the number of IOPS per storage account. Each account is limited to 20,000 IOPS. To avoid hitting the storage account limitation, make sure to distribute drives across accounts when needed.

Virtual machines access data disks over the network, which can add latency to your I/O operations. To minimize the latency between your virtual machines and data disks, make sure to define the storage account and the virtual machines in the same affinity group. If you're using a virtual network for your virtual machines, make sure to define it in the same affinity group as your storage account.

Network Configuration

Microsoft Azure Virtual Machines are created inside a container called a cloud service, much like the virtual machines that are created using the Cloud Service PaaS model. Cloud services provide a single external IP address behind a firewall as well as a load balancer that can be mapped to any number of servers internally. Because Couchbase clients access nodes directly, this setup is not suited for Couchbase Server clusters, unless the clients reside inside the cloud service.

Another problem with deploying Couchbase inside a cloud service is the way name resolution works. The cloud service provides hostname (short machine name) resolution, but does not guarantee that VMs will keep the same IP address, and the cloud service tends to change the DNS suffix when all machines in the cloud service are stopped and restarted. Due to a limitation of Erlang, Couchbase Server can only use IP addresses or Fully Qualified Domain Names (FQDN), both of which can change within the cloud service, which makes them unusable in a production deployment.

The optimal way to deploy Couchbase on Microsoft Azure is by using the Virtual Private Network service, called Virtual Networks. Microsoft Azure Virtual Networks provide the following capabilities:

- *Custom name resolution*: When setting up the virtual network, you can specify the IP address of a DNS server, which will provide your network with name resolution. You can use public DNS services, such as Google DNS, to resolve external domains. Or you can set up and manage your own DNS server to provide custom name resolution for your virtual network. You can use any DNS software, such as Microsoft DNS on Windows Server, or bind9 on Linux.

- *Static IP addresses*: A new and simpler option for maintaining consistent names or addresses within your virtual network is to assign static, private IP addresses to your virtual machines.

- *Connectivity:* Microsoft Azure virtual networks are designed first and foremost to securely connect networks and computers. You can use virtual networks to connect your Couchbase clients to your cluster, either by connecting a network they belong to, such as a Microsoft Azure Cloud Service, or by connecting single machines to the virtual network.

Now that you understand the capabilities and limitations of hosting Couchbase Server on Microsoft Azure, let's take a look at how to set up virtual machines for Couchbase Server.

Setting Up Couchbase Server on Microsoft Azure

Setting up Couchbase Server on Microsoft Azure boils down to setting up a virtual network and then creating the virtual machines correctly. You can set up the virtual machine manually through the Microsoft Azure management console or CLI tools, or by using third-party tools such as Chef or Puppet to automate setup and deployment.

Creating a Virtual Network

Creating a virtual network is a relatively simple process: you can create a virtual network using the command-line tools or the Microsoft Azure management portal. To create a VM using the management portal, simply log on to the Microsoft Azure management portal using your account credentials, click on the plus sign at the bottom of the page, as shown in Figure 12-17, and then select Network Services ➤ Virtual Network ➤ Quick Create to set up the virtual network, as shown in Figure 12-18.

Figure 12-17. *The New menu in the Microsoft Azure portal*

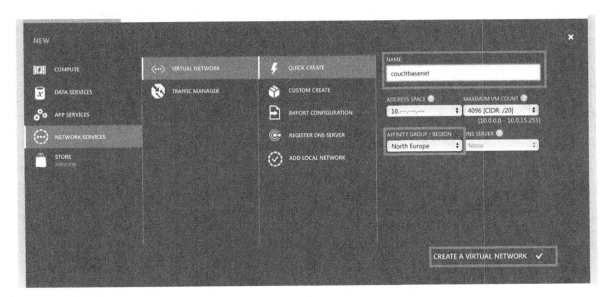

Figure 12-18. *Creating a new virtual network*

There are a few things you can control using the Quick Create option. First, set the virtual network's Name. Then specify the Region or Affinity Group where the virtual network will reside. We strongly recommend selecting the same location as the cloud service where your Couchbase cluster is located, to minimize latency. You can also change the address space for the network, the maximum amount of VMs that will be associated with this virtual network, and the DNS server address.

Manually Creating Microsoft Azure VMs

Creating a Microsoft Azure VM is a straightforward process. Just as with virtual networks, you can create a VM using the command-line tools or using the Microsoft Azure management portal. To create a VM using the management portal, simply click on the plus sign on the bottom of the page and then select Compute ➤ Virtual Machine ➤From Gallery, as shown in Figure 12-19, to start the virtual machine creation wizard.

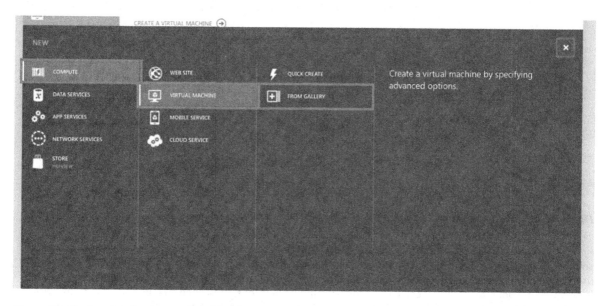

Figure 12-19. *Starting the Create virtual machine wizard in the Microsoft Azure portal*

Next, you will need to select an image from the Images Gallery. You can select any of the operating systems supported by Couchbase. In this walkthrough, we have selected OpenLogic Linux, which is based on CentOS 6.5.

Next, we need to configure the virtual machine. At this point, you need to set the machine name and size and then specify a username for login, as well as set up the authentication method. For brevity, uncheck the Upload a Compatible SSH Key checkbox and check the Provide a Password checkbox to connect through SSH with a username/password combination, as shown in Figure 12-20, before clicking on the Next button.

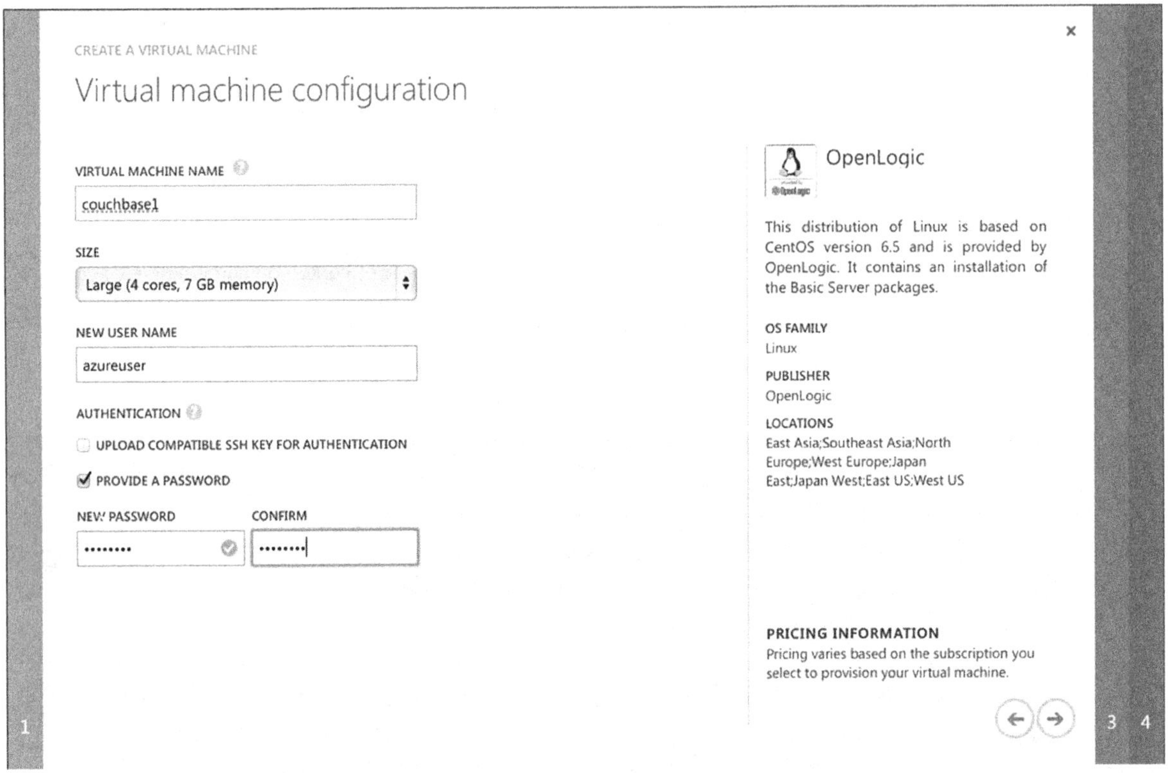

Figure 12-20. *Configuring password authentication for a virtual machine*

Next you need to set up your cloud service (Figure 12-21) on the virtual machine configuration dialog. To do so, select the Create a New Cloud Service option and give the cloud service a DNS name. This DNS name is a publicly used sub-domain of the *.cloudapp.net domain and therefore must be globally unique. You also need to set the location for the cloud service—this can be a region, an affinity group, or a virtual network. Because you need a virtual network for name resolution, select the virtual network we created before. In addition, you can select a storage account that will hold your VM disks. Lastly, create a new availability set for the Couchbase Server nodes before clicking Next.

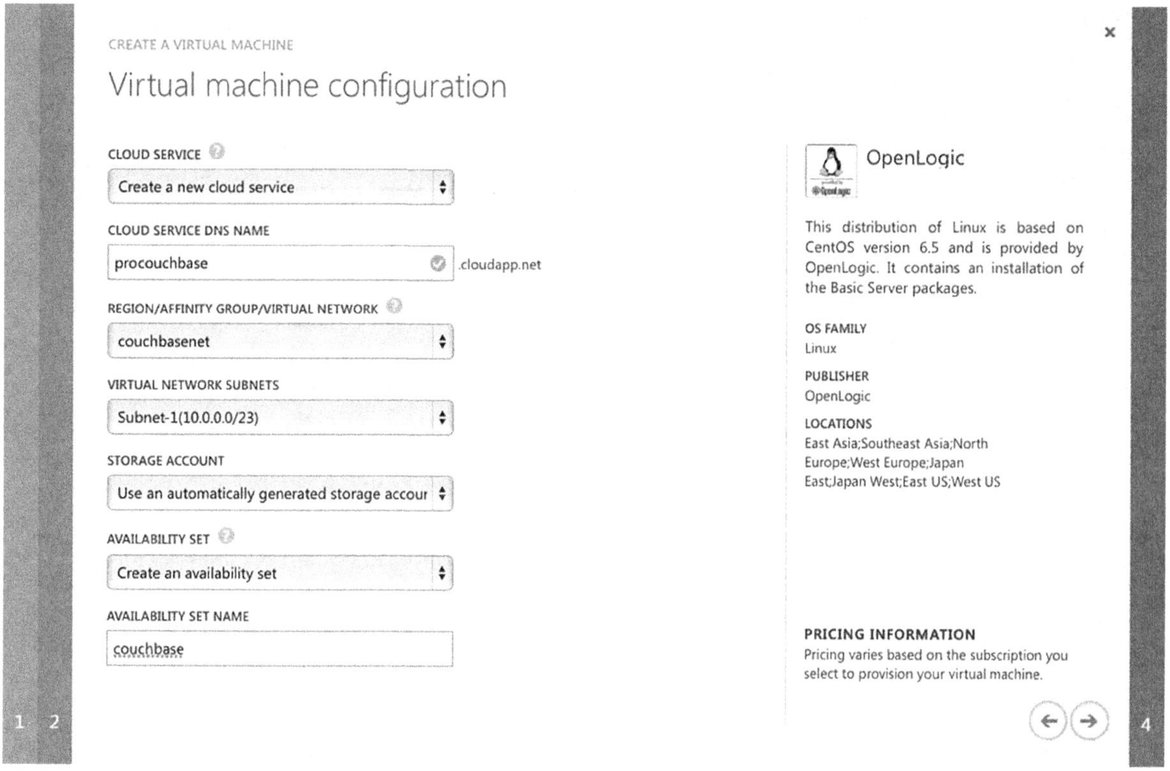

CREATE A VIRTUAL MACHINE

Virtual machine configuration

✕

CLOUD SERVICE ⓘ

Create a new cloud service ⬍

CLOUD SERVICE DNS NAME

procouchbase ✓ .cloudapp.net

REGION/AFFINITY GROUP/VIRTUAL NETWORK ⓘ

couchbasenet ⬍

VIRTUAL NETWORK SUBNETS

Subnet-1(10.0.0.0/23) ⬍

STORAGE ACCOUNT

Use an automatically generated storage accour ⬍

AVAILABILITY SET ⓘ

Create an availability set ⬍

AVAILABILITY SET NAME

couchbase

🐧 OpenLogic

This distribution of Linux is based on CentOS version 6.5 and is provided by OpenLogic. It contains an installation of the Basic Server packages.

OS FAMILY
Linux

PUBLISHER
OpenLogic

LOCATIONS
East Asia;Southeast Asia;North Europe;West Europe;Japan East;Japan West;East US;West US

PRICING INFORMATION
Pricing varies based on the subscription you select to provision your virtual machine.

1 | 2   ← → 4

Figure 12-21. *Setting up a new cloud service for a virtual machine*

You will be prompted to set up firewall and load balancer endpoints. Because you're using virtual networks for your communication, you just need to add an endpoint for the web console on port 8091, as shown in Figure 12-22. Make sure you keep the public port on AUTO to allow Microsoft Azure to open a different port for each VM in the cloud service.

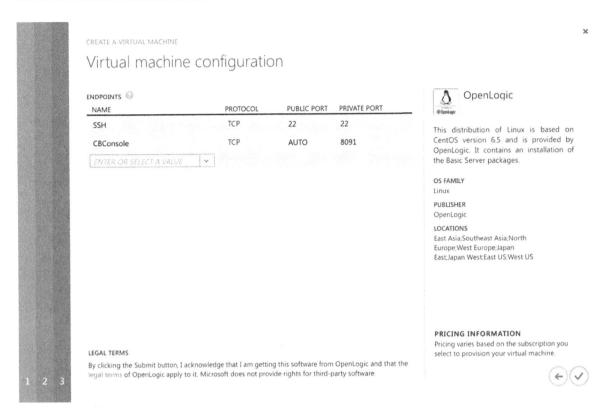

Figure 12-22. Setting up an endpoint for the Couchbase web console

---

■ **Note**   Microsoft Azure creates an SSH port by default for Linux VMs and an RDP port for Windows VMs.

Configure VMs to Use Static IP Addresses

Reserving static IP addresses for VMs is a relatively new option. In fact, at the time of this writing, it is only available using the Microsoft Azure PowerShell tools. You can use these tools to create VMs with a static IP assigned to them, or to configure a static IP for existing VMs, which are a part of a virtual network. The following PowerShell cmdlets update the VM we have created with the 10.0.0.4 static IP address.

```
> $vm = Get-AzureVM -ServiceName procouchbase -Name couchbase1 > Set-AzureStaticVNetIP
-VM $vm -IPAddress 10.0.0.4 | Update-AzureVM
```

If you're using a PowerShell script to automate VM creation, you can use the Test-AzureStaticVNetIP cmdlet to check whether a specific address is available and get a list of alternative address suggestions if it's unavailable. For example, after assigning the IP 10.0.0.4 to your first VM, you can get a list of available addresses with the following PowerShell command:

```
> Test-AzureStaticVNetIP -VNetName procouchbase -IPAddress 10.0.0.4
```

That command will return something similar to the following output:

```
IsAvailable         : False
AvailableAddresses  : {10.0.0.5, 10.0.0.6, 10.0.0.6, 10.0.0.7...}
OperationDescription : Test-AzureStaticVNetIP
OperationId         : e5f50ca4-bb47-7907-9c7e-bc1c2e925fdd
OperationStatus     : Succeeded
```

You can then use an address from the AvailableAddresses array to assign static IPs to any further VMs you create.

■ **Note** Make sure not to mix dynamic and static IP addresses in the same subnet. During reboot, machines with dynamic addresses might receive the reserved IP if the machine it was assigned to is shut down. We recommend creating a separate subnet that will contain only VMs with static IPs.

Best Practices for Running Couchbase in Microsoft Azure

There are some aspects specific to Microsoft Azure that have a major impact on the cluster performance. Assuming your cluster has enough RAM allocated, the number one bottleneck you will face is storage throughput. Because Microsoft Azure stores all your VM drives to blob storage, your storage will have both relatively high latency and limited IOPS performance. Creating striped volumes can improve IOPS, but in practice this scales less than linearly with the number of blobs in the volume. After storage, your next bottleneck may be CPU, depending on how many views and XDCR replications you have configured.

As is always the case, your Couchbase performance will depend on your particular use case, including the data set size, working set size, the ratio of reads to writes in your application, and more. Test multiple VM configurations and combinations with a test workload that is as close to your real production workload as possible. Be generous when sizing your cluster—you can always scale it down later, and over-provisioning is far preferable to discovering the hard way that you under-provisioned, when the cluster stops accepting new data due to being out of memory.

■ **Note** There is no substitute for thorough performance testing!

Because Microsoft Azure has planned VM downtime for OS updates on the host OS, not to mention the potential for unexpected VM failure, you should take care to optimize your cluster for quick recovery. Configuring your buckets to index replicas will save a lot of time in the event of node failover. The time to re-index a very large data set—tens of millions of items—on Microsoft Azure VMs is measured in hours, not minutes. You may want to forgo automatic failover and use a combination of external monitoring tools and software design to handle VM restarts.

Also, for large data sets, adjust the server warm-up parameters to begin serving requests earlier. As discussed in Chapter 11, normally Couchbase loads all keys and metadata into RAM and then proceeds to read documents into memory until it either fills 75% of RAM or loads all the documents, and only then does it begin serving client requests. Changing the warm-up threshold to be much lower than 100% will shorten the startup time considerably.

Some specific configurations you may want to consider:

- For write-heavy workloads, consider using smaller VMs, each with three or more data disks combined into a single striped volume. Place the disks for each VM into a separate storage account to ensure that they do not have to compete with other VMs or services for storage throughput. Use the maximum number of read/write threads to maximize disk utilization.

- For read-heavy workloads with a large working set, test whether you get better performance by using disks with no caching or by using the built-in Azure read caching. This will depend on your particular data access pattern and size.

- For CPU-heavy workloads, such as when using a large number of views or XDCR streams, you may have to use standard instances instead of the memory-intensive instances we normally recommend. This means that you will need twice as many VMs for the same amount of RAM, but you will then have twice as many CPU cores available.

- As a follow-up to the previous point, if your views do not need to be updated in close to real-time, such as when you use views to aggregate statistical data, you can set up a separate Couchbase cluster and define your views there. The main cluster will replicate data to the second through XDCR. The second cluster can use less RAM, because it doesn't need to hold the entire working set in memory, and more CPU cores, to compute the indexes. The benefits of this approach are twofold. You allocate resources to your two clusters based on their purpose, improving the respective performance of both. And in addition, the second cluster serves as a hot backup for the primary, adding another layer of resilience to your database solution.

Summary

Cloud computing is a big part of the rapidly growing modern computing environment. More and more applications of all scales use either private or public cloud infrastructure to provide elasticity and high availability. Couchbase Server is built to provide seamless scaling and simple failover, which makes it a great fit for cloud deployments.

Cloud environments behave differently from on-premises environments and from one another. We have seen how to deploy Couchbase Server on two of the most common public cloud platforms today: Amazon Web Service and Microsoft Azure. However, you can deploy Couchbase Server on other platforms as well, as long as you are aware of the caveats and standards of the platform you are using.

Additional cloud and infrastructure tools such as Chef and RightScale offer management capabilities for Couchbase and can be used to simplify deployments everywhere.

We can expect Couchbase as a service to become a major part of Couchbase Server deployments in the cloud. At the time of this writing, KuroBase, a cloud data platform, offers an early version of Couchbase Server as a service, which is hosted on AWS and is integrated with Heroku. Couchbase also offers Couchbase Cloud, a developer "sandbox" service.

CHAPTER 13

■ ■ ■

Cross-Datacenter Replication (XDCR)

As you've seen throughout this book, Couchbase Server can replicate bucket data internally. This allows Couchbase to prevent data loss in the event of node failure. However, there are several cases in which you might like to replicate your data to another cluster. For example, you might need to provide your application with cluster-level failover, otherwise known as a hot backup. Another reason for cluster-level replication in often found in applications that are distributed across data centers in different geographic regions. For such applications, it makes sense to replicate your data between clusters, providing local replicas of your data. Cross-datacenter replication (XDCR) is a bucket-level, cluster-to-cluster replication. You can use XDCR to synchronize data in a bucket between different clusters.

XDCR can be either unidirectional or bidirectional, and it will provide reliable, continuous replication between clusters. Every change made to documents in the source cluster will be replicated to the destination cluster. If a document gets updated multiple times before it gets replicated, only the latest version will be sent. The XDCR mechanism is push based—the replication source sends changes (also called mutations) to the target cluster. To ensure that replicated documents are persisted, XDCR manages periodic checkpoints. This allows XDCR to resume from the last-known checkpoint in case of communication failures, thus providing reliable and resilient delivery of data.

XDCR uses multiple datastreams—32 by default—to replicate data between vBuckets. Couchbase shuffles the streams between buckets to balance the replication evenly across the cluster, which allows XDCR to scale linearly when nodes are added. XDCR supports replication between different-size clusters, and because it is aware of changes to your cluster topology, you can just add nodes to clusters that are connected through XDCR as you would normally.

Prerequisites

Before you start configuring XDCR, there are a couple of things to note. First of all, we need to make sure that the clusters can communicate with each other. Since XDCR runs locally on all the nodes in the source cluster and writes directly to the nodes on the destination cluster, we need to make sure that all nodes can communicate with each other. Couchbase Server v2.0 introduced version 1 of the XDCR protocol, which used HTTP for standard communication (this is referred to as the REST protocol, or CAPI, in the Couchbase documentation). Couchbase v2.2 and newer use version 2 of the XDCR protocol, which works over the memcached protocol, instead of HTTP, and is known as XMEM mode. And starting with Couchbase v2.5 Enterprise Edition, XDCR communications can be secured with SSL. Depending on your protocol configuration, you need to open the following ports:

Protocol	Port Numbers
Version 1	8091, 8092
Version 2	8091, 8092, 11210
SSL (Versions 1 and 2)	18091, 18092, 11214, 11215

In addition to network communication, you need to make sure that the Couchbase version and platform for both clusters is the same. Last, before creating the replication, you need to verify that the target bucket exists on the destination cluster.

Setting Up Unidirectional XDCR

Setting up XDCR is a fairly straightforward process and can be done completely from the XDCR tab in the Couchbase admin console. The first thing you need to do to set up XDCR is create a cluster reference. To do so, click on the Create Cluster Reference button in the XDCR tab, as shown in Figure 13-1.

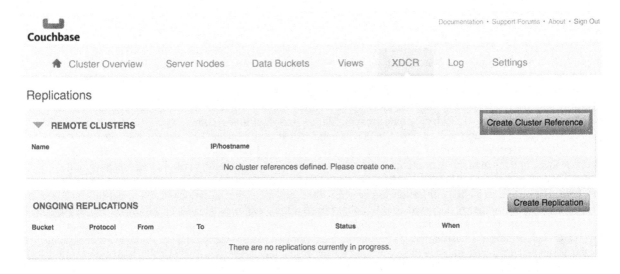

Figure 13-1. *Creating a cluster reference in the admin console*

Next, you need to configure the cluster to which you wish to replicate your bucket. Give the cluster a friendly name, as this might prove to be important in complex replication scenarios when you have multiple clusters you need to track. In the IP/hostname field, enter the address of one of the nodes in the destination cluster. Finally, provide the username and password for authentication against the destination cluster.

At this point, you can also enable SSL encryption between the clusters. To do so, check the Enable Encryption box, as shown in Figure 13-2. You will then be asked to provide the SSL certificate from the remote cluster.

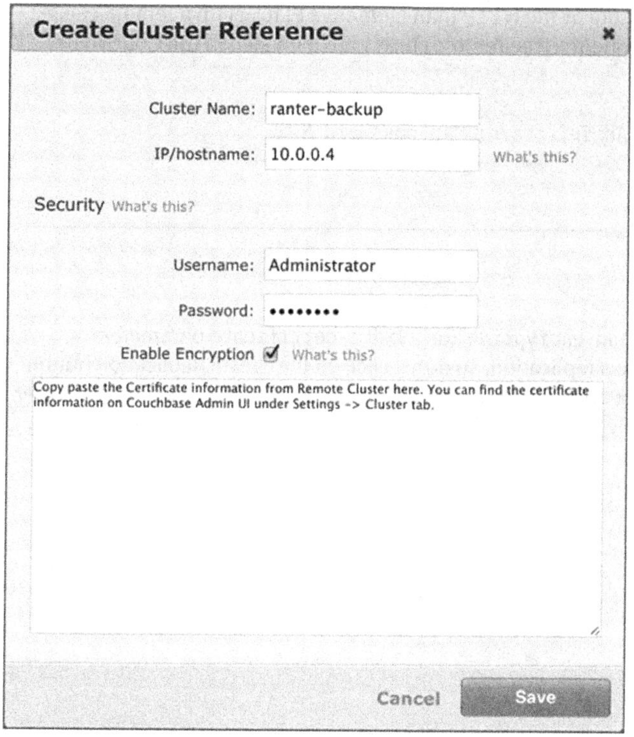

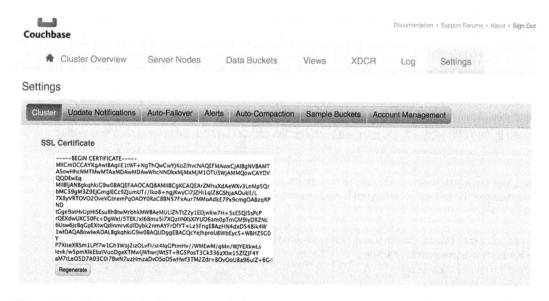

Figure 13-2. *Creating a cluster reference*

To get the certificate information from the remote cluster, simply open the remote cluster's admin console and copy the SSL certificate from the cluster configuration in the Settings tab, as shown in Figure 13-3.

Figure 13-3. *SSL certificate information*

You can also use the couchbase-cli command-line tool or the HTTP management API to set up a remote cluster reference. For example, the following command is equivalent to the remote cluster creation step in the Couchbase admin console:

```
> couchbase-cli xdcr-setup -c 10.0.0.5:8091 -u Administrator  -p password \
  --create \
  --xdcr-cluster-name=ranter-backup  \
  --xdcr-hostname=10.0.0.5:8091  \
  --xdcr-username=Administrator  \
  --xdcr-password=password
```

To enable encryption, you can use the --xdcr-demand-encryption and --xdcr-certificate parameters.

Now that you have a cluster reference, you can create a replication. To do so, click on the Create Replication button in the XDCR tab. In the Create Replication window, select the bucket you want to replicate, select the destination cluster, and set the name of the destination bucket, as shown in figure 13-4. Click the Replicate button, and XDCR will activate.

Figure 13-4. *Creating a replication*

■ **Note**   You can click on the Advanced Settings link to further configure XDCR. Most of the settings can be changed after creating the replication (we cover them next). One setting that can only be changed during the creation of XDCR is the protocol version. If you need to run XDCR version 1, you will need to change the protocol version during the replication creation.

Once again, you can also use the couchbase-cli command-line tool or the HTTP management API to create a replication. For example, the following command is equivalent to the replication creation step in the Couchbase admin console:

```
> couchbase-cli xdcr-replicate -c 10.0.0.5:8091 -u Administrator -p password
      --xdcr-cluster-name ranter-backup
      --xdcr-from-bucket ranter
      --xdcr-to-bucket ranter
```

In addition, you can specify the protocol version with the `--xdcr-replication-mode` parameter. To use version 2 of the protocol, pass the value xmem, and for version 1 pass the value capi.

Advanced XDCR Settings

You can further configure XDCR to control its behavior. The advanced XDCR settings can impact replication performance and durability and will allow you to make the most of your cluster's capacity. The advanced XDCR settings options are as follows:

- *XDCR Max Replications per Bucket*: The max replications per bucket controls the number of XDCR streams that perform replication in parallel. You can set any value between 8 and 256, with a default setting of 32.

- *XDCR Checkpoint Interval*: The checkpoint interval is the timeframe, in seconds, between checkpoints. This setting affects the amount of data that will need to be re-replicated in a case of XDCR communication failure. Setting a long interval will potentially result in re-sending a lot of documents that were already replicated, but were not yet persisted. On the other hand, having frequent checkpoints can negatively affect client (i.e., not XDCR) writes on the destination cluster. The checkpoint interval can be any value between 40 and 14,400 seconds, with a default setting of 1800 (30 minutes).

- *XDCR Batch Count*: XDCR copies documents in batches. You can use this setting to specify the number of documents to be transferred in each batch. Increasing this number can improve replication throughput, at the cost of increasing the delay until a change gets written to the destination. It also makes the disk queue on the target cluster experience larger write spikes. The batch count can be any value between 500 and 10,000, with a default setting of 500.

- *XDCR Batch Size (KB)*: The batch size in KB also limits the size of batches in XDCR. If you decide to change the size of the XDCR batches, make sure that the batch size matches the expected amount of data that needs to be replicated in every batch. The batch size can be any value between 10 and 100,000, with a default setting of 2048.

- *XDCR Failure Retry Interval*: The retry interval is the time, in seconds, before XDCR tries to resume replication after failure. The retry interval can be set to any value between 1 and 300, with a default setting of 30.

- *XDCR Optimistic Replication Threshold*: This specifies the maximum document size, in bytes, for optimistic replication. In order to understand the optimistic replication threshold we need to first understand how XDCR resolves conflicts, which we will explore in the next topic.

You can configure the advanced settings during replication creation by clicking the Advanced Settings link, or after creation by clicking the Settings button for the ongoing replication in the XDCR tab on the Couchbase admin console, as shown in Figures 13-5 and 13-6.

ONGOING REPLICATIONS						Create Replication
Bucket	Protocol	From	To	Status	When	
ranter	Version 2	this cluster	bucket "ranter" on cluster "ranter-backup"	Replicating	on change	Settings Delete

Figure 13-5. Ongoing replications view

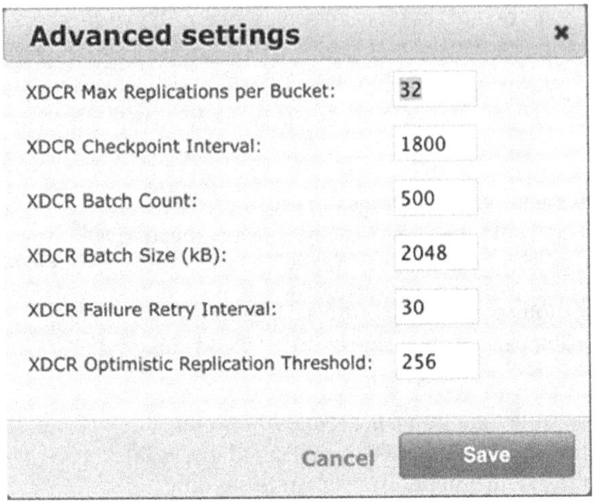

Advanced settings   ✕

XDCR Max Replications per Bucket:	32
XDCR Checkpoint Interval:	1800
XDCR Batch Count:	500
XDCR Batch Size (kB):	2048
XDCR Failure Retry Interval:	30
XDCR Optimistic Replication Threshold:	256

Cancel   Save

Figure 13-6. *The XDCR advanced settings*

In addition, you can use the couchbase-cli command-line tool or the HTTP management API to configure the advanced replication settings. For example, the following command sets the replication to the default values:

```
> couchbase-cli setting-xdcr -c 10.0.0.5:8091 -u Administrator -p password
        --xdcr-cluster-name=ranter-backup
        --max-concurrent-reps=32
        --checkpoint-interval=1800
        --worker-batch-size=500
        --doc-batch-size=2048
        --failure-restart-interval=30
        --optimistic-replication-threshold=256
```

Conflict Resolution

When the same document key exist in both clusters, XDCR needs to determine whether it should replicate the document from the source cluster or keep the version on the destination cluster. As a rule of thumb, XDCR will replicate a document if the version on the source cluster has more mutations than the one on the destination cluster. To figure out which document has the most mutations, XDCR looks at the metadata of both documents.

The first metadata item that XDCR checks is the revision number, which is incremented on every mutation made to the document. If both documents' revisions are the same, XDCR compares the CAS values, document flags, and TTL to see if they have been changed using touch operations.

For small documents, XDCR performs conflict resolution on the destination cluster; for documents larger than 256 bytes, XDCR compares the document's metadata before replicating the document to the destination cluster to save on network bandwidth. The default threshold for performing the check on the source cluster is 256 bytes, and we suspect this number was selected due to the common belief that 256 bytes ought to be enough for anybody. However, if you feel that your network can stand larger documents being sent across before resolving conflicts, you can change this threshold with the XDCR Optimistic Replication Threshold advanced setting.

In particular, if your replication is entirely unidirectional and documents are only changed on the source cluster, you should increase the optimistic replication threshold to be larger than the document size. This will increase the XDCR throughput, because Couchbase will not perform the extra step of retrieving the document metadata from the destination cluster for each document, and since there will be no conflicts to resolve, all documents will only be sent once.

Even if documents can be changed on the target cluster, or the replication is fully bi-directional, it might make sense to increase the optimistic replication threshold if the network connection between the clusters has high latency and high bandwidth. This means that some documents will be sent more than once, wasting bandwidth, but on the plus side, most documents will be sent in a single operation without the metadata request step. You will be trading increased bandwidth use for a reduction in replication latency. There are no hard and fast numbers for the correct setting, so you will have to experiment with something similar to your expected production data traffic to see how the optimistic replication threshold affects throughput and latency.

■ **Note** Most cloud providers charge for traffic between data centers, so that's a point against setting a very high optimistic replication threshold—increased bandwidth cost.

Bi-Directional Replication and Advanced Topologies

XDCR can be set up in various topologies; for example, you can set up bi-directional replication simply by defining a second replication from the destination cluster back to the source cluster.

Bi-directional replication is useful when you expect both clusters to be accessed in the same manner from your applications (see Figure 13-7). That means writes might be performed on both clusters. Since conflict resolution in XDCR is based on the number of mutations, you might need to plan ahead when you expect more-complex needs.

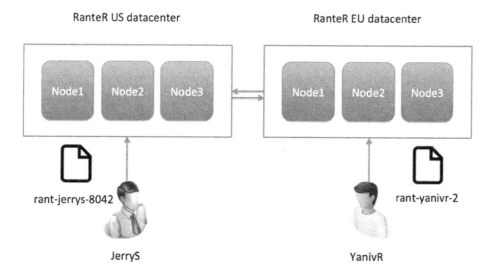

Figure 13-7. Simple bi-directional replication

Let's take a few examples from our RanteR application. The first example we will look at is creating rants, with the not-entirely-realistic assumption that each user always connects to the data center closest to them. Rants are actually quite simple, because each rant can only be edited by the person who created it, and therefore there is no chance for conflicts between clusters as far as rants are concerned. This allows users to both read and write from the cluster closest to their geographic location.

Rantbacks present a more complex problem because they can be edited by any ranter in the system. When RanteR was running on a single cluster, we relied on CAS to manage concurrency. However, we cannot use CAS to resolve collisions in XDCR, because the CAS value is maintained by each cluster separately.

To resolve this, we can introduce a third, write-only cluster for documents that might experience conflict between clusters (see Figure 13-8). Clients can still read locally, and can even use get-with-cas, since the CAS value is always generated by a single cluster—the third one we introduced. One thing to note here is that documents can also be written locally, so we can still write rants to the local cluster and use the write-only cluster for writing rantbacks.

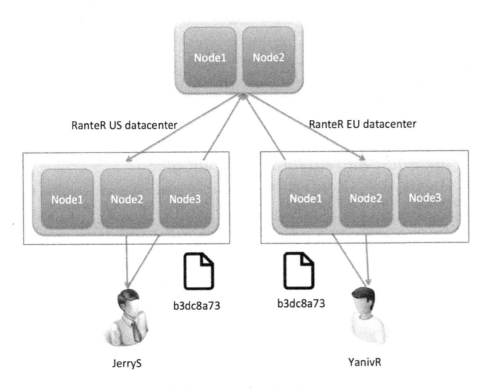

Figure 13-8. *Using a write-only cluster to synchronize writes*

We can use this kind of mixture between replications for other scenarios; for example, global companies can set up local clusters for their branches and have replications updating a global HQ cluster. They can also write data that they need to distribute globally into the global HQ cluster, from which it will be replicated to the local clusters.

Monitoring XDCR

Setting up XDCR is easy. However, in production environments you need to monitor and govern replications in order to ensure data integrity.

Outbound XDCR Operations

As you learned in Chapter 11, the web console displays detailed statistics in the bucket monitoring view, which you open by clicking the name of the bucket you want to track in the Buckets tab. For each outgoing XDCR replication you have configured, you will see a monitoring category similar to what is shown in Figure 13-9.

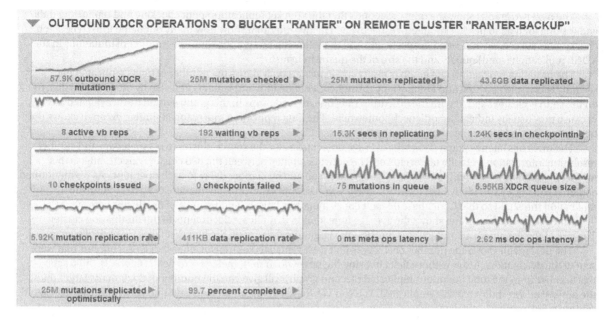

Figure 13-9. Outbound XDCR operations

The first graph in the outbound XDCR operations category shows the number of document changes (mutations) in the replication queue waiting to be sent to the target cluster. This is an important indicator of whether the source cluster is able to keep up with replicating data to the destination. The amount of data that can be replicated is capped by the available bandwidth and CPU and is also affected by the network latency and disk-write speed. If the replication rate is too slow, the outgoing mutations queue will keep growing, and the data at the destination cluster will gradually fall out of sync with the source. If your data traffic rate is fairly constant, you should expect the outbound mutations indicator to be very close to zero at all times. If you normally experience traffic spikes, then the queue should fill up and drain back to zero after a short while.

The next two graphs show the number of mutations that were checked on the source cluster and the number of mutations that were sent to the replication cluster. Normally, both of these graphs should go up continuously as data gets written to the source cluster. A discrepancy between the checked and replication mutation counts means that XDCR can't replicate data fast enough. The last graph in the top row shows the total amount of data that was replicated.

The active vb reps graph shows the number of active vBucket replicators (XDCR streams) that are sending data to the destination cluster. Each vBucket has a replicator that is either active and sending data or waiting to send. The maximum number of active replications is controlled by the XDCR Max Replications per Bucket advanced setting that we talked about earlier. In Figure 13-8, you can see the effect of setting this value too low; in this case, we've set it to the minimum value of 8. As you can see, the active vb reps graph is capped at 8, and the next graph—waiting vb reps—is climbing up as more and more vBuckets are forced to wait until their replicator can become active. The outbound XDCR mutations graph is also rising, which makes sense, because the source cluster is unable to send data to the destination fast enough.

If at this point you're asking yourself "Why shouldn't we just set this to the maximum 256 concurrent replications?" You have a good point. Keep in mind, though, that each replication costs CPU and memory resources, and the setting is per-bucket, so if you have multiple buckets, you'll actually have up to 256 * <num buckets> concurrent replications. Additionally, if your destination cluster is not as powerful as the source, you may want to limit the amount of data that can be streamed to it over XDCR. If your incoming data traffic is spiky, it might make sense to let it queue up on the source side and be sent over to the destination at a slower, more even rate.

The next two graphs show the time in seconds that the vBucket replicators spent checking and replicating data, and waiting for data to be checkpointed, respectively. The two after that show how many out of the most recent ten checkpoints succeeded and failed, respectively. And the following two graphs show the number of mutations in the XDCR replication (send) queue, and the size of the queue in bytes.

The mutation replication rate graph is pretty self-explanatory: it shows the number of items replicated per second. This is affected, first and foremost, by the network bandwidth and latency, and also by the CPU and disk I/O on the source-cluster side. As with the disk drain rate, unexpected drops in this graph should be investigated closely, because they usually indicate a bottleneck somewhere. The data replication rate graph is similar, except it shows the replication rate in bytes rather than in number of items.

The meta ops latency graph shows the average time it takes for the source cluster to get metadata and conflict resolution information from the target cluster. The network latency between the two clusters directly affects this metric. In addition, excessive load on the target clusters can add even more delay to each operation. As we mentioned earlier, if you have particularly high meta ops latency, you should experiment with increasing the optimistic replication threshold so that Couchbase doesn't check metadata before sending most of the documents over.

The doc ops latency graph shows the average time it takes to replicate documents to the destination cluster. The size of the document also affects this metric—the larger the document, the longer it takes to send, of course.

The next graph shows the number of changes that were replicated optimistically—that is, documents that were sent to the destination cluster without first checking the target document metadata to detect conflicts. Subtracting this number from the total mutations replicated (second graph) will give you the number of documents larger than the optimistic threshold that were replicated. You can use these two parameters to calibrate your optimistic threshold setting based on real-world data.

The last graph shows the percentage of changed items that were replicated successfully out of the total number of changed items.

Incoming XDCR Operations

The receiving side of the XDCR replication shows far fewer statistics about the incoming data. As you can see in Figure 13-10, we are presented with graphs for the number of metadata reads per second—these are the metadata that the source cluster requests for conflict resolution—as well as the number of sets, deletes, and total operations per second. These are all pretty straightforward. Couchbase replies to metadata requests from memory, which take very little bandwidth to send, so a high number of reads is nothing to worry about. Sets are equivalent to regular write operations, which go into the disk-write and replication queues as normal. It is much the same with deletes.

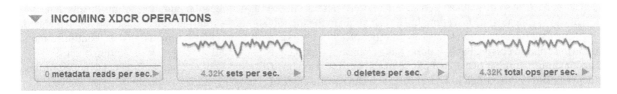

Figure 13-10. *Incoming XDCR operations*

The one thing that XDCR monitoring doesn't tell us is how long it takes from the moment we write something to the source cluster until it becomes available on the destination. This interval is composed of multiple parts, including the time it takes to persist the item to disk on the source cluster, the time it takes for the XDCR engine to detect the mutation and read it into the outgoing XDCR queue, the time the item spends in the queue, the latency for checking target metadata, and finally the transmission delay. However, it's quite simple to check programmatically: write a script or program that inserts a test object with a known unique value into the source cluster and then repeatedly polls the target cluster until it gets the object with the correct value. Just measure the time between the two events to find the XDCR replication interval.

This is often a very useful piece of information because it tells us how "fresh" the data in the target cluster is. It can mean all kinds of things for your application. For example, if there is a large delay between the source and target clusters, it might make sense to retrieve time-critical data directly from the former; this is something you can have your application decide programmatically, according to the most recent freshness check. Alternatively, you can write time-sensitive data to both the source and target clusters, if the XDCR delay between the two is too high. Even in a simple use-case, such as keeping the second cluster purely as a hot backup, it's useful to know how much data you would lose if something were to happen to the main cluster.

Recovering Data from a Remote Cluster

As mentioned, XDCR is useful for backing up your cluster. Let's consider a failure scenario in which there are fewer replicas than failed nodes—in this case some of the active vBuckets will be lost. In Chapter 10, you learned how to use the cbbackup and cbrestore tools to recover lost vBuckets from the data files of an offline node.

A trivial example would be a 2-node cluster with no replicas at all—each node holds 512 out of the total 1024 active vBuckets, and if one of them fails its 512 active vBuckets will be permanently lost. You can see what that looks like in Figure 13-11, which shows what happened after we failed over one node in a cluster that held 1 million items with no replicas. Note that after the failover it only has 512 vBuckets and 500k items in the single remaining node.

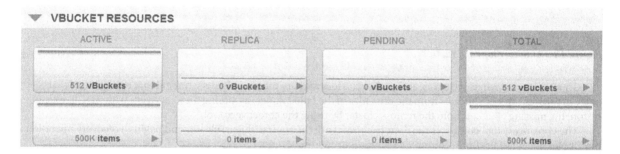

Figure 13-11. *vBucket loss due to failover*

Any active vBuckets on the failed-over node, which had no corresponding replica vBuckets, were lost and are no longer be available in the cluster. Operations with keys that belong to those buckets will return an error. The server log will show how much data was lost, similar to what you can see in Figure 13-12.

Data has been lost for 50% of vbuckets in bucket "ranter".	ns_rebalancer001	ns_1@procouchbase1.local	**19:11:06** - Thu Apr 10, 2014
Lost data in "ranter" for [512,513,514,515,516,517,518,519,520,521,522,523,524,525,526,527,528,52 9,530,531,532,533,534,535,536,537,538,539,540,541,542,543,544,545,546,5 47,548,549,550,551,552,553,554,555,556,557,558,559,560,561,562,563,564, 565,566,567,568,569,570,571,572,573,574,575,576,577,578,579,580,581,582 ,583,584,585,586,587,588,589,590,591,592,593,594,595,596,597,598,599,60 0,601,602,603,604,605,606,607,608,609,610,611,612,613,614,615,616,617,6 18,619,620,621,622,623,624,625,626,627,628,629,630,631,632,633,634,635, 636,637,638,639,640,641,642,643,644,645,646,647,648,649,650,651,652,653 ,654,655,656,657,658,659,660,661,662,663,664,665,666,667,668,669,670,67 1,672,673,674,675,676,677,678,679,680,681,682,683,684,685,686,687,688,6 89,690,691,692,693,694,695,696,697,698,699,700,701,702,703,704,705,706, 707,708,709,710,711,712,713,714,715,716,717,718,719,720,721,722,723,724 ,725,726,727,728,729,730,731,732,733,734,735,736,737,738,739,740,741,74 2,743,744,745,746,747,748,749,750,751,752,753,754,755,756,757,758,759,7 60,761,762,763,764,765,766,767,768,769,770,771,772,773,774,775,776,777, 778,779,780,781,782,783,784,785,786,787,788,789,790,791,792,793,794,795 ,796,797,798,799,800,801,802,803,804,805,806,807,808,809,810,811,812,81 3,814,815,816,817,818,819,820,821,822,823,824,825,826,827,828,829,830,8 31,832,833,834,835,836,837,838,839,840,841,842,843,844,845,846,847,848, 849,850,851,852,853,854,855,856,857,858,859,860,861,862,863,864,865,866 ,867,868,869,870,871,872,873,874,875,876,877,878,879,880,881,882,883,88 4,885,886,887,888,889,890,891,892,893,894,895,896,897,898,899,900,901,9 02,903,904,905,906,907,908,909,910,911,912,913,914,915,916,917,918,919, 920,921,922,923,924,925,926,927,928,929,930,931,932,933,934,935,936,937 ,938,939,940,941,942,943,944,945,946,947,948,949,950,951,952,953,954,95 5,956,957,958,959,960,961,962,963,964,965,966,967,968,969,970,971,972,9 73,974,975,976,977,978,979,980,981,982,983,984,985,986,987,988,989,990, 991,992,993,994,995,996,997,998,999,1000,1001,1002,1003,1004,1005,1006 ,1007,1008,1009,1010,1011,1012,1013,1014,1015,1016,1017,1018,1019,102 0,1021,1022,1023]	ns_rebalancer000	ns_1@procouchbase1.local	**19:11:06** - Thu Apr 10, 2014
Starting failing over 'ns_1@procouchbase2.local'	ns_orchestrator000	ns_1@procouchbase1.local	**19:11:05** - Thu Apr 10, 2014

Figure 13-12. *Server logs of data loss*

This is the point where we either accept the data loss and fire the consultants who said that replicas are for sissies or try to recover the lost vBuckets from the data files of the failed nodes, assuming they survived. With XDCR, we can restore the missing vBuckets from the remote cluster by using the cbrecovery tool.

The cbrecovery tool compares the remote cluster with the source (failed) cluster and begins a recovery operation that copies any missing vBuckets over. The syntax is as follows:

```
> cbrecovery http://<remote>:8091 http://<failed>:8091 -u <remote_user> -p <remote_password> -U
<failed_user> -P <failed_password> -b <remote_bucket> -B <failed_bucket>
```

The preceding command will begin recovering all missing vBuckets, in all buckets, from the remote cluster to the failed cluster. There are additional parameters you can specify to better target the recovery process:

- `-b <bucket>`: Remote bucket name to recover from

- `-B <bucket>`: Failed bucket name to recover to

- `-i <vBucket id>`: ID of the vBucket to recover

- `-n`: Perform a dry-run, which will validate the input and then print out which vBuckets can be recovered

- `-t <threads>`: Number of concurrent threads to use in the recovery process

- `-v`: Print more verbose messages

- `-x`: Extra optional config parameters, same as for the cbbackup and cbrestore tools. You can find the full list in Chapter 10, in the section "Using cbbackup to Back Up Data"

Before you begin recovering the lost vBuckets, make sure to add sufficient nodes to replace the ones that were failed over, but do not rebalance the cluster. Rebalancing the cluster before running recovery will create new active vBuckets and destroy all information about the missing data. Then run cbrecovery in dry-run mode to make sure you've entered the correct parameters and to see which vBuckets will be recovered, which will produce an output similar to the following:

```
Missing vbuckets to be recovered:[{"node": "ns_1@procouchbase2.local", "vbuckets":
[512, 513, 514, 515, 516, 517, 518, 519, 520, 521, 522, 523, 524, 525, 526, 527, 528, 529, 530, 531, 532,
... more vBuckets ...
1021, 1022, 1023]}]
```

When ready, run cbrecovery for real and monitor the progress in the bucket monitor view. You should see the number of active vBuckets and items go up as they get copied over from the remote cluster, which will continue until the bucket reaches the expected 1024 vBucket count. You can cancel and resume the recovery process at any time either by stopping the command-line tool with Ctrl-C or by clicking on the Stop Recovery button, which will appear in the Server Nodes tab, next to the Rebalance button (see Figure 13-13).

Figure 13-13. *Stop Recovery button*

After cbrecovery finishes copying vBucket data from the remote cluster, it will print out a summary report similar to this:

```
Recovery :              Total |   Per sec
batch    :               2057 |      4.2
byte     :           35844328 |  72973.1
msg      :             500000 |   1017.9
512 vbuckets recovered with elapsed time 491.20 seconds
```

All that's left is to rebalance the cluster, which will re-create missing replica vBuckets and re-distribute data between nodes in the cluster.

Summary

This chapter showed you how XDCR gives you even greater flexibility to create complex distributed systems with Couchbase Server. As we move towards cloud-powered global applications, XDCR allows us to provide our clients with local access to their data in a simple, manageable manner. Bi-directional replication with XDCR opens the door for deploying applications globally by seamlessly connecting data centers across the globe. Finally, we have seen how XDCR can be used to back up and recover data when needed using the cbrecovery tool, giving us yet another layer of data resilience.

PART IV

Mobile Development with Couchbase

CHAPTER 14

Couchbase Lite on Android

Mobile devices have become such an integral part of modern life that most of us cannot imagine life without them. Forty years after Motorola introduced the first commercial handheld phone, there are now an estimated 6.8 billion cellular subscriptions in the world, nearly equal to the total world population of 7.25 billion. In addition to a rapid growth in usage, mobile devices experienced an evolution, becoming a premier computing platform connected to the Internet and packed full of applications.

While mobile devices are becoming one the most common means for accessing the Internet, they do have one major drawback in comparison to traditional computer systems: connectivity. Traditional server-backed applications can assume that connectivity between the client machines to servers exists, at least for the duration of their use. This allows them to communicate directly with servers without storing data locally.

It is important to know that connectivity is still an issue in connected systems. This is why we've always had mechanisms for caching data locally. For example, looking at the World Wide Web, the HTTP protocol has built-in caching, which also helps tremendously with scalability. HTML5 added local storage, which is implemented in most modern browsers.

With mobile applications, connectivity is becoming more of an issue. We all use our mobile apps (that's what the kids call them these days) on the go, sometimes losing access in closed spaces, such as the subway or an elevator. And some areas of the world, mostly upstate New York, still do not have proper coverage.

Over the years there have been several mobile databases, all of them relational. The most common and best known is SQLite, which is not only deployed on mobile operating systems such as iOS, Android, and even Symbian, but is also used by multiple desktop-based programs such as Skype and McAfee anti-virus. Astute readers might also recall that the first versions of Couchbase Server (and Membase before that) used SQLite for storing documents locally on each node.

Couchbase Lite is the first NoSQL mobile database. Just like Couchbase Server, it is a JSON-based, document-oriented database. Couchbase Lite runs as a part of your application process and provides several key features:

- *Access to storage*: Couchbase Lite provides a set of APIs to manage, store, and query documents locally on a mobile device. Currently there are iOS and Android native APIs, cross-platform HTTP-based APIs for hybrid HTML applications using PhoneGap, a portable Java API, and a C# API for creating cross-platforms applications with Xamarin.

- *Indexing capabilities*: Couchbase Lite provides the same MapReduce-based views as Couchbase Server. You can write the views using either JavaScript or the native language used by your platform (Objective-C for iOS and Java for Android). Normally, you will use the native language option to create your in-app views.

- *Synchronization to a backend server*: Couchbase Lite also maintains a thread in charge of data synchronization with a backend Couchbase Server cluster. To do so, you also need to have an additional cluster of the Couchbase Sync Gateway, a product that manages the synchronization of data between a Couchbase Server cluster and its mobile clients. In addition to updating the server-side database, Couchbase Lite also provides an event-based mechanism for updating the application UI based on changes to the data, initiated by the server.

- *Authentication and authorization*: Couchbase Lite can be used to authenticate users, using an identity provider such as Facebook or any service that supports OAuth, against the Couchbase Sync Gateway. In addition to communicating changes between the server and clients, Couchbase Sync Gateway provides a set of channels associated with different clients that can be used for routing data to clients based on these channels.

- *Conflict resolution*: Couchbase Lite uses document revisions to track changes and resolve conflicts. It uses UUIDs as revision values and, unlike CAS in Couchbase Server, actually allows users to resolve conflicts by comparing the conflicting versions in the client.

Just like with Couchbase Server, a major part of the functionality of Couchbase Lite is implemented in client libraries. In fact, Couchbase Lite is built entirely as a library that is designed to wrap pluggable key-value storage implementations. The current implementation of Couchbase Lite uses SQLite as its underlying storage mechanism, which might be subject to change in the future.

By now, you've probably noticed that we strongly believe that the best way to understand new libraries is to use them. So without further ado, we are going to start building the RanteR mobile application(s) using the various client environments. There are a lot of similarities between the different environments. If you are interested in a specific environment, you can just skip directly to the environment of your choice.

■ **Note** The following section assumes minimal prior knowledge of the different mobile development environments.

Getting Started with Couchbase Lite

As mentioned, Couchbase Lite is implemented as a client library, and, as such, the first step should be adding Couchbase Lite to your project.

■ **Note** The code samples in this section are all part of the RanteR-Android sample application, which can be found through the book's page at www.apress.com and in the Github repository.

Adding Couchbase Lite to an Android Project

You have several ways of adding Couchbase Lite to your Android project; for example, you can download and add it manually. Couchbase Lite is also available from Couchbase itself via a Maven repository. This means you can just add a Maven dependency to your pom.xml file. However, we are going to use Android Studio for the development of the RanteR mobile app, and Android Studio projects use Gradle—a modern build-automation tool that, in addition to other advanced capabilities, can manage Maven dependencies without the excruciating process of managing XML configuration files.

Before configuring your project to work with Couchbase Lite, you must also make sure that the right Android SDK components are installed. This can be done in Android Studio using the SDK Manager and selecting the following:

- Tools/Android SDK Tools

- Tools/Android SDK Platform-tools

- Tools/Android SDK Build-tools

- Android API (currently recommended: API 19)

- Extras/Google Repository

- Extras/Android Support Repository

If you are working with Eclipse, you need to download and install the Android Developer Tools (ADT) Bundle or configure ADT for your existing installation. Both the package to download and instructions can be found here: http://developer.android.com/sdk/index.html

The first step when working with Gradle is adding the Maven repository to the project. To do so, open build.gradle on the root level of your project and add the Couchbase Maven repository to the repositories block inside the allProjects block, using the following code:

```
maven {
    url "http://files.couchbase.com/maven2/"
}
```

Once you are done, your build.gradle file should resemble the following:

```
buildscript {
    repositories {
        mavenCentral()
    }
    dependencies {
        classpath 'com.android.tools.build:gradle:0.9.+'
    }
}
allprojects {
    repositories {
        mavenCentral()
        maven {
            url "http://files.couchbase.com/maven2/"
        }
    }
}
```

You are now ready to start writing code that uses Couchbase Lite in your Android application.

Creating a Couchbase Lite Manager

The first component we need to create is an instance of the Manager class, which can be found in the com.couchbase.lite.Manager namespace. The Manager class is a container for Couchbase Lite databases that is responsible for managing access to multiple databases and adding database-level functionality such as replacing a database with a version stored on file.

Because our Manager instance contains all the application's databases, we would like to be able to access it from different activities throughout our application. One of the ways to do this in Android applications is to extend the Android Application class and add our Manager instance to the application. To do so, add a new Java class to the project and then add the following import commands at the top of the class file:

```
import com.couchbase.lite.Manager;
import com.couchbase.lite.android.AndroidContext;
import com.couchbase.lite.util.Log;
```

The com.couchbase.lite.Manager namespace contains the Manager class, and the com.couchbase.lite.android.AndroidContext contains the AndoidContext class, an implementation of the android.content.Context interface. This interface is a part of the Android APIs designed to expose information about an application environment. In addition, Couchbase Lite has a global logging infrastructure that can be configured using the Manager class. The log infrastructure is implemented in the com.couchbase.lite.util.Log namespace.

Now we can start implementing the RanteRApplication class. The first step is to extend the android.app.Application class using the following code:

```
public class RanteRApplication extends Application{
}
```

Next, we need to create the Manager instance. To do so we will create a private variable called manager and instantiate the Manager class inside the onCreate method:

```
private Manager manager;

@Override
public void onCreate() {

    StopWatch watch = new StopWatch();
    final String TAG = "RanteRApplication";

    try {
        manager = new Manager(new AndroidContext(this),
    Manager.DEFAULT_OPTIONS);
        manager.enableLogging(TAG, Log.INFO);

        Log.i(TAG, "manager created");
    }
    catch (Exception e) {
        Log.e(Log.TAG, "Error: " + e);
    }
}
```

The preceding code example creates a new Manager instance. In addition, it also enables and configures global logging using the Couchbase logger and uses that logger to emit log messages. You might notice that creating the Manager is done inside a try/catch block. This is because the Manager constructor can potentially throw an IOException.

Before we move on, we need to make sure that the application instance created by our Android app will be of type RanteRApplication. This can be archived by setting the name property of the application element in the AndroidManifest.xml file:

```
<application
    android:allowBackup="true"
    android:icon="@drawable/ic_launcher"
    android:label="@string/app_name"
    android:theme="@style/AppTheme"
    android:name="com.example.ranter.app.RanteRApplication" >
    <activity
        android:name=".MainActivity"
        android:label="@string/app_name" >
```

```
    <intent-filter>
        <action android:name="android.intent.action.MAIN" />
        <category android:name="android.intent.category.LAUNCHER" />
    </intent-filter>
  </activity>
</application>
```

Creating a Couchbase Lite Database

Once we have our Manager instance, we can start creating Couchbase Lite databases. To create a new database we simply call the getDatabase method of the Manager class. Let's create our ranter database in the MainActivity class. We'll need to add the following import statements:

```
import com.couchbase.lite.Database;
import com.couchbase.lite.Manager;
import com.couchbase.lite.util.Log;
```

And then add the following code at the end of the onCreate method:

```
Manager manager = ((RanteRApplication)getApplication()).getCouchbaseManager();
try {

    // create a new database
    Database ranterDb = manager.getDatabase("ranter");

}
catch (Exception e){
    Log.e(Log.TAG, "Error: " + e);
}
```

In the preceding code sample, we created a database named ranter and got a Database object, which can be used for accessing that database. It is important to note that if the database already exists, the getDatabase method simply creates a new reference to the existing database object. This allows us to use the Manager instance to access databases in different parts of our application without having to pass the Database instances around.

The one assumption we are making here is that the database name is valid. Couchbase Lite database names can contain only lowercase letters, numbers, and the following special characters: _ $ ( ) + - /. If you want to validate your name before attempting to create a database, you can use the static isValidDatabaseName method of the Manager class as shown in the following code:

```
String dbname = "ranter";
if (!Manager.isValidDatabaseName(dbname)) {
    Log.e(TAG, "Bad database name");
}
```

Now that we have a database, we can put it to good use and let unhappy people complain about, well, everything.

Using Couchbase Lite

As in earlier parts of the book, we're going to skip most of the glue code that goes into making an app and just show the interesting parts that are relevant to using Couchbase Lite. You can find the complete application code through the book's web page at www.apress.com and on GitHub.

CRUD Operations

The first thing we want to do is to store a new rant in the database. We have added some UI elements, including a Button control with the ID rantButton and a TextEdit element with the ID rantText, to the activity_main.xml file in the RanteR-Android application. Now all we need to do is to add an OnClickListener to the rantButton by adding the following code to the onCreate method:

```
Button button = (Button) findViewById(R.id.rantButton);
button.setOnClickListener(new OnClickListener() {

@Override
public void onClick(View view) {
    }
}
```

Unlike the Couchbase Java SDK, in Couchbase Lite we are not going to create an object that we will later serialize into a JSON document. Instead, we will store our document as a set of keys and values in a HashMap, as shown in the following code:

```
// creating the document as a map
Map<String, Object> doc = new HashMap<String, Object>();

doc.put("id", UUID.randomUUID());
doc.put("userName", ((RanteRApplication) getApplication()).getUserName());
doc.put("type", "rant");
doc.put("rantText", ((EditText)findViewById(R.id.rantText)).getText().toString().trim());
```

One thing you might have noticed is that we did not set an ID property. This is because, by default, Couchbase Lite creates an ID automatically and stores it as a property named _id when it creates a new Document object.

To create a Document object we need to use the ranter database. Since this code is in a different class, we do not have access to the ranterDb variable or even to the Manager variable we created in the onCreate method, so we need to get a new reference to them. Just like in the onCreate method, we are going to do this using the getApplication method. Then, once we have a database reference, we can create a document using the getDocument method and set its properties as shown in the following code:

```
Manager manager = ((RanteRApplication)getApplication()).getCouchbaseManager();

try {
    Database ranterDb = manager.getDatabase("ranter");

    Document document = ranterDb.createDocument();
    document.putProperties(doc);

    Log.d (Log.TAG, "Document written to database ranter with Id = " + document.getId());

} catch (CouchbaseLiteException e) {
    Log.e(Log.TAG, "Cannot write document to database", e);
}
```

In the preceding code sample, we create a new document using the createDocument method of the Database class and then use the putProperties method to save its data. We also call the getId method to retrieve the _id property that was generated for us. Alternatively, you can use the documentWithID of the Database instance to create a new document with a user-specified ID. Document objects in Couchbase Lite are unique, meaning that retrieving the same document ID multiple times will return a reference to the same object in memory. This makes comparing documents easy, since you can just compare the objects by reference, and also saves memory, which is pretty important on a mobile device.

Once we have the document ID we can retrieve the document and get its properties. We can even update the properties and then update the document by simply calling the putProperties method as we have done previously:

```
// retrieve the document from the database
Document retrievedDocument = ranterDb.getDocument(document.getId());

// display the retrieved document
Log.d(Log.TAG, "retrievedDocument=" + String.valueOf(retrievedDocument.getProperties()));

Map<String, Object> updatedProperties = new HashMap<String, Object>();
updatedProperties.putAll(retrievedDocument.getProperties());

// perform updates and changes...

retrievedDocument.putProperties(updatedProperties);
```

Another way to update a document is to use the update method, which takes a callback function that receives a mutable copy of the original document and updates its properties:

```
Document retrievedDocument = ranterDb.getDocument(document.getId());
retrievedDocument.update(new Document.DocumentUpdater() {
    @Override
    public boolean update(UnsavedRevision newRevision) {
        Map<String, Object> properties = newRevision.getUserProperties();
        properties.put("rantText", "<some text>");
        newRevision.setUserProperties(properties);
        return true;
    }
})
```

The main difference between putProperties and update is the way they handle document revision conflicts. Because a local Couchbase Lite database is often synchronized with a remote database through the Couchbase Sync Gateway, which is covered in Chapter 16, it's possible that while your code is updating a document, the background replication process has already downloaded a newer version of the same document. If a newer revision of a document exists, the putProperties method simply returns an error, which you must handle in code. Most likely, you'll have to write some sort of update-with-retry logic, similar to what you've seen in Chapter 4 with CAS and optimistic concurrency. The update method, on the other hand, already contains the retry logic. When a conflict is detected, update calls itself recursively with the newest revision of the document until there is no longer a conflict. Within the update method, your callback code performs the conflict resolution, possibly several times if the document is changing rapidly in the background.

To delete a document, simply call its delete method:

```
Document retrievedDocument = ranterDb.getDocument(document.getId());
retrievedDocument.delete();
```

This actually creates a new revision of the document with the _deleted property set to true to make sure the deletion eventually gets replicated to the Sync Gateway.

Lastly, you can listen for changes both at the database level, or on individual documents, so that you can, for example, update the UI or perform some other action in response. Use the addChangeListener method of either the Database or the Document classes to add a change listener.

Attachments

Mobile applications might need to store more than just a JSON document. For example, many apps need to store and share media files, such as images, videos, and sound. Couchbase Server supports storing either JSON documents or binary data, but managing binary data manually from a mobile device might call for a lot of manual coding. Couchbase Lite has support for attachments: binary files that are saved outside of the JSON document, but are managed as part of the document.

Besides storing binary data, attachments have few additional capabilities:

- Attachments are saved with a Multipurpose Internet Mail Extensions (MIME) type, which can help applications to determine their type.

- Attachments are only replicated to the Sync Gateway if they have been changed since the last synchronization, which saves bandwidth.

- On the mobile device, attachments are stored with a filename that is a SHA-1 digest of their content. This means that if different attachments contain the same binary data, they will be saved to disk only once, which saves on storage.

Before saving an attachment, you need to have the following:

- *Name*: The name of the attachment

- *Content Type*: The MIME type of the attachment's content

- *Attachment*: An InputStream or Uri instance, which can be used to read the attachment

To add an attachment to a document, you first need to create a new revision of that document. Besides being used in conflict resolution, the Revision class also exposes the setAttachment and removeAttachment methods for dealing with attachments.

The following code in the RanteR app attaches a picture taken with the Android camera API. This API returns a byte array that is passed into an InputStream:

```
if(image != null) {
    // Create a media file name
    String timeStamp = new SimpleDateFormat("yyyyMMdd_HHmmss").format(new Date());

    String fileName  = "IMG_"+ timeStamp + ".jpg";
    InputStream stream = new ByteArrayInputStream(image);

    UnsavedRevision newRev = document.getCurrentRevision().createRevision();
    newRev.setAttachment(fileName, "image/jpeg", stream);
    newRev.save();
}
```

As you can see in the code example, if the image variable returned by the camera API is not null, the code creates a new, unsaved revision of the document, attaches the byte stream of the image, and—because this is an unsaved revision—saves the new revision in the database.

Views

Similar to Couchbase Server, Couchbase Lite supports secondary indexes, advanced querying, and aggregation via MapReduce-based views. Couchbase views are covered in depth in Chapter 5, so if you haven't read that chapter, we recommend that you do so before continuing.

Defining Views

To create and query views we use the View class. You can get a new view by calling the getView method of the Database class. Once we have a view, we need to create a map function, as shown in the following code sample:

```
// Note: because the view definition is built with the userName
// of a specific user, we need to delete and recreate the view
// if we wish to support multiple users on the same device.
db.deleteViewNamed("Stream");
View streamView = ranterDb.getView("Stream");

streamView.setMap(new Mapper() {

    @Override
    public void map(Map<String, Object> document, Emitter emitter) {
        if (document.get("type").equals("rant") &&
            document.get("userName") != null &&
            !document.get("userName").equals(ViewsInit.userName) ) {
            emitter.emit(document.get("date"), null);

        }
    }
}, "1");
```

This code sample uses the getView method to create an instance of the View class. Once you have a view you can use the setMap function to create a map function. This is done by creating an anonymous class that implements the Mapper interface, which defines a map function. This implementation has three aspects, which are slightly different than the implementation of Couchbase Server views:

- Unlike Couchbase Server views, views in Couchbase Lite are written natively in the language used by the platform, which in the case of Android is Java.

- Since the view is running locally, we can build the view specifically for the user. In the preceding example, one of the conditions of the map function is that the userName parameter is different from the userName of the current user.

- The second parameter to the map is the version number; you must update the version number if you wish to update the map function.

Note If you intend to create a user-specific implementation of the map function in an application that might be used by multiple users on the same machine, you need to either update the version number every time or delete the view and recreate it whenever you start the application. Alternatively, you can also create multiple databases for multiple users.

Similar to Couchbase Server views, you can also define a reduce function by calling the setMapReduce method of the View class.

Querying Views

To query views, we will use the Query class. The following code sample shows a query that retrieves the ten latest rants in a ranter's stream:

```
// Creating a query to get the latest rants:
Query query = ranterDb.getView("Stream").createQuery();
query.setDescending(true);
query.setLimit(10);

QueryEnumerator rants = query.run();
```

Once the query is executed, it retrieves the relevant documents immediately and returns an instance of the QueryEnumerator class. The QueryEnumerator class implements the Iterator<QueryRow> interface and therefore can be used for iterating over the results:

```
int i = 0;
for (Iterator<QueryRow> it = rants; it.hasNext(); ) {
    QueryRow row = it.next();
    Document doc = ranterDb.getDocument(row.getDocumentId());

    ranters[i] = doc.getProperty("userName").toString();
    rantTexts[i] = doc.getProperty("rantText").toString();
    i++;
}
```

Summary

In this chapter you saw some of the capabilities of Couchbase Lite, including basic CRUD, views, and attachments. However, some of the greater strengths of Couchbase Lite lie in the way it is integrated with Couchbase Server, which uses a process called the Couchbase Sync Gateway to synchronize data between the local Couchbase Lite database and the remote server. If you are not interested in iOS development with Couchbase Lite, we recommend you skip directly to Chapter 16 and learn how to install, configure, and use the Sync Gateway.

CHAPTER 15

■ ■ ■

Couchbase Lite on iOS

Chapter 14 introduced Couchbase Lite, the first mobile NoSQL database. During the first part of that chapter, we discussed Couchbase Lite's use cases and architecture. In this chapter, we are going to dive immediately into the technical aspects of using Couchbase Lite on iOS. If you haven't read Chapter 14 yet, we strongly recommend you read at least the first section as an introduction to this chapter.

Getting Started with Couchbase Lite on iOS

Chapter 14 explains that Couchbase Lite is implemented as a client library. As such, the first step would be adding Couchbase Lite to your project.

■ **Note**   The code samples in this section are all part of the RanteR-iOS sample app, which can be found can at the book's web page at www.apress.com and Github repository.

Adding Couchbase Lite to an iOS Project

The first step in adding Couchbase Lite to an iOS project is to download the latest version of Couchbase Lite from the download page at the Couchbase website: www.couchbase.com/download

Once you download and extract Couchbase Lite, drag the CouchbaseLite.framework folder, shown in Figure 15-1, into the Frameworks folder in your project navigator, as shown in Figure 15-2.

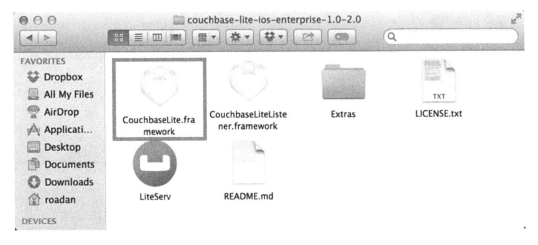

Figure 15-1. *The CouchbaseLite.framework folder*

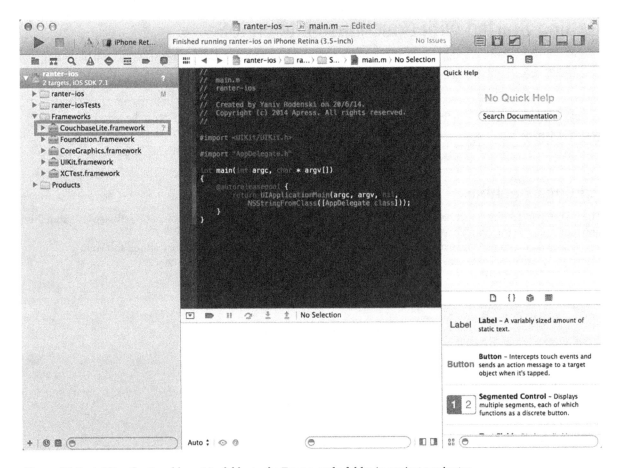

Figure 15-2. *Adding the Couchbase Lite folder to the Frameworks folder in project navigator*

Just as in Android, Couchbase Lite in iOS is dependent on additional libraries that need to be added to the project. Before we add those, we also need to configure the Objective-C linker to load classes and categories from static libraries. To do so, click on the project file for your project in the project navigator. This will open the project editor. In the project editor, go to the Build Settings tab and set the Linking -> Other Linker Flags property to the value -ObjC (with capital O and C).

Next, click the Build Phases tab and expand the Link Binary With Libraries section. Click on the + sign and add the following libraries:

- CFNetwork.framework

- Security.framework

- SystemConfiguration.framework

- libsqlite3.dylib

- libz.dylib

You are now ready to start writing the code that uses Couchbase Lite in your iOS application.

Creating a Couchbase Lite Manager

The first component we are going to use is the CBLManager class. The CBLManager class is a container for Couchbase Lite databases, managing access to multiple databases and adding database-level functionality such as replacing a database with a version stored on file.

Because our manager contains all the applications databases, we would like to be able to access it from different activities throughout our application. However, unlike the Android Java implementation, the Objective-C manager is designed as a shared instance—the Objective-C convention for a singleton, which has two implications:

- We can simply access the same instance of the manager from every class, including all of our view controllers.

- The manager can only be accessed from the main thread.

To get access to our manager, simply call the sharedInstance method of the CBLManager class. The following code sample is part of the initWithNibName method defined in the UIFirstVC.m view controller:

```
// Creating a manger object
CBLManager * manager = [CBLManager sharedInstance];
if (!manager) {
    NSLog(@"Cannot create Manager instance");
    exit(-1);
}
```

To have access to the Couchbase Lite APIs, including the CBLManager class, we need to import the Couchbase Lite header file as follows:

```
#import "CouchbaseLite/CouchbaseLite.h"
```

Creating a Couchbase Lite Database

Once we have our CBLManager instance, we can start creating Couchbase Lite databases. To create a new database we simply call the databaseNamed method of CBLManager, which returns an existing database by its name, or creates a new database if no such database exists. Let's create our ranter database in our view controller. First, we will add a private variable of type CBLDatabase so we will be able to access it from different methods in the view controller. To do so, use the following code:

```
CBLDatabase * database;
```

Then add the following code inside the initWithNibName method, right after we get the manager instance:

```
database = [manager
            databaseNamed:@"ranter"
            error: &error];
if (!database) {
   NSLog(@"Cannot create or get database ranter");
   exit(-1);
}
```

In the preceding code sample, we created a database named "ranter" and got a CBLDatabase object, which can be used for accessing that database. It is important to note that if the database already exists, the databaseNamed method simply creates a new reference to the existing database object. This allows us to use the CBLManager instance to access databases in different parts of our application without having to pass CBLDatabase instances around.

The one assumption we are making here is that the database name is valid. Couchbase Lite database names can contain only lowercase letters, numbers, and the following special characters: _ $ ( ) + - /. If you want to validate your name before attempting to create a database, you can use the static isValidDatabaseName method of the CLBManager class, as shown in the following code:

```
NSString* dbname = @"ranter";

if ([CBLManager isValidDatabaseName:dbname]) {
   NSLog(@"invalid database name ranter");
   exit(-1);
}
```

Now that we have a database, we can put it to good use and let unhappy people complain about, well, everything.

Using Couchbase Lite

Just like in the earlier parts of the book, we're going to skip most of the glue code that goes into making an app and just show the interesting parts that are relevant to using Couchbase Lite. You can find the complete application code on the book's page at www.apress.com and on GitHub.

CRUD Operations

The first thing we want to do is to store a new rant in the database. We have added some UI elements. including a Button control with the outlet doRant and a TextView control with a referencing outlet called rantText, to the UIFirstVC view controller in the RanteR-iOS application. One thing that is important to notice is that unlike the Couchbase Java SDK, in Couchbase Lite we are not going to create an object that we will later serialize into a JSON document. Instead, we will store our document as a set of keys and values in an NSDictionary, as shown in the following code:

```
NSDictionary* properties = @{@"type":      @"rant",
                             @"userName":  self.userName,
                             @"rantText":  self.rantText.text,
                             };
```

One thing you might have noticed is that we did not set an ID property. This is because, by default, Couchbase Lite creates an ID automatically and stores it as a property named _id when it creates a new CBLDocument object.

To create a CBLDocument object we need to use the ranter database. We create a document using the createDocument method and set its properties as shown in the following code:

```
CBLDocument* document = [database createDocument];
NSError* error;

if (![document putProperties: properties error: &error]) {
    NSLog(@"Failed to save document");
}

NSLog(@"Document written to database ranter with Id = %@", document.documentID);
```

In the preceding code sample, we create a new document using the createDocument method of the CBLDatabase class and then use the putProperties method to save its data. We also use the documentID property to retrieve the _id property that was generated for us. Alternatively, you can use the documentWithID of the CBLDatabase instance to create a new document with a user-specified ID. CBLDocument objects in Couchbase Lite are unique, meaning that retrieving the same document ID multiple times will return a reference to the same object in memory. This makes comparing documents easy, since you can just compare the objects by reference, and also saves memory, which is pretty important on a mobile device.

Once we have the document ID, we can retrieve the document and get its properties. We can even update the properties and then update the document by simply calling the putProperties method as we have done before:

```
CBLDocument *retrivedDoc = [database documentWithID:document.documentID];

NSLog(@"retrievedDocument=%@", [retrivedDoc properties]);

// adding a date property. In order to do so we need an NSMutableDictionary
NSMutableDictionary* updatedProperties = [[retrivedDoc properties] mutableCopy];
updatedProperties[@"date"] = [NSDate date];

if (![document putProperties: updatedProperties error: &error]) {
    NSLog(@"Faild to save document");
}
```

Another way to update a document is to use the update method, which takes a callback function that receives a mutable copy of the original document and updates its properties:

```
CBLDocument* retrivedDoc = [database documentWithID: document.documentID];

if (![retrivedDoc update: ^BOOL(CBLUnsavedRevision *newRev) {
    newRev[@"date"] = [NSDate date];
    return YES;
} error: &error]) {
    NSLog(@"Error updating the document");
}
```

The main difference between putProperties and update is the way they handle document-revision conflicts. Because a local Couchbase Lite database is often synchronized with a remote database through the Couchbase Sync Gateway, which is covered in Chapter 16, it's possible that while your code is updating a document, the background replication process has already downloaded a newer version of the same document. If a newer revision of a document exists, the putProperties method simply returns an error, which you must handle in code. Most likely, you'll have to write some sort of update-with-retry logic, similar to what you've seen in Chapter 4 with CAS and optimistic concurrency. The update method, on the other hand, already contains the retry logic. When a conflict is detected, update calls itself recursively with the newest revision of the document until there is no longer a conflict. Within the update method, your callback code performs the conflict resolution, possibly several times if the document is changing rapidly in the background.

To delete a document, simply call its delete method:

```
CBLDocument* retrievedDoc = [database documentWithID: document.documentID];
[retrievedDoc deleteDocument: &error];
```

This actually creates a new revision of the document with the _deleted property set to true to make sure the deletion eventually gets replicated to the Sync Gateway.

Lastly, you can listen for changes both at the CBLDatabase level or on individual documents so that you can, for example, update the UI or perform some other action in response. Use the addChangeListener method of either the CBLDatabase or the CBLDocument classes to add a change listener. For example, you can listen for changes that cause conflicts and then implement your own custom strategy for examining the two conflicting versions and resolving the conflict.

Attachments

Mobile applications might need to store more than just a JSON document. For example, many apps need to store and share media files, such as images, videos, and sound. Couchbase Server supports storing either JSON documents or binary data, but managing binary data manually from a mobile device might call for a lot of manual coding. Couchbase Lite has support for attachments—binary files that are saved outside of the JSON document, but are managed as part of the document.

Beside storing binary data, attachments have few additional capabilities:

- Attachments are saved with a Multipurpose Internet Mail Extensions (MIME) type, which can help applications to determine their type.

- Attachments are only replicated to the Sync Gateway if they have been changed since the last synchronization, which saves on bandwidth.

- On the mobile device, attachments are stored with a filename that is a SHA-1 digest of their content. This means that if different attachments contain the same binary data, they will be saved to disk only once, which saves on storage.

Before saving an attachment, you need to have the following:

- *Name*: the name of the attachment.

- *Content Type*: the MIME type of the attachment's content.

- *Attachment*: an NSData or NSURL instance which can be used to read the attachment.

To add an attachment to a document, you first need to create a new revision of that document. Besides being used in conflict resolution, the CBLUnsavedRevision class also exposes the setAttachmentNamed and removeAttachmentNamed methods for dealing with attachments.

The following code in the RanteR app attaches a picture taken with the UIImagePickerController class, which returns a UIImage instance. We use the UIImageJPEGRepresentation method to convert it to an NSData object:

```
CBLDocument* document = [database documentWithID:documentId];
CBLUnsavedRevision* newRev = [document.currentRevision createRevision];
NSData* imageData = UIImageJPEGRepresentation(chosenImage, 0.75);
```

```
NSDateFormatter *dateFormater = [[NSDateFormatter alloc] init];
[dateFormater setDateFormat:@"yyyyMMdd_HHmmss"];
NSString* fileName = [NSString stringWithFormat:@"IMG_%@.jpg",[dateFormater stringFromDate:[NSDate
date]]];

[newRev setAttachmentNamed: fileName
        withContentType: @"image/jpeg"
                content: imageData];
// (You could also update newRev.properties while you're here)
NSError* error;
assert([newRev save: &error]);
```

As you can see in the code example, the code creates a new, unsaved revision of the document, attaches the image data, and—because this is an unsaved revision—saves the new revision in the database.

Views

Similar to Couchbase Server, Couchbase Lite supports secondary indexes, advanced querying, and aggregation via MapReduce-based views. Couchbase views are covered in depth in Chapter 5, so if you haven't read that chapter, we recommend that you do so before continuing.

Defining Views

To create and query views we use the CBLView class. You can get a new view by calling the viewNamed method of the CBLDatabase class. Once we have a view, we need to create a map function, as shown in the following code sample:

```
// Note: because the view definition is built with the userName
// of a specific user, we need to delete and recreate the view
// if we wish to support multiple users on the same device.
CBLView* streamView = [database viewNamed: @"stream"];
[streamView setMapBlock: MAPBLOCK({
    if ([doc[@"type"] isEqualToString: @"rant"] &&
        doc[@"userName"] &&
        ![doc[@"userName"] isEqualToString: self.userName]) {
        emit(doc[@"date"],nil);
    }
}) version: @"1"];
```

This code sample uses the viewNamed method to create an instance of the CBLView class. Once you have a view you can use the setMapBlock method to create a map function. This is done by wrapping the block of code in a function defined in the MAPBLOCK macro. This implementation has three aspects which are slightly different than the implementation of Couchbase Server views:

- Unlike Couchbase Server views, views in Couchbase Lite are written natively in the language used by the platform, which in the case of iOS is Objective-C (or Swift, if you are reading this book from the future).

- Since the view is running locally, we can build the view specifically for the user. In the preceding example, one of the conditions of the map function is that the userName parameter is different from the userName of the current user.

- The second parameter to the map is the version number; you must update the version number if you wish to update the map function.

■ **Note** If you intend to create a user-specific implementation of the map function in an application that might be used by multiple users on the same machine, you need to either update the version number every time or delete the view and recreate it whenever you start the application. Alternatively, you can also create multiple databases for multiple users.

Similar to Couchbase Server views, you can also define a reduce function by passing the reduceBlock parameter to the setMapBlock method in addition to the mapBlock.

Querying Views

To query views, we will use the CBLQuery class. The following code sample shows a query that retrieves the ten latest rants in a ranter's stream:

```
// Creating a query to get the latest rants:
CBLQuery* query = [[database viewNamed: @"stream"] createQuery];
query.descending = YES;
query.limit = 10;

CBLQueryEnumerator* result = [query run: &error];
```

When the query is executed, it retrieves the relevant documents immediately and returns an instance of the CBLQueryEnumerator class, which implements the NSEnumerator interface and therefore can be used for iterating over the results:

```
CBLQueryEnumerator* result = [query run: &error];

for (CBLQueryRow* row in result) {
    // getting the original document id in order to query the document
    NSString* docId = row.documentID;
}
```

Summary

In this chapter you saw some of the capabilities of Couchbase Lite, including basic CRUD, views, and attachments. However, some of the greater strengths of Couchbase Lite lie in the way it is integrated with Couchbase Server, which uses a process called the Couchbase Sync Gateway to synchronize data between the local Couchbase Lite database and the remote server. The Couchbase Sync Gateway is covered in the next, and final, chapter of this book.

■ ■ ■

CHAPTER 16

Synchronizing Data with the Couchbase Sync Gateway

The preceding two chapters covered how Couchbase Lite is going to change the lives of upstate New York residents (and the rest of us as well) by bridging the gap between connected and offline mobile apps. A local database is very useful for all kinds of apps, but it becomes truly awesome when given the ability to synchronize data between the mobile database and a centralized server. The Couchbase Sync Gateway is a server-side component of the Couchbase ecosystem that provides connectivity and synchronization between Couchbase Server and any number of Couchbase Lite instances.

Couchbase Sync Gateway

The Sync Gateway is a server-side component that runs as an optional add-on for Couchbase Server. It exposes an HTTP endpoint that instances of Couchbase Lite can use to send and receive data. On the back end, the Sync Gateway uses a dedicated Couchbase bucket as its data store. The Sync Gateway bucket can only be used for mobile app synchronization and replication—not for regular Couchbase clients—because it stores additional metadata about mobile users, permissions, and document routing. A mechanism for replicating data between a Sync Gateway bucket and a regular bucket is covered later in this chapter. Alternatively, the Sync Gateway can use an in-memory database called Walrus for data storage instead of a Couchbase bucket. Walrus is useful for development and testing, but should not be used in production.

Sync Gateway uses a system of users and roles to track and control access to data, and a set of channels to route documents to relevant users. Each document in the sync bucket belongs to one or more channels, each Couchbase Lite instance authenticates itself with the Sync Gateway as a specific user, and each user has access permissions to specific channels. This system serves to limit the amount of data synced to each mobile device, and to control who has permission to access this data.

The Sync Gateway exposes two REST API endpoints:

- *Sync API*: Used to communicate with clients, defaults to port 4984.

- *Admin API*: Used to manage users and roles and to retrieve the contents of the data store in superuser mode. By default, it opens on port 4985 and is only accessible from `localhost` for security reasons.

Installing the Sync Gateway

To get started with the Couchbase Sync Gateway, download the appropriate version from the Couchbase download page at `www.couchbase.com/download#cb-mobile`.

On Ubuntu, install the *.deb file you downloaded with dpkg:

```
> sudo dpkg -i couchbase-sync-gateway-<version>.deb
```

Replace <version> with the version of the installation package.
On RHEL or CentOS:

```
> sudo rpm -i couchbase-sync-gateway-<version>.rpm
```

The sync_gateway binary is installed into the /opt/couchbase-sync-gateway/bin directory by default. In order to be able to run it from anywhere, either add this directory to your shell path or add a symbolic link from some location in the path to the /opt/couchbase-sync-gateway/bin/sync_gateway binary.

On Windows, simply run the couchbase-sync-gateway-<version>.exe installer and follow the instructions. Note that, for some reason, the 64-bit version of the 1.0.0 installer puts the files in c:\Program Files (x86)\ Couchbase instead of c:\Program Files\Couchbase.

On OS X, unzip the archive into your Applications folder.

Running the Sync Gateway

To start the Sync Gateway, run the sync_gateway executable. Running the server without any additional parameters will create an in-memory Walrus database called sync_gateway and will open the synchronization and administration HTTP endpoints on default ports.

You can configure the Sync Gateway through a combination of command-line options and configuration files. It accepts the following command-line arguments:

- *-adminInterface*: The admin API port, default 4985.

- *-bucket*: The name of the Couchbase bucket to use as a data store, default is sync_gateway.

- *-dbname*: The name of the database exposed to clients by the sync API, defaults to the same name as the Couchbase bucket used for back-end data storage.

- *-help*: Prints the help.

- *-interface*: The sync API port, default 4984.

- *-log*: A list of subsystems to log, as a comma-delimited string. Possible subsystems are: Access, Attach, Auth, Bucket, Cache, Cache+, Changes, Changes+, CRUD, CRUD+, HTTP, Shadow, and Shadow+. Logging for the HTTP subsystem is enabled by default.

- *-personaOrigin*: The base URL for Persona authentication, must match the URL that clients use to access the Sync Gateway server.

- *-pool*: The name of the Couchbase pool that contains the data-store bucket. Default is default.

- *-pretty*: Returns JSON responses in human-readable format. Useful for debugging, but should not be used in production due to incurred performance overhead.

- *-url*: The location of the Couchbase server or built-in Walrus database. HTTP://<host> URLs are interpreted as Couchbase, walrus: URLs are interpreted as in-memory Walrus.

- *-verbose*: Prints more verbose messages, default is false.

To use the Walrus in-memory database, pass a URL with the `walrus` schema to the `-url` parameter. The URL can be blank or can contain a path to a local file that Walrus will use for data persistence. For example, to start a development Sync Gateway with a persistent Walrus database and HTTP and CRUD operation logging in order to expose a database named ranter to clients, you can use the following command:

```
> sync_gateway -url walrus:///tmp/sync -bucket ranter
```

This command will create a file named `/tmp/sync/ranter.walrus` that will be used to periodically save the data stores in Walrus. Note that on Windows the URL syntax is `walrus:c:\temp`.

Here's how to start the Sync Gateway with a Couchbase bucket named ranter as the data store in order to expose it as a database with the same name and to enable verbose logging for HTTP and CRUD logging:

```
> sync_gateway -url http://<host>:8091 -bucket ranter -log HTTP,HTTP+,CRUD,CRUD+
```

Note that there are no spaces between the log subsystems, and the `<host>` in this case is (any) one of the nodes in the Couchbase cluster.

You can also specify a configuration file to read as part of the command.

```
> sync_gateway config.json
```

The configuration file is (mostly) in JSON format and, in addition to the options that are available from the command line, it can specify multiple databases and buckets to serve. For example, the following sample configuration file specifies default ports for the sync and admin APIs, enables all logging categories, and serves two databases: a Walrus in-memory database named default and a Couchbase bucket–backed database named ranter. The ranter database defines two users, `ranter` and the built-in `GUEST`. Users and permissions are covered later in this chapter.

```
{
    "log": [ "Access", "Attach", "Auth", "Bucket", "Cache", "Cache+", "Changes", "Changes+", "CRUD",
"CRUD+", "HTTP", "HTTP+", "Shadow", "Shadow+"],
    "adminInterface": ":4985",
    "interface": "localhost:4984",
    "databases": {
        "ranter": {
            "server": "HTTP://localhost:8091",
            "sync": `function(doc){
                channel(doc.channels);
            }`,
            "users": {
                "ranter": {
                    "admin_channels": [ "all" ],
                    "admin_roles": [ "ranters" ],
                    "password": "12345"
                },
                "GUEST": {
                    "disabled": false,
                    "admin_channels": [ "*" ]
                }
            },
            "roles": {
                "ranters": {
                    "admin_channels": [ "rants" ]
                }
```

```
            }
        },
        "default": {
            "server": "walrus:",
            "sync": `function(doc){
                channel(doc.channels);
            }`
        }
    }
}
```

Unlike standard JSON, the configuration file format accepts the special character ` to specify a multi-line literal string, which is used for defining the sync function. The sync function is used for processing document changes and is discussed in depth later in this chapter.

If you use both a configuration file and command-line options, the Sync Gateway will do its best to combine the two while giving priority to the command-line arguments.

Working with the Sync Gateway

Setting up replication between the local Couchbase Lite database and the Sync Gateway–fronted Couchbase Server is quite straightforward.

To create a new Replication object for Android, use the instance of the Database class you learned to create in Chapter 14. To do so, call either the createPullReplication or createPushReplication methods of the Database class to create a pull replication from the Sync Gateway or a push replication from the local database, respectively.

Using the example code from Chapter 14, you can add replication from the local ranter database to the Sync Gateway, like this:

```
ranterDb = manager.getDatabase("ranter");
URL url= new URL("http://<host>:4984/ranter");

Replication pull = ranterDb.createPullReplication(url);
Replication push = ranterDb.createPushReplication(url);
Authenticator auth = new BasicAuthenticator("<username>", "<password>");
pull.setAuthenticator(auth);
push.setAuthenticator(auth);
pull.start();
push.start();
```

The example code will initialize and start two new replications, one to pull data from the Sync Gateway and the other to push local changes to the Sync Gateway. It uses basic HTTP authentication with a username and password provided by the user.

By default, a replication runs long enough to synchronize all the existing changes and then stops. Instead of starting and stopping the replication manually, you can have the replication run continuously, meaning that it will replicate new changes whenever they occur and then enter an idle state when there are no changes to replicate. Simply add the following code to the preceding example before starting the replications:

```
pull.setContinuous(true);
push.setContinuous(true);
```

Just like the Database and Document classes, the Replication class can also raise notifications to let you know about changes in documents and the replication state. To receive notifications, add a change listener to the Replication class instance by calling the addChangeListener method with any instance of an object that implements the Replication.ChangeListener interface, as follows:

```
pull.addChangeListener(this);
push.addChangeListener(this);
```

Make sure to implement the changed method in the change listener, which receives a ChangeEvent object that you can use to retrieve information about the replication state:

```
@Override
public void changed(Replication.ChangeEvent event) {
    Replication replication = event.getSource();
    android.util.Log.d("Sync", "Replication : " + replication + " changed.");
    if (!replication.isRunning()) {
        String msg = String.format("Replication %s is stopped", replication);
        android.util.Log.d("Sync", msg);
    }
    else {
        int processed = replication.getCompletedChangesCount();
        int total = replication.getChangesCount();
        String msg = String.format("Changes processed %d / %d", processed, total);
        android.util.Log.d("Sync", msg);
    }
}
```

For iOS, assuming you created the ranter database connection earlier, as shown in Chapter 15, you can create a bi-directional replication, which uses basic HTTP authentication to log into the Sync Gateway, as follows:

```
CBLDatabase *ranterDB;
CBLReplication* _pull;
CBLReplication* _push;

NSURL *url = [NSURL URLWithString:@"http://<host>:4984/ranter"];
_pull = [self.database createPullReplication: url];
_push = [self.database createPushReplication: url];
id<CBLAuthenticator> auth;
auth = [CBLAuthenticator basicAuthenticatorWithName: @"<username>"
                                           password: @"<password>"];
push.authenticator = pull.authenticator = auth;
[_push start];
[_pull start];
```

To specify that the replication runs continuously:

```
_pull.continuous = _push.continuous = YES;
```

To get notifications about changes in the replication:

```
NSNotificationCenter* nctr = [NSNotificationCenter defaultCenter];
[nctr addObserver: self selector: @selector(replicationProgress:)
            name: kCBLReplicationChangeNotification object: _pull];
[nctr addObserver: self selector: @selector(replicationProgress:)
            name: kCBLReplicationChangeNotification object: _push];

- (void) replicationProgress: (NSNotificationCenter*)n {
    if (_pull.status == kCBLReplicationActive ||
        _push.status == kCBLReplicationActive) {
        unsigned completed = _pull.completedChangesCount + _push.completedChangesCount;
        unsigned total = _pull.changesCount+ _push.changesCount;
        NSLog(@"Changes processed %u / %u", completed, total);
    } else {
        // Sync is idle
    }
}
```

■ **Note**   Because Couchbase Lite runs within the app process, replication only works as long as the app is running. Replication will resume from the same place when the app is restarted.

In addition to the Couchbase Lite SDKs for mobile apps, you can use the REST API to work with the Sync Gateway directly. You can find the details of the API here: http://developer.couchbase.com/mobile/develop/references/couchbase-lite/rest-api/index.html.

Channels

As you learned earlier in this chapter, the Sync Gateway uses channels to specify which documents should be synched to which users. In essence, channels are a way to partition the data stored in the Couchbase bucket and only sync a small portion of the total to the relevant users. When connecting to the Sync Gateway to replicate documents, the client can specify which channels it wants to sync. By default, the replication will exchange all the documents in all the channels to which the user belongs.

Channel names are case-sensitive and can contain alphanumeric characters, plus the following special characters: = + - / . _ @. You can use the wildcard * to mean *all channels*. A document that belongs to the channel * can be read by all users. Conversely, a user or role with access to the channel * can read all documents in the bucket. There is no need to pre-create or configure channels, as they are created dynamically by the Sync Gateway at run-time.

The Sync Function

The sync function is a server-side JavaScript function that the Sync Gateway calls for at every document change, including creation and deletion. It is somewhat similar to the map function used in Couchbase Views, but serves several different purposes. First and foremost, the sync function is used to assign documents to channels. If you do not specify a sync function explicitly, then the Sync Gateway uses the following by default:

```
function (doc) {
    channel (doc.channels);
}
```

The default sync function uses the built-in channel function, :which assigns the document in question to one or more channels. This means that, by default, the Sync Gateway expects documents to have a property named channels, which can be a string or an array of strings. The channel function ignores undefined and null values, so if the channels property is missing or is null, nothing happens. Calling channel on an existing document (such as when the document is updated) overwrites the document's channel assignments. Note that changing the sync function for an existing bucket will cause Sync Gateway to re-run the function for every document in the bucket (just like changing the map function in a view will re-index that view.)

Using the example from Chapter 14, you could assign documents to the channel of the ranter who posted the rant with the following code:

```
Map<String, Object> doc = new HashMap<String, Object>();

// ... set other properties ...
doc.put("channels", ((RanteRApplication)getApplication()).getUserName());
```

In addition to mapping documents to channels, the sync function can also programmatically grant users and roles, which are discussed later in this chapter, rights to channels. The built-in access function accepts two parameters: :

- A user name or array of user names

- A channel or array of channels

Usernames that begin with "role:" are interpreted as roles, while undefined, null, or non-existent usernames and channels are ignored. The access function grants the specified users and roles access to the specified channels, as in the following example:

```
access (["davido", "yanivr", "role:admins"], ["all_rants", "admin_rants"]);
```

Using the RanteR mobile app as an example, if you want to grant a specific ranter access to the feeds (i.e., channels) of the ranters they're following, you can add the following code to the sync function:

```
function(doc) {
    // ... other stuff here ...

    if(doc.type == 'follows') {
        // Give a ranter access to the channels of the ranters they follow:
        access(doc.userName, doc.followsChannels);

        // Assign this document to its ranter's channel:
        channel(doc.ranter);
    }
}
```

■ **Note**   As you'll recall from the beginning of this chapter, you can specify the sync function in the Sync Gateway configuration file.

The sync function in the preceding example checks whether the document it received is the special "follows" document that means a ranter has followed someone new. If so, it grants the ranter (userName) access to all the channels that they follow. In this case, the names of the channels for each ranter are assumed to be the same as the name of the ranter itself. Because you are not using the default sync function, you can use other properties to set the channels, such as the follows property in the example.

Next, the sync function can also assign users to roles using the role function, which accepts a username and a role (or arrays of either) as parameters, like this:

```
role ("davido", ["role:admins", "role:ranters"]);
```

It's important to note that, unlike channels, roles and users cannot be created dynamically in the sync function. They have to be created in the server configuration or through the admin API.

Lastly, the sync function is also used for document validation and authorization. When a document is created, updated, or deleted, the sync function accepts both the new and old versions of the document as parameters. You can use the following built-in functions to check whether the user who is trying to perform the operation has the rights to do so:

- requireUser(<name>): Throws an exception, which will return the HTTP 403 "Forbidden" status if the user performing the operation is not <name>. Parameter can be a string or an array of strings (for multiple users).

- requireRole(<role>): Throws an exception if the user performing the operation doesn't belong to the specified role(s).

- requireAccess(<channel>): Throws an exception if the user performing the operation doesn't have access to the specified channel(s).

- throw(exception): Throws an exception with the specified exception object. If the exception object contains the property forbidden, the REST API will return the HTTP 403 "Forbidden" error code with the value of the forbidden property as the status message, otherwise it will return 500 "Internal Server Error".

Using one of these functions to throw an error stops the rest of the sync function from executing and prevents the Sync Gateway from persisting any document changes or channel and role assignments to the database.

■ **Note** The Sync Gateway allows *any user* to perform *any operations* (CRUD) on *any document*, so it's up to you to make sure that the user changing the document has the rights to do so.

For example, to validate that the user updating a rant has the rights to do so, you would add the following code to your **sync** function:

```
function(doc, oldDoc) {
    if(doc.type == 'rant') {
        if(oldDoc) {
            requireUser(oldDoc.userName);
        }
    }
}
```

> ■ **Note**   The code checks the userName property of the original document (oldDoc), because the new document has to be treated as untrustworthy—after all, it could have been submitted by anyone.

When a document is deleted, the first parameter to the sync function will only have a single property called _deleted with the value true. This means that you will need to check whether the document is being deleted before trying any of the other validations in the sync function:

```
if (doc._deleted) {
        // Only the original ranter can delete the rant:
        requireUser(oldDoc.userName);
        // Skip the rest of the sync function:
        return;
}
```

Sync Gateway Administration

By default, the admin API binds to the loopback interface (127.0.0.1, i.e., localhost) and is not accessible remotely. You can specify which network interface to bind to in the command-line and configuration file for the sync and admin APIs separately.

Authenticating Users

The preceding section discussed how to authorize specific actions for users and roles, which presupposes a mechanism for authenticating these users in the first place. The Sync Gateway supports three forms of authentication: basic authentication, Facebook login, and Mozilla Persona. Basic authentication simply sends the username and password over HTTP. Facebook login gets a token from the Facebook authentication service and uses that to log into the Sync Gateway. You can read about Facebook login here: https://developers.facebook.com/docs/facebook-login/v2.0. Mozilla Persona is a cross-platform authentication system that uses an email to authenticate the user with the specified origin server. You can read more about it at https://developer.mozilla.org/en-US/Persona.

When using the REST API to authenticate, all three methods will set a session cookie following a successful authentication. Basic authentication is enabled by default, and clients can use the REST API endpoint /<database>/_session to perform regular HTTP authentication. To enable Facebook authentication, add the following to your Sync Gateway configuration file:

```
"facebook" : {
  "register" : true
}
```

Clients can then log in by issuing a POST HTTP request to the /<database>/_facebook API endpoint with a JSON body that contains the following properties:

- access_token: The access token you got from the Facebook authentication service.

- email: The user's email.

- remote_url: The replication endpoint for your Sync Gateway.

To enable Persona authentication, add the following to your Sync Gateway configuration file:

```
"persona" : {
  "origin" : "http://example.com/",
  "register" : true
}
```

Only users who have the (optional) `email` property set can use Persona login. Clients can log in by issuing a `POST` HTTP request to the `/<database>/_persona` API endpoint with a JSON body that contains the `assertion` property, which is the signed assertion you got from the Persona identity provider.

If the `register` property is set to `true` when using Facebook or Persona authentication, the Sync Gateway can register (create) new users. If the user (email) does not exist yet and the server successfully verifies the token or assertion, a new user will be created with the name and email properties set to the email specified in the authentication request. The newly created user will have a randomly generated password, which cannot be retrieved, so they will only be able to log in using Facebook or Persona authentication in the future.

To authenticate with the Sync Gateway from a mobile app using Couchbase Lite, use the `AuthenticatorFactory` class in Java or the `CBLAuthenticator` interface in Objective-C. Call the appropriate method—`createBasicAuthenticator`, `createFacebookAuthenticator`, or `createPersonaAuthenticator`—with the relevant arguments to create an `Authenticator` object that will be used to authenticate with the Sync Gateway.

Access Control

Each document tracked by the Sync Gateway belongs to one or more channels (document that don't belong to any channels are ignored). Users and roles are granted access rights to channels either through the admin API or programmatically by the sync function, which you've already learned about in this chapter. Users can have any number of roles, which grant them access to any channels that are assigned to those roles.

The admin API endpoint for managing users is `/<database>/_user/<username>`, where `<database>` is the name of the database served by the Sync Gateway and `<username>` is, obviously, the name of the user. The endpoint responds to `GET`, `PUT`, and `DELETE` requests: `GET` returns the user, `DELETE` deletes the user, and `PUT` creates a new user. To create a new user, send a JSON document in the following format in the body of the `PUT` request:

```
{
    "name": "<username>",
    "password": "<password>",
    "admin_channels": [
        "<channel1>", "<channel2>"
    ],
    "admin_roles": [
        "<role1>", "<role2>"
    ],
    "disabled": "false",
    "email": "<email>
}
```

The name and `password` properties are self-explanatory, the `admin_channels` array holds a list of channels to which the user is granted access, and the `admin_roles` array holds the roles to which the user belongs. The optional `disabled` property can be used to set the user as disabled or enabled—the built-in `GUEST` user is disabled by default, while all other users are enabled unless otherwise specified. The optional `email` property sets the user's email, which is used by Persona authentication.

Getting the user from the endpoint will also return the properties all_channels and roles, which are calculated properties that hold all the channels and roles that the user has been associated with either through the admin API or programmatically. This property cannot be set through the endpoint.

The admin API endpoint for managing roles is /<database>/_role/<rolename> and works in the same way as the user endpoint. When creating roles you can only specify the name and admin_channels properties. Retrieving the role document also returns the all_channels calculated property, which works the same as in the user endpoint.

Shadowing Couchbase Server Buckets

So far, you've learned how to use Couchbase Lite as a local database for a mobile app, and the Sync Gateway to synchronize changes between the mobile database and a dedicated Couchbase Server bucket. However, what if you wanted to use a regular Couchbase bucket, because in addition to the mobile apps, you have clients using the bucket with the regular Couchbase SDKs? Unfortunately, you cannot mix a regular Couchbase bucket and the Sync Gateway data-store bucket directly, because the latter holds a lot of extra metadata about the replication process, document revisions, and user management.

Luckily, the Sync Gateway includes a feature called Bucket Shadowing, which lets it "shadow" a regular bucket, meaning that the sync bucket will hold a copy of all the documents in the shadowed bucket. Whenever a document in the regular bucket changes, the Sync Gateway copies it into its own bucket, and vice versa. Sync Gateway doesn't do any advanced conflict resolution when copying documents between shadowed buckets; if a document is changed in both the regular and the sync bucket, the Gateway stores both as different revisions in the sync bucket and then arbitrarily picks one version as the default.

To enable bucket shadowing in the Sync Gateway, add the following section to the configuration file:

```
"shadow": {
  "server": "http://<host>:8091",
  "bucket": "<regular_bucket>",
  "doc_id_regex": "<regex>"
}
```

The server property specifies the Couchbase server that holds the bucket you want to shadow, and the bucket property is, of course, the name of the bucket to shadow. The doc_id_regex property is optional and lets you specify a regular expression to filter the documents. If you specify the doc_id_regex property, only documents whose keys match the regular expression will be replicated in either direction.

■ **Note** If you have a cluster of Sync Gateway instances, make sure to only enable shadowing on a single one of them. Otherwise, you'll have multiple processes competing to try and replicate the buckets at the same time.

Deploying the Sync Gateway

For development and testing, you can deploy the Sync Gateway pretty much anywhere. The official recommendation is to use a dual-core machine with 4 GB of RAM, but for small-scale testing you can get away with less than that. For production, you will want at least a quad-core machine with 4 GB of RAM for the machine that hosts the Sync Gateway, and then follow the normal sizing guidelines for the Couchbase Server cluster. Because the Sync Gateway behaves like a regular Couchbase client internally, you will need to place it close (in network terms) to the Couchbase cluster that hosts its data store to get the best performance. You can even co-locate the two on the same machines, as long as they meet the combined hardware recommendations.

Instances of the Sync Gateway are completely independent of each other, built in what's known as a shared-nothing architecture. You can safely deploy multiple instances of the gateway with the same configuration file; you will have to provide your own HTTP load-balancing solution for clients to access the gateways. If you don't have a preferred load balancer already, nginx and haproxy are two popular choices. According to the official hardware recommendations, a single Sync Gateway on a quad-core, 4 GB machine can support up to 5,000 users. This amount scales almost linearly, both vertically with machine size and horizontally with the number of gateway instances.

Summary

The Sync Gateway server lets you synchronize data between the mobile Couchbase Lite database and a central Couchbase Server instance. Setting up a replication between the two databases only takes a few lines of code. Sync Gateway offers document syndication and access control while scaling linearly with the number of running instances.

Index

■ D

Get the eBook for only $10!

Now you can take the weightless companion with you anywhere, anytime. Your purchase of this book entitles you to 3 electronic versions for only $10.

This Apress title will prove so indispensible that you'll want to carry it with you everywhere, which is why we are offering the eBook in 3 formats for only $10 if you have already purchased the print book.

Convenient and fully searchable, the PDF version enables you to easily find and copy code—or perform examples by quickly toggling between instructions and applications. The MOBI format is ideal for your Kindle, while the ePUB can be utilized on a variety of mobile devices.

Go to www.apress.com/promo/tendollars to purchase your companion eBook.

Apress®
THE EXPERT'S VOICE™